Names on the Globe

NAMES
ON
THE GLOBE

GEORGE R. STEWART

New York
OXFORD UNIVERSITY PRESS
1975

To
Chuck and Sally
Friends Indeed

Contents

IV *Place-names as Sources of Knowledge,* 369

I
Man, the Namer

I

The Place and the Name

A sense of place is older than man. What is a "haunt" or a "lair" but a place known and remembered—known, remembered, and set apart from other places?

My dog, finding a door shut, goes around and enters the kitchen by another door, not even pausing to consider. He knows the house and the lot as well as I do, or better.

Once I snagged a trout, jerking it from the water. But it fell from the hook into a shallow pool, opening to the main stream by an inch-deep passageway only a hand's breadth wide. I sprang forward to retrieve my catch, but the fish, without a moment's hesitation, wriggled snake-like through the skim of water, directly toward and through the narrow opening, and escaped. I could only conclude that at time of high water the trout had learned how to enter and leave that smaller pool, and had remembered.

We could cite the miracles of return, as performed by spawning salmon, honey-harvesting bees, and homing pigeons.

To judge, then, by such actions of animals, we can believe that the earliest men—or even the anthropoids—must have recognized particular places. As we say, "They knew their way around."

A place, therefore, is any area which an observing consciousness, whether human or animal, distinguishes and separates, by whatever means, from other areas. The boundaries may be precise or vague; they may be physical and concrete or mental and imaginary. A place may be a natural feature or a human construction. It may be a continent, a county, an inn, a prison, a forking of streams, a grove of trees, a lake, a grave.

There is no need for much size. A rock-shelter into which one man can barely crawl for cover is large enough to fulfill the requirements, and, in fact, may be on occasion all-important. Considering common usage, there is even a connection between the size of a man and his idea of a place. In an area where a mouse might recognize a hundred places—and an ant, ten thousand—a man might find only one or two.

In addition, places may pile up, as if in strata, as when a particular district also bears the name of a town, a county, a state, and a nation.

Both from smallness and from superposition the number of places in a given area of normally variegated terrain is large, and in a single square mile there may be hundreds of them. Over the whole world the total of potentially discernible places—chiefly existing on the land—reaches a kind of meaningless "astronomical" figure, far into the billions.

Topographers, geographers, and physiographers have written much about the earth's surface, but that is not, as such, our present theme. Here we consider not the places themselves, but the names by which they are distinguished, what are commonly known in English as place-names.

Name, in the abstract, can raise troublesome problems for even the most acute philosopher, but the more restricted conception that is a place-name need not become thus deeply involved. With *place* already defined, a place-name may be considered to be—superficially, perhaps, but practically—a word or words used to indicate, denote, or identify a place.

Though a place may be conceived as existing in itself or as standing in the consciousness of an animal, a place-name exists only with men, being a part of language—"No names without people!" The converse also is true, "With people, names!" At least no tribe has ever been discovered so primitive as to be without names, both for people and for places. Man has been defined as "the thinker," "the tool-maker," and in many other terms. We can also describe him as "Man, the namer."

In the beginning, if we may think of a beginning, how the naming of places started is beyond our knowledge, and always will be. Anthropoids, developing speech, could have applied some series of sounds, such as "river," to the large expanse of moving water beside which they lived—knowing no other such body of water. In that situation "river" is doubtless to be considered a proper noun, that is, a place-name, since it refers only to a single and particular entity. At some later time these anthropoids—or even, we may say, people—wandered more widely and came to a second large and flowing body of water. Now they faced, though unconsciously, a choice. The new stream was similar to the original one, but it was not the same. They might have referred to it by an entirely different series of sounds, originated by whatever system of word-coinage they employed. But having language of a sort, they had also some power of classification, since language is essentially allied with that logical process. So they could have said, "new river," with "river" denoting the class and "new" distinguishing the individual within the class.

These primal names thus arising—we may say in the "folk-mind"—seem to spring from some unconscious and communal process, as if through an unpersonalized linguistic development. No one can declare at what moment a mere designation or description thus crystallized into a name, any more than a biologist can pontificate at what moment, or even in what year or century, a new species arose by the process of evolution. By biological analogy, then, these names may with justification be known as *evolved*.

At an early stage of human development, however, the namer made his appearance—the individual who consciously took his stand and declared, "This place I call ———!" In such comparatively simple societies as those represented in the Old Testament, the Norse sagas, and the Maori folk-tales, the ideas of the namer and the consciously given place-name are already commonplace. Such names may be known as *bestowed*.

Between the two of them, *evolved names* and *bestowed names* divide the total field. Theoretically, the distinction may be considered clear. Usually, however, actual documentation is lacking, and it is necessarily lacking for all names that arose before writing. Because of the lack of evidence of conscious naming, there has been, unjustifiably, a tendency to consider the evolved name as the normal one, and to push the conscious namer into a far secondary position. This conclusion, however, means that mere ignorance is being made the basis of judgment. In such a situation as this one, "There are no documents" cannot be made, logically, to lead to the conclusion, "Therefore, I believe."

Actually, the case for the early development of conscious naming can be based not only upon such early documents as are preserved, but also upon folk-lore and anthropology. Country-people and peasants, often themselves illiterate, show interest in names and their origins. The Maoris have ancient tales dealing with the journeys of primitive or mythological heroes and their giving of names. (See Book III, Chapter 13.)

In the end, though the principle of place-naming is simple enough, its workings have become almost miraculous. By a single term, often a single syllable, by the utterance of some conventional sounds or the shaping of a few characters, we evoke the idea of the place. And this need be no little rock-shelter. By merely saying "Rome" (probably Etruscan, original meaning unknown), we call up not only the teeming modern metropolis of rich and poor, but also a whole panoply of popes, emperors, consuls, senators, and kings, clear back to some little huts upon a hilltop.

From another point of view, however, as those who deal in the philosophy of names have often emphasized, this all-inclusiveness of the place-name is disadvantageous, preventing, as it does, any description or concentration upon special qualities. Thus pent in, people adopt the crude practice of qualifying, so that they speak of "Augustan Rome," or "the Rome of Rienzi." Or, sometimes, they take refuge in an epithet, such as the Eternal City.

Nonetheless, place-names enshrine both the history and the

poetry of man upon the earth, much of his folk-lore, something of his religion. His daily life proceeds among the "little" names; the "great" names echo with the power and the glory—and, sometimes, with the shame.

The attempt of this book will be to demonstrate how this great work of naming was consummated, with emphasis upon human motivation—that is, upon the reasons for which the names arose or were bestowed.

2
What Is Named?

As to what is named, the question may be taken in two senses—the first, external or physical; the second, internal or psychological, or even philosophical.

In the external sense, that which is named may be stated in a principle so universal as possibly to merit being called a law—"the Principle of Entity and Use." To be named, a place must first be conceived as an entity, that is, as being separable and identifiable from other places. But the number of such identifiable places is so great that in actuality only a small fraction of them can bear names, or need do so. The comparatively few to be named will be the ones for which names have proved, in daily life, to be useful, from the point of view of whatever persons are involved.

Because of the vast number of recognizable places, entity might seem to create no problem. The question, however, may become practical. Many regions of the earth—such as the more arid parts of the western United States—have salt-flats which stretch for miles without any identifiable landmark. So also, once "out of soundings," the always-wave-broken surface of the ocean is without "places." Similarly, the surface of a lake, or of a large river, remains without names.

The failure to recognize entity even functions to make the

name-pattern of a primitive people different from that of a more developed one. The difference is not in the small features. The most untutored of men can recognize a spring or a cave. But, lacking maps, ignorant of physiographic studies, his capacity for travel limited to the length of his own legs, the primitive man cannot usually conceive of a mountain, though he may recognize and name meadows and rocks upon its slopes. He may, indeed, recognize a towering peak from a distance, especially if it is snow-covered and arouses feelings of religious awe. But anything like a mountain range or a mountain system is far beyond him. To us the Appalachian Mountains stand out clearly on the map as a unit fit to bear a name. But no Indian so recognized them. Even the English colonists had their difficulties, and the unity of the mountains, with a single name, was not achieved until the nineteenth century.

Similarly, primitive man could not conceive of "an ocean," though he could apply the term "ocean," or "the ocean," in a vague sense, to that whole continent-embracing body of salt water. But only after Magellan and Vasco da Gama had made their voyages could men begin to recognize and distinguish the individual oceans.

Concealed things, like large units, are not recognizable. Ancient and modern seamen alike sailed across the unnamed (and to them unnameable) surface of the sea, and were unknowing of the variegated topography that lay far below—submarine basins, sea-mounts, oceanic ridges. "Deeper than ever plummet sounded" was not only a poetic phrase, but also a practical line of demarcation.

Even when a place is recognized as an entity, the idea of it may remain vague. Until our era of laws, treaties, surveyors, and governmental regulations, most boundaries were hazy. A stream may have marshy edges. Are they a part of what is to be included under the conception "river," or are they part of the land? Besides, at springtime freshet the flowing water reaches far across the spaces where the stones offer dry footing in the summer drought.

Some natural features show what we may call clean-cut

edges—an island sharply rising from the water of a lake; a standing rock; a tarn, deep-set in granite boulders. But most features in nature show less sharp delineation. Where does the slope of ground become marked enough for anyone to say, with authority, "Just here the hill begins"?

Because of such vagueness, many primitive "places" are to be conceived as consisting of something that might be termed a central nucleus, and around it and radiating from it an area that is also of that place but in some way not so completely or so strongly.

Largely for this reason there are, characteristically, among primitive peoples, many of what may be called *spot-names*. Let us imagine that there exists a broad and quiet and deep part of a river that is known as Big Pool. Two men walk through the forest along a crude trail that they know will lead them to that pool, where they can fish. At a certain point, recognizing a landmark tree, one of them says, "We are near Big Pool." Walking a hundred paces more, they see the glint of water. The other one says, "Now we are at Big Pool," and the reply is, "Yes, here is Big Pool." Thus to speak, they do not wait until they stand at the bank, much less step into the water, but the influence of the place, along with its name, oozes outward. If, later, a village is built anywhere in that neighborhood, it will naturally be known as Big Pool, even though not very close to the pool itself.

Some places by their very nature cannot be clearly delimited. Stony Forks and Sandy Rivermouth must be taken as possessing entity chiefly by a kind of abstraction or metaphor, rather than as a physical thing.

Entity is thus one influence in determining what is named. The other influence is *use*. This term, however, must be taken to mean that the name, not necessarily the place, is useful. A man-trapping quagmire or a canoe-breaking rock is the opposite of useful in itself, but each can be advantageously named in warning. Generally, however, profitable places are those that bear the names.

What is of use naturally differs among communities. A tribe

of hunters places its names freely upon grassy glades and meadows that are the haunt of deer. A tribe of food-gatherers finds use in having names for its berry-patches and for its oak-groves where acorns dot the ground.

Use, however, is not to be taken in any narrow economic sense. "Man does not live by bread alone," and a name may be useful to keep alive in the tribal consciousness the memory of some great exploit, or even of a humorous incident. So also it is with religion, and even with play, as when various names of certain American Indian tribes are to be translated as "ball-ground," because they denoted the scenes of vigorous athletic contests.

The principle of entity and use, therefore, is basic for ex-plaining what is named, but the psychological or philosophical implications of the question "what is named?" still remain for consideration.

When someone names, for instance, a river, what is he nam-ing? The water? But the water passes by and is never twice the same. The bed? But if the river runs dry in midsummer, a man then refers only to the stream-bed and no longer considers it a river. Or, what is a mountain? Do we consider it to be the millions of tons of rock that compose it? Or is it the peculiar quality possessed by these rocks that have piled up high in the air? How deep does the mountain extend into the earth? Or, what is a mountain pass? Is it something in itself, or only the absence of something—that is, an emptiness between two solidi-ties?

But, if natural features raise questions of naming, man's own creations do so even more strikingly. When we speak the name of a town, we may refer, first, to a certain area of land. Or, sec-ond, we may refer to the artificial entity—often compared to a person—which constitutes the corporate unity and has the power to make contracts and enforce laws. Or third, we can refer to the people of that town, as when we say "That city is strongly Democratic." Finally, the name of a town sometimes refers to the physical equipment, the streets and buildings. Thus we can speak of "a deserted town," but when the buildings have fallen and grass grows where once the streets were, then we can speak only of "the site of the town," since the town no longer exists and the place by itself is scarcely enough to hold the name.

Abstraction, one of the capacities of human thought that makes naming possible, shows in all naming, but most clearly in the usage of such a word as *cape*. Common practice in the United States sometimes applies the term to a whole area, as with Cape Cod. Ordinarily, however, *cape* represents a point (and a point has no area) at which the coastline makes a major change. Cape Horn, for instance, is a notable feature upon every map of the world, but in itself it scarcely exists, being actually upon a small island to the south of Tierra del Fuego.

This philosophical approach is rarely of "practical" value in the study of place-names. But somewhere, at a very basic level, it must have exerted an influence upon the kinds of names placed upon various features. Very striking in Europe, and to a less extent in other continents, is the practice of preserving the same name for a river clear into its headwaters, where it is often traced to a "true source." Eager adventurers struggled to discover this source of the Mississippi, and then coined a name for it. The controversy over the source of the Nile led explorers to hard feelings and vituperations. Yet, by the test of length, the source of the Mississippi should be found in the present headwaters of the Missouri, and the Nile (the heat of controversy having faded) is generally conceded to arise from more than one source.

Apparently, people looked at a river at any point along its course, and found it possessing a strong entity. Having named it, they then, as they moved up or down the stream, insisted upon taking the name with them.

Some have seen in this practice, and plausibly, the belief in a river-god. If there is such a god, he must be essentially indivisible, since he is usually regarded as having the form of a man. Thus Achilles fought against the river-god Scamander at Troy, and the Romans commonly spoke of Father Tiber. Now, obviously, you should not insult the god by decapitating him by means of another name, but you should trace him as far as possible and give him respect by bestowing his proper name upon the highest headwaters, until you come to the spring in which he emerges from underground.

"What is named?" also raises the question of what kinds of entities are commonly named, although that is tantamount to asking "What entities are most commonly found useful?" Here, however, we arrive at a primary classification of place-names— the division into feature-names and habitation-names.

"Feature-names," which is merely a briefer way of saying "place-names of natural features," must be taken to mean the names bestowed upon entities which already exist in nature, and were merely recognized by men and afterwards named. They include (to use a technical word) *hydronymy*, that is, names of all water-features, such as seas, streams, lakes, swamps, and springs. The counterpart to *hydronymy* is *oronymy*, that is, the names of all "uplift" features, such as mountains, hills, capes, promontories, and rocks.

Broadly interpreted, hydronymy and oronymy may be made to include almost all feature-names. But we should still probably have to include at least one other major classification—one for such entities as meadows, glades, and groves, that is, places set off by natural growth.

Under the broad classification of habitation-names must be included, as the term suggests, places such as cities, towns, and villages, which primarily supply habitations for man. The term, however, may be used for entities which have been created and used by men, though not strictly speaking as habitations, such as counties and townships, states and provinces, and even fields. Without too much sophistry, we may think that such places became entities as the result of habitation.

Much study of place-names, particularly in continental Europe, has dealt merely with habitation-names, and the French phrase *nom de lieu* has been commonly so restricted. On the other hand, usage in the English language has generally included feature-names under place-names. The continental classification has the advantage of greatly reducing the scholar's responsibility, but it seems to be too culturally oriented.

Moreover, the mingling of the two kinds of names is intimate. Innumerable villages took the names of natural features at or near which they were located. On the other hand, innumerable brooks and hills have, in the course of time, taken their names from near-by villages. In recent times, therefore, this compartmentalization of name-study has tended to break down, even upon the Continent.

3
How Many Names, and Why?

The question, "What is named?" leads on to "How many names?" or what is known as "place-name density," and is expressed, for any given district, as the number of names to a unit of area, such as the square mile.

As a beginning, however, one must resolve an ambiguity, that is, that "How many names?" may be taken to mean either "How many named places?" or "How many different names?" Obviously the named places are more numerous, many times over, than are the names, since some terms, such as Big River and Sand Lake, are commonly repeated. By ordinary usage, however, the question of place-name density is not concerned with the number of different names, a problem in which scholars have scarcely, as yet, displayed any interest.

Even the establishment of the number of named places has not been of primary interest. To date, few investigators have undertaken the laborious countings upon which any authentic determination of density must be based, and the information available is spotty. Moreover, the supporting data are not highly reliable. Countings from maps show the number of names on those particular ones, but map-makers, hard pressed for space, may omit names for their own convenience. Gazetteers and lists of post offices permit easy estimates of habitation-names, but are of no value for natural features.

Moreover, even professional scholars differ among themselves as to what should be accepted as being a place-name. Some American scholars exclude street-names, but others admit them. In many parts of the United States rural schools and churches are landmarks and are noted on many maps. They may reasonably be considered place-names, since they designate places, but they may just as reasonably be considered buildings, and the names of buildings are, conventionally, not included among place-names. On the other hand, Europeans may omit the names that are often described as "minor"—*Flurnamen, lieux dits*—designating such insignificant units as fields and other unofficially named localities.

In many instances the limitation is primarily for the mere reason of economy. The number of names within any given area is usually so overwhelming that the worker accepts any means by which his task may be legitimately eased. Still, to open a book entitled *The Place-names of X——* and to discover that it omits all names of natural features is to provoke disappointment and to raise a question of mistitling—at least in the United States.

In any case, though everything may be omitted that can possibly be, the number of named places remains appallingly large. About 1945 the U.S. Board on Geographic Names attempted to arrive at the sum-total of place-names for the world. The method was the rational one of sample-counting from maps, but the final figure passes the limits of credibility. It requires that the surface of the globe should give shelter, so to speak, to place-names totaling three and one-half *billion!*

One hesitates to dispute such an eminent authority, but the figure seems far too high. The water-surface of the globe has only a negligible number of names, and the land-surface amounts to no more than fifty-seven million square miles. To attain the Board's figure we must assume that the average density is about seventy to the square mile. This figure seems greatly excessive, especially since we must include in the land-surface the whole of Antarctica, the polar regions, and the deserts, all of which have few names.

If we write off the total at the round number of one billion, the requirement is for twenty names to the square mile, a figure that does not seem impossible.

Calculated figures are available for a few haphazardly scattered areas, and may be considered moderately reliable. The density for the United States has been a topic of inquiry. As far as the contiguous states are concerned, the best approach is by way of careful counting, from maps, such as was conducted by Thomas P. Field for Kentucky. The conclusion to be drawn from this project is that the place-name density of that state is just about one to the square mile.

Since Kentucky, at least for place-names, is apparently a fairly average area, we may assume that the same density holds for the forty-eight contiguous states in general, and that they would therefore present a total of about three million named places. In addition, perhaps a million other names have been recorded, but are not in current use.

Some states have a higher density, some a lower. For instance, a fairly good estimate for South Dakota yields a figure of 0.8 to the square mile.

As compared with other regions for which estimates are available, the United States is so low as to approach a desert. The island of Tonga, for instance, is an area of about 250 square miles, and scholars have listed 4776 place names on it, or thirty-three to the square mile. The commune of Archon in northern France yields a figure of 62.0. Ukrainia, with the considerable area of 223,000 square miles, has an estimated twenty million place-names, for an average of about one hundred. But even these figures are not the highest.

Japan shows a count of 140. The province of Bohuslän in Sweden rises a little higher, to 150. The record, however, seems to go to the island of Fetlar in the Shetlands. Only four square miles in area, it possesses about 2000 place-names, 500 to the square mile. Though this figure should probably be somewhat reduced, because some of these names are presumably those of off-shore rocks and shoals, still the figure is the highest so far available.

Several factors working together produce this exceptional variation in place-name densities. The first is certainly the environment, that is, chiefly, the topography. A salt-flat in a desert is almost perfectly level, lacks vegetation, and is without streams or even noticeable water-courses. It thus has almost no landmarks on which to attach a name. On the other hand, a variegated topography invites many names—on hills, streams, groves, parks, meadows, and many other features. The optimum for place-name density (the works of man not considered) is probably a jagged coastline—with coves, beaches, reefs and rocks, headlands, points, shoals, arches, capes, and so forth.

Second, we may consider density of population, on the general principle "The more people, the more names are needed." Extreme density of population may, in some small degree, work in the opposite direction, as when the builders of a city scrape the hills down and run the brooks into sewers. Usually, however, density of place-names bears a somewhat proportional relationship to density of population, because of the proliferation of habitation-names.

Third, the length of settlement is of some importance. In the occupation of Iceland, for instance, the names of many of the farms were not fixed until the second or third or fourth generation. A similar situation exists when one tribe or people is replacing another. At such a time the old names of many of the smaller natural features are not passed on to the newcomers, and they themselves do not place new names immediately.

Fourth, and most important, is the cultural pattern of the people inhabiting the area. Here, for instance, we probably find the basic reason for the low density of the United States. The American people overran the land rapidly, seldom naming their fields and smaller streams and hills. A man's holdings were large compared with the peasant farm of Europe. Even in cities the streets might run for many miles without change of name, in contrast to European practice. One can maintain that the average American saw things in a larger way than did his European ancestors.

High density of place-names seems most often to coincide with a cultural background of an agricultural peasantry. In most of the European countries, and in many countries outside of Europe, the peasant held tenaciously to his land, cultivating it in small parcels, to the despair of modern agricultural economists. In a mountain area such as Andorra a field of wheat may be no larger than a good-sized living-room in an American private home, and it can be an entity marked off by stone walls, and given a name. A similar situation accounts for the high density of Japan. If we had figures for agricultural regions of China and India they also would undoubtedly be high. A similar situation, with a name placed upon every little plot of taro, existed in Hawaii before the modernization of its agriculture.

Curiously, the high density of the Shetland Islands, and of Fetlar in particular, is not based primarily on crops. There the economy depended chiefly upon the keeping of cattle and sheep, and a name was placed on every nook, mound, point, rock, brook—any minute place in which an animal might take shelter. A part of the training of every boy was to learn these names, so that he could function efficiently as a herdsman.

The study of place-name density, however, is still in its beginnings. Most interesting, in the present state of ignorance, are the tremendous variations from country to country and region to region.

4
Generic and Specific

Anyone observing place-names across many lands and in many languages is likely to be struck by a curious and haunting thought. He comes to realize that the place-names of any land or language, though wholly unrelated in vocabulary and superficially showing almost infinite diversity, actually seem to be based upon the same system of formation. Their structure, whether in English or Polynesian or Eskimo, is commonly two-fold. One part expresses the class to which the place belongs, such as river, or mountain, or town. The second part restricts the meaning, being most typically an adjective, such as black, or big, or muddy.

The analogy with the biological system of nomenclature is obvious. On the basis of this analogy, "generic" has been applied to the term that indicates the class, and "specific" to the modifying or restrictive term.

An often-repeated name may serve for illustration. Probably all peoples have a word for a stream of water, and find it convenient to distinguish one or more of these streams as being larger than the others. Thus we have many times repeated in the United States the place-name Big River. In Spanish this is merely Río Grande, with the specific following the generic, as is customary in many languages. In South Africa we find Groote

Rivier; in China, Ta Ho. The names of some of the world's largest rivers amount to nothing more than that in some local language, such as Yukon, Mississippi, and Zambesi. So also Paraguasso in South America and Murrumbidgee in Australia. Streams that are big only in local thought bear the same name, as with the Avonmore in Ireland and the Wadze among the Kwakiutl of British Columbia.

In its near universality the specific-generic system is in marked contrast to the great diversity of systems shown over the earth in the naming of individual persons.

Three possibilities, none with any great certainty, can be assigned for the existence of this apparently super-linguistic system. First, there is the possibility that it may represent something very early and primitive. We might suppose that it came into being at the very birth of language, and was transmitted down, still preserved, even after vocabularies and grammars diverged. An objection here is that no one has any proof or any strong belief that language developed only once and that all languages are descended from that parent source. A second idea is that the system was passed from language to language until it thus became almost ubiquitous. Again, the possibility seems slight. The third and most likely hypothesis is that the system is not so much linguistic as logical. The human mind, we may suppose, merely sees the places in this kind of relationship. Thus being seen, they are thus named. In any case, the system seems to be super-linguistic. Nonetheless, it has to function within a particular language, and to accommodate itself to the vocabulary and grammar of that language. (See Book I, Chapter 5.)

The specific, being a modifier or restrictive element, is most typically an adjective, as we have already illustrated with *big*. In many languages, however, it can be a noun, though the situation is usually saved for the grammarian by the insertion of the phrase "noun used as an adjective." Or the specific may be a noun in some special case-form, usually a genitive. Thus English has no trouble with such names as Thunder Mountain, Gold Lake, and Rabbit Spring. In Russian, however, the specific assumes the adjectival form and is so declined.

The specific may also be a phrase or a clause, since these are modifying devices. We have in English such names as the Gulf of Mexico and the Cape of Good Hope. In languages such as Spanish, which do not readily admit the noun used as adjective, these prepositional phrases are common.

The clause appears less often, but in French, for instance, it may occur because of the lack of an easily usable present participle. Thus in Minnesota a Siouan name which would be translated into English as Talking Lake has passed into French as Lac Qui Parle.

One of the greatest advantages of the system is its extreme flexibility. In ordinary usage, if advantageous, either the generic or the specific may be used alone. Thus, in a country dominated by one example of the generic, that term by itself is sufficient, so that people say merely "the city" or "the mountain." But if one example of a class is to be distinguished from another, then merely the specific is sufficient.

A man living in New Orleans, for instance, will ordinarily say merely "the river." On occasion, if the context involves other great rivers, he will say "the Mississippi" to distinguish it from the Nile and the Danube. Only on special occasions will he say "the Mississippi River."

The possibility of thus omitting the generic has sometimes led to the assumption that no generic exists for that particular name. This is especially the situation with regard to cities, towns, states, and provinces. But, though we may think of Massachusetts or Chicago as complete names, in legal language or more formal discourse they appear as The Commonwealth of Massachusetts and The City of Chicago. Large, important, and historical features also tend to be used generally without the generic. Thus we would commonly speak of the "the Rhine" and "the Thames." On occasion, however, the generic will be supplied.

In English the definite article itself sometimes displays the characteristics of a specific. This tendency may be seen with rare generics, some of which meet no competition from others near by. In the United States a sharp cliff may be known as The

Jump-off, and the article carries the meaning of "the well-known" or "the principal" or even "the only." In Nevada, though many hot springs exist, one group of them was known for many years, and was recorded on official maps, merely as The Hot Springs. This particular group lay on the chief route of communication, was an important source of water for emigrant trains, and was correspondingly well known.

A tendency toward amalgamation, in speech as well as in writing, also helps to obscure the situation. So we have -ton and town appearing as mere unaccented syllables in speech and as suffixes in writing. Most of them, however, were originally generics. In such a situation a new generic is likely to develop automatically, with a resulting tautology, that is, a repetition of the idea, which may be distressing to purists but only produces an additional interest for the connoisseur of names, as when we speak of the City of Charleston or of the Sierra Nevada Mountains. The situation is particularly common when a name passes from one language to another, without being understood. In this way Mississippi contains an Algonquian term *sipi,* meaning river, and many other such examples exist.

These situations are also obscured by the occurrence of double specifics. Usually the second specific (in English the one to appear first in the word-order) modifies the whole name, so that Little Red River distinguishes this stream from one that would be Big Red River or, perhaps, merely Red River. Occasionally the second specific modifies only the first one. In California an investigator of Little Pete Meadow would look in vain for a Big Pete Meadow. In this instance, the feature took its name from a man who was known as Little Pete.

Specifics sometimes occur even in higher multiples. During the Gold Rush of 1849 in California, the country was explored rapidly by men who were chiefly advancing upstream. They were thus very conscious of stream-forks, and when they came to one, they were likely not to give a new name, but merely to assume that the stream had split into two. Most rivers thus came to have a North Fork, a Middle Fork, and a South Fork. This meant that for complete identification one had to say the Middle Fork of the American River, and we attain a triple specific with the North Fork of the North Fork of the American River. The situation even reached a quadruple stage with the East Fork of the North Fork of the North Fork of the American River, and there are several comparable examples. The map-makers, in the interest of brevity, then tended to simplify these original namings. Thus the North Fork of the North Fork of the Yuba River has been given a name in its own right, becoming the Downie River, from the name of an early settler who also had given his name to the town of Downieville at the mouth of the stream. Originally, however, the cumbrous older system had its advantages, for it supplied both a name and a kind of gazetteer, which located the stream geographically.

The system of multiple specifics, however, is not harmonious with the general customs of place-naming in English, where exactness is usually counted as second to brevity. In many so-called agglutinating languages the number of word-elements may be loosely attached, the one to the other, until a long and highly descriptive name results.

In a language such as English, in which the specific often has the form of a noun, the same word may now serve as a specific and again as a generic, so that we should not think of even such usual generics as *river* and *mountain* as being necessarily and always generics. Granted, such terms may in the beginning have been only generics, though even this proposition is not susceptible to any proof. In various languages, including English, they now can function as specifics, in names like Riverview and Mountain Lake.

Less commonly, a word that is typically a specific becomes a generic. The process usually occurs over some period of time, and may involve a certain degree of misunderstanding. Even an adjective may sometimes be so treated or be thus turned into a noun. In northern California something of the sort has happened with "craggy," which has come to be conceived as meaning "a craggy place" and occurs in Paradise Craggy and other features.

In modern times the name Alps has displayed a shift toward becoming a generic. In the earliest usage preserved, the name referred to the central mountain mass of Europe. In modern usage it has been applied to particular parts of this mass, such as the Dinaric Alps, but it has also come to mean, in a generic sense, any group of high and rugged mountains, so that we have the Lingen Alps of Norway and the Trinity Alps of California.

In general, though the combined generic-specific or specific-generic forms the complete place-name, the two differ in their nature. The generic is ordinarily a common noun in a current or dead language, and as such is to be found defined and explained in whatever dictionaries of that language are available. Such will also be the case with a considerable number of common specifics. Many specifics, however, are not to be found thus explained, and are not to be considered as simple common nouns. They are, instead, highly distorted forms, often ancient, representing combinations of words and even incorporating former generics. Most of the interest in the study of place-names, as well as most of the difficulty of elucidation, therefore concentrates on the specific.

The all-important generic-specific system, even if it may be considered essentially super-linguistic, necessarily becomes involved with the subject of the following chapter, on place-name grammar.

5
Place-name Grammar

Place-names, existing in a language, must exist also in harmony with the usages of that language, which are included under the general term "grammar." Thus in English, the modifier usually precedes the term which is modified, and place-names commonly follow this procedure, as illustrated by Red Rock, Rising River, Chestnut Hill, and millions of others. Nonetheless, some place-names show the opposite, as with Mount McKinley and Lake Ontario. The description and codification of such practices, in any particular language, constitutes "place-name grammar." Anyone who is repelled by the term "grammar" may substitute a more romantic one, such as "spirit of the language."

Actually, grammar is so fundamental to language that no one can consider place-names at all without being concerned with it. Thus the practice already discussed of using either the specific or the generic alone (see Book I, Chapter 4) is a grammatical problem. So also is the partially discussed problem of the adjectival or prepositional name in English (see Book I, Chapter 4). This latter question, however, calls for further presentation.

In general, the adjectival (including the noun as adjective) place-name so predominates in English that it may be considered regular. The prepositional place-name occurs in rare instances as a descriptive, as with the Bay of Whales, but it appears chiefly in two situations. The first is for habitation-names with which the generic is not commonly expressed, as in the already illustrated cases of The Commonwealth of Massachusetts and The City of Chicago (see Book I, Chapter 4). Such an expression as Chicago City, though not impossible and occasionally heard, may be considered uncharacteristic.

Second, the prepositional place-name occurs in secondary, or "transfer," names. Thus Mexico is the original name, and the Gulf of Mexico arose later from association. We may even think that in the future the logically shortened Mexico Gulf may arise. The prepositional name, in fact, may even be said to occupy a kind of halfway stage, not yet being quite a place-name in its own right.

Occasionally a sort of evolution may be traced, as a prepositional name "advances" toward an adjectival one. Thus Chesapeake occurs first in records as the name of an Indian village. Soon the name was transferred to the large body of water lying to the north of that village, the English having approached from the south. We then have records of the Bay of Chesapeake. Only after continued usage, and the disappearance of the original village, did the term Chesapeake Bay become established. Still, the name is apparently not quite wholly evolved, and the form "the Chesapeake Bay" is sometimes used.

Place-name grammar may be said to divide languages, superficially, into two groups, depending upon whether the specific precedes or follows its generic. Thus English, in the "preceding" group, falls in with Turkish and Chinese, while French takes its place with Celtic, Maori, and Choctaw. In fact, one of the first things to be done in attempting to become familiar with the place-names of any language is to determine to which of these groups it belongs.

Though in English the specific regularly precedes, there are so many special cases that the matter becomes of considerable complexity. Obviously, with the prepositional name the specific must follow. Even with the adjectival name the specific follows in a number of instances. Usage differs regionally, individually, and even, it sometimes seems, by mere whim.

The British, thus, say the River Clyde. Americans prefer the opposite.

In usage in the English language throughout the world a tendency exists for certain generics to precede—Mount, Cape and Lake being the most notable. The closest approach to universality occurs with Mount, for the simple reason that this idea when following the specific is naturally expressed by Mountain. Still, there are places in the United States called Rocky Mount, Merry Mount, and others. While Cape precedes in Cape Horn and Cape Cod, it follows in North Cape, Icy Cape, and many others. Lake precedes in Lake Baikal, Lake Michigan, and Lake Victoria, but follows in Great Salt Lake and in hundreds of names using such simple adjectives as Big, Little, or Reedy. A few other generics precede rather commonly—Fort, Camp, Key, Point, and Port. Still others may be found occasionally, as with Bay Marchand, Pass Cavallo, and Canyon Diablo.

The real explanation is that English here is undoubtedly being affected by foreign borrowings. All of these particular generics entered the language from French or Spanish, and there was a natural tendency to take the word-order along with the name. The original borrowings, we may say, were of the names and not of the words. With the passage of time, the term came to be used independently as a word and new names were formed with it. There was—and probably still is—a tendency for the normal English word-order to reestablish itself. But linguistic conservatism has often maintained the original usage.

With some generics this process can be traced historically. Fort, for example, came into use in the seventeenth and eighteenth centuries when professional armies were dominated by French military usages. Lake is also a latecomer, scarcely existing in the British Isles and being rare in New England. It developed after the colonists came into contact with the French, and the names of the five Great Lakes, and many smaller ones, entered English as names already fashioned and therefore with the generic preceding. On the other hand, the French did not settle the country thickly and thus failed to give names to many of the smaller bodies of water. When the American settlers had to give such names, they reverted to their familiar word-order, as in Blue Lake or Mud Lake.

Thus arose a rather curious situation in the United States. Lake, when preceding its specific, is generally associated with a larger and more important body of water than is the same generic when it follows.

A third interesting grammatical usage in English is the question of the omission or inclusion of the definite article in place-names. It is regularly included with the prepositional name and with the plural name, so that we have the Bay of Biscay, the Thousand Islands, and the British Isles. It also occurs in the rather rare instances when the name consists of a single term, usually to be considered a generic, as in The Jump-off (see Book III, Chapter 4).

Scholars have attempted—as with the question of the generic-specific order—to associate the use of the article with particular generics. Certainly, such a one as River very commonly calls for the article, whereas the article does not commonly appear with Lake or Mountain. The question, however, is of considerable complexity, and cannot be solved merely by reference to generics. Quite possibly the whole language is, in this respect, in the process of shifting. In the long run, it seems likely, the use of the article will disappear with the ordinary place-name and may even disappear with the prepositional name and the plurals. It actually serves no good purpose, and its omission is useful as a signal that the words to follow are to be considered a proper name, not a mere description.

The process is capable of demonstration, at least in theory. We may consider a series of sentences:

1. They met at the black rock.
2. They met at Black Rock.
3. They met at Blackrock.

Theoretically we might also have two others:

4. They met at the Black Rock
5. They met at the Blackrock.

The last two, however, would probably not be used in practice for any additional nuance of meaning. The other three are clearly distinguished in speech. The first includes the article and has approximately equal stresses on *black* and *rock;* the second omits the article but maintains the equal stresses; the third omits the article and subordinates the stress of -*rock* to that of *Black.*

Semantically, in the first sentence we have a straightforward description of a landmark. In the second we have a place-name, in a somewhat halfway stage, with the idea of description still preserved. In the third the idea of description is wholly—or almost wholly—replaced by a full-fledged place-name, which probably identifies a habitation instead of a rock, and will survive after the blasting away of the rock in the building of a highway.

The grammatical implications of inflection are also of interest. In the Anglo-Saxon period the English language was much richer in inflected forms than it now is, and many place-names preserve, for instance, the traces of the dative case, either singular or plural. But Modern English limits the inflection of the noun to the singular and plural forms with their possessives.

In place-names the use of the possessive is almost wholly with personal names. Thus we have Johnstown and John's Creek. But, as with the definite article, usage seems to be moving against the possessive. In the first place, there is very little to be gained from it, since the difference between John Creek and John's Creek is not notable. Before long the apostrophe disappears in most instances, because of either ignorance or mere carelessness or because it no longer serves any particular function, especially after the original possessor of the name has died or moved on, leaving someone else as owner. Eventually, the *s* itself meets the same fate, for much the same reasons.

Place-names, being such a small part of a language, necessarily adapt themselves to the grammar of the particular language in which they exist. This fact should be clear enough from the presentation of the situation in English, but can be further illustrated from other languages.

Xenophon's *Anabasis* is an excellent source-book on place-names in ancient Greek, though the original texts could not make the distinction between capital and small letters.

A passage from the *Anabasis* which is full of place-names is translatable with a minimum of difficulty, although a few of the definite articles would not be expressed in English, here being put into parentheses:

> From there they marched through the Troad, and crossing over the Ida [a mountain range], they arrived first at Antandros; then going along the sea, they reached the Valley of Thebe of (the) Mysia. From there proceeding through Adramyttion and Kytonion, they came to the Valley of Kaïkos, and took possession of Pergamon of (the) Mysia.

The place-name grammars of Greek and English thus show much in common—such as the specific-generic distinction (Valley of Thebe). Greek also follows the custom of using only the specific when the meaning is thus clear. As the equivalent of the noun as adjective, Greek easily makes use of the genitive case, which also serves for the possessive. Xenophon writes, for instance, of *Marsyou potamos,* Marsyos' River, or, as it would more likely stand in English, Marsyos River. Approximating to English construction, one sentence reads: "The breadth of the Marsyos [generic omitted] is twenty-five feet."

Greek is fonder of the article than is English, using it with names of countries and districts, much as French does. As in modern English, Xenophon's use of the article seems to be a little uncertain and even inconsistent, probably varying because of slight personal nuances which are difficult for a reader to distinguish.

The lack of any distinction between capital and small letters, however, seems to have caused the writers of ancient Greek some slight embarrassment. Thus Xenophon often inserts the expression "by name," or an awkwardly long participle, "called," *kaloumenos.*

The same difficulty apparently was at work in the famous passage in the Book of Acts in which Paul is instructed to "go into the street which is called Straight." Mark Twain poked fun at this passage, on the ground that the writer was not guaranteeing the street to be straight, but only that it was so called. Actually Twain is stating the approximate fact, but he did not realize the difficulty of the lack of capitalization. One would suspect that in colloquial speech oral signals sufficed to indicate a place-name and the clumsy *kaloumenos* was not necessary.

In Hebrew, as in Greek, place-name grammar offers little difficulty to anyone familiar with English. But in Latin the situation is considerably different. Like Greek, Latin lacked a distinction of lower-case letters, and it also lacked both the definite and the indefinite articles. It had therefore no way of distinguishing between "We crossed a big river," "We crossed the big river," and "We crossed Big River." Even in ordinary speech some difficulties would thus have arisen, and for writers there would have been more problems.

Perhaps because of these difficulties the language preserved an archaism. As a signpost "This is a place-name," the Romans preserved an ancient device of using the locative case alone, no preposition being used, with the names of cities and some other geographical features. A Latin author thus wrote merely Romae (though he could use no capital letter), thus expressing the idea "at Rome," or "in Rome." So also, by using the accusative case without a preposition, he could write Romam to mean "to Rome." Possibly, in speech, the Romans had a way of distinguishing feature-names from mere descriptions, just as speakers of English do when they shift "black rock" into "Black Rock," but there is no obvious way in which they could do so.

Among modern languages Spanish is particularly interesting for the many contrasts which it offers to English. Spanish, like English, has both the definite and the indefinite article, but it makes little use of either of them in separating descriptive terms from place-names. In general, Spanish retains the definite article for a natural feature, and thus lacks the useful device of omitting it, which English has. Spanish also lacks the possessive case and the capacity of employing the noun as an adjective, though in place-names it sometimes uses an abbreviated form, such as Punta Arenas, instead of Punta de las Arenas. The language may thus seem less well-qualified than English to deal with place-names, but actually it is in many ways superior.

Unable to employ the noun as an adjective, Spanish has re-course to the prepositional place-name, and the English Bear River has for an equivalent El Rio del Oso. But to call this the equivalent is not altogether accurate, for Spanish can use various forms, gaining much in accuracy and variety. El Rio del Oso indicates that the stream was named for bears in general or for a single male bear. We may also have Osa for a single she-bear, and the plurals Osos and Osas. If someone had happened to see a bear cub there, the name could be El Rio del Osito. There are also the possibilities of Osita, Ositos, and Ositas. Spanish thus offers six possibilities, where English has commonly but one. True, such names as She-bear River and Bears River are not impossible, but they certainly are not in the spirit of place-name usage in English.

In practice, actually, there is not as much difference as is theoretically possible. Few namers have the opportunity or desire to name anything for a number of female bear-cubs. But such terms as Osos and Osito occur—for example, in California.

Also, it can be argued, what Spanish gains in variety and accuracy it loses in prolixity. Speakers of English certainly are not likely to see advantages in abandoning their curt, emphatic, and all-purposive Bear River.

As languages exist by dozens and scores over the face of the earth, so also do the variations of place-name grammars. In Chinese, for instance, the system is much like that in English, so that Peking, "North Capital," and Hoangho, "Yellow River," raise no difficulties. Languages of the agglutinating type, such as Turkish and Eskimo, tend to pile one qualifier upon another. Even more difficult are the languages which incorporate verbs or whole sentences into their place-names. Thus we have the Australian name Culkinewarinedinelup, "place-where-palms-grow-thickly" and the Navajo name Lukachukai, "white-patch-of-reeds-extends-out." In general, the basic point at issue seems to be brevity as opposed to specificity. English, along with a few other languages, stands at the extreme point in the practice of brevity.

6
Names Within a Language

Although the chief topic of this study is the actual genesis of place-names in whatever language, each such name necessarily exists in some particular language. Indeed, most investigation of place-names has focused not upon their origin by human action and from human experience, but upon their linguistic changes and developments. Obviously, this present study must also consider what thus happens to a name after it has once taken form in some language.

Historically, such investigation of place-names within a language has started with three assumptions.

The first of these, which is based upon much evidence, is that every existing place-name is derived eventually from a word (or words, or a linguistic element) which originally was an ordinary term (not a name) in some language. Briefly put, the dictum has been "Every place-name has a meaning." Even place-names derived from personal names need not be considered exceptions, since the denotation of an individual or group by a term is a kind of meaning.

In general, this assumption is a proper one, though the name-patterns of the United States, and of some other countries to a lesser degree, show exceptions. (See Book II, Chapter 8, etc.) Still, even in the United States, the scholar should at least test every name against this standard.

A second assumption—at least tacitly current among European scholars—is that place-names regularly either describe the site or record some human occupation or ownership of the place. Again, non-European examples supply many exceptions.

A third common assumption is that a name, once established in a language, follows in its phonetic development the main stream of the development of that language. Thus, if the sound usually written as *a* changes to *o* in ordinary words, the same sound in place-names will also so change. Though, once again, certain exceptions occur, this doctrine of "phonetic parallelism" is a cogent one.

To illustrate the whole process of names within a language, we may consider England. That country has been intensively studied, and the situation is a fairly typical one—at least for the longer-settled areas of the world. The English people have, predominantly, spoken the same language for well over a thousand years, and, since this book itself is written in that language, the names fit into the text harmoniously.

From the investigations of English scholars, five basic conclusions may be drawn as to the history of the English place-names in the last millennium.

1. A place-name pattern of England was already established in Anglo-Saxon times, and apparently the majority of presently recognized places were then known by established names.

2. These names were prevailingly Anglo-Saxon in language, that is, in form and spelling, and (presumably) in pronunciation.

3. As what may be considered a kind of corollary to 2, these names, by a great majority, were Anglo-Saxon in meaning, and therefore intelligible to the ordinary person, that is, the Anglo-Saxon warrior or farmer of King Alfred's time lived in what we may call a familiar environment, where he knew what the names "meant."

4. These names have survived, and they form the present main body of place-names in England.

5. To the ordinary twentieth-century Englishman these same names, in a great majority of instances, are not intelligible.

These five propositions, thus stated succinctly, call for some annotation.

1. Although the documentation is not full enough to make certain a negative statement, as-yet-unnamed "places" were, probably, most of the less important natural features, such as small streams and hills. Certainly unnamed were entities still not in existence, such as the numerous country-houses which were established after 1700. Many field-names also date from the last three centuries.

Still, in spite of these exceptions, the generalization holds, and the situation serves to demonstrate the solidity of Anglo-Saxon culture.

2. As regards being Anglo-Saxon in form, spelling, and pronunciation, allowance is to be made for dialects and for change of language with time. "Anglo-Saxon" as a linguistic term is not altogether precise.

Yet, again, the main proposition is tenable. Even names derived from Celtic and Latin (and possibly even from earlier languages) had been absorbed. Thus, some names were derived from the Latin *castra,* "camp." These names, however, appeared in such spellings as *ceaster* and *cester,* far removed from Latin, but good Anglo-Saxon. (See Book III, Chapter 11.)

3. The proposition that the names were generally intelligible is demonstrable from the spelling actually preserved in numerous documents. Thus any ordinary person doubtless knew the meanings of Acton and Blacwaelle, just as a present-day American would know their equivalents—Oakville and Black Creek.

By the year 1000—or, indeed, by any particular year chosen—certain names would have been unintelligible already. Thus Thames, Severn, Avon, and most of the other names for larger streams, together with some of the older habitation-names, such as London and Kent, were already "just names," having been taken over from earlier languages and never, in a strict sense, having been Anglo-Saxon, just as with such American equivalents as Mississippi and Schenectady.

Moreover, some names had come to be unintelligible because of social changes which had resulted in certain words becoming obsolete and therefore meaningless, when preserved, like fossils, in names. For instance, by the year 1000 the Anglo-Saxons had long been Christians, and were using the word *cirice,* "church," having no further need for *hearg,* which had been their word for a heathen temple. Such a place-name as Harrow, therefore, must have become obscure to anyone except an antiquarian, of whom there were few among the Anglo-Saxons.

Nonetheless, the ordinary person lived in a familiar world of intelligible place-names.

4. That most of these names have survived is demonstrated by mere inspection of any comprehensive list of modern English place-names. Actual records of changes of names are rare, such changes having been, apparently, against the generally stable nature of English culture. Henry VII replaced the old name Sheen with Richmond when he built a new palace there, a short distance up the Thames from London. Perhaps for "public relations," Mechingas became Newhaven when it developed into a Channel port. But no weighty list of such examples can be compiled.

Much more numerous, naturally, are names that have merely been added, such as those of country-houses and fields, already mentioned. The Norman conquerors sprinkled a few French names, especially for newly built castles and newly founded monasteries. The development of modern civilization also shows its influence. On the whole, however, a study of the English place-name pattern leaves one with amazement and admiration at the thoroughness with which the Anglo-Saxons did their work of naming and at the tenacity of the English tradition through ten centuries.

5. The fifth proposition is of outstanding interest in the present chapter. It may, therefore be re-stated: "To the ordinary twentieth-century Englishman, these same names, in a great majority of instances, are not intelligible."

Admittedly, the wording is vague. What is "ordinary"? What constitutes "a great majority"? Does "not intelligible" mean partially or wholly so? What, even, is implied by "these same names"?

These questions, fortunately, can be fairly well answered.

By an "ordinary person" of the present time is meant one who has made no study of linguistics or of the Anglo-Saxon language, probably 95 per cent of the population. "These same names" are those which scholars can demonstrate to be Anglo-Saxon. "Unintelligible" may mean wholly so, or partially so, as in such names as Barford and Blackrod. By "great majority" some such figure as 80 per cent is implied, though it has not been soundly established by statistics.

The main topic of this chapter thus emerges as the attempt to explain the present situation of mixed intelligibility and unintelligibility that has become established in a well-studied region, considered as representative of those where the same language has been spoken for a long period of time.

Along with the mere tenacity of the English names, the chief influence to ensure some intelligibility has been phonetic parallelism. Thus Aeppelford, recorded c. 900, has become Appleford. So also it has gone with Bridebroc to Birdbrook, Blakeheth to Blackheath, Aelm to Elm, Fourstanys to Fourstones, Fercesford to Freshford, Wallesende to Wallsend. In all of these instances—and hundreds more could be added—the meaning has presumably remained clear and constant through the centuries.

At work in some of these examples, as an aiding influence, is what may be called the Principle of Final Attraction (see Book I, Chapter 7). Thus the Aeppel of Aeppelford might just as well have remained Aeppel. Being already so close to a common word, however, it was attracted by analogy to exactly that same spelling. This principle has generally been effective with this particular word, and places named for an apple-tree or an apple-orchard throughout the country generally appear as Apple. As an exception one may note Appuldurcomb, where an older spelling survives.

The counter-influences, those producing unintelligibility, are both numerous and complicated. They may be divided into phonetic and semantic.

The phonetic influences are those working primarily as shifts of sound (expressed, often, in the spelling) without affecting the meaning, except in a kind of secondary result, and commonly working toward loss or obscuration of meaning.

The most common of such influences is the tendency toward shortening. In general, people tend to shorten names as much as is possible without the risk of too constant ambiguity. The tendency is strongest with personal names, which are commonly reduced to a single syllable, as in Katherine to Kate and Frederick to Fred. Place-names are similarly treated, especially when long. Thus in the present-day United States we have Chi, Philly, K.C., and L.A.

In England we find Bede, about 730, recording a town as Eoforwicceaster. By 1300, with some help from the Danes and Normans, this had worn down to the single syllable York.

Actually the English have avoided extreme shortening (at least of their official forms), and many of their place-names remain of three or more syllables—Canterbury, Nottingham, Glastonbury, Liverpool, and many others. Even these names, however, show some shortening, as with Glastonbury, which has at least pulled itself together from the Glaestingeberia of Domesday Book.

A particular phase of shortening is to be connected with the general evolution of the language. The numerous and varied inflectional endings of Anglo-Saxon leveled to a final *e* in Middle English, and even this vestige disappeared in modern English speech. Though phonetic parallelism largely took care of the process, many remnants of the old inflections remained to obscure the meaning.

Bathum, as a dative plural, appears in 796, but later is given as Bath, the idea of there being more than one bathing-place having been sacrificed for brevity.

The Anglo-Saxon spellings Oxnaford, Oxenaford, and Oxeneford all show a genitive plural and indicate that the meaning was "ford of [the] oxen." Chaucer, about 1390, wrote Oxenford, thus keeping the plural but losing the genitive. Eventually the name shortened to Oxford.

Similarly, the initials *n* and *r* are to be viewed with suspicion, being often mere vestigial fossils from the phrase *atten* or *atter*, where *ten* and *ter* are forms of the inflected definite article. Thus Nash is what is left of *atten ash,* "at the ash-tree," and Rea and Ray, both rivers, are from *atter ae,* "at the river."

Even more numerous are the phonetic obscurations resulting from the amalgamation of specific and generic. A common specific, for instance, is the Anglo-Saxon *hwit,* which was pronounced like the Modern English *wheat,* and developed by regular phonetic change into *white.* As a descriptive this word was coupled with numerous different generics, such as *bourne, acre, chester, cliff, hill, ford.* Amalgamation in common speech resulted in forms in which the long *i* of *hwit* was followed by two or more consonants. In that situation there was a strong tendency toward a shortening of the *i* with resulting forms, unintelligible to the modern Englishman, such as Whitbourne and Whitford. The shift did not always occur, so that Whitecliff, Whitefield, and a few others survive. Before a vowel or *h* the long vowel usually maintained itself, as with Whitehill, but even in Whitacre and Whittaker the vowel shortened—probably here because it was the first syllable of a trisyllablic term.

Similarly, *green* is commonly *gren,* and *sheep* is *shep.* Particular confusion, even for the expert, arises with *read,* "red," and *hreod,* "reed." Only by inspection of early forms, or by a guess as to appropriateness, can the expert decide that Redbourn is "reed stream," but Redcliff is "red cliff."

The process of assimilation also works toward unintelligibility. Thus *suth,* "south," not only shortens the vowel, but suffers assimilation of its final consonantal sound, becoming *sut* before -*ton* in the common Sutton, "south town." Before other consonants with other generics it takes different forms, as in Sudbury and Suffield. The combination of vowel-shortening and assimilation shows also in Shefford, "sheep-ford."

Probably of much greater importance than phonetic processes in removing English place-names from the realm of common speech are changes which may be classed as semantic, or cultural. Basically these arise because of the conservative nature of place-names, which cling on tenaciously even after meaning has deserted them. In fact, some onomatists have promulgated the theory that the only true place-names are those that have thus ceased to mean anything!

In the thousand years of our survey perhaps as many as half of all the English place-names have wholly or partially become obscured because the language has, so to speak, changed beneath them, and left them stranded but firmly in place, like boulders, dropped by a shifting and melting glacier, whose places of origin only the geologist can determine.

The loss of words with the passing years and the substitution of new ones as needed are universal throughout languages. Both tendencies were at work in Anglo-Saxon times, as illustrated already by the loss of *hearg* and the use of *cirice*. Other casualties of the adoption of Christianity were the heathen gods. Woden, Thor, Frig, and Tiw were forgotten, but they remained firm-set as place-names, though meaningless in the current language, as with Woodnesborough, Thursley, Frobury, and Tysoe.

Changing social or political customs also had their effect. One Anglo-Saxon land-unit was the *hid,* an area thought sufficient to support one free family. It survives, fossilized, in many places called merely Hyde, as well as in Nynehead, "nine hides," and others.

Other terms that disappeared were those dealing with forests and their clearance. As the woodland shrank back before ax and fire, the word *leah* went out of use, but it survived as one of the commonest place-name elements—most often as -*ley.* So complete was its disappearance as a common noun that even the experts argue about its meaning. It may be connected with the word for *light,* and have meant "light-place," that is, a natural glade or a man-made clearing. When the forest was forced back and the open places coalesced, *leah* lost its significance. There was no longer such a thing. Instead, groves and woods stood isolated in the midst of open country throughout much of England. As would be expected, however, *leah* survived in the names of towns and villages, just as *prairie* survives in town-names of the American Middle West, though the passerby can no longer identify the boundaries of the original treeless area that was called a *prairie.* Now that the landmarks over much of

England had become the groves or clumps of trees, *leah* sometimes shifted, apparently, from the open spaces to the trees that
remained. As a result it seems, in some instances, to be applied
to a place without trees and, in others, to a wooded place. Either way, it came to be a term without modern significance,
often clipped to a mere -*ly* or almost to nothing, as in Acle and
Eagle, "oak-glade," and Bradle, "broad glade."

Place-names, however, may be meaningless, not because the
thing that they denote has vanished, but because a new word
has taken over. The term for a large stream was *ea*. It was so
short that by mere usage it wore down to a vestige, showing up
as a single sound in Eton, "river town," and by itself yielding
such stream-names as Eye and Yeo. Perhaps because of this
vanishing nature, or for other reasons, *ea* yielded to *river*, a generic that still shows its French origin by often standing in front
of its specific, as with the River Thames. The many names
formed from *ea* thus became, as it were, orphans.

Many other terms, used both as specifics and as generics, either disappeared or were replaced by new terms, usually of
French origin.

The process of change by analogy or folk-etymology also has
had its effects. An uncommon name—especially one that has
wholly or partially lost its meaning—tends to be made over in
common speech (and eventually in writing) to something that
may or may not make sense, but at least is composed of familiar
elements. Thus Finnsheved, "Finn's head (i.e. hill)," came to be
Fineshade. These names are especially interesting because they
are actually misleading, persuading anyone to believe that he
knows the origin, when he does not. Ferryhill, for instance,
suggests the plain idea of a hill near a ferry, but is from *fiergen*,
"wooded hill," with an additional *hill* added later. Arrowfield
seems reasonable enough, but actually contains *hearg*, "heathen
temple." Badsaddle has nothing to do with horsemanship,
being from "Baeddi's hazel-bush." The list could run on indefinitely.

In spite of all this change, however, certain terms hung on bravely. Scarcely put into doubt as to meaning have been such common generics as *ford, cliff, brook, house, land, pool, ridge, water, wood.* Even when coupled with cryptic specifics these terms provide a certain comfort of familiarity.

Some of the specifics, similarly, remain generally clear in meaning—*sand, old, new, long, ox, west.* Coupled with clear generics we get wholly clear names—Sandford, Oldland, New-land, and Westbrook.

As the result of all of these processes, and even of others which are not so easily classifiable, the Englishman came to live, year by year, in a land with names of unknown meaning, though scarcely to be called alien or foreign, since the names themselves remained firmly English; the language, it was, that changed.

So also the history runs, typically, for much of Europe, and for many regions over the globe in which the same language has been continuously in possession throughout long periods of time. Both a language in general and its place-names continually change with time. But the two, to use a comparison, may be considered as following separate paths—and the paths inevitably diverge.

7
Research Within a Language

In the present chapter, as in the preceding one, England provides the examples. The discussion here will attempt to demonstrate something about the giving of names, by means of a consideration of scholarly methods in their study. Such study has been chiefly European, and the prestige of European scholarship has been such that even many non-European scholars have tended to emphasize the established methods.

The European approach begins with the acceptance of the three assumptions, or hypotheses, which were outlined at the beginning of Chapter 6. The scholar's energy is involved particularly with the first assumption, "Every place-name has a meaning." If he can establish the meaning—that is, the name's etymology—he has done his work successfully. With few exceptions these scholars would consider an "interesting" name to be one involving a complex problem of language. The orientation is thus almost wholly linguistic. There is little interest in the *giving* of names.

This situation is understandable, and, indeed, almost inevitable. In the development of research in place-names, the scholar has found a rigorous linguistic discipline to be essential. "Etymology" it has been, and, most attempts at "etiology," the problem of the reason why, have seemed mere amateurish speculation.

If the matter merely stopped at this point, no positive error would result. Unfortunately, it does not so stop. Being so exclusively interested in etymology, the European scholars follow a second assumption, that place-names must be either descriptive or personal. One scholar, for instance, argues that a certain height cannot be Stag Mountain because it does not look like a stag! Even a little study of name-giving in America or Australia would have taught him that an animal-name may be given for a number of reasons—and, indeed, is rarely thus literally descriptive.

With place-names derived from personal names, the same *caveat* must be posted. Bodiam in England can be analyzed roughly as "Boda's meadow," but this does not establish that Boda ever owned it or lived there. The name may, for instance, mean that he met with an accident or was killed at that place. There may be even other reasons, as the testimony of American place-names shows clearly.

As for the third assumption—that place-names follow the phonetic development—the European scholar is nearly always deeply trained in phonology, and therefore able not only to apply the general principles but also to make allowance for special situations. A century ago, when such study was just beginning, the conception of linguistic "laws" was rigid, and had a good influence in largely suppressing the uninhibited imagination—which, in the old epigram, "paid very little attention to consonants and none at all to vowels."

Thus oriented, the competent scholar approaches the study of place-names by, first of all, collecting the early forms of each name. He may find one of them in a charter of the reign of Henry II (*c.* 1175), a second in Domesday Book (*c.* 1070), and a third in a passage of the Anglo-Saxon Chronicle (*c.* 990). In later years, after 1400, many occurrences are to be noted, but these are of little interest as compared with the older ones. To these early forms, therefore, the scholar addresses himself. He determines the likely spelling (with allowance for dialect and date) which the element in the names would assume in "standard" Anglo-Saxon. He establishes the apparent meaning. If this meaning makes sense as a place-name, his work is well along. Otherwise, he tries further, perhaps postulating a personal name, which he uses with an asterisk to show that it is not actually recorded but merely constructed as a likely name for a man or woman, and one which can explain the place-name in question.

He also, in a difficult case, visits the place itself, in instances where the modern preservation of the name makes the site known. If he has postulated a meaning "steep slope," and finds a steep slope there, he feels himself confirmed. If there is no such slope, he may still maintain that the building of the railway in the nineteenth century destroyed the slope, or he may return, disappointed, to his studies for further hypotheses. At this point, possibly, he may consider more meticulously the possible influence of other languages.

In the end he will either establish a reasonable etymology or he will go no further than a suggestion which he himself will label questionable. In very rare cases, he will not even make a suggestion, but will be forced to comment, "Origin unknown."

Having satisfied himself with an etymology, the European scholar, figuratively, releases a sigh of relief and satisfaction, and murmurs, "That one's done!" He may indeed append a trite "explanation." If the etymology comes out as "ash-ford," he will note "ford where ash-trees grow." If it is "fox-stream," he will put it "stream haunted by foxes."

Though we must pay the very highest tribute to this linguistic research, the explanatory note is at best what anyone could have supposed for himself, and at worst it does positive harm by oversimplification. Is it really "ford where ash-trees grow"? Or may it not be a ford marked by a particular ash, doubtless notable for its size or because it was a rare species and thus conspicuous among the predominant oaks of the region? As for "stream haunted by foxes," American experience shows that the names of native animals are usually given because of some special incident involving that animal, and may even, paradoxically, spring not so much from abundance as from rarity.

In general, however, the European scholar's lack of interest in the causes of name-origin is understandable and obviously springs from necessity. In dealing with the ordinary place-name, he simply has no historical data that will give him the slightest clue as to the particular reason—or even the occasion—for the naming. There is no getting blood out of a turnip. The scholar cannot be blamed for this situation. He can, however, be blamed for his assumption that the most commonplace cause must be assumed in all cases, and for his general lack of interest in the process of naming, as it can be studied in "newer" regions, such as the Americas and Australia.

As a corollary to this exclusively etymological interest, European scholarship has become fixated on the older names, the newer ones being generally clear and obvious in their linguistic origin. In place-name dictionaries such names are commonly thrust aside with the mere label "Recent," or 'Of obvious meaning.' Also thus occurring is the seemingly derogatory "Fancy name." Just what "fancy" is supposed to mean I have never seen defined, but I would take it to be applied, generally, to any name that arose by conscious naming-process after the year 1500, especially if anything a trifle unusual or imaginative appears in it. Even the monumental works of the English Place-name Society pay minimal attention to post-1500 examples. The great Eilert Ekwall, in his *Oxford Dictionary of English Place-names,* does indeed include Blenheim, but with the almost insultingly terse comment, "Named from the victory of Blenheim in 1704," thus not telling when the name was applied, by whom, or for what specific reason, though on the facing page, under the entry Blean, he devotes fifteen lines to the details of an etymological problem. The names Lover's Leap and California occur several times in England, and the reasons for their existence there are of interest to an American—but not to conventional European scholarship.

One unfortunate effect of the predominantly etymological approach has been the reduction of the semantic explanation to a kind of least common denominator, so that, as already pointed out, names are *en masse* considered as originating by description or from a person. As a result, our ancestors are made to appear extraordinarily dull and unimaginative people. Did not the ancient Gauls possess some of the wit and alertness for which their descendants, the French, are notable? Did not

certain Angles and Saxons display at times a humorous attitude toward life that crops up now in the Cockney and in the
humorist of the pub? If so, we might expect at least a few
names in France and England to reflect some alertness, wit, and
humor.

As an example of the excellence of the European scholarship—and, in a smaller way, of its limitations—we may take the
English names beginning with the element *Fair-*. When the meticulous investigations of the English Place-name Society shall
have been finished and tabulated, the total of these names may
well pass the hundred mark. Actually listed in gazetteers are
about twenty-five of them. Treated by Ekwall are ten examples.
We cannot know precisely his reason for the omission of the
others, but may suppose that he considered them of too little
importance as places to be included in a "concise" dictionary, or
that they were post-1500, no earlier forms having been discovered.

To that useful though mythological person known as the ordinary Englishman, the names in *Fair-* would naturally, as a
group, be referred to the common adjective *fair,* and probably
in the archaic meaning, "beautiful." Ekwall in his dictionary,
however, by the collection and analysis of early forms, none
later than 1300, has been able to establish three (or four) origins:

1. To explain Farnburn (1242), Farenburne (*c.* 1030), Ferne-
leghe (Domesday Book), and Farnleg (1249) he demonstrates
an origin from the word appearing in Modern English as *fern,* a
common-enough descriptive specific for natural features.

2. Forfeld (817) demands a connection with an Anglo-Saxon
for, "pig," a word surviving in its derivative, *farrow.*

3. The Anglo-Saxon *faeger,* "beautiful," surviving as *fair,* Ekwall assigns as the source of Fairefeld (*c.* 1250), Fairefeld
(1203), Fayrelye (*c.* 1250), and Fairsteda (Domesday Book).

4. Also from *faeger,* but with the specialized (and non-esthe-
tic) meaning "clear," is Fareforde (Domesday Book).

Semantically, these conclusions offer no difficulty, and *fern* is
actually commonplace. *For,* indeed, is rare as a specific, but

other terms for swine are of frequent occurrence, and *for* cannot be said to raise any serious problem. Esthetic terms do not appear commonly among Anglo-Saxon names, but there is no reason why *fair* should not be present occasionally. Besides, as seems to happen with such words among primitive peoples, *faeger* may have been a general commendatory, with the broad meaning of "fine, good." As such it could easily assume its other meaning, "clear" as applied to water. *Clear* is especially applicable when coupled with *-ford,* as being a counterpart to the common Fulford, that is a ford that is "foul, dirty, muddy."

In these cases examination of the sites could not be of help. If a place, in 1200, was beautiful or ferny or a pigpen, that same place may or may not show the same qualities in the twentieth century, but neither way is anything to be proved.

Thus far, then, the method is triumphant, in working back to the oldest forms and then separating and distinguishing the various origins.

This procedure, obviously, does not tell us everything, and nothing such is to be expected. It assumes the commonplace origin, with no allowance for the namer's whim or humor or for accident or incident. Nonetheless, Ekwall's analysis determines much, and makes its statement with clarity and authority.

The method, however, has a particular limitation. In the analysis, the Fairfield in Worcestershire, on the basis of an early (817) Forfeld, is referred to *for.* But Fairfield in Derbyshire and in Kent, along with Fairlee and Fairstede, are all referred to *faeger.* These four, however, lack recorded early forms, none antedating 1200, and thus being, as far as record goes, four hundred years later than Forfeld. The suspicion thus arises that the one Fairfield is distinguished from the others only by the accident of the preservation of a single ninth-century form.

In such a situation controversy can arise, if the name is one to engage scholars' special interest. All the battery of historical phonetics may be brought into action. The rarity of *for* among Anglo-Saxon names may be cited in favor of *faeger.* On the opposing side, this same rarity may be brought forward as favoring the substitution of *fair,* as *for* became obsolete. Moreover, *fair* is used here with *field, ley,* and *stead,* common generics which are readily or naturally associated with swine but not likely to be very beautiful or to be so identified. We should expect an esthetic term to be used with *brook, mere,* or *hill.* But such couplings are missing. The method of historical linguistics therefore has its limitations.

American material, as so often, supplies interesting sidelights and commentary.

In the United States the first element *fair* occurs more than one hundred times in current gazetteers, thus being, in comparison with the size of the country, not nearly so common as in England. Etymologically, the name offers no problem worthy of the European scholar's attention. It is of interest, however, in other areas—semantics, history, social customs.

The name Fairfield was applied in Connecticut in 1667, probably being taken, as the custom then was, from the name of one (or more) of the English villages. The older meaning of *fair,* that is, "beautiful," was, however, still in use, though obsolescent, and an additional reason for the application in Connecticut was certainly a commendatory one. Since a meadow or an Indian "old field" may have marked the site, there is also a descriptive possibility.

From this start Fairfield was propagated across the country—in most instances echoing the first one. Thus, a man who had once lived in the town in Connecticut was responsible for the name in California. Generally, also, we may assume, most of the towns being in agricultural country, there were descriptive and commendatory suggestions.

Fair as a common adjective, moreover, has displayed semantic changes in the last two or three centuries, and some of these developments show in place-names—considerable numbers of them, such as Fairbanks in Alaska, originating from personal names.

The old meaning, "beautiful," which had become obsolete in common speech, lingers as a kind of poetic archaism, preserved through such diverse sources as nursery rhymes and the King James Bible. It remains not only in Fairfield, but also, half-fossilized, in a number of repeated town-names, such as Fairview, Fairmont, Fairmount, Fairoaks.

In the specialized sense of "fair weather," the word has stayed in active use, but this meaning was not prolific of names. It stands, however, in Cape (and Mount) Fairweather in Alaska.

Also in common use was *fair* meaning "just, equitable," and settlements known as Fair Play were thus named.

From a different origin, but still not raising an etymological problem, is the use to mean a gathering for sales and exhibitions, and Fairground in Vermont (and elsewhere) preserves this meaning.

In this investigation of Fairfield and its kindred names the American scholar need not even have special linguistic training, since he works by the methods of history. Like his European co-workers, also, he is dependent upon early records, sometimes being able to find testimony of the actual time, occasion, and reason for the naming.

The necessary conclusion might seem to be that the problems of research in place-names are so diverse as to constitute two separate topics or disciplines—the one focused upon etymology, the other upon the motive of the naming. Some European scholars, indeed, seem content thus to view the situation.

Nonetheless, the objective is to elucidate place-names, and so we must recognize essentially one field of study—operating for advancement of the whole, and, as occasion requires, by different disciplines.

Moreover, the situation has been presented, for ease of demonstration, in an oversimplified form. In America the native Indian names present etymological problems as difficult as those of Europe. The too-common attitude that one should solve such names by the historical approach (as when the opinions of "old-timers" are solicited) has resulted in much compounded ignorance. In the Indian field basic training in the necessary languages and dialects and thorough grounding in historical linguistics are as mandatory as for European study, and have too seldom been evidenced.

On the other hand, the proper study of European place-names requires at least a historical appendix to treat the large numbers of place-names that have been traditionally swept under the rug and curtly assigned to oblivion under such labels as "Recent" and "Fancy."

The situation is similar to that which occurs in science when two groups work toward the solution of one basic problem, one group using the discipline of a particular science (let us say, physics) and the other using another discipline (let us say, biology). Advance is more likely to come, not through ignorance and mutual lack of respect, but through cooperation and understanding.

8
Names Between Languages

Place-names possess a marked capacity to outlive the displacement of one language by another, by being passed from the speakers of the original language to those of the succeeding one.

Before the invention of writing (and normally, indeed, after that time also) inter-linguistic traffic in place-names required some verbal exchange between the speakers of the two languages—in most cases, as we can roughly state it, between conquerors and conquered. Occasionally some horde may have descended upon a district and slaughtered the inhabitants so quickly and so totally that the killers learned no names. Generally, however, as historical examples illustrate plentifully, conquerors are not so bloody-minded, or perhaps merely not so efficient. Captives may at least be allowed to give information and thus buy a little time before having their throats cut. There are spies and renegades, comely captive women, slaves. Human inertia and laziness are aids. The giving of new names is an act of labor, and it also requires some imagination. Easier to take the names already in use! Religion must be regarded. A river and its god or goddess bear the same name, and to replace that name may have unfortunate results. Safer to learn the old name!

The ancient Israelites, according to their own tradition, received precise orders from the Lord to exterminate the Canaanites. But their moralists, some centuries post-conquest, kept querulously complaining that the people had not obeyed the Lord's order. Certainly the occupiers of the land adopted many Canaanitish names.

We even have preserved for us in the Book of Joshua some indication of one way in which the name-transfer could have occurred. The two spies who entered Jericho must have been able to speak the local language, or they would have been of little use as spies. They apparently talked freely with the double-dealing prostitute Rahab, and they would have been interested in learning the names of places, so as to facilitate the campaign.

Fortunately, however, we need not depend upon such ancient and possibly legendary materials. The contacts of English with Mexican Spanish, American French, and the various Indian languages in the United States, along with many other modern situations, supply a wealth of material for demonstrative examples.

Names may be transferred from one speech to another, orally, in three different ways. In addition, under the influence of writing—and, even more, of printing—another possibility is added. They are: 1. phonetic transfer, 2. translation, 3. folketymology, and 4. visual transfer.

1. The method of what is here termed phonetic transfer is generally considered the normal one—that is, the commonest. This method is natural when neither party understands much of the other's language, and communication is at a minimum.

In such a situation the newcomer hears the name and then renders it in his own language in what may be called a reasonable approximation of what he has heard or thinks that he has heard. The sound-system of any language differs from that of another. If the name as pronounced to the newcomer contains sounds that do not exist in his own language, he renders them as somewhat similar sounds in his own language, or may even ignore them.

In the Southwest of the United States many names (some of them originally Indian, but having assumed Spanish form) passed orally from Mexican Spanish to American English in the nineteenth century. The situation is useful for illustration because it is a simple one, the Spanish-to-English transfer raising few difficulties, since all but a few Spanish sounds have close equivalents in English. First of all, it must be recognized, phonetic exactitude is not to be expected. The Spanish vowels and such consonants as *d* and *t* differ more or less from the roughly corresponding English sounds. In colloquial speech, however, such minor differences are ignored. The Spanish sound which most often raises a problem is the one commonly represented by *j,* though sometimes by *g* or *x.* The speakers of English usually approximated an initial *j* sound by *h,* as in Gila or Jacalitos. But an intervocalic *h* is difficult and not "natural" to speakers of English. Accordingly, in many cases, though it may have been sounded at first, the *j* simply disappeared, as in Vallejo. The same loss occurred with Bexar in Texas, and the two vowels then coalesced to produce a colloquial pronunciation close to the English *bear.*

In the transfer of a new name the speaker retains his general speech-habits. In taking such a name as San Francisco, the Americans transferred it, broadly speaking, phonetically. In so doing, however, they altered the length and quality of the vowels to correspond with English speech-habits. To Mexicans, this American pronunciation, though generally intelligible, is definitely foreign.

Since the nature of the contact between the speakers may vary greatly, we have difficulty in reconstructing anything like a typical situation, and the actual sound that the name takes in the new language may feel the influence of the particular circumstances.

If the transfer occurred in haste and under stress, as during a warlike invasion, we should expect less care in the rendering than if it took place during friendly and leisurely contacts of trading. Certainly the degree of mutual understanding between the two parties is an important influence. So also is the continuing contact between the languages, as in a border-zone.

The relations of the Americans with the Indians is illustrative of the complexity of the situation, and the amount of variation occurring as the result of differing dialects and of personal idiosyncrasies in pronunciation on the one hand and of perception on the other. A repeated name in New England is one that literally seems most probably to be "little field," which was used with reference to unforested places where the Indians had once cleared the land for their agriculture. Granting that some of the confusion is mere spelling, the name occurs in various forms, such as Pequonnock, Poquomock, Poquonock, Pequannock, and Peconic.

As one should always remember, such a phrase as "transfer from one language to another" is a figure of speech. The actual transfer is not between languages, but between individual persons, along a sinuous and sometimes uncertain path, involving perception and speech as well as physical sound-waves, with chances all along the line for what may be termed "error."

The case of an important river of the United States demonstrates the personal quality and the difficulties resulting. As it happens, personal testimony is preserved. In 1607 Captain John Smith landed with the colony at Jamestown. He was alert and intelligent. Having traveled widely, he had doubtless developed some facility at picking up the rudiments of a language, and during the first year he had some contact with the local Indians. Still, he was a busy man, and we cannot think that he, lacking time, as well as teachers and books, had made much progress with the highly difficult Algonquian speech, totally alien from any language that he could previously have known.

In 1608 he led an exploring party to the upper Chesapeake Bay, where he discovered a large inlet or river. From the Indians he determined—or, at least, he so stated—that its name was Patawomeck, which he thus wrote down in his report but for which he gave no meaning. From this origin Potomac has developed.

Various scholars have expended much erudite labor in attempts to elucidate this name. Even excellent linguistic methods, however, have failed to yield conclusive results. The problem, in fact, becomes not a linguistic, but a human one—John Smith.

Even granting that he had learned at Jamestown the useful traveler's phrase, "What's its name?" or "How is it called?" did these Indians, a hundred miles north, speak the same dialect, or even the same language? Even if they understood him literally, did they really know what he wanted? Indians did not conceive of a large river as having a name as a whole. Obviously, being friendly and interested in the strange newcomers, they made a reply, but they may have been saying something entirely different. On the other side, Smith was not a trained linguistic anthropologist, but only a clever young Englishman. He wanted a name for his report. So, without analyzing the process himself, he performed several actions. First, he assumed some particular sounds, as uttered by an Indian, to be the name. Then he repeated these with what seemed to him the proper sounds, though Algonquian (it may even have been Iroquoian) was not easily equatable with English. Finally, from those sounds he wrote the name in the uncertain orthography of Jacobean English.

2. Translation provides the second method for the transmission of place-names between languages. It indicates—and, we may almost postulate, requires—a fair ability, at least in one of the parties, to communicate across the language-barrier, and it therefore works more readily in times of peaceful contact and along linguistic boundaries, where some degree of bilingualism exists. It cannot always be assumed to have occurred even when forms of identical meaning for the same place are known in two languages. If a stream bears such a common name as Big River or Red River in both languages, the situation may only indicate that the speakers of the second language applied an obvious and easy descriptive term from their own observation, without even knowing what name their predecessors had used.

Translation is likely to occur with more important names, since they circulate at greater distances and among men who are commonly conscious of linguistic differences and may be, themselves, to some extent bilingual. Large features, moreover, are less likely to be classified as the property of some individual tribe or nation than to be considered as international.

Through the centuries the English name Red Sea has been Erythre Thalassa in Greek, Mare Rubrum in Latin, Rothes

Meer in German, Mar Rojo in Spanish, and so on. The Black
Sea, the North Sea, and the Dead Sea have been generally
translated. A striking example is the Cape of Good Hope,
which began its career in fifteenth-century Portuguese as Cabo
da Boa Esperança. The Spaniards soon rendered this as Cabo
de Buena Esperanza, and the other nations followed with their
own translations, as if unwilling to admit a Portuguese name-
monopoly for a great international landmark. Such multiplicity
of names creates a problem for international chart-makers, but
their difficulties are not likely to change popular usage.

As may be expected in onomastics, there is much irregularity
in practice. On the analogy of the names already cited, we
should expect Greenland, Iceland, Cape Verde, and many
others to be subject to translation, but they usually are not, or
may be translated in some languages and subject to phonetic
transfer in others.

In any case, translation is a common enough practice to be
considered as a possibility in any case of doubt.

3. The third mechanism for the transmission of names between languages is that known as folk-etymology, which in its
widest sense is to be associated with the process of assimilation.
Since it is based upon sound, it has a relationship with phonetic
transfer, but it is essentially different.

Though folk-etymology is probably less active in inter-
linguistic shiftings than are phonetic transfer and translation, it
is a regular process. It cannot be dismissed as a mere vagary,
chiefly modern and self-consciously humorous.

As a means of transmission, folk-etymology is most active
when the languages differ markedly in sounds. In the United
States, for example, Spanish names are easily absorbed into English by phonetic transfer, but French names are much more
difficult. As a result, folk-etymologies originating from Spanish
are almost lacking, but French supplies many well-known examples—Smackover from Chemin Couvert; Picketwire from
Purgatoire; Lemonfair from Le Mont Vert.

Folk-etymology has also been active in the Americas between
the various Indian languages on the one hand and English,
French, Spanish, and Portuguese on the other.

The whole process of folk-etymology is more fully treated in Book II, Chapter 7.

4. From the point of view of onomatologists who are concerned only with medieval and more ancient names, into which classification most of the European scholars fall, the influences of writing—and even more markedly, of printing—are of little or no interest, or may be termed inconsequential. Since the invention and the increasing importance of printing, however, names have more and more often shifted by visual process. From the very invention of writing, moreover, certain influences upon name-transfer became possible, and the specialists in medieval names are fully conscious of so-called scribal problems.

In England, during several centuries after the Norman Conquest, the great mass of the people continued to speak Anglo-Saxon (or Middle English, as it is called from about 1150), but the ruling classes, civil and ecclesiastical, spoke Norman French. Most of the clerks, who conducted the correspondence and wrote the documents, were attached to the ruling classes and therefore spoke French, and wrote either in French or in Latin.

One curious result of the situation was that the linguistic majority did not altogether rule, but in the long run the ordinary people adopted many French forms for names. One reason, certainly, was that the written spellings tended to remain fixed from generation to generation, and were inscribed in deeds, wills, charters, and other documents which served as established points of reference and with which no one wished to tamper without good cause. Naturally, French exerted no influence upon the vast majority of minor names, but such influence has helped determine the names of important towns, where the speakers of French chiefly lived, in the service of their feudal lords and the church.

Thus a Norman preference for *r* over *n* resulted in the Anglo-Saxon name Dunham becoming Durham. So also, we have Salisbury in place of a possible Sarisbury, along with Exeter and Gloucester, where they might have been Exester and Glouchester.

An illuminating later example of the influence of print

occurs with Florida. The Spaniards in the New World applied this term widely, as a descriptive, "flowery," and also to record a naming in the Easter season (Pascua Florida). In Spanish the accent is upon the second syllable. That pronunciation offers no difficulty to speakers of English, and has been used for the Florida Mountains of New Mexico. In English, however, the name of the district and state has borne the accent on the first syllable—at least as its occurrence in verse shows—from the early seventeenth century, and probably from its entrance into the language. The most reasonable explanation would appear to be that the transmission was not by word of mouth, as happened in New Mexico. Instead, the name apparently became known in England through a written or printed form, probably as it appeared on maps or charts. People unfamiliar with Spanish would then have been likely to follow the common English practice of accentuation. In addition, they might have taken the name to be Latin, and therefore have put the accent on the first syllable.

In more recent times the importance and prestige of the written word (especially in print) has increased greatly. Many people—we might even say, people in general—have come to hold the opinion that the printed form is "official," or "proper," and that the pronunciation should conform to the spelling.

Many exotic names in the United States have been introduced from books or maps in their established spelling, and then pronounced according to popular American conceptions. Thus, when applied to American towns, Berlin, Madrid, and Pekin are accented on the first syllable; Genoa and Modena on the second.

A complicated example of the influence of printing occurs with the name of the great city of Los Angeles. Founded by the Spaniards in 1781, the village and town remained Spanish-speaking for many years. Even after annexation by the United States in 1848, English took over slowly. There continued to be much bilingualism, and a large segment of the population still remains Spanish-speaking, and naturally—in a Spanish context, at least—they use their own pronunciation for the name of the city. The speakers of English, therefore, have never lacked a model.

In the course of the development almost every sound in the name became controversial. Should the first syllable be *loss* or *lohs?* Should the final one be *luss* or *leeze?* The struggle, however, centered upon the *-ng-*, and we may confine ourselves, for simplicity, to this problem.

The Spanish sound of *-ng-* is difficult for speakers of English. Partly because of this difficulty, a great diversity of pronunciations developed as the city became more and more Americanized in the late nineteenth century. Some pro-Spanish enthusiasts set themselves to use and to propagandize for others a pronunciation approaching the genuine Spanish one—a quixotic attempt which was bound to fail. Others paid some gestures of respect to Spanish, usually by maintaining the so-called "hard *g,*" as if deriving the name from *angle*—a procedure which might be called normal and one that might well have succeeded. Eventually, however, during the rapid growth of the city in the twentieth century, these Spanish and pseudo-Spanish speakers were overwhelmed by newcomers who arrived from non-Spanish areas in tens of thousands, had no interest in Spanish, assumed that the pronunciation should conform to the spelling, and had already been using, before coming to California, a pronunciation based upon spelling.

The essence of this pronunciation was the assumption that the *-ge-* spelling should be taken, after the common English language practice, as standing for the so-called "soft *g,*" or *j.* As a corollary, the *n* was disassociated from the *g*—or, as it had become, the *j.*

Besides the support drawn from the written form, the *j*-party took strength from the fact that the name was literally "the angels," and that *angel* has the *j* sound in English. Rather curiously, no one seems to have advocated a change of spelling, the written form being legally and governmentally "official."

The controversy (and confusion) extended over half a century, often with rancor. It even entered into politics.

As might have been predicted, the full Spanish pronunciation, though remaining in use among the Spanish-speaking people, had no chance of general victory as the English speakers came more and more to predominate. In the end (if such words can ever be written), the *j*-sound has prevailed.

A possible secondary result of the long period of uncomfortable doubt is the variety of ways in which the people have avoided using the name at all, for fear of getting into controversy. Politicians, not wishing to take sides, have referred to The City of the Angels. The shortening *Loss* has been heard among some citizens. Others have begged the question by saying Loss-an-less. Almost universal, however, has become the simple acronym L.A.

The present listing of methods for transmission of place-names from language to language may be an oversimplification, in that the methods may sometimes work together or be superimposed. Such complications need not be associated with important places; an insignificant stream in the western United States may be used for demonstration.

The name Raft River, in what is now southern Idaho, probably originated with the Alexander Ross expedition of the Hudson's Bay Company in 1824, and was first recorded, as Raft, in 1826. In the next few years, however, the stream was mentioned under a different name, with various spellings—Cassia (1832), Casu (1832), Ocassia (1832), Cassie (1837), Cozzu (1838). Obviously, these transcribers were struggling to reproduce a strange, orally transmitted term, and at the same time they were doubtless themselves uncertain spellers. Not until 1843 was this term correctly spelled, and explained, by J. C. Frémont, the noted explorer. The son of a French father, he spoke French fluently, and most of his men were French-speaking. He, therefore, may be considered to write authoritatively when he notes "a stream called Raft River (Rivière aux Cajeux)." In actuality, *cajeux* is a dialectal term in American French (not occurring in standard French), meaning "raft(s)." Obviously, therefore, Raft translates Cajeux, or *vice versa*. As far as the record goes, Raft is six years older, but this small precedence is inconsequential. Since Ross's expedition included speakers of both French and English, Raft and Cajeux may have come into use at about the same time, even on the same day.

Though the Raft-Cajeux coupling makes the meaning unquestionable, the name is strikingly unsuitable, a fact that was noted in a record of 1834. The stream, in near-desert country, is too small for the use of a raft.

An origin by folk-etymology (from earlier Indian, English, or French forms) is possible. An early French trapper in the region is recorded as Casseau. A connection with common French *cache,* "hiding-place," is attractive, but this last hypothesis violates the general principle of folk-etymology by progressing from the more common to the less common.

Lacking definite information, we can only suppose that the inappropriate name originated from some minor incident, even with a touch of humor or irony—a common enough process in the early West.

Within a decade or two, Americans replaced Canadians in this area, and the name Raft River was securely fixed. The French term, however, survived on a tributary, being recorded as Casua (1846), Cashier (1848), and Casier (1848). These are, again, obvious attempts to render orally transmitted material, with Cashier influenced by folk-etymology.

In 1849, at the time of the Gold Rush to California, a large number of emigrants passed that way, many of them keeping journals. From the sources of journals that have survived, Raft River is commonly written in plain English. The name of the tributary, however, turns up in a bewildering multiplicity of forms, indicative of the fact that the emigrants were still writing down the name from what they heard—Cache, Cachia, Caggeen, Cajaux, Cajing, Cano, Carus, Cash, Cashire, Cassue, Cayiux. A few of these forms are uncertain in some details because of obscure handwriting.

From this almost utter confusion a standardized form finally arose by folk-etymology. Cassia—actually recorded once at the early date of 1832—was certainly not a common word among Western Americans, but it would have been known to some from its pharmaceutical use and from its occurrences in the

King James Bible. As it happens, a plant of the cassia family grows in parts of the West, but it is inconspicuous and useless, and its existence and biological relationships would scarcely have been known except to a skilled botanist. Probably, therefore, it has nothing to do with the naming, and the present Cassia Creek must be credited to folk-etymology.

To add to the complication there is the possibility that one part of a name may pass over in one fashion, while another does so in some other way. The English-speaking frontiersmen found the Algonquian-speaking Indians, especially in Pennsylvania, using a name to designate a salt-lick, where game was likely to be abundant. This name they rendered by phonetic transfer as Mahoning, and it still thus stands upon two streams. They must have learned that in literal meaning *mahon-* was "salt-lick." They may or may not have learned that *-ing* was a locative ending. Certainly, however, the name Licking developed, and still exists. It apparently represents a translation of *mahon-* and a phonetic transfer of *-ing*.

9
The Name and the Tribe

The word "tribe" as here used, after common custom, designates any discernible group of people larger than a family, sharing a sense of long-enduring entity, and practicing some joint action. No attempt need be made to distinguish tribes from sub-tribes, clans, septs, and so forth, on the one hand, and from nations and confederacies, on the other.

In general, the toponymist should not carry the investigation of tribal names to the point of inquiring into their etymology or cause of origin. Such study constitutes an interesting field in itself, but its introduction into place-name study not only complicates and vastly extends that study, but also is likely to lead to confusion and error.

In the vast majority of instances, the existence of a place-name that is derived from a tribal name means nothing more or less than a close association of that tribe with that region—commonly, its occupation or domination. Therefore, the basic conclusion as to origin can merely be "From a tribal name," with the assumption that the tribe or some of its members once lived there, or still do.

Other origins may now and then occur—usually because of incidents. The Mohawks, for instance, lived in what is now the state of New York, where they have left their name upon a large river. The name also appears, however, throughout the United States upon places which are commemoratively named from that river. The name also occurs upon some features in New England, where it probably denotes spots associated with forays of the Mohawks against the local Indians.

An analogy appears between tribal names and personal names. When we ascribe the name Bolivia, along with many similar ones, to a certain Bolívar, we should identify him and indicate why his name was so used, but we need not present its etymology, any more than we do for Jones and Mary in Jonesboro and Marysville.

The question then arises, "Why grant any space at all to the special problems of tribal names?"

The justification rests in the extraordinary number of place-names that are derived from tribal names. Among these are many uncertain cases, and some knowledge of the characteristics of tribal names may help with the solution. Moreover, the methods of the shiftings and transmissions, from tribal names to place-names, and *vice versa,* are pertinent.

As illustrative of the close connection of the two, one may point out that as a rule the tribal names show the same derivation as the associated names of nations, provinces, and the larger habitation areas, including strongly marked natural features such as islands, peninsulas, and isolated valleys.

As the historical record shows plentifully, the derivation may proceed in either direction—that is, the tribe may give its name to the region, or the region may give its name to the tribe. The former is probably the more common, and may even be termed regular. Thus Scotland, England, France, and, indeed, most of the names of the European nations sprang from those of tribes. The same is true for the smaller regions and provinces and for the cities—as abundant examples demonstrate in Book III.

Not infrequently a double transfer has occurred. Thus, at the beginning of historical record a tribe known as Siculi held much of the great island off the toe of Italy. As a result the island came to be known by a name which English still preserves as Sicily. From Sicily, then, the term for the inhabitants of the island came to be Sicilians, the Siculi having lost their identity.

Many tribal names, however, are certainly derived from place-names—the land having been named independently of the people, and earlier. There was no tribe ever known as the Ices to produce Iceland and Icelander. Many other such instances occur. Some of these are obvious, as is Icelander, but careful study may be necessary to reveal some of the others.

Names of tribal derivation are also common on natural features. Such a statement may almost be taken as a truism. If a region in general bears a tribal name, the chief river or mountain is likely to be so called.

The situation in Europe, however, is exceptional, in that its more important natural features rarely bear tribal names. More strictly speaking, they rarely bear names which can be clearly distinguished as tribal—doubtless, in many instances, because they are old and are derived from unknown languages. When the Indo-European tribes took the land over, their names came to stand upon the cities and the provinces, but many of the chief streams and mountains already had names, some of which were probably tribal. These, however, remain unrecognized.

The situation in the United States is vastly different. There the English settlers regularly transferred the name of the local tribe to various natural features, especially the chief river. Thus we have not only Seneca Lake and the Adirondack Mountains, but also the long roll of great rivers, among them the Mohawk, Susquehanna, Alabama, Missouri, Iowa, Illinois, Arkansas, and Kansas, many of which eventually provided state-names.

An interesting and curious case is that of Delaware. Originally the partly French title ("de la Warr") of an English lord who was briefly the governor of Virginia, the name was bestowed in his honor upon a bay. It passed to the chief river that entered the bay. Since the river-tribe equation was well fixed in English minds, the Indians inhabiting the river-basin came to be known as Delawares. Eventually these people were forced to move farther west, and they took the name with them, inevitably placing it upon various places as far west as Oklahoma.

The basic identity between the name of the tribe and the name of its inhabited territory is, in fact, so close as to approach 100 per cent, no matter which of the two names may have originated first. In some cases, indeed, depending partly upon linguistic usage, there is actually no differentiation. Thus Xenophon in his march through Asia encountered many tribes without using place-names for their countries. He writes, "through the Kardouchoi," or "into [the] Makronas." But he uses both Armenoi and Armenia, probably because Armenia was a Persian satrapy and in official usage.

The same manner of speech was in common usage on the American frontier, where the backwoodsmen spoke of going "to the Chickasa," or "to the Illinois." Eventually, but only by gradual evolution, many of these tribal names became place-names.

Like place-names, tribal names are long-lasting. A people clings tenaciously to its own way of identifying itself. As a result, these namings tend to survive linguistic and geographical shifts, and to be difficult, often impossible, to decipher.

Some tribal names can be interpreted, and we may group their manners of origin into five classes: 1. from the idea of "people"; 2. from location; 3. from description; 4. from an ancestor; 5. from religious ideas, especially totemism.

1. Many tribal names are—at least, in primitive stages of culture—not formal designations, but merely equivalents of the pronoun "we." Such a situation is wholly natural, since there is little need for people to refer to themselves if they are living in their own group and lack important contacts with other tribes. Similarly, members of a family rarely use its name, but commonly say "we" or "our family."

At a slightly advanced stage, with more outside contacts, the appellation may develop into meaning "people," with the implication that those of other tribes are not human in quite the same sense. At a still later stage this kind of name takes the meaning of "men" in the sense of "outstanding people."

Names of this type may be found over the earth—Ainu in Japan; Bantu in South Africa; Berber in North Africa; Inuit and Chuchi in the polar regions. They are common in North America—Leni-Lenape, Salish, Yokut, Washoe, Tlinkit, Illinois.

2. Tribal namings from geographical location are common. In California, from the time of the English-speaking trappers, about 1820, a stream was known as Pit River, from the pitfalls dug there by the Indians. Soon the tribe itself was called the Pit River Indians, or the Pit Rivers.

The Angles, most probably, had their name from a region on the Continent known as Angel, which itself meant something in the nature of "river-bend, land in a river-bend."

Both the Senecas and the Oneidas of the Iroquois confederacy took their names (the first in Algonquian speech; the second in Iroquoian) from a standing rock.

Often the name is vague, or states the location relatively. The Quapaw and the Omaha (by tradition and by evidence of language) divided at a river, and the Quapaw then were "downstreamers," as against the Omaha, who were "upstreamers," their territories being separated by some hundreds of miles.

Etymologically, the Mercians were the "borderers," though in historical times they occupied the central third of Anglo-Saxon England. The name must have started at an early period, but the particular boundary they lived along cannot now be surely known.

Alsace takes its name from a tribe, probably meaning "those of foreign parts," which would be a term applied to a German tribe by other Germans because the Alsatians lived to the west of the Rhine.

3. Many tribal names are descriptive, if we allow a broad interpretation to the word. Physical and racial names, however, are rare. Such an extensive term as Blacks may be applied, but it usually fails to have tribal specificity. In general, tribes are small, and there is not enough difference, physically, from one to another near-by group to make such a distinction useful.

On the other hand, distinction by food or eating habits is common, though not always rationally based. The Paiutes of the deserts of Nevada were notorious among early travelers for their omnivorousness. Nonetheless, their sub-tribes were distinguished as eaters of some particular food. Many such names appear to be derogatory, given by neighboring tribes. Thus the Sheep-eaters of the Rocky Mountains had been driven into the fastnesses, and were, allegedly, forced to live poorly and exclusively on the mountain-sheep, shut off from the buffalo of the plains.

The general term "foreigner" occurs frequently, obviously not being applied by the people themselves. Thus the common Anglo-Saxon word *walh* became the name Welsh, and it also appears in Cornwall, of which *Corn-* was originally a tribal name.

Similar in nature are names springing from the idea of uncouth, foreign speech. Thus Hottentot is the Dutch term for stutterer, the Hottentots' own name for themselves being a proud "men of the men."

Not very common are names which specify some occupation or way of life—probably because neighboring tribes do not usually differ much in such respects. According to Strabo, however, the Georgi of the Caucasus—hence, the modern Georgia of that region—were literally so called from the Greek "farmers"; other tribes in the area, unlike them, were nonagricultural nomads.

Much controversy has raged as to whether certain peoples were named for a characteristic bit of clothing, ornament, or equipment. Livingstone reports of the Banyamwezi that their name,' "people of the moon land," was derived from an ivory pendant in the shape of a new moon that the people wore around their necks. Long-maintained, tantalizingly attractive, but never fully demonstrated is the theory that Saxon is from *seax,* a type of knife, dagger, or sword, which was a favorite weapon.

4. Many tribes assume their name to be derived from an ancestor, and such belief is often clearly signaled by a linguistic element, in the usual patriarchal society, with the meaning "son, sons." Thus we have the often-repeated Arabic element Ben, Beni; the Irish O'; the Scottish Mac. Among many Indians of South and Central America the tribe has been regularly known by the name of the chief.

The Children of Israel, (Beni-Israel) as well as the Tribe of

Benjamin (probably Beni-Amin) display this type of patro-
nymic. Whether the ancestor is real or legendary or mythological makes little difference as far as the name is concerned. Generally, however, we can be credulous. From many actual
examples we know that a man's followers become known by his
name. In the Mexican revolution of the early twentieth century,
Villa, Zapata, and other *jefes* gave rise regularly to such names
as Villistas and Zapatistas. Given proper conditions, such names
could have become tribal, and eventually even national. So also,
every petty Anglian or Saxon leader seems to have advanced
inland against the Britons with his followers—probably both
men and their families—distinguished by his name with the suffix *-ingas*. Thus from Haesta, Reada, and Beorma we have the
Haestingas, the Readingas, and the Beormingas—and eventually the cities of Hastings, Reading, and Birmingham.

5. The tendency of people to identify themselves with animals is marked at all levels of culture. Even the athletic teams of
the modern United States go by such names as Tigers and
Bears. In many cases such names indicate the actual beliefs that
are known as totemism, or else the worship of theriomorphic
gods.

Identification with plants (usually, trees) is rare, but can be
seen in the Lemovices of ancient Gaul (hence, Limoges) who
took their name from the elm, presumably a sacred symbol.

Among some peoples, naming for animals is systematic and
nearly universal. The Bechuana of South Africa thus divide
themselves into "they-of-the-monkey," "they-of-the-crocodile,"
and so forth. Clear on the other side of the globe, the Chilkats
of Alaska named their tribes the Ravens, Wolves, Eagles,
Hawks, and Bears. Some of the more important Indian tribes
of the United States are the Crows, Snakes, and Foxes.

From classical sources, animal-names are preserved on
enough tribes to suggest that the practice was once widespread.
Ancient Italy had the Picentes, "woodpeckers," Lucani,
"wolves," and Hirpini, "wolves" in another dialect. The ancient
Lycians, prominently mentioned in the *Iliad*, were literally "wolves" in Greek speech, and probably to the Lycians themselves.
Hyrcania, near the Caspian Sea, was from an Iranian word for

wolf, and is sometimes rendered "wolfland," as if notable for those animals. More likely, it was from still another tribe known as "wolves" whose name resembles that of the Hirpini.

One important and pervasive influence upon tribal names is the internal-external distinction, that is, whether the name originates with the people bearing it, or whether it originates with other people and is imposed upon the people thus named.

An internal name is neutral or commendatory; an external name ranges from neutral to derogatory, and may even be downright insulting. Obviously, the whole class of "we" names is internal. The really boastful name is internal and rare, but occurs in some of the ancient Gallic peoples, as in Bituriges (hence, Bourges), meaning "world-kings."

Tribes are likely to bestow names upon their neighbors. Often the relationship is hostile; at the least, it may be patronizing, involving much prejudice. Newcomers, advancing toward a tribe, are likely to learn its external name first, and eventually that name may become the general one.

A famous case occurs with the ancient people who knew themselves as Hellenes, but became known to the Romans as Greeks. Eventually the Romans passed this on, and it became a modern name. Although much controversy is involved, the most likely supposition is that some of the Italic peoples who lived to the north and west of the Greek-speaking peoples first made contact with a small tribe of the northwesterly Hellenes— possibly before the general term Hellene came into use. These Italic peoples learned the name of this tribe to be Greeks (Graeci), and applied it inclusively as they became acquainted with others who spoke the same language.

One of the most important North American tribes had its own name, Dakota. The French and English, however, advancing from the east, learned of these people from the Ojibways, the Dakotas' enemies, and thus got Nadowessioux, which they shortened to Sioux. The name is hostile and derogatory, probably meaning "snakes," and by implication "treacherous enemies."

Strabo lists a number of names so derogatory as scarcely to be adopted by a people for themselves, no matter how unusual we may consider their habits to have been. Scordisci appears to contain the Greek *skor,* "dung." The Cynamolgi and the Phtheriophagi, to credit their names, were the "bitch-milkers," and the "lice-eaters." Of the latter Strabo comments that they received their name (he means, apparently, not giving it to themselves) from their squalor and filthiness.

Since the subject of the present study involves place-names primarily, the discussion of tribal names cannot, at this point, be carried further. In later chapters (see, especially, Book II, Chapter 4) it will furnish a topic for renewed discussion. As in the study of names in general, the many thousands of tribal names render selectivity the basic art in their treatment. The Spanish chronicler Herrera deserves our praise and our emulation for his self-control in writing about some South American tribes: "Beyond these are twenty-seven nations of different names, languages, and customs, which are not named to avoid tediousness."

10

Some Ways of the Namer

In the course of the millennia the giving of names has progressed under the influence, or guidance, of certain habits of
thought which may be called principles. Most of these have affected the namers unconsciously, and only as phases of the general processes of thought working through language. But some
of the principles—at least, with certain namers and on particular occasions—have exerted their influence through conscious
channels.

In the self-confident nineteenth century the term "law" was
often used in such a context. The word is an apt one, if we recognize that the fate of laws is to be broken, just as it is the fate
of rules to have exceptions. Principle, however, is a safer term,
implying nothing more than a general tendency to move in a
certain direction as the result of continuously acting forces,
with full opportunity for conflicting forces to reverse the course
in special situations.

Two of these principles, presented already, need only be reit-
erated—the Principle of Entity and Use (see Book I, Chapter 2)
and the Principle of Generic-Specific (see Book I, Chapter 4).

To these we here add other principles: 1. Rarity, 2. Special
Vocabulary and Repetition, 3. Analogy and Final Attraction, 4.
Counterpart and System, 5. Point of View, 6. Dual and Multiple
Origin, 7. the "Fossilized" Generic.

1. The Principle of Rarity we may state thus: "The namer is more likely to use the uncommon term than the common one."

Illustration serves the purpose here better than does an attempt at abstract definition. McArthur, in his excellent *Oregon Geographic Names,* comments upon the rarity of Fir among Oregon names, though that is the commonest tree in much of that state. In writing of Oklahoma, Gould makes an analogous statement about the oak. Both of them have missed the point. A very common and therefore undistinguished phenomenon, such as a tree of the prevailing species, does not impress the namer, and also it does not serve to provide a differentiating landmark. A name such as Fir or Oak fails to provide distinction in a country overgrown with firs or oaks.

Far too many "explanations" of place-names have failed to take into account this simple principle. For instance, the common (to the point of being the established) explanation of animal place-names runs, "It is called Wolf Creek, because in early times there were many wolves there." But where authentic records survive, they nearly always show some other reason.

Equally fallacious is the counter-argument, "We cannot accept the meaning 'wolf creek,' because there were very few wolves in that area." Surely, if there were "very few," each one became highly notable and name-worthy.

The importance of rarity also displays itself, especially with plants and animals, in "edge-of-range" names. Hickory Township in Minnesota has little reason to be so called, except that it stands at the very northern limit of the growth of the hickory tree.

Toad River in British Columbia is so far north that toads can never have been numerous or individually large. But to see a toad at all in such latitudes is surprising and could have been the occasion of naming.

Even the obtuse observer—perhaps he more than the acute one—is likely to note what is unusual, and thus to give the name. Failure to recognize the Principle of Rarity has been too common among scholars.

2. The Principle of Special Vocabulary and Repetition may be stated: "In the giving of place-names, the namer is likely to

employ a specialized and conventionalized vocabulary, and therefore these special words are much repeated."

Namers frequently wish to express the idea of size to distinguish one feature from another of the same class, as with two streams. In English a number of words express this quality— *large, big, great, broad, wide.* In actual practice, however, *large* and *wide* occur so rarely in place-names that they may really be considered to be unused. An English-speaking namer simply did not think of saying Large Creek or Wide River. *Broad* also is rare. *Great* occurs as a heritage from earlier times, and with a somewhat specialized meaning "grand, very large." *Big,* on the other hand, is the usual term, and the maps of the United States bristle with *Big*—Big Creek, Big River, and Big Run. That term, after *Great* had begun to be obsolete, became the natural adjective to couple with a stream. Certainly the namers were familiar with the other words, but these terms were not considered as place-names for streams—or, indeed, for features generally. Thus Big Mountain (not High) and Big Pond (not Large) are common.

Another example in the United States is Troublesome, commonly coupled with Creek. Its actual history is not known, but its geographical distribution indicates that it began near the Atlantic seaboard and worked west, and that it is thus to be connected with the westward-moving migration. It suggests a stream that gave trouble to emigrants trying to ford it, or was in some manner associated with minor misfortune. Yet it is, unlike Big, not a very common word in ordinary speech, and no more likely, it would seem, to stand as a name than Unlucky, Dangerous, or some related term such as Trouble or Troublous. Yet, once applied as a place-name, it satisfied a need, became conventional, and even supplied, to unimaginative namers, a convenient *cliché.*

3. The Principle of Analogy and Final Attraction has already been considered to some degree, insofar as assimilation is a process working within a language. By "analogy" is meant the tendency of one form to become like another form. The reason is usually that the second form is more frequently used, because it occurs on numerous places or because it is the name of an important place. (For examples, see Book I, Chapter 6.)

"Final attraction" is merely the last stage of analogy, resulting from a process somewhat comparable to that of such natural forces as magnetism and gravity, becoming stronger as the two reacting bodies come closer together. With names this principle means that, once the two names have become nearly alike, there is a powerful and almost irresistible tendency for them to go the whole way and become identical.

The process is best illustrated by the spelled forms, though it applies equally to the pronunciations. In the United States there are no fewer than five place-names, widely scattered, which are spelled Miami. Three of these (Ohio, Florida, and California) are derived from wholly unrelated Indian languages. One (Arizona) originally honored a girl called Mima. In Oregon the name is from Chinook jargon, "downstream." The statistical probability against five identities thus occurring is stupendously high. (In fact, even the occurrence of two examples of the same five-letter sequence is improbable.) What has certainly happened is that one of the names became what may be called dominant. This one must have been that in Ohio, which was originally the name of an important Indian tribe, and had assumed the spelling Miami as early as 1791. An influence of settlers from Ohio is historically evidenced for the Miami in Arizona. The others, originally, would have been only somewhat similar. Thus in California the name is recorded as Me-ah-nee; in Florida as Maymi, Mayami, and Aymai; in Oregon as Mi-me. From such beginnings, analogy and then final attraction have produced the identity with the well-known Ohio name.

One feature of importance in this principle lies in the suspicion that it casts upon the identity of spelling as indicating identical origin. Though we cannot dismiss such identities as "mere coincidence," yet neither can the identity be taken as of much importance in its etymological evidence. In Italy the spellings of Reggio Aemilia and of Reggio Calabria do not supply strong evidence for an identical etymological origin, even though the possibility of a six-letter sequence by sheer coincidence is very small. The principle of final attraction is better invoked.

4. The Principle of Counterpart and System is of much importance. Ordinary linguistic usage supplies few absolutes. How big is big? It means one thing as applied to a mosquito; another

as applied to a man; still another as applied to a river or a mountain. Many descriptives on place-names are fitting only when applied against another near-by example of the same class. Big River might, in many cases, be Bigger River—that is, it is big only by comparison with smaller streams. Similarly, Red Mountain is not usually to be so called by the standard of roses or arterial blood, but only as it displays a reddish tinge when seen against a background of drab-colored mountains in the vicinity.

Naming by system is only a pluralizing of naming by counter-part. The giving of numerous names has seldom been the work of professionals. Called upon to bestow a number of names, the ordinary person finds himself somewhat at a loss. He has a vague feeling that he should give "good" names, but he is not likely to be a man of much imagination, and a variety of names fails to come to his mind. So if he calls a place after St. Paul today, he will probably honor St. Peter tomorrow, and some other saints on the following opportunities.

One of the most striking occasions of the use of a naming system can be dated as July 3, 1790, when a board of three Commissioners, plus an auditor, met in New York, and faced the duty of dividing a certain region of the state into twenty-five townships, for each of which they had to supply a name. Instead of following a random or whimsical course, they naturally fell into a system, and used (with some exceptions) the names of notable men from ancient history. Thus arose much of the so-called "Classical belt"—Lysander, Hannibal, Cato, and the others.

The United States supplies many examples of system, probably because its rapid extension of population in the nineteenth century made the finding of new names a chore for the unimaginative people who were usually responsible. Thus the counties of Oklahoma were originally distinguished merely by the letters of the alphabet, and Kay County still survives.

Railroad officials had to name their stations on new lines, and sometimes used an alphabetical system. California has such a series, running from Amboy to Goffs.

Numerical systems also appear, especially with chains of

lakes—First, Second, and Third. The islands in the Mississippi River were once called officially by numbers, and an important river-battle of the Civil War occurred at Island Number 10.

Though thus flourishing richly in English on American soil, counterpart and system are universal to the human mind and are super-linguistic. The Latin names for the two chief Balearic Islands were Major and Minor, which have given rise to the modern Majorca and Minorca. In Latin they were simply "bigger" and "smaller"—a perfect counterpart, of especial interest as displaying the comparative form, rare in naming.

In various parts of the world an island and a smaller one "following" it are likely to be called The Cow and The Calf. But in the Mergui Archipelago off the Andaman Islands we find The Cat and The Kitten.

Captain Cook during his visit to New Zealand named Poverty Bay because it was "an unfortunate and inhospitable place." Some distance away, because the Maoris were living there prosperously, he named the Bay of Plenty.

George Vancouver, a patriotic English explorer, named Point St. George on the California coast for his country's patron saint, and then named the near-by Dragon Rocks.

Sometimes the mere juxtaposition of names, without historical evidence, provides enough testimony, as with Harewood and Houndwood, close together, in Scotland. In that same country, near Buccleuch, which is "buck-glen," we find also names meaning "doe-glen," "wolf-glen," and "wildcat-glen," a grouping scarcely to be attributed to coincidence.

5. The Principle of Point of View indicates merely that the name in many cases is determined by the point of view of the namer. An excellent and important example is that large body of water which to the English and the Scots should be the East Sea, but which they call the North Sea. Historically, the name preserves the Dutch point of view, and its acceptance elsewhere is a tribute to Dutch activities in navigation and trade. It is also an excellent case of counterpart naming, since the Zuider Zee, "south sea," complements it in Dutch usage.

Most of the directional names, such as those involving points of the compass or the right-left distinction, are related to point of view, and often make sense only when the direction of the naming is determined. By a fine anomaly Sutherland, which is "southern land," is at the northern tip of Scotland, but owes its name to the Norse settlers, who viewed it from the sea-approach or from the Orkney Islands.

Mountains, being seen and often named from a distance, are likely to bear point-of-view names, which may be inappropriate from certain directions. Thus South Mountain in Pennsylvania and Maryland is really "North" for the many people seeing it from the south. Partly for this reason, some landmark peaks bear several names, according to the direction from which seen—a circumstance noted from as differing places as Norway and equatorial Africa.

Such names as Saddle Mountain and Camelback can have been named only from particular points of view.

6. The Principle of Dual and Multiple Origin must be invoked in the explanation of many names. In human life a man must have, biologically, one father and only one, and a strong tendency has always existed to extend the analogy to the origin of place-names. Much argument has thus resulted in attempts to establish "the," that is, "the single" source of a name. But, when details of naming survive in the records, we often find more than one reason. In fact, one influence may supplement another, combining to prevail against a second proposed name where singly they might have failed.

A revealing original passage is that in the narrative of Richard Hawkins's voyage in 1594. The chronicler wrote that a small bay in the Straits of Magellan was called Crabby Cove:

> It brooked its name well for two causes; the one for that all the water was full of a small kind of red crabs; the other, for that crabbed mountains which over-topped it; a third, we might add, for the crabbed entertainment it gave us.

A few other examples are pertinent. In New Zealand the Maori name for the stream Te Waitere is "the-water-swift," but it was named (1905) both from description and also in commemoration of John Whiteley, *waitere* being the Maori pronunciation of his family name.

Captain William Bligh, on his famous return voyage after the mutiny on the Bounty, noted as of May 29, 1789:

> This being the anniversary of the restoration of King Charles II, and the name not being inapplicable to our present position (for we were restored to life and strength) I named this Restoration Island.

In Canada, Campobello Island was named partly in compliment to the governor, Lord William Campbell, by a pun, and partly because its soil and fine appearance merited the Italian name, "field-beautiful."

A case about which needless controversy has arisen is that of the important Columbia River. Captain Robert Gray gave the name in 1792. "Columbia" was at that time new and commendatory in the United States and, being used by Gray as the discoverer, constituted a territorial claim to the river-basin. But it was also the name of Gray's ship, and many shipmasters have thus commemorated their vessels. There seems to be no reason, however, why Gray should not have felt double motivation.

A whole class of names involves dual origin. In founding their counties and towns the American colonists frequently gave names of counties or towns of "the old country." This furnishes a good example of a naming-system, but it is also much complicated. The choice of one name rather than of another for commemoration had to be decided, and often what might appear to be the secondary cause was in reality the chief cause. Thus York is an English county and town, but the giving of that name to New York in 1664 was primarily a compliment to the Duke of York, whom King Charles II had appointed governor of the colony. Similarly, Huntingdon County in Pennsylvania followed the established system of giving English names, but was in special compliment to the Countess of Huntingdon, who had been a patroness of the colony.

English place-names were also common as family names among the colonists, and the presence of such a family doubtless helped in some choices, as is a traditional belief of the Hart family about Hartford.

7. The Principle of the "Fossilized" Generic may be illus-

trated by Avon, which occurs in England as the name of so many streams that Ekwall's *Dictionary* lists it as "a common river-name." Scholars have long recognized that Avon is from the Celtic, "river," a word well attested in modern Welsh *afon*. These fossilized generics thus come to be specifics of unknown meaning (unless, as with *avon*, the language of their origin is known). They commonly arise from the contacts occurring when one language supersedes another.

The usual process is clear enough, as Avon may serve for illustration. Though there is no detailed record of the Anglo-Saxon conquest of England, we may suppose (and the evidence from place-names strongly confirms) that the Britons were far from exterminated, many of them being absorbed as slaves or serfs, or possibly as allies. In the early stages of this mingling, mutual knowledge of language must have been scanty. If a Saxon asked a Briton the name of the near-by stream, the Briton may simply have answered "Avon" to the generalized question "What is it called?" not distinguishing "What is its name?" from "What is the word for it in your language?" Certainly, in the course of the years, as people of the two languages lived there, the Saxon would have said *ea* for river and the Briton *avon*, but Avon would have been convenient for the Saxon as a term by which to distinguish the particular stream. If the process had been universal, the result would merely have been that *avon* would have entered the English language as a borrowed word for stream. As the situation developed, however, Avon merely became the specific of some streams. And, as the British speech became extinct in Saxon territory, no new Avon could arise. "Fossilized" can be considered an apt term for a specific that is clearly in evidence and even common, but inactive—that is, not increasing in numbers.

Less frequently, the fossilized generic develops wholly within a language as the result of linguistic change with time. Actually the Anglo-Saxon *ea*, "river," may serve as an example, since it eventually was replaced by *river* and, concomitantly, in many names, coalesced with the specific to form a new and longer specific, joined with *river* as a generic. Even if Anglo-Saxon were an unknown language, the many river-names ending in

-ey would require us to postulate a former generic. Thus we have Waveney, Wissey, Mersey.

No matter by which process it arises, the principle of the fossilized generic has been the great reliance of scholars working with names that have arisen in ancient and pre-literate periods (see Book III, Chapter 9). They have thus postulated old generics such as *cuci*, "mountain," *car*, "rock," *ar*, "river."

Needless to say, in their enthusiasm some of these scholars have gone too far. Undeniable though the theory is in some instances, it can be treacherous, as certain examples can demonstrate. (See also Book III, Chapters 9 and 10.)

In California three near-by rivers are the Mokelumne, the Cosumnes, and the Tuolumne. Lacking anything except the place-name evidence, any scholar would be likely to think that *umne* represents an ancient generic which, being applied to three streams, is doubtless to be taken as "stream, river." Our knowledge of the local Indian (Miwok) language, however, is enough to establish that *-umne* means "people, tribe," so that each of the rivers was named for the tribe living near it.

Another California situation is of interest. Throughout a large area in the northwest of the state the term Bally, Bolly, or Bully occurs upon mountains or high hills, such as Bally Peak, and appears also as a quasi-generic, as in Shasta Bally. Apparently by folk-etymology it occurs as Indian Creek Baldy, Billy's Peak, and Bailey Hill. The term is certainly connected with the Wintun *buli*, "peak," and the association with mountain is strong. Another Wintun word, however, is *bola*, "spirit," and the possibility thus exists that these peaks were named with the common belief that gods or spirits are associated with high places. Or does the association extend further back into language, so that *buli* and *bola* are eventually the same word?

This far-western example has peculiar interest for its analogies with Greek mythology. Olympus, a high mountain, was known as the abode of the gods, and it was a name borne by a succession of high peaks extending into Asia Minor. The temptation to take it to mean, linguistically, "high peak" has been strong and is supported by its intimate linkage with mountains. But the California analogy would suggest that it might be taken, as the Greeks supposed it actually to be, in the literal meaning, "abode of the gods."

The principles here enunciated and briefly illustrated may be considered as acting in or upon the human mind in its processes of selecting and establishing names. Generally they represent unconscious influences. But, as will later be demonstrated (see, especially, Book III), much naming is consciously motivated, even in comparatively simple cultures.

II
The Mind of The Namer

Introduction:
The Classification of Place-names

Since place-names exist by so many millions, their division into classes becomes essential, and many methods have been used.

1. Most common of all has been a territorial classification, as when one writes of the place-names of England. Such a system is of great practical use and has much flexibility. Its shortcoming is that it is a classification of places rather than of names, and lumps together all sorts of naming processes.

2. Names have been often classified by means of chronology, as when we speak of pre-Revolutionary names. In England the notable work of the English Place-name Society has been in general restricted to names of which the record appeared before the year 1500.

3. The classification of place-names by language of origin is common and useful. It is especially valuable to the specialist, who must be deeply erudite in the particular language.

4. Many books on place-names have been based upon a classification according to the kind of place which is named, that is, more or less, according to generics. Thus we have studies of town-names, of field-names, and of river-names.

5. In the ordinary dictionary of place-names, where an alphabetical order is used, the classification actually becomes one of specifics. This is especially notable when an "entry" system is

used, by which all the occurrences of a name are included under the heading of the specific. In such a work a single entry would occur, for instance, with Ash, and the entry would then elucidate the use of that term, whether rising from the tree, from a person, from volcanic ash, or from some other source.

6. A loose but sometimes useful classification springs from the attempt to determine the motivation of the namer. Thus we have such classes set up as "humorous names," "religious names," and so forth. Enough similar to be grouped along with these are divisions set up according to cultural background— for example, "place-names from the cattle-industry."

Against such a background, then, subdivision may occur either in depth or in breadth; that is, we may further divide according to the original principle or may set up a cross-classification, such as that by territory, and then further subdivide it according to provinces or counties. On the other hand, we may set up a cross-reference by such a category as "the town-names of England before 1500."

Although convenient, useful, and even to be called essential, these methods of classification of place-names fail to grapple with the actual *giving* of place-names. The present work, moreover, is directed primarily at the elucidation of the naming-process. I will therefore make use of a still different system of classification. Many features of this classification—such as the use of "descriptive names"—have been in use for many years. The actual formulization of the system, however, does not appear to precede my article "A Classification of Place-names," published in *Names,* of March 1954. Since then I have further elucidated the system in my *Encyclopedia Britannica* article (Names, in Linguistics) and in *American Place-names* (1970).

This system of classification rests, basically, upon the proposition that all place-names arise from a single motivation, that is, the desire to distinguish and to separate a particular place from places in general. To accomplish this end, the namer must employ some linguistic process. A spring of water may be notably clear, and will therefore be named Clear Spring. The motive still remains the basic one of distinguishing that feature from others of the vicinity, but the method which is used for this distinction may be called descriptive.

The advantages of this system of classification may be briefly outlined.

1. It deals with specifics, not generics, and thus particularly with the name as a distinguishing feature.
2. It is close to and in harmony with the namer's approach to giving names, and to his feelings.
3. It is complete, that is, it allows for the classification of every individual name. At least, I have worked with it over a period of about twenty years, and I have found no body of names anywhere in the world which fails to fit into the system.
4. The system easily allows for dual or multiple origins or for borderline cases.
5. It allows for both evolved and bestowed names.
6. The system accommodates both the name-giving of primitive peoples and that of sophisticated peoples.

The chapters of Book II will be devoted to the elucidation and exemplification of the various classifications. They are here listed:

1. Descriptive names
2. Associative names
3. Incident-names
4. Possessive names
5. Commemorative names
6. Commendatory names
7. Folk-etymologies
8. Manufactured names
9. Mistake-names
10. Shift-names.

Wholly to accord with the approach here offered, these listings might have used "namings," instead of "names." Ordinary custom, however, as well as the convenience of brevity, make "names" more practical. The emphasis of this treatment will remain upon the process of naming.

The order in which the kinds of names are here presented can be said to reflect, roughly, their chronological development. Descriptive, associative, and incident-names occur among very primitive peoples—therefore, we must believe, from very early periods. Possessive names spring from the idea of the particular ownership of land. Commemorative names arise among peoples who have developed some sense of identity and of their history. Commendatory names, also, arise only with self-conscious namers, people who have an interest in the future. The last four classes, however, do not fall into this rough chronological scheme. Manufactured names, indeed, are to be considered the most recent of all, but the others may occur at any period.

I

Descriptive Names

A descriptive name originates when the mind of the namer, consciously or unconsciously, fixes upon some permanent or semipermanent quality of a place for its identification, as with Big Mountain, Yellow River, and Long Lake. The quality may be recurrent rather than continuous. Thus Roaring Creek may roar only after a rain, but may still be thus descriptively named.

Ideally, the quality must be distinctive, serving to identify the particular place among other places of similar nature near by— especially those using the same generic. Thus, in a certain region the streams may generally be muddy and thus reddish in color. One stream, however, flowing over a country of different soil, may be dark in color, and it will then be called Black River.

In such a situation, theoretically, no stream should be called Red River or Muddy River, since that name would not be distinctive. Actually, a single stream in the area may be so called, since the namer works from what he experiences at a particular spot, not after having explored the whole region and established a rational system of naming. We can, however, be fairly certain that no more than one stream of the region will be known as Muddy or Red, even though many might well be so described. Repetition of a name within the ordinary radius of communal human activity destroys its basic distinguishing value.

Since the namer is not ordinarily trained to scientific exactitude, the so-called descriptive names are often vague or even inaccurate. The namer's *black* may in many instances be more aptly described as merely *dark*.

In addition, standards differ. There is no set criterion for rivers or mountains. What can pass for Big River or Big Mountain in one part of the world cannot do so in some other setting. All is comparative.

Counterpart-names can serve for illustration. When Big River and Little River stand (so to speak) in opposition, they measure up to no standard of feet or meters, but the one is merely so named in comparison with the other.

Descriptive namings are numerous everywhere. They represent a basic and natural method of naming. They may be termed super-linguistic, that is, in spite of varying vocabulary and grammar, a general idea of distinction of places by means of a characteristic quality seems to appear in all languages. Descriptives are especially common upon natural features, less so upon habitations.

One reason, however, for the predominating position of descriptives is that some scholars have tended to extend the class until it has become a general catchall. Given a broad enough definition, the term can become almost a universal.

Even with all possible delimitation the descriptive class remains both large and complicated. It is here presented under eight headings—according, very roughly, to the impression made upon the namer's mind. These are descriptives which may be termed: 1. Sensory, 2. Relative, 3. Intellectual, 4. Metaphorical, 5. Subjective, 6. Negative and ironic, 7. Hortatory, 8. Repetitive.

1. *Sensory Descriptives.* Most commonly, and most simply, a description springs from a sensory impression. Since man is primarily sight-oriented, names based upon that sense are predominant, but names from the other senses are important enough to call for brief presentation.

Although man is well equipped for hearing, names from this sense are rare—obviously because neither natural features nor habitations commonly emit distinctive sounds. An exception occurs with noisy streams, which in recent naming in English are usually termed Roaring. Traces of an older usage survive in the River Loud in England and in another known as Loudwater. Wind-currents producing sounds have occasioned Moaning Cave. Since surf is noisy, one would expect names derived from it, but they are rare. The Shetlanders have placed some such names, for example, Bomba, "drum," and Bruler, "roarer."

Names from smell are even rarer than those from hearing, but Stinking Spring, in any language, indicates a water-source afflicted with the odor of carbon disulfide. The Irish-derived Scecoor, "fragrant bush," is highly unusual.

Names to be included under the general idea of touch are commonly those based upon temperature, and are applied to water-features. Cold, Warm, and Hot seem almost to exhaust the possibilities in English.

Namings from taste are chiefly applied to water-features— Bitter, Salt, Fresh, Sweet (in the sense of "not salt"), and a handful of others.

In contrast, namings from sight occur literally by millions, and the specifics employed are too numerous for more than a sketchy exemplification. The group itself demands sub-classification.

A. Namings from size, which is determined by sight, are everywhere common. The vocabulary, however, is likely to be limited to a few words, such as Big and Little.

B. Namings by color are also numerous. Black, White, and Red are most often employed, but Blue and Green are also common. Yellow is not generally favored, but the Irish have been fond of their term "boy." Neutral tones, such as Gray and Brown, are rare. Either they are too common, as in desert regions, or they are not in themselves eye-catching enough to be picked for a distinguishing feature.

C. Another large group consists of what may be called configuration-names. Hills, mountains, and islands are thus designated as High, Flat, Steep, or Sharp. Lakes and islands are

Long or Round, or even Square, or Crooked. A rock may be Sharp, Steep, or Round.

D. Names based upon material (identified by sight) supply many examples, such as Muddy Ford, Sand Point, Rocky Ridge, and Granite Pass.

2. *Relative Descriptives.* The namer often works not by direct sense-impression, but by expressing the relationship of the place to other places, or to the position of the namer at the time. Such a name is descriptive only from a particular point of view. Here fall the compass-point names, such as North Cape. Others are sufficiently indicated by mere listing—Far Rockaway, Left Prong, Fourth Crossing, Back Bay, Upper Volta, Lake Superior. Many relative descriptives fall naturally into counterparts, as with North-South, Upper-Lower, and Right-Left.

Relative descriptives can also be based upon time. In such usage New is often the counterpart of Old. Commonly, the original name remains unqualified, as with Mexico and New Mexico. Occasionally, however, the reverse may be true. When the Hopi moved the site of their ancient town Oraibi, they preempted the name for the new establishment, and the settlement on the original site has become Old Oraibi.

Distinction according to time is especially a feature of habitation-names, and some famous cities have merely developed from an original "new town." We may thus derive Carthage, Naples, and Novgorod.

Since natural features are commonly fixed, the old-new distinction is rare with them. A channel developing from a shift in a stream may result in New River. Occasionally a newly discovered feature may be so called—as, apparently, with New River in West Virginia. More surely we may cite Newfoundland.

Under relative descriptives we may also group names which express position within another entity, such as an island or county or state. The numerous names with Middle and Center are to be here included. Land's End is a pertinent example. The small town of Northeast, in Pennsylvania, is nearly at the northwestern corner of the state, but it takes its name from being at the northeastern corner of its county.

3. *Intellectual Descriptives.* Still descriptive, but beyond mere sense-impression, are names that are based upon special knowledge or belief. Ecuador is a good descriptive name for a country lying on the equator, but it depends upon astronomical data and a knowledge of the sphericity of the earth, not to be observed by the primitive Indian of the Ecuadorian jungles. The city of Cuzco in ancient Peru was "the navel" to the Incas, but the idea must have resulted from more than immediate local observation and upon some belief that the earth might be supposed to have a navel. So also, Pliocene Ridge, Silurian Hills, Pentamerus Point, Brachiopod Mountain, and many other such names are descriptive, but can have been named only after geological investigations. A mountain in South Africa is Horologieberg because its shadows fall on certain features in such a way as to be used in telling time, a fact not to be known without experience and reasoned deduction.

Here also are to be included those names for which the sense-impression was not direct, but sprang from a map. Vogelkop, "bird-head," as used by the Dutch for the eastern end of New Guinea, could scarcely have been grasped as the shape of the area until after it had been charted. Long Island, off the eastern coast of the United States, was so called by the explorer Adriaen Block in 1614, apparently after he had sailed along it and taken his observations. From the point of view of one of the local Indians it could only have been Big Island.

4. *Metaphorical Descriptives.* In giving a name, the namer may express himself metaphorically, that is, by making a comparison without the help of such a word as *like*. Originally someone may have said, "The outline of that ridge is like a camel's hump," or "That two-topped mountain reminds me of a saddle." The step is then easy to Camel Ridge or Saddle Mountain.

Essentially, such naming picks out one quality of the thing and uses this as an abstract term. The camel thus becomes merely "humpishness," its other qualities, such as its ability to go without water, being quite ignored.

World-wide, the most famous metaphorical name is Sugarloaf. Its history cannot be ancient, for it must have arisen after the beginnings of the sugar-trade in the seventeenth century. Apparently the world lacked not only a sweetener but also a word for a conical or conoidal form. Until the later nineteenth century the product was commonly marketed in sugarloaf form—*pan de azúcar* in Spanish and *Zuckerhut* in German. As a metaphorical descriptive for an up-standing hill, mountain, or rock it came to dot, in appropriate languages, all the newly explored parts of the world, and even to make incursions into the regions already named. A Sugarloaf Hill appears in Kent.

The sugarloaf itself finally became obsolete, but by that time the use of the word in topography had become established. Eventually, as must happen in such a case, the word lost its metaphorical quality, and became merely a descriptive for that sort of hill, and even a generic. People who used the name, and even people who bestowed it, had never seen a sugarloaf and did not even know what one was, or that such a thing had existed.

5. *Subjective Descriptives.* Some names identify the place by the effect that it produces upon the namer. In most languages the descriptive words themselves are likely to be ambiguous in this respect. In English such terms as Dismal or Happy may apply either to a place or to a person, though no one would be likely to suppose that the place itself had any feelings. So also, the term Desolate or Desolation may be taken of a place in its literal sense "deserted, uninhabited," but commonly supposes some emotional effect upon the observer. Mount Remarkable, in Australia, was named by the explorer Eyre because that was the way it looked to him. The Remarkable Mountains are also a feature of New Zealand.

Many of these names are definitely and strikingly subjective. Arid Flat can be taken to be an ordinary descriptive, but Thirsty Flat is a description by implication. So also it goes with Mount Disappointment in Australia, the descriptive quality of which is vivid, but is expressed subjectively, in terms of the effect upon the namer.

Flinders, in 1798, looking shoreward from his ship at the northwest tip of what is now Tasmania, noted "a steep, black head, which from its appearance, I call Cape Grim." But the grimness was not in the dark rock, but in his own mind. His naming still stands.

In other languages the universal feelings of mankind are echoed. The Golfe Triste, off South America, "sad," or "sorrowful," is the Spaniards' commentary on a body of water which presents problems for navigators because of tidal currents.

On the other hand, Joyeuse in French stands not only for the fictional castle, Joyeuse Garde, of King Arthur's Lancelot, but also for real places, which in some way warranted being known as "happy," or "joyous."

In the Scottish Highlands, Muirneag stands for "joy," it being a landmark hill for fishermen making for harbor, and Larig Ghruanach is "pass dreadful."

The widespread use of a word for devil often seems to indicate primarily the effect produced on the namer's mind by a difficult stretch of terrain.

6. *Negative and Ironic Descriptives.* These are not common, but there are some interesting examples. In English the element "no" usually signals the negation, as in Nowood Creek. Since naming is a practical activity, misleading names are rare and seldom endure, even when given. An established example, however, is Straight Creek in Alaska, named because it is very crooked. Happy River, also in Alaska, was so called in 1898, ironically, by a party of men who were having a very unhappy experience at trying to navigate it. This name is, therefore, at once subjective and ironic.

7. *Hortatory Descriptives.* A rare but interesting type of name describes by essentially asserting, "This is the kind of place at which you should perform a particular act." Linguistically the name is couched in imperative or hortatory form. Here we

have the Spanish and Portuguese repeated namings Abreojo and Abrolho, "Open your eye!" an advertisement to the ship-pilot that the place is a dangerous one. Somewhat similar is Quitasueno Rock in Alaska, a name given by a Spanish expedition of 1775, and describing the place as being of such a character that the pilot should "Quit sleeping!" or "Wake up!" So also Alargate Rocks in Alaska is an announcement "Keep your distance!" or, in nautical terms, "Give this a wide berth!" To other names given by seafarers the Spanish contributes Parece Vela, "Furl sail!" and the English, Avoid Bay, a signpost name which Flinders placed on the south coast of Australia in 1802 as a warning to shipmasters who came after him—"from its being exposed to the dangerous southern winds."

Leaving the sea, we can mention the common Spanish descriptive Salsipuedes, applied to a small stream or ravine, "Jump if you can!"

Some seeming hortatories are not really such, but come from phrases which have already been construed as nouns before being used for place-names. Thus the amusing Kiss Me Quick Hills of South Dakota arose because the road across them was full of the kind of irregularity which might give excuse for a girl to throw herself into her lover's arms, and was thus known to American country-folk as a kiss-me-quick.

8. *Repetitive Descriptives.* One type of descriptive seems to be highly restricted, or to be limited to conventional examples. It identifies a place by a repetitive action or activity. Thus many villages in Japan bear such a name as Friday, because they have habitually held their market on that day. An overactive dog may continue his activity long enough to result in a place known as "where the dog barks."

In the end any attempt to classify descriptive place-names tends to break down as the result of their overwhelming number and variety. But the continued existence of a small miscellaneous group can be taken as merely a demonstration of the almost infinite variation of the human mind.

A general quality of descriptives, however, may be noted in

conclusion. More than any other kind of name they identify the place and thus serve a practical purpose. Some of them, indeed, may even be termed "landmark names." Such a one is Pilot Peak, a recurrent name in the American West, arising because it served as a comforting guidepost to early explorers and covered-wagon emigrants.

Perhaps a personal anecdote is allowable. Once, in a small plane with a friend as pilot, I was flying across Nevada, with the ground below, except for the mountaintops, obscured by low-lying clouds. Though my friend was using instruments, the situation for me was not altogether a happy one. I felt a corresponding comfort to recognize, thrusting plainly up into the clear sky, the unmistakable profile of Broken Top Mountain, a landmark that demonstrated clearly to me, even though I was only a passenger, our approximate position and the route that we were following.

2

Associative Names

Such names as Mill River and Dome Lake compose a class to be usefully known as Associative Names. They differ from descriptives in that they do not offer an actual description, but identify by means of something with which the place is conveniently associated and by which it can be distinguished from other places bearing the same generic in the area.

Mill River uses the circumstance that a mill stands (or once stood) on the stream, but not upon streams near by. Dome is actually impossible for a descriptive of a lake, but can arise because that body of water is near a dome-like mountain or rock.

In the present classification, associative names are postulated as a major grouping. Besides seeming to be truly distinct from descriptives, the separate class is useful, at the very least, in setting up a distinction within the over-large descriptive group.

Naturally, some borderline cases exist. Rock River may be judged as supplying a description of the stream's course, but it may also be taken only to express the association of the stream with a rock at some single point. Even Mill Creek describes by implication, telling us that the stream is big enough to turn a mill-wheel—or, at least, that someone thought it to be so.

Associative names may spring from natural or from man-made sources. Natural association can be topographical, mineral, or vegetable—less frequently, animal. A stream flowing near a natural spire of rock may be known as Spire Creek, and similarly we may have streams with such specifics as Pinnacle and Arch, which by their very nature are non-descriptive of streams. The occurrence of a particular mineral in the vicinity gives rise to Gold Lake, Copper River, and many others.

Man—primitive or civilized—is much impressed by natural vegetation, and names thus derived are generally associative. Such specifics as Grassy, Moss, Brush, and Berry are common, but the names from trees are even commoner. The general term Tree is rare, though such a name as Wood Creek (compare the French *boisé*) may indicate the mere presence of unspecified trees. Such names as Oak, Ash, Pine, and Fir commonly occur. Typically, these names stand upon the smaller natural features, such as brooks and hills, but one large European river, the Beresina, bears the Slavic name for the birch-tree.

Tree names usually fail in themselves to make clear a basic distinction. Is the name Oak, in a particular instance, given because of a single landmark tree or because of the notable presence of many oaks? Languages like Spanish allow the names to distinguish easily between singular, plural and collective (del Pino, de los Pinos, del Pinar), but in practice the difference is not well maintained.

In general, the plural idea would be expected along botanical boundary lines or in arid areas where any appearance of trees is noteworthy. On the contrary, in such a well-wooded region as northern Europe a vast number of names must have originated from single trees. Ashford, for instance, is probably not to be explained (as it conventionally is) as "ford where ash-trees grow," but as "ford marked by the presence of a large (or in some way notable) ash-tree." In the course of the centuries the original tree inevitably disappears, but the name, thus orphaned, remains.

With sedentary animals the situation is much the same as with plants. Gopher Meadow and Prairie-dog Mesa may be considered associatives. Most notable in supplying such names has been the beaver. The animal itself is easily seen swimming about during the twilight, and is heard because of its loud tail-slaps; it also builds dams, houses, and canals, besides leaving conspicuous stumps of gnawed-off trees. A beaver-dam is almost as noticeable as a man-made dam, and is itself the origin of many names, such as Beaverdam Creek. All across northern Europe and America the beavers and their work were once noteworthy. England has Beversbrook, Bevercotes "houses," Barbourne "stream," Beverley "glade," and others. The beaver-names dot their way across France and Germany, and on east to mingle with Slavic namings in *bober*. In Canada and the northern United States the beaver-names run into the hundreds or even thousands.

Probably no other animal equals the beaver as an inspirer of names, since no other is comparably conspicuous, useful (for furs, and even for meat), productive of visible works, widely distributed, and sedentary.

Other specifics that are obviously based upon more or less enduring works of animals include Otterslide, Beartree (for a tree marked by clawings), Pigeonroost, Eaglesnest, Buffalowallow. The concentration of animals at salt-licks leaves clear marks, and has given rise to numerous American names ending in *-lick*.

With animals which are neither sedentary nor given to leaving permanent and conspicuous traces, the case is vastly different, but under unusual conditions some names may arise by association. Thus in desert areas of the western United States the mountain-sheep maintained (and still do, to some extent) what might be called an "islanded" habitat, living only in high and rocky country where they find the proper forage and can escape the attacks of wolves. Such places became known to men, and have yielded Sheep Rock and Sheep Range Mountain.

Such an animal as the elephant—being large, conspicuous, and generally unafraid of men—yields some true association names. Ilheta dos Elefantes on the west coast of Africa was so called, in Portuguese, specifically "because of the many elephants there."

Commonly, however, names with such elements as Deer, Bear, Wolf, and Fox arise from incidents and must be catalogued under that head. By unwarranted assumption, an opposite derivation is frequently allowed to stand, that is, for Foxford, "ford frequented by foxes." Such an "explanation" seems unconsciously humorous. One sees, in imagination, a kind of convention of foxes, assembling nightly. What early man, we wonder, took the census to establish that foxes "haunted" this place rather than some other, and in larger numbers? Such names spring regularly from incident (see Book II, Chapter 4).

Associations with man-made works also supply numerous names. In many instances such names replace earlier ones, descriptive or otherwise.

Interesting as a source of names are words, in various languages, for bridge. In primitive times the word may have meant causeway or dike or may have referred to a natural passageway, such as is afforded over a stream by the trunk of a fallen tree. Whether natural or—much more commonly—man-made, a bridge is of the greatest importance for communications, and a place is readily thus designated. The city of Bristol in England is first recorded, in 1063, as Brycgstowe, which is merely "bridge-place." Since the river there is a good-sized one, the bridge was presumably man-made. No record is available as to whether the place had a name before the building of the bridge.

Many English town-names appear first in some form meaning merely "bridge," convincing testimony that even as late as the Norman Conquest bridges were so rare that one of them was not likely to be confused with another. Later, distinctions had to be added. Thus Bridgerule in Devonshire set itself off by adding the name of a certain Ruald, who seems to have owned it (charging toll?) in 1086.

The anomalous but repeated English name Bridgeford seems to require the existence of a ford near a bridge. Perhaps the more frugal travelers still used the ford, especially in times of low water, rather than pay a toll. Or the bridge (possibly a Roman one) may have fallen into disrepair.

France has at least one village which is simply Pont, and

dozens which used the term with a differentiation, such as Pont-de-l'Arche "arch," Pont des Moulins "the mills," and Pont-de-Planches, "of planks." Pontoise, "bridge of [the river] Oise," is recorded from the fourth century, when it was Briva Isarae, using Celtic words for bridge and for the river's name.

In the United States the associative names on natural features but springing from human activity yield a kind of history of the country. Trail Creek usually indicates a stream-route followed in most primitive times. Road Creek and Dugway Creek show a developing civilization. Pounding Mill Creek indicates the now long-forgotten site of a factory for gunpowder, and Powder House Hill a place where the product was stored. Cabin Creek and even House Creek are names placed when a single habitation served for identification. Bridge Creek is comparatively late. Acid Factory Brook in Rhode Island and Paper Mill Creek in California testify to a higher specialization in products. Still Creek may indicate calm water, but, more likely, a primitive industry—whiskey-making.

Superficially considered, associative names appear commonplace and generally uninteresting. Emotions, however, may become involved.

In California a small hill rising conspicuously from the flat land close to San Francisco Bay had been known for many years by the simple Spanish term El Cerrito, "the little hill." In 1909 a town, including the hill within its incorporated limits, took the name Albany, selected for no better reason than that the mayor of the town happened to have been born in Albany, New York. As population increased in the area another town was founded, just to the north, and in 1917 it took the name El Cerrito.

Several decades passed, and no one paid much attention. Then the Albanians began to feel that they had been in some way cheated and wronged. The hill was within their limits, and to be considered their property. Therefore it should not be called by the name of the other town. The only argument, actually, was one of association, since the name of the hill, being that of a natural feature, did not come under municipal jurisdiction, as if it were a man-made work such as a street or

bridge, but was under federal control, insofar as anything official was concerned. Nonetheless, the power of association was
so well established that the movement seemed just and proper
to the people of the area in general, and Albany Hill it now is
on the tongues of most people.

On a much larger scale, an incident culminating in 1921
shows the power of association in determining people's feelings
about names. The state of Colorado (admitted in 1876) had occasioned some controversy in Congress over its name, since the
general area lacked any apt and popular appellation. An old
tradition was to name states after rivers, and so Colorado was
adopted. The inhabitants and the country in general seemed to
approve of the melodious Spanish term, and only after almost
half a century did the problem of association (or lack of it)
arise. The Colorado River nowhere flowed through Colorado!

The name-situation, however, offered a possibility. Because
of the vagaries of explorers the name was applied only to the
lower part of the stream. As happens not too infrequently, the
river was "formed" by the junction of the Green and the
Grand, two rivers of comparable size and length. Of these, the
Grand rose in the mountains of Colorado, and flowed for most
of its length through that state. The legislature of the state
therefore voted in 1921 that the name Grand should be
changed to Colorado. Congress and the legislature of Utah con-
curred. After the passage of a half century the change is so
firmly rooted that many Coloradans fail to realize that things
ever were different.

Association is to be suspected when a name seems inappropriate, or what might be called anti-descriptive. Such a one is
Broken Bay in Australia. How, we may ask, can a bay be described as broken? Fortunately, Captain Cook himself supplies
the answer, writing that it took the name from the "broken
land" near it. Here we have an instance of metaphoric description superimposed upon association—a complicated process by
which to arrive, finally, at what is a very simple name.

3
Incident-names

In 1793 the Revolution was gripping France, but the people of the community of Selongey supplied an incident of their own to talk about. On September 7, near a certain spring or fountain, a wolf killed and ate a six-year-old boy named Nicolas Roth.

Even in the eighteenth century such predators were not expected in September. Possibly the Revolution had already broken down the common ways of life, and given an unusual chance to wild beasts, so that the unfortunate little Nicolas may be listed as a far-off and unintended victim of the Terror.

His horrible fate impressed the villagers. What may have been the name of the spring, if it had one, is unknown. It came, however, to be called Fontaine au Loup, "wolf spring."

The name serves excellently as an example. It is based upon an incident which is recorded in history. It is of France, where incident-names have been rejected or left unrecognized by scholars to the point of hardly being admitted at all. In its final form it has been reduced to the single word *wolf,* so that it can be established as an incident-name only by the historical record.

In one other respect, also, it demonstrates a possible way of namers, in that the wolf, and not the person, stands recorded. The positive actor remained in the folk-memory, not the recipient of the action. Lacking the written record, a scholar would have made some facile conclusion, "Wolves frequented the fountain."

On the other hand, Nicolas Roth cannot have been an important person, and was doubtless the child of peasants, allowed to stray away from home with no nurse or protector. If he had been of importance his name might well have been fixed on the place, as has happened in innumerable instances when a person has died on some particular occasion and his comrades have remembered the place by his name, not by the manner of his death.

Thus we first probably had something like, "The spring where the wolf ate Nicolas Roth," which would quickly have shortened. The members of the child's family might have said, "The spring where Nicolas was eaten," and soon "Nicolas Spring." But the villagers in general considered the incident more than the boy, and so Wolf Spring was the result.

An incident-name is one which arises from a particular event occurring at that place, thus identifying it and distinguishing it from other places in the area.

Commonplace happenings such as may be observed anywhere at any time do not serve for distinction. Therefore, a high proportion of incident-names are colorful—Battleford, Murder Pool. Hurricane River, Earthquake Creek, Massacre Rock.

We must distinguish true incident-names from those that spring from repeated or habitual happenings, and so are to be considered associative or even descriptive. For instance, if a tribe holds a council, the place may be known afterwards as Council Meadow, taking its name from the incident. But if that place should become one of an annual council meeting and then be named, the name can be held to be associative. (See also Book III, Chapter 1.)

What seems to be an illustration occurs with Runnymede in England, famous as the island on which King John met with the barons and signed the Magna Carta. The name actually occurs in that famous document as Ranimede and Runingmeth (from the Anglo-Saxon *runieg*, "council-island") and the assumption, therefore, must be that the place had been habitually used for the holding of councils, and even, partly for that reason, was selected in 1215. Enough evidence thus seems to be available to classify the name as an associative rather than as an incident-name.

On the other hand, the city of Council Bluffs in Iowa takes its name from a single meeting, in 1804, between the leaders of the Lewis and Clark expedition and some Otoe Indians. It serves, therefore, as an excellent example of an incident-name.

Naming from incident is considered to be highly primitive. The first place-names are as likely to have sprung from incident as to have been descriptives. Many primitive peoples, as the record indicates, seem to have been fond of such names—the Tonganese, the Maori, the Eskimo, and (to judge from the Bible) the ancient Israelites. On the other hand, in the name-patterns of England and France incident-names seem to be comparatively rare.

To establish the type, the readiest procedure is to present, first, the names for which some historical record is available. With the general principles thus established, the less well authenticated examples become acceptable.

Incident-names may be analyzed into seven classes, for convenience of presentation: 1. "Acts of God," 2. calendar-names, 3. animal-names, 4. names from human actions, 5. names from an event associated particularly with a person, 6. names from feelings expressed by the namer, 7. names from sayings, especially from exclamations.

1. What is known as an "Act of God," experienced by people at a certain place, may impress them sufficiently to result in that place being thus named.

On July 28, 1769, some Spanish explorers were halted near a stream in California, and the camp was shaken four times by violent earthquakes. They named the stream Río de los Temblores. (It is now known as the Santa Ana River, and, in fact, names from earthquakes are rare, perhaps because they suggest an ill omen.)

The Bay des Chaleurs in Canada was so named by Cartier in April 1534 because he suffered from what must have been very unseasonable hot weather.

Eclipse Harbor in the Canadian Arctic was named by Captain John Ross, explorer, because he observed an eclipse of the moon when anchored there on September 12, 1829.

Foulweather Cape in Oregon was named by Captain James Cook on March 7, 1778, because of a storm.

2. What may be called calendar-names spring from the circumstance that the namer happened to be at that place on a certain day and thus gave the name.

Christmas is a name repeated many times throughout the English-speaking area. On December 24, 1777, Captain Cook bestowed it to an island off the coast of Australia, "as we kept our Christmas here."

Spanish explorers, both by land and by sea, were assiduous namers by the calendar. If the record of Vizcaíno's voyage along the California coast in 1602 should be lost, its progress might be reestablished by the religious namings. He named a bay for Saint Didacus on November 12, and it has remained as San Diego. By November 25 he had sailed farther north, and the saint's day had become that of Saint Catherine, remaining as Santa Catalina Island. So he went, dropping names for Saint Barbara and Saint Lucy, and for the Immaculate Conception. Point Reyes still informs us where he was on the Day of the Three Kings.

Another voyager given to calendar-naming was Amérigo Vespucci, who apparently confused a bay with a river, which he sighted on January 1, 1501, and thus gave the name Río de Janeiro, "river of January."

3. As with Fontaine au Loup, many places have received names from incidents springing from animals. In fact, the majority of animal-names originated thus. Only with sedentary animals such as the beaver (see Book II, Chapter 2) can an origin from association be assumed.

Plants, on the other hand, rarely produce incidents. Poison Creek, however, may not indicate polluted water, but merely a

stream on whose bank someone ate a poisonous plant or suffered from poison ivy. Loco Meadow may record the happening that someone's horses were affected by eating locoweed.

Many incident-names from animals, however, are fully authenticated from many parts of the world. Arsenjew, in Siberia,
tells of Wildboar River, so named because, along its course, wild
boars tore two hunters to pieces. He tells also of Tiger River,
named for a well-known and particular tiger who raided the
natives' trap-lines. In South Africa, Stream Conyama (a Hottentot word for lion) was named for a particular lion which was
shot there in 1858. In the same area, Elandskraal sprang from
the shooting there of the first eland killed by an expedition of
1685.

The United States is especially rich in both animal-names and
preserved records of the incident causing them. At Bear River
in California in 1850 Lewis K. Wood was badly mangled by a
grizzly. At Bear Creek in Oregon a sheepherder reported
seeing nine bears frolicking by the stream. At Bear Gulch, also
in Oregon, an excited bear once jumped upon a pack-horse,
causing well-remembered confusion.

Many incident-names from animals make use not of the general term, such as *deer,* but of some special term, such as *buck,
doe,* or *fawn.* In 1837 William Grant came upon an Iowa stream
where a large buck had taken to the water, and was standing at
bay against a wolf; Grant, unchivalrously, shot the buck, and
then called the stream Buck Creek.

Similarly, any kind of special detail suggests an incident. Oso
Flaco Lake in California, translatable as "thin bear lake," obviously refers to a particular animal, and the record actually
stands that the men of the Portolá expedition, marching northward in 1769, killed a thin bear here.

Though the examples so far given are all of larger mammals,
the smaller ones and even the so-called lower forms of life also
supply incidents and therefore names. In California alone
about two hundred natural features bear the name Rattlesnake,
and many others that are merely called Snake originate from
the same reptile. Only the grizzly supplies more names in that
state. Insects also provide names, as in the numerous places

called Mosquito, many of them because of tormented nights spent there by unfortunate campers.

The number of names for a certain animal in a particular region may be put down, indeed, as being proportional not to its numbers, but to what we might call its incident-producing capacity. The rabbit, the deer, and the crow are so common as scarcely to be noted, and they rarely or never surprise, startle, or threaten. Shakespeare expressed it; such creatures become "as the cuckoo is in June," and no one pays them any attention. On the other hand, though a grizzly or a rattlesnake might not be seen every day, an encounter with one was likely to be hair-raising, serious, or even fatal. The place was often remembered as "Where we met that grizzly," or "Where I almost stepped on that rattler," and eventually such reminiscences consolidated into names.

4. Human activities of all imaginable kinds may give rise to names, and many such stories are reliably reported.

In Australia we have Accident Inlet, because a man was accidentally shot in the ankle; Disaster Inlet, because Lieutenant Gore of the *Beagle*, when hunting, was shot in the hand; Mount Destruction, because an early expedition had several of its horses die of thirst: "It was a day that threatened to destroy every living thing of the party."

Good luck as well as bad luck can be effective. For example, also in Australia, Escape Cliffs arose because two members of the *Beagle* expedition were here threatened by the aborigines, but escaped.

The incident may be trivial. Cheese Rock in Massachusetts was named by Governor John Winthrop on February 7, 1652; he was on a journey and, his servant having neglected to pack a lunch, had nothing but cheese to eat. Deathball Rock in Oregon is a humorous reference to an unsuccessful attempt of an amateur cook to bake some biscuits.

Reading the accounts left by explorers, whether by land or sea, shows that these men, time and again, gave a name because of some incident, most often based upon some activity of the expedition's personnel.

5. Many incident-names have been reduced merely to a per-

sonal name. Therefore the assumption cannot be made that all places are thus named because of ownership. In the great majority of cases, however, no documentation exists by which to connect the name with the incident, or even to know what the incident may have been. Most common, probably, is the death of some person at that point, and his burial there.

A mass of high hills in Nebraska preserves the toponymic record of a famous and tragic story of the early West. Hiram Scott fell ill when he was traveling eastward with a party of trappers. His comrades apparently abandoned him—callously, though the record is not altogether clear. Scott, with a grim will to live, dragged on for sixty miles, until he came to some rough hills near the River Platte. There, finally, he died. The next summer another party (including the very men who had abandoned him) came over the same route, found his body, and identified it by the clothing and equipment. The name survives as Scotts Bluff.

Such naming was common and perhaps can even be called conventional among the early trappers. George Ruxton, an English army officer who traveled in the Rocky Mountains during the 1840's, noted in his narrative that many of the streams bore familiar personal names. He added: "These are invariably christened after some unfortunate trapper, killed there in an Indian fight, or treacherously slaughtered by the lurking savages."

Obviously such names cannot be classed as possessives. In many instances the man would never before even have been at the place. Only in a kind of spiritual sense did his name eventually come permanently to possess the stream or the hill.

6. Names that are merely expressed by a word denoting emotion are comparatively rare, but are highly interesting.

In 1585 Sir Richard Grenville was exploring the coast of what is now North Carolina, and his ship became embayed behind a long spit of land. At the thought of being wrecked and cast away on an unknown and uncivilized coast some of the seamen went into a panic. As the result, we have Cape Fear.

In Siberia, as Arsenjew reported, a snowstorm prevented his party from crossing some mountains, and they were compelled to wait. As he wrote, "We named this height 'Terpenija,' that is, 'patience.' "

Pigafetta records of Magellan that at a certain landfall "The captain-general wept for joy, and called that cape, Cape Deseado, for we had been desiring it for a long time."

7. Names consisting of an exclamation uttered at the time of the naming are rare, but cannot be altogether neglected. Such names must regularly be held under suspicion, as being the product of a lively folk-imagination. No one, for instance, needs to take seriously such an "explanation" as that Mooselookmeguntic originated from the excited words of a hunter, "Moose! Look! My gun, quick!" Such "etymologies" spring up by thousands.

On the other hand, Goshelpme Creek in Alaska is of recent origin, arising from someone's exclaiming "Gosh-help-me!" "God-help-me!" may have been the actual words.

Among folklorists incident-names have held the position of favorite children. Place-name scholars, on the contrary, have tended to treat them as stepchildren, or even as illegitimates. Equally, these tendencies have produced bad results.

Folklorists, by the bases of their discipline, have focused their interest upon the story, not upon its truth as an explanation of the name. This attitude, in turn, has reacted upon the scholars. "If so many of these stories," they conclude, "are thus untrue and even fantastic and merely humorous, we cannot then be bothered to investigate the others." Many studies of place-names omit the idea of incident entirely.

The justification for such procedure seems to come, especially, in areas where little historical record of place-naming has survived, such as over most of Europe. Even in such areas, however, many names bespeak an origin from incident—by their very meaning. (See Book III, Chapter 11.)

4
Possessive Names

Names, in vast numbers, arise from the idea of the ownership of a place. In a firmly established society this ownership is usually formal and legally based. In a primitive society—and even, under some conditions, in a highly organized society—the ownership is informal and recognized only in the folk-mind.

The owner from whose personal name the place-name is derived may be an individual or may be a group, such as a family, clan, tribe, or nation.

In many regions (probably in most regions) possessives form the largest class of place-names, and in some instances a majority.

On the other hand, possessives are not primitive as are descriptive, associative, and incident-names. Primitive peoples generally lack the conception of the personal ownership of land, and under such circumstances personal names can be used for place-names only because of some temporary and unusual relationship which can often be classed as incident. Even the idea of a tribal land which is clearly enough defined to be given a name is probably not extremely ancient. Once the possessory idea has been grasped, however, such names rapidly take over.

Possessive names arise generally by the evolutionary process, as thousands of well-recorded examples in the United States can testify. A settler named Smith might acquire some land legally or he might merely "squat" at some site. In the course of a few years, out of mere convenience, people would be speaking of Smith's creek, Smith's hill, and Smith's ford. Such designations, as the failure to use capitals with their generics is supposed to indicate, are scarcely to be considered names, but are merely identifying notations. At this point, however, Smith dies, or moves west with the frontier. What we might call a naming crisis then ensues, though such a word as "crisis" is hardly apt when, probably, no one is conscious of it.

When Smith disappears, the tendency of the community (if it is at all stable) will be to continue to use his name on the natural feature even though the original Smith may be soon forgotten. Moreover, a new settler named Brown arrives. On the site of Smith's cabin (now burned), Brown builds his own cabin. Will the stream, the hill, and the ford now take Brown's name? Such an outcome is possible, especially if Brown himself turns out to be a permanent settler, of strong personality, becoming a community leader. But the name of Smith may already be too firmly implanted to be thus removed. Perhaps Brown himself is conservative and unimaginative, sticking to the old ways, and preferring the original name.

But with Smith gone, there comes an almost necessary change. The idea of his actual possession is no longer there, so that Smith's hill becomes, symbolically, Smith's Hill, and even Smith Hill. This survival of a name after the removal of its original cause may be taken as a test as to whether the name is actually so to be considered, and should not be classed as a temporary makeshift.

With habitation-names the tendency of survival for possessives is especially strong. A man's title to hills and streams may be questioned—as to whether, for instance, he owns the game and fish on those hills and in those streams. But a man's ownership of a house or other building on his land is very much less likely to be challenged. On the American frontier the evolution of names from mere buildings is common.

In 1852 a certain William Hayward opened a hotel on a California stage-route. Such an establishment would be known in common speech as "Hayward's place," or merely "Hayward's." In 1854 Guillermo Castro, local landowner, laid out a town at the site, but retained the name. In 1860 a post office was established, named Haywood, probably in error since it was later changed to Haywards. By this time a village was growing up at the spot of the original hotel. In 1911, in accordance with its general policy, the Post Office Department changed the name to Hayward. Its residents, however, continued generally to say Haywards. In the later twentieth century the village has grown into a city—some of its citizens probably still using the possessive form which indicates the long-destroyed hotel of the long-dead William Hayward. The whole process had been an evolutionary one, based upon established folk-ways, with a minimum of conscious action. It can be paralleled in thousands of instances in the United States alone, and by thousands or millions in all the more developed countries of the world.

The case of Hayward is of some special interest, since Castro, not Hayward, seems to have been the actual landowner, and that name still stands upon the near-by Castro Valley. By his ownership of the hotel and its appurtenances, however, Hayward produced the effect of ownership, and in popular speech the place became thus known.

The evolution of another possessive stems from an early California settler bearing the rather pretentious name Royal Porter Putnam, and usually known as Porter. In 1859 he established, like Hayward, a stage-station, and it, naturally, came to be known as Porter's Station. Being something of a businessman, the proprietor began to expand into dealing in various goods, and the name shifted to Porter's Trading Post, or Porter's Store—in ordinary speech, we can be sure, merely Porter's. Developing beyond being a storekeeper, Porter laid out a town on his land in 1864, calling it Portersville, thus employing one of the commonest nineteenth-century American suffixes for "town." As the strong tendency of the time ran, the unnecessary and cumbersome possessive form was eventually eliminated for simplification, and the town survives as Porterville, though Royal Porter Putnam has long since vanished from the scene.

Ownership by groups of people is also a very important source of possessive names, especially because it has given rise to many names of outstanding historical entities, such as nations, provinces, and large cities. (See Book I, Chapter 5.)

A naming for two proprietors is very rare, but may be seen in such a case as Foss and Knowlton Brook, in Maine, so called from two men who, as partners, once maintained a lumbering operation in the area.

The naming for a family is common, and in many instances no conclusive judgment is possible as to whether a particular place was called for the family as a whole or for one particular member of it. There is no reason, indeed, why even the original namer or namers should have made any firm decision in such a matter. Castro Valley (mentioned above) is generally assumed to be named for Guillermo Castro, who certainly owned land in that vicinity. But the Castros were a large and widespread family of early California, and some of its members were much more widely known than was Guillermo. The solution, if any, of such problems must commonly be passed into the province of the local historian.

The family itself merges into the clan or tribe, many primitive tribes being essentially nothing more than a slightly extended family. Such small units hold their land by merely inhabiting it, and their rights (and lives) are rarely respected by their more powerful and warlike neighbors. Such a small tribe named Canarsie (of Algonquian background) inhabited a spot near the western end of Long Island in the colony of New York in the earlier seventeenth century. They suffered from raids by the militant Mohawks, (of Iroquoian background), who really subjected the Canarsie to tribute. In 1655, however, something upset the situation, and the Mohawks massacred the Canarsie, almost annihilating them. Their name and the name of their territory had become known already to the Dutch settlers, and Canarsie still survives as a district in the city of Brooklyn. It may be considered a possessive, arising from a recognition by the Dutch that the Canarsie at one time had "owned" that region, however weakly and uncertainly.

With larger tribes the situation has not been very different in this dog-eat-dog world. Most of the great tribes (or even peoples) of antiquity have vanished. They were not, we may think, actually wiped out, and their bloodstreams must survive. But as entities they have lost identity, and disappeared. Where are the Goths, the Gauls, the Illyrians, the Iberians? Even as place-names they survive principally as vague modern abstractions, such as Iberia. As in so much else, something seems to turn upon the mere luck of the game.

The name Italy illustrates how tenuous a bond may be. The Greeks, advancing by sea toward the west, came upon a tribe which was known locally as Vituli. It was apparently not of much importance, and its land must have been somewhere around the Italian heel. The Greeks, following their own established speech-habits, made the name into Italoi. The Romans borrowed it back in that form, and found it a useful term to denote the inhabitants of the various tribes of the peninsula. Before long the place-name Italia resulted. In the process the original Vituli seem to have become completely lost. During the long centuries of Roman decline and the Dark Ages, Italy still maintained itself as a "geographical expression," though not a unified nation. In the end unification caught up with the name, and the altered name of the long-vanished tribe was applied all the way north to the Alps.

What we may call the more successful tribes established their domains strongly and planted their names upon their possessions. One thinks of the Franks and of modern France, whose people call themselves Français, which is nothing more than a development of the original name. Yet the name France itself cannot really be understood except in the background of history. In the early Middle Ages the name commonly referred only to what is now known as the Ile de France, the district around Paris. A few miles to the westward the dukes of Normandy maintained what was essentially an independent state, and did not consider it to be part of France. Only after some centuries of warfare and diplomacy did the so-called kings of France extend their own holdings and the prestige of their crown to include more or less what is now France.

The triumph of the kings of France thus assured a kind of overlordship of the name of the Franks, but did not result in any annihilation of other tribal names. The Normans still gave their name to the large province of Normandy, and most of the names of the traditional French provinces still go back to the possession exercised in that region by some tribe.

A large proportion of place-names that include a personal name may safely be considered to be possessives. On the other hand, we cannot accept what seems to be the basic assumption of European scholars, that is, that all such place-names can be classified as possessives, except for the handful that may historically be otherwise established. Evidence from the Americas and elsewhere shows that place-names from personal names, in an appreciable number of instances, arise from incidents, are commemoratives, or may even stem from some loose association not involving ownership.

Normally, as the present discussion should have made clear, possessive names arise after the act of taking possession. They constitute, therefore, a kind of recognition of an already existing state, and they establish themselves by what we have called the evolutionary process. A personal name, however, may be put upon a place before its occupation or simultaneously with its creation. These names are bestowed by a conscious act. Such naming processes are classifiable as commemorative or commendatory. (See the following chapter.)

5
Commemorative Names

The common human desire to conserve a memory and to do honor gives rise to what may be called commemorative names. Examples are the South American countries Colombia and Bolivia, named for Christopher Columbus and Simon Bolívar, together with the thousands of places in the New World which bear their names in memory of places in the Old World—from Boston to Guadalajara and far beyond to north and south.

In most regions such names are not numerous, as compared with those stemming from other motivations. Nonetheless, commemoratives are clearly enough marked to form a distinct class.

Unlike descriptive, associative, and incident-names, but somewhat resembling possessives, the commemoratives are not much used among primitive peoples. What they require is a well-established tradition or a personal domination which approaches kingship. Still, commemorative naming can be exemplified from the usage of various peoples who would generally be considered to be of simple culture.

The Indians known as the Creeks had held their lands in what is now Alabama for at least some centuries, and possessed well-established towns. In the 1830's, after wars with the Americans, they were forced to move to the so-called Indian Territory—the present state of Oklahoma—where they made new settlements. Just as the English re-planted names such as Worcester and Lancaster, so the Creeks took their old town-names along with them and placed them commemoratively on their new-founded habitations; thus the modern city of Tulsa derives its name.

Similarly, the Polynesians took their names with them on their Pacific voyages and re-planted them, so that the name Hawaii, in varying linguistic form, appears in several far-flung island-groups.

In one interesting detail the process of naming commemoratively shows a difference from the kinds of naming previously discussed. In descriptives and the others a conscious attitude may exist, a person or several persons considering the question, "What shall we call this place?" With commemoratives, however, the conscious process is universal and necessary. Obviously, moreover, such names are bestowed, and do not originate by evolution.

Commemoratives also differ from the other classes in that they are commonly placed only upon the more important habitation-names or upon a few kinds of natural features, especially mountains and lakes. The reason is clear enough: small settlements without much chance of a future and many unattractive or unpleasant natural features cannot be considered as having much possibility of bestowing honor by means of the name.

Many towns, however, are founded with the definite idea that they are to be capitals or great cities. New Orleans was one such, and the namers could justly feel that they were honoring the Duke of Orleans. The capitals of the Australian states all bear commemorative names. Though they may have been miserable little settlements in their origins, they obviously had possibilities for the future, and could with dignity and propriety be named for a queen or a prime minister.

With natural features the situation, also, is obvious enough. Through history and even before it, human beings have looked upon great peaks, perhaps with feelings of esthetic pleasure, but certainly with wonder, and even with religious awe. To put a person's name upon such a towering mass is to bestow out-standing honor and seeming immortality upon him. It is almost to make him a god. The idea, however, was not grasped in early times. Even Alexander the Great named cities for himself, not mountains. Only in the nineteenth century did the practice become common. With the twentieth century, in the United States, such namings have exhausted all the higher peaks, and later heroes have to be content with lower summits. Inevitably some great peaks have been named for people whose names seem unmatched to the snowy loftiness. The highest mountain of all bears the name of Sir George Everest, an estimable man. But who can even identify him?

The placing of a person's name upon a lake has also been thought to be an apt means of paying honor. Rarely, indeed, has this been true of the larger ones, though Lake Victoria and the others in central Africa provide striking exceptions. The French in the eighteenth century named one of the Great Lakes after their famous Governor Frontenac, but with the En-glish conquest of New France the name became Lake Ontario.

Small lakes, however, are not overpowering in their size, and are beautiful in their mountain-setting, blue and tranquil. Throughout the later nineteenth century and on into the twen-tieth, enthusiastic American mountaineers called lakes after their wives, sweethearts, or sisters—or even their mothers-in-law or grandmothers—until Lake Mary, Lake Eleanor, and Lake Elizabeth spot the map thickly.

The exploring voyagers of the eighteenth century, such as Cook and Vancouver, commemorated in their namings the royal family, their higher officers in the Admiralty, and the pa-trons of their voyages, placing these names upon capes, bays, and other seacoast features.

A modest man was General John A. Rawlins, Grant's Chief of Staff in the Civil War. In 1867, dying of tuberculosis, he camped with some companions near a spring in the Rocky Mountains. He remarked that if anything should be called after him he would like it to be a spring. After his death his comrades named that particular spring for him, but the name, ironically, is now preserved as the town of Rawlins.

Many natural features, by their very nature, fail to suggest honor. Who would feel complimented to have a swamp named for him? There are, however, a few instances. Ickes Slough in Alaska is named for H. L. Ickes, Secretary of the Interior. He was notable for a short temper and for having little respect for other people's feelings. The naming, therefore, may well be with derogatory suggestions.

Another interesting case is a California swamp which was officially named Willis Hole in 1965. The honoree, Willis Jepsen, was a renowned botanist, and may have had a special interest in the swamp as a source of rare plants.

An interesting point with regard to commemoratives involves who or what is commemorated. In general, four classes may be postulated: 1. persons, 2. other places, 3. abstractions, 4. miscellaneous groups.

1. As the examples already presented go far toward demonstrating, the honorees of commemorative names are an extremely mixed lot. About all that can be generalized is that they are equally as variegated as the namers. A fisherman camped beside a little mountain lake compliments his lady by calling it for her. A legislature, having a hundred counties to be established, honors the national heroes, such as Washington and Franklin, adds a selection of Civil War generals, several congressmen who had helped in the establishment of the new state, and some of its own members. Surveyors, overburdened with dozens of new natural features to name, select the Surveyor General to whom they owe their jobs and a number of locally prominent citizens.

2. As already illustrated in the cases of Tulsa and Hawaii, places may be commemorated by having their names placed upon new foundations, such as states, counties, and towns.

At the primitive level the situation is complicated in that the name of the people and the name of the habitation are commonly the same, even in grammatical form. If the tribe moves, the name goes along. Locroi, the ancient Greek colonial city in the south of Italy, is in form a plural, meaning the members of that tribe, which was well known in Greece itself. There was apparently no distinction between "going to the Locrians," and "going to Locroi."

A few of the other Greek colonies show commemorative naming more surely; that is, the name of the city itself is placed upon the new foundation—as with the Sicilian foundations of Megara and Naxos.

In this transporting of the name of a town, the motivations of the namer or namers are so natural as scarcely to call for elucidation. In early New England, as that name itself indicates, the desire of the immigrants was to set up, anew, an English community. Though they learned from the Indians the place-names, the settlers regularly abandoned them—at least, for town-sites. One reason, undoubtedly, was that they feared lest these strange and unintelligible words might contain an invocation to the Devil, since the assumption was that the Indians worshipped the Devil or many devils. But the names of "the old country" also had positive attractions. They were of familiar sound and spelling; they suggested an established government; most important of all, they were Christian in association. The colonist found little enough that was comforting and familiar in this new land of thick forest, wild animals, and heathen Indians. He cherished the old names.

Although the custom of commemorative naming was associated with New England in particular, it was almost as well established in the other English colonies, not only those of North America, but clear around the world, to Australia and New Zealand. The other colonizing peoples—Spanish, Portuguese, Dutch, and French—also placed the old names upon new settlements. The practice may be considered normal and universal.

Commemorative naming of natural features for the already-known features of the mother-country is much less common. The east coast of the United States has its Thames and its Severn. But that is about all. Canada has a Thames, an Avon, a Severn, a Don, and a few others. The custom of commemorative naming of streams is somewhat commoner in the Antipodes, reaching its climax in Tasmania. There the English or Scottish fisherman may cast a fly into homelike-sounding streams—the Tamar, Clyde, Esk, Derwent, Mersey, and several others. An important reason for this situation is that the English contact with the Tasmanian aborigines was almost wholly hostile. (In fact, the Tasmanians are now extinct.) In New Zealand, where peaceful contacts were customary, the stream-names are almost universally Maori. (See also Book III, Chapter 13.)

With other natural features commemorative namings occur, usually, by a different process. They are not brought to the new land directly from the old one, but are what may be called literary. The widespread use of Alps need not be counted, since that name (as pointed out in Book I, Chapter 4) has become a generic. Though several peaks in the United States are called Matterhorn, there is no evidence that any of the namings were made by Swiss. In fact, the namers may never have seen that peak, but could have learned of it from books. Also, the numerous examples of Mount Hermon and Mount Pisgah are taken from the Bible. They are not the less commemorative for that reason, but the mechanism of transmission involves no nostalgia.

3. A third class arises from abstractions, which may be said to commemorate an idea or an ideal. Here are to be assigned patriotic namings such as Independence or Union and religious namings such as those of the numerous Spanish foundations which translate as "sacrament," "holy faith," or "body of Christ." Here also may be placed certain more general abstractions—Concord, Amity, Friendship, and others.

In many instances the distinction is not great between the naming for a person or place and the naming for an abstraction, because the person or place symbolizes the abstraction. Thus Washington is roughly equivalent to Independence, and Waterloo stands for a symbol of defeat or victory, not for a place in Belgium.

The names of saints (if they do not merely originate from the calendar) are usually motivated by the idea of commemoration, so that the common usage may be expressed by the formula "in honor of St. ———." Some saints, moreover, especially those now officially desanctified, raise the question of reality. From the point of view of the study of names, however, this problem is not serious. The proviso need only be added, "including fictional and mythological names" thus to accommodate St. George, St. Christopher, and St. Nicholas.

Many fictional characters and places, indeed, seem to possess more life than most real people do. The map of the United States shows the influence of Shakespeare, along with that of Swift, Scott, Longfellow, Dickens, Thackeray, Kipling, Gilbert and Sullivan, and many others. A town in Pennsylvania is named Apollo. Whether Hiawatha was a man or a myth may be argued, but Longfellow's poem is second only to the Bible as a literary influence upon American names. The question of whether a character really lived makes no difference as far as names are concerned.

Typically, the person or other entity appearing in a commemorative name has no immediate connection with the place, and had not had in the past. A ship may fix its name upon some shoals where it has been wrecked, but such a naming is rather to be classed as from an incident. So also possessive names are not inspired primarily by the idea of commemoration.

Also characteristic of commemoratives is the formality associated with them. Often, indeed, a ceremony accompanies the bestowal, sometimes with the analogy of a christening. A considerable amount of champagne has been destroyed on such occasions. In 1770 Captain Arthur Phillip, the first governor of New South Wales, decided to plant on that still-uninhabited coast the name of the Secretary of State for Home and Colonies, a gentleman who was far off in England. On January 26 the name was officially bestowed with a ceremony on the beach, a flag raising, and a toast to the royal family. Sydney Cove thus originated, to pass on by transfer to one of the world's great cities.

4. Almost anything capable of being conceived as an entity can bear a name—an animal, a doll, a ship, a corporation or society, a star or constellation, a book or a painting, a holiday. Once named, any of these can become, commemoratively, a place-name. Alexander's favorite horse, Bucephalus, died in

India, and his master founded there the city of Bucephala—not concerned, apparently, that the name could be translated literally in the homely terms, "cow-head." Cincinnati commemorates the society of that name. Cook named the Society Islands in honor of the Royal Society.

Most commonly, the sources of names in this miscellaneous group are ships. Almost any unusual seacoast name may with some confidence be ascribed to a ship, whose captain in early times left its name there as a memorial. During the War of 1812 a flotilla of British gunboats operated on the St. Lawrence River, and most of them had their names placed upon natural features along the stream, with such colorful results as Bloodletter Island, Deathdealer Island, Belaborer Island, and Active Pass. An occasional shipmaster has recorded his feelings, as did Captain M'Clure in 1850 when he named Investigator Sound in the Arctic, "that the name of our ship might be perpetuated in those icy seas, she had hitherto navigated in safety."

One problem has never been satisfactorily solved. Should you name a place for yourself? Obviously, the namer may be deserving of a name fully as much as the people whom he is honoring.

With egomaniacs like Alexander the Great, who founded a swarm of cities named Alexandria, the situation scarcely arises. Even ordinary emperors and kings are not subject to the pressures of public opinion. Besides, some sycophantic courtier is always close at hand to propose the imperial or royal name. In addition, the monarch is already so heavy with honors that he cannot much care whether his name is placed upon some rough new colony or town. Was Louis XIV appreciably pleased that La Salle complimented him with Louisiana, though the area was larger than France? Technically, we might decide that Charles II named Carolina for himself, though the statement would mean little.

But explorers and heads of expeditions have felt some embarrassment. One method has been to record in the official journal that by general acclamation of the company such-and-such a place was declared to be named for the commanding of-

ficer. Captain Cook used a different device by failing altogether
to put a name upon one of the most prominent features that he
explored and described. Thus conspicuously lacking a name,
this feature went to the Admiralty, where it was declared to be
Cook Inlet.

Many records of name christenings are preserved, and thousands of others may be assumed.

Such a ceremony does not necessarily involve an ancient date.
On October 11, 1970, a dedication occurred for Gudde Ridge
in California. The ridge is about five miles long, but not outstanding. The honoree had lived quietly as a professor and
scholar, and had written the authoritative book on the place-
names of California. Such activity made the preservation of his
name seem particularly fitting. As is required, the name was au-
thorized by the state and federal boards on geographic names.
Its dedication attracted to the hilltop members of the local historical society, a brass band, legislators, officials of the local
park, and many friends. Mrs. Gudde attended, and became the
recipient of no fewer than four framed diplomas or certificates,
two of them having been passed by the branches of the state
legislature. Professor Gudde had not owned the ridge nor had
he been in any special way connected with it. The procedure,
however, is typical of commemorative names—in a country
where the giving of place-names is still actively practiced.

Though not very common in comparison with most other
classes of names, commemoratives have a special interest, in
that they so generally stand upon places of note.

6

Commendatory Names

Many namers select a name of such a nature that it will, primarily, create a "good" effect, that is, that it will affect people as being pleasant, attractive, lucky, or inspiring. These names may be called commendatory.

Obviously, such names cannot result from evolution, but must be consciously bestowed. They are commonly habitation-names, but also stand upon natural features.

In distinction from commemoratives, which recall the past, commendatories look to the future. Since really primitive people have little sense of what has not yet existed, commendatories scarcely exist among such tribes. They become common, however, at a somewhat more advanced level of culture, with the development of religion, along with what we more commonly call superstition and magic. In such a milieu namers work with the purpose of influencing the future for the better. Names are then bestowed for good omen. They are, as the apt French phrase goes, *de bon augure*.

Naming a place for a god, with the idea that the god will then be favoring, constitutes one of the commonest manifestations of commendatory naming. The more dominating the religiosity of a culture, the commoner is this type of naming. India is an outstanding example, a numerous pantheon making it possible for names of good omen to be placed even upon the smaller natural features. The names of the larger cities, although they date from the far and recordless past, are prevailingly of this type. Calcutta is "Kali's dwelling place," and this name of Shiva's consort appears on many other towns. Madras is "Manda's realm." Bombay has arisen from Mombei or Bumbai, a goddess (see also Book III, Chapter 14).

Among European examples we may cite cities of the Greeks and the Celts, both being among those peoples possessing a strong sense of the other world (see Book III, Chapters 4 and 8).

The innumerable namings for saints, however, are better classed as commemoratives, since they seem rather to honor the past than to try to influence the future. In special cases, however, they are commendatory. Commendatories need not all be religiously oriented. Nonreligious commendatories have flourished in the modern world of explorers, colonizers, and town-founders.

Commendatories are rarely given to natural features unless the feature is viewed as having potential for a habitation. Such a name as Blue Lake or Silver Lake may thus arise.

Commendatories are closely allied both to descriptives and to commemoratives. The distinction really abides in the namer's mind, and cannot always be determined. Blue Lake may be a good-enough descriptive, but chosen over an equally possible Long Lake because of the suggestion for the future.

One might even venture a generalization that all bestowed namings of habitations have at least some suggestion of being commendatory. Just as parents do not deliberately choose an unpleasant name for a child, so namers of villages and towns are likely to reject Stinking Spring or Murder Gap, and choose a name that either is neutral or has some pleasing suggestion. The United States is thick-set with name-changes, as carelessly or derogatorically named natural features shifted to something more attractive when a village developed on the site. Nebraska shows, among others, Poverty Ridge changing to Prosperity; Poorman's Bottom to Sunshine Valley; Crazy Hollow to Pleasant Valley.

A Japanese regulation of the ninth century ordered that lucky names should always be selected for districts and villages.

Miners, being among the most superstitious of all people, often name mines to invoke luck and good fortune, often by re-using the names of those that have been successful. Thus Potosí has been echoed in the city of San Luis Potosí in Mexico, twice in Nicaragua, and in other places.

In the United States, from the nineteenth century on, material is plentiful for a whole study of commendatories, with accompanying elucidation of the dreams and aspirations of the people as they shift with time and development. When individuals were few and suffered from isolation, such names as City and Center were attractive. Later, when people began to suffer from crowding, they preferred Acres and Estates. The association of altitude with a cooling breeze and a view has produced, by the dozens, such names as Vista Heights, The Uplands, Rolling Hills. Glade and Prairie might be in fashion when people still disliked the darkness of the thick and enveloping forest. When the forest was slashed back, home-buyers felt the attractiveness of Maplewood and Greengrove. With such sites the namers cared little whether the trees might be maples or oaks or elms, and whether the grove, after the ravages wrought by the bulldozers, might consist of only a few scattered saplings.

Along with commendatories we may class the few names that may be termed counter-commendatories, that is, pejoratives or derogatives. Any stretch of bad trail in the early years of the United States was likely to be known as the Devil's Half-mile, and that Satanic name exists upon many spots over the world. Certain uncomplimentary obscene terms also appear, although they are usually censored out of the modern records.

Derogatives are less common for habitation-names, but occur in certain areas, especially for small settlements. In Wallachia many villages bear names meaning "cursed," "hostile," "naked," or "miserable." Just why and how they were so called is uncertain. One possibility is that such names were taken to ward off bad luck and to make the place seem too poor for ravagers to pay it any attention. We may compare mines and mining-districts such as Poorman Gulch and Poverty Flat, named with the hope of keeping rival miners away, so that the original discoverers could reap the reward.

Another possibility with derogatives, such as those in Wallachia, is that the villages were named by outsiders who enjoyed poking fun at their neighbors, or insulting them. In many regions of the United States, especially the Southeast, "rural derogatives" still exist—Hardscrabble, Bug Tussel, Rabbithash, Possum Trot, Starve Goat Island, Lickskillet, Needmore, Seldom Seen. Probably such a recurring name as Sodom is to be placed in this class, since there is generally no historical record or likelihood that these places were any more the haunt of wickedness (or of any particular practice) than were places near by. With encroaching civilization the rural derogatives have tended to die out, and the communities took other names, if they became post offices.

In still another sub-group we may place euphemistic names, that is, those in which a name is altered or bestowed for the particular purpose of covering up what really exists, and thus, in one way or another, making an improvement or preventing trouble. In Domesday Book a village is recorded as Fulepit, "dirty hole." A hundred years later it had become Bealmont, "beautiful hill." The ancient Greeks and Romans were alert to good and bad omens, and believed that words and manners of speech could bring fortune or misfortune. The Romans even had the ritual phrase, "Favor with your tongues," which warned all present to be careful of what they said at times of sacrifice and omen-taking. When, therefore, we come upon the Promontorium Pulcrum, "cape beautiful," we probably should not consider that the Romans were esthetically moved by the view, but rather that they were trying, by the name, to prevent disaster to ships which were rounding a dangerous headland. The Romans would scarcely have tolerated such modern names as Disaster Inlet, Cape Fear, and Point Anxiety. So also the Greeks used Kale Akte, "beautiful cape," and apparently for the same reason.

Although difficult in some cases to differentiate from the other types of namings, commendatory names provide a useful classification. Their looking to the future is perhaps their most individual quality, and they flourish upon words thus oriented. Of all of these *hope* is probably the most characteristic.

We have it in small instances, as when a German village is Gutehoffnung, "good hope." The same meaning turns up (in many different languages) in one of the world's great land-marks, the Cape of Good Hope, changed euphemistically from the Cape of Storms.

In 1848 some Mormon pioneers were struggling to make their way eastward by an unexplored route across the Sierra Nevada. Having crossed a high summit, they came to a small valley through which a stream flowed toward the east, a favor-able sign to the trail-breakers that they had surmounted the crest of the mountains. A diarist recorded that they camped at a place "which we called Hope Valley as we began to have hope."

Not only does Hope Valley survive, but it has given rise by counterpart to Faith Valley and Charity Valley.

7
Folk-etymology

The formation of a new name by the action of the principle of Analogy and Final Attraction (see Book I, Chapter 10), is here termed folk-etymology. Other terms have been used to denote, roughly, the same process—for example, popular etymology, false etymology, and paronomasia. To be of interest in this present work, the result must be a place-name, but folk-etymology can also result in a personal name or in an ordinary word.

Some may wish to maintain that folk-etymology yields, not a new name, but the alteration of an already existing one. In typical instances, however, the original and later forms have lost semantic contact, and such a term as "new" can be employed conveniently and with sufficient accuracy.

The process is better illustrated than theoretically presented. We may begin with a famous and highly illustrative American example.

In the early nineteenth century English-speaking and French-speaking trappers mingled as they penetrated the area which is now southeastern Colorado. They found there a river which the speakers of French, translating the already established Spanish name Purgatorio, easily rendered as Purgatoire, and the speakers of English must first have accepted it in the French version. It was, however, too far from their own *purgatory* to be readily recognizable. In any case, most of them were of Protestant background, and were not very familiar with the word. At the same time Purgatoire had difficult non-English sounds and combinations of sounds. As already pointed out (Book I, Chapter 8), such a situation may be solved by phonetic adaptation, by translation, or by folk-etymology. This last was the solution of the Americans.

The word *picket* was familiar to them, a horse being commonly tied by a picket-rope. Picket is not too far from *purgat-*, in which the French *r* is scarcely sounded. The rest of the name, *-oire,* was close to English *wire*—a word known even then, before the invention of the now ubiquitous barbed wire. So the name came out as Picketwire.

We may note here a kind of desperate attempt to make sense. A rope, not a wire, was used for picketing, but a wire did not seem wholly incredible. The transfer, however, is not primarily semantic. On the contrary, it is phonetic, the sounds being preserved, after a fashion. The final result is determined by attraction to a familiar word (or words) in the receiving language. The total process has much in common with the play on words commonly known as a pun.

Such a procedure violates the "laws" of linguistic process as laid down by nineteenth-century scholars, who called for an orderly transfer by phonetic units. Semantics, too, in their theory, should become involved only by reasonable translation, not by gloriously irresponsible shifting, such as from *purgat-* to *picket.* Indeed, even in the nineteenth century a few indubitable instances had to be acknowledged, but the scholars of that time and the twentieth-century followers in their tradition conceived folk-etymology as a rare and quasi-illegitimate practice, to be explained away whenever possible.

On the contrary, folk-etymology is a regular and common process, whenever two languages are impinging and one of them is superseding the other. It will be most in evidence when the phonetic structures of the two languages display considerable and difficult differences. As already pointed out (Book I, Chapter 8), Spanish sounds are easily, if not exactly, handled by speakers of English. Probably as a result, Spanish-English folk-etymologies are rare. But French sounds are difficult, and French-English names resulting from folk-etymology are numerous.

Wherever the conditions are fulfilled, names arise by folk-etymology, much to the delight of the numerous persons who enjoy unusual names.

Thus, in Australia, as English replaced aboriginal languages, we have Wahlmoorun becoming Mt. Maroon. Colegdar yields Collector; Dilliget, Delegate; Cambowra, Gunblower. Charam, "spear," has become Lake Charm.

English-Gaelic contacts have been productive in Scotland, where an-Fharaid, "projecting cape," has become Far Out Head. Apur-Crossan, "mouth of [the river] Crossan," has produced Applecross. In some notable instances the original name was given by the Norsemen, and probably passed through the Gaelic. Fitful Head was originally a Norse naming for the sea-bird that they knew as the *fitfugl.*

Canada, too, has its folk-etymologies, both from French and from the Indian languages. Newfoundland even adds Portuguese and Basque, from the early visits of explorers and fishermen—Cabo Razo, "bare," becoming Cape Race, and the sixteenth-century name Cabo de Peña, "cape of punishment," being reduced to a commonplace Cape Pine. On the other hand, Arenhosa, "sandy," has become the enigmatical Renews. Even further afield is the curious repetitive name Port au Port, which represents in French spelling a Basque legacy—Apphorportu, a word of uncertain meaning.

The predominance of English examples here presented should not be taken as evidence that folk-etymology is a specialty of the English language, but it has arisen rather from an attempt to escape some of the awkwardnesses of continual translation.

Certainly the Spanish-speakers of Latin America have been much given to the practice. Such common words as *agua,* "water," often prove to be evidence not of a spring or a lake or a river, but merely of some transformed Indian term. So also the syllable *guad,* from the Arabic but appearing in many Spanish place-names, turns up constantly by folk-etymology. The simple name Paz, "peace," in Honduras has developed through a form Paza from the Indian name of a plant, *pachtli*. Río Bueno in Chile is not a commendatory "good," but slightly transforms an Indian term *hueno,* indicating a stream descending from the highlands. A region in Chile is known as Los Ulmos, "the elms," but a folk-etymology is involved and no elms grow there.

On a larger scale, folk-etymology is responsible for the fearful term Mosquito Coast, with all its suggestions of fever and death. This name came to the Spaniards first as that of a local Indian tribe, being rendered Miskito. Almost inevitably it made the small shift. Undoubtedly the coast has mosquitoes, but whether they are worse there than elsewhere has not been established, and is not actually the point.

This mere proliferation of examples need not, however, be continued further. By those already presented we can see that folk-etymology occurs as a common and regular process, widely distributed over the world. It can be put down as a universal human trait, requiring only, for its appearance, the proper contacts of two languages.

By "two languages," moreover, can be meant a single language reacting to contacts with its own older forms and obsolete words. Thus a certain English name, Badecanwelle, would have been easily understood in the middle of the tenth century to be "Badeca's spring," but by a century or two later it was being recorded as an unintelligible Bauquell. Then, by a typical shift of folk-etymology it finally became Bakewell, composed of easy and comfortable English syllables, but making no real sense unless the town were to be conceived as having a proficient baker.

Similarly derived by folk-etymology from an Anglo-Saxon personal name is such a fine example as Owlpen—and, probably, Sixpenny Handley.

In different linguistic areas, which of necessity have different cultural backgrounds, origins by folk-etymology vary considerably. In France, for instance, they seem to be less numerous than in England. Partly this situation may merely be the result of the inhospitality of French place-name scholars, who seem to prefer to postulate the name of some early proprietor rather than to admit the seeming irregularity of folk-etymology. In addition, from the time when the inhabitants of Gaul began to speak Latin, the French-speaking area has suffered no serious break in its linguistic evolution, with correspondingly less chance for folk-etymology.

Still, Flèche clearly means "arrow" to a modern Frenchman, but has been attracted away from a Latin *fiscus,* "treasury." Terrehault (a somewhat archaic "land-high") has suffered a severe change from the name of a saint, recorded about 1200 as Errehaud. Dieudonne, "God gives," arises from a German personal name, Deudon. Longjumeau, showing a desperate attempt to make sense by meaning, literally, "long twin," can be traced back through Longjumel, Mongimel, and Negemello, and probably at last to Noviomagus, the common Celtic "new-market."

In the roll of French names we may also observe those which display a partial shift by folk-etymology and those which merely suggest French words. Coupesarte displays its first form as Courbe Essart, "curved-clearing," but the first element has been attracted to *couper,* "cut," a reasonable joining with "clearing." Aquenove, however, only looks French. It shows a violent attempt to escape from an uncongenial Germanic *eskin-holt,* "oak-wood."

La Manche, the French term for the English Channel, means "the sleeve," and is commonly classed as a descriptive. But anyone looking at the shape of that body of water on a map will have difficulty in making the identification. It looks about as much like a sleeve as it does like a loaf of bread. Moreover, the name is an old one, which must have been placed before maps became common, and when a shipmaster who sailed that water could have had only the vaguest conception of its general shape. More likely, the name represents a reworking by folk-etymology of a Celtic term for channel, which is also the name of a body of water off Scotland, The Minch.

In what probably amounts to a great majority of instances, folk-etymology changes only a part of the name, commonly leaving the generic without change. From a brief look at a small fraction of English names under L we can come up with such a list as Leftwich, Legbourne, Ladbrooke, Landford, Latchford, Lawford, and Laughterton. In every instance the first part of the name has been attracted toward a current word, in an attempt to make sense out of a syllable that had become unintelligible. In the same part of the alphabet we find a few names that have been totally affected—Lemon, Lark, Landcross.

Some American namings have carried out this process elaborately. One New Jersey name can be traced back to a seventeenth-century Algonquian name, Allametunk, probably meaning "within-hills-at." It has been shifted, however, to what may be called the perfect semblance of an English town name, and stands as Lamington. No such English town-name exists, though Leamington and others are close to it.

In similar fashion a Pennsylvania town began with an Indian tribal name and ended as Sewickley, which seems to consist of three common English place-name elements, though again, no such combination exists as an English place-name.

Such names as Lamington and Sewickley may be said to have been attracted to a mere collection of place-name elements rather than to actual meaningful words. Here, as elsewhere, familiarity is the great attractive quality. The Americans involved in the process would not, probably, have known the meaning of *wick* or *-ing* or *ley*, but they recognized them as much-used parts of commonly known names.

In situations involving closely related languages there may be difficulty as to whether mere phonetic transfer sufficiently explains the case or whether folk-etymology is involved. Thus Bushkill Creek in the state of New York has as its specific a Dutch name, Bosch-kill, "forest-stream." The sounds, however, are so similar in the two languages that folk-etymology can scarcely be demonstrated.

Folk-etymology must be distinguished from what may be called false etymology, that is, an explanation given after the establishment of the name. A classical example is the ancient

Cape Palinurus in Italy (still Cape Palinoro), explained by Virgil as having originated from the loss there of Aeneas' pilot, Palinurus. But the name seems to consist of Greek elements—*palin,* "backward," and *ouros,* "fair wind," so that the reference is probably to wind conditions to be expected off the promontory, and the name is to be considered a descriptive.

Virgil may have picked up this story from some local source, or may have invented it himself. However it may have been in this instance, fictitious etymologies have been fabricated liberally in modern times, usually being the fancies of conscious humorists. The original maker, of course, knew that the story was his own creation. As it was passed along, however, literal-minded people believed it to be true, and many such "explanations" worked their way into local histories and even into books on place-names. Although the result has been somewhat to increase the gaiety of life, the existence of so many of these untrustworthy stories has tended to put into disrepute the whole idea of origin by folk-etymology.

The term itself suggests that an unconscious "folk-process" is the normal procedure. Actually, there is and can be no proof for such a postulate. Conscious humor is no exclusive privilege of the well-to-do and the well-educated. In many instances, a village wit may have shifted the name consciously and on a particular occasion—for his own amusement or to get a laugh.

In very rare instances the name itself preserves some testimony of conscious origin. In London a small brook was first recorded as Tyburn, "boundary-stream," but by 1490 had become Maryborne, by association with a church of St. Mary. By that time, however, the generic *burn* in its different spellings was obsolescent in southern England. Nevertheless, it was preserved in many names, usually as *bourne.* In this instance, however, it was shifted to *bone,* for the French *bonne,* and the whole name became, as it remains, Marylebone, "Mary the good." Although ascribed by Ekwall to "popular etymology," it can only be classed as "popular" in a very broad sense. Though *burn* may have been obsolescent, even more strongly can it be said that the London populace was not French-speaking. The responsibility must rest upon some individual with a knowledge (ap-

parently slight) of French, who by conscious act made the transformation—whether he was a tavern-wit or a pious churchman.

The influence of writing must also be considered. In an illiterate society, when a name shifts there is then no going back
beyond the memory of living persons. Writing and printing
preserve the older form, and give to pedants and purists the
chance to discover the "original" and "correct" spelling, and
then to clamor for its restoration. Many charming folk-
etymologies have thus been destroyed. Among them, lamen-
tably, is the famous example with which this chapter began.
Purgatoire has been restored to the official usage, and Picketwire maintains nothing more than a kind of underground existence.

Very rarely a false etymology may arise from the written
name, as when the British soldiers referred to Ypres as Wipers,
a form which obviously has little to do with the original pronunciation.

Folk-etymology, to sum up, is a pervasive influence in the giving and transforming of names. Scholars, however, have
frequently failed to recognize this importance, and have considered it a kind of illegitimate linguistic process, producing only a
few "exceptions" to the orderly course of phonetic development. Not only, however, are names of this class numerous, but
they are also likely to be colorful, poetic, and humorous. The
very strangeness of their origin captivates the public, and some
scholars as well.

Folk-etymology, however, cannot flourish except orally, and
in a literate society it is likely to wither. In this quality it differs
sharply from the class of names to be next considered.

8

Manufactured Names

Tesnus, Romley, Wabowden, Pringhar, Tolono—the scholar may feel the challenge of such names, and turn to his dictionary. But what dictionary? The ending of Tesnus suggests Latin; Romley seems definitely Anglo-Saxon; Wabowden might be from some American Indian dialect; Tolono could be Italian; Pringhar is baffling.

Actually no dictionary will be of value. These are manufactured names, constructed of sub-semantic elements. Any suggestions of meaning are incidental and even deceptive. Such names refute the venerable dictum, "Every place-name has a meaning."

Tesnus results from sunset, spelled backwards. Romley is from the personal name Morley, with the first three letters reversed. Wabowden commemorates a man named W. A. Bowden. Pringhar represents eight initial letters of family names, arranged in such an order as to be pronounceable. Tolono was created in a conscious attempt to form a useful and beautiful name, as stated by J. B. Calhoun, its originator, "by placing the vowel *o* three times, o-o-o, and filling in with the consonants t-l-n."

The results of such practices are here termed manufactured names, but could equally well be called coined names. Not altogether inappropriate would be the term creative names, since this type of naming frees the namer from tradition and enables him to exercise his originality.

A typical manufactured name is devoid of meaning in any ordinary sense of the word. Only by an extreme shift of approach can one find semantic significance in such a name as Pringhar or Tolono.

On the other hand, except for far-out cases such as Tolono, each manufactured name may be considered to constitute a cipher. Once solved, the elements of the name, though not the name itself, have at least a relationship to meaning and can generally be treated like ordinary names. Thus, if we learn that Remlaw in Australia is the reversed spelling of Walmer, we can then set out to discover who Walmer was and why his name was thus placed.

The older school of scholars tended to denigrate such manufactured creations, and to dismiss them with the single and scornful epithet "Fancy name." But the process cannot be merely thus written off as illegitimate, and its practitioners classed under the common term for illegitimates. Such names are numerous in the modern world—especially in the United States, Canada, and Australia. Some important places bear manufactured names. The city of Texarkana on the boundary of Texas and Arkansas takes its -ana ending from near-by Louisiana; it is a center for more than a hundred thousand people. The Delmarva Peninsula is a geographical entity, 150 miles long, deriving its name from abbreviations of the names of the three states from which it is composed.

Although the results of name-manufacture may seem strange and even bizarre, the chief basic methods are comparatively few.

1. Alteration of spelling may be considered a transitional stage resulting in nothing more than a slightly modified name, and possibly not worthy of notice in the present context. Thus Somerange in Oregon is merely from "summer range." Some interesting practices arose in the English colonies in America, in connection with a tendency to shift spellings and thus to create,

in a minor way, new names. Thus Hertford became Hartford. As with this name, pronunciation was usually involved, and the spelling employed in America may have been a phonetic one already used in England—spelling in the seventeenth century being uncertain. But in some more extreme instances we have what almost amounts to a new name. Indeed, mere consultation of a gazetteer will not solve the problem of what towns in England were the originals of certain towns in America. Thus Burlington and Killingworth do not readily reveal that their parent-towns are now Bridlington and Kenilworth.

2. Blends, as they are commonly called, represent another step in the process of manufacturing names. Again the development of the process points to America, with the naming of Saybrook in Connecticut, dating from 1635. The coinage was simply the joining of the titles of Lord Say and Sele and Lord Brook, being applied to a fort which was built on land held under patent by the two noblemen.

Though name-manufacture has not been common in France, an early example of blending occurs with Henrichemont, recorded in 1644, but possibly as early as 1609. Here the personal name Henri, probably for King Henry IV, has been joined with the otherwise-occurring Richemont.

A now-obsolescent coinage of the nineteenth century was Senegambia, for a West African region, from the names of the two principal rivers—Senegal and Gambia.

In Australia two miners were named Coster and Field, and in 1862 their names produced Costerfield. Such a name or name-element as Field is likely to be so used for its punning quality. In Minnesota the name Northfield springs from early settlers, North and Field.

The situation becomes more complicated when only parts of the name are preserved, often with a telescoping effect. Caribou Crossing in Canada became Carcross for simple brevity, but with the passage of time has come to suggest automobiles.

3. Fully developed name-manufacture arises with the manipulation of syllables or similar small groups of sounds. Actually, the unit is better described as a group of letters, since the practice seems to be limited to these visual symbols.

In Canada a new name was to be placed near Kewatin, Norman, and Rat Portage. By taking the first two letters of each of these, the namers produced Kenora—not only unique, but also convenient and euphonic. In Texas an early settler had sons, Bickham and Jerome. Favoring neither over the other, he produced Birome. In New Mexico a company town of the Gallup American Coal Company became Gamerco.

4. Another step involves the actual manipulation of individual letters, sometimes in combination with an established name or word. Theoretically the practice could be oral-auditory, but actually it seems always to arise from writing or printing. The analysis of sounds within a word, in fact, is a sophistication not likely to be attained by an illiterate person.

Sometimes letters can merely be run together, as when a certain coal-company president, I. T. Mann, gave his name to a West Virginia town, Itmann. At the opposite end of the nation, in Oregon, Alice Ladd gave a name to Alicel. As these examples indicate, single letters may be joined with whole words or with syllables to produce a viable place-name. Or we may have a combination of letters and syllables, as when the W. E. Steward Land Company yields Weslaco.

An often repeated practice is the reversal of the order of the letters, already illustrated by Tesnus. The United States supplies many examples, a few of which need only to be listed— Senoj, Lebam, Seloc, Rolyat, Reklaw, Notla, Sacul.

5. Some names arise, as far as can be determined, from mere shuffling of letters. Such a one is Tolono, already listed. Its companion, by the same coiner and produced by the same method, is Panolo. Here, however, mere coincidence seems to arise. Panolo in Illinois is doubtless to be thus explained, but in Alabama and Oklahoma it is the Choctaw word for cotton.

Names that cannot otherwise be explained can be suspected of being manufactured. Such a one is California. It first appears in a fictional work, the romance *Las Sergas de Esplandián* (*c.* 1500), by Garcí Ordóñez de Montalvo. In such fictional works as this the coinage of names is to be expected. Diligent scholars have located similar names, such as Calaforno and Calafornina (minor places in Sicily) and Californe (in *The Song of Roland,* but itself uncertain). There are also analogies with such Spanish names as Calahorra. The possibility remains, however, the California may be essentially nothing else than a coinage by the romancer for his own purposes.

In practice there are really no rules to the game, and these "standard" methods may appear in combinations of all kinds, and may even be linked with ordinary words or names.

A miscellany from Canada yields Jacam from J. A. Campbell, Bartstow from F. W. Stobart, Antross from Anthony Ross, Reco from Reliance Coal Company, Weno from "We Know!"—a company motto.

Sarben in Nebraska is from the first six letters of the state name, reversed. Pawn in Oregon is from the initials of four men, Poole, Akerly, Worthington, and Nolen. Adamana in Arizona, though suggesting *adamant,* is from Adam Hanna, an early settler.

The records of certain name-coiners and their methods have been preserved. J. G. W. Wilmot practiced the art in the state of Victoria in Australia. Since he was a surveyor, he had many opportunities for naming. He named Dundonnell because a settler named Donnell had been "done" in a land-deal, and Dunneworthy because he thought Judge Dunne to be worthy. Miepoll arose from the custom of a certain husband to refer to his wife as "My Poll." (See also Book III, Chapter 22.)

Operating in an aura of erudition was the American scholar H. R. Schoolcraft. He had some knowledge of Algonquian, but his names seem coined rather than derived. Algoma, for instance, used the first syllable of Algonquian, plus the word for *lake.* Some of his other names have never been explained, but they were successful. Alcona is a county in Michigan; Iosco stands on towns in several states. Schoolcraft's most famous production, however, was Itasca, known as the source of the Mississippi River. The name was coined in 1832, when Schoolcraft and his companion, W. T. Boutwell, camped by the lake and decided that it was the "true source." Boutwell rendered this in crude Latin as *veritas caput.* Schoolcraft then coined what he probably conceived to be an Indian-appearing name, taking the last four letters of *veritas* and the first two of *caput*.

Unless actual record of the naming is preserved, the identification of a manufactured name is impossible. Therefore names which have descended from the past may be manufactured and yet remain indecipherable by the most acute scholar. We have no reason to assume that men such as Wilmot and Schoolcraft only appeared on the earth in the last two centuries.

We have, indeed, at least one hint. St. Jerome, writing about A.D. 400, stated that Jordan was coined, being formed physically by the union of tributaries named Jor and Dan, and thus taking its name. Although we cannot accept this origin for Jordan, Jerome's idea became well known, and other such etymologies were suggested. With the idea being in circulation, names may have been thus coined, and, in fact, the two branches of the Jordan were certainly known to medieval pilgrims as the Jour and the Dan.

A situation which may owe something to Jerome came into existence in Virginia. There, in the seventeenth century, the Mattaponi River had taken its name from an Indian tribe. At some time later (the history is not well known) the two chief forks took the names Matta and Poni, and finally, at two higher forkings we have streams known as the Mat, Ta, Po, and Ni.

Lake Wagejo in Michigan would have no trouble in passing as merely another of the Indian names of the region, except that the record stands of its naming from the first and second letters of the first names of Walter Koelz, George Stanley, and John Brumm. On the other hand, Chickawaukee Lake in Maine lacks a record. It looks convincingly Algonquian, but one has the uneasy feeling that it may be merely some joker's combination of the Chicago and Milwaukee, with a *k* introduced for slight deception.

Three special types of coinage exist, especially in the United States. Of these, the boundary names are so numerous as to become almost conventional. They are blend-names from the names or abbreviations of two (occasionally, more than two) geographical areas such as states and counties. Texarkana has already been cited as a three-way coinage. Around the circuit of the California boundary-line the prefix *Cal-* or *Cali-* has been so frequently used as to become conventional—all the way from Calor on the north to Calexico on the international boundary to the south. Canalaska Mountain supplies a Canadian example.

Many of these boundary-names are euphonic, as may be claimed for most of the *Cal-* and *Cali-* examples, and for Texarkana. Others, like Tennga, scarcely warrant that praise, but serve effectively as names.

A second type of manufactured name derives from a visual symbol. The name of a brand for livestock often has become the name of the ranch or station and then of a settlement. Thus Odart in Arizona is from a brand composed of a circle and a dart-like symbol. Others among American examples are Ucross, Bar M Canyon, and Teedee. A lagoon in New South Wales is Deewhy, because of its resemblance to the letters D and Y. Even the Greek alphabet has been of use—for example, with Ypsilon Mountain in Colorado, on which the snow in the gullies at certain times of year is in the shape of that letter.

A third and highly important group is that formed from the names of companies. In fact, across the map of the United States, the suffix *-co* is thickly placed, and it usually represents a company town. Gamerco and Weslaco have already been cited. In Alcoa, from Aluminum Company of America, the *-co-* is internally preserved. An Australian example, doubtfully aesthetic and perhaps humorous, is Chewko from Chewing Tobacco Company.

There is every reason to think that the manufactured name will come more and more into use with the passage of time. It may, in fact, be termed congenial with modern civilization, which has taken more and more to the manufacture of names, from pure necessity. In every year hundreds of new names are coined by various processes and for various ends—often for products of all kinds, from Kodak to Coca Cola. Some of these names inevitably pass into place-names. Kodak, in fact, already appears on the map of the United States at least three times. The formation of new names from initials has become so common that a new word, *acronym,* has been coined for the result.

Although manufactured names may represent a break with linguistic process and with linguistic studies, they seem to point to the future. Eventually some of these names will become the names of famous places, will be effectively used in poetry, and will become symbols of patriotism or other abstractions. Far from being written off as a sign of New-World crudity, the manufactured names of the United States should be recognized as a creative achievement, and as the only basic contribution to place-naming within the historical period.

Even aesthetically, such names do not seem wanting. Perhaps not much can be said in favor of Jacam, Chewko, and Drofwal. On the other hand, Alicel and Willaura are musical enough for anyone. Even Pringhar has its guttural strength, a place where battles might be fought. Any lover of names may find comfort in Itasca, Henrichemont, and Kenova.

9

Mistake-names

George Davidson, though English-born, is to be reckoned as a remarkable American of the later nineteenth century. In commemoration of his many-sided career as hydrographer, geographer, and astronomer, his name stands on Mount Davidson in his home-city of San Francisco, on Davidson Seamount, and on other features in Washington and Alaska. Routine duties never satisfied his wide-ranging mind, and he felt the charm of both the practice and the theory of place-names. In compiling his *Pacific Coast Pilot* he gave many names, and satisfied his curiosity about the origin of many others. But one of them intrigued and baffled him.

Nome was a famous Alaskan gold-mining district. As Cape Nome, the name of a near-by headland, it had appeared on British charts since about 1850. But what was its meaning and significance, and what, even, was its language? Historically it might most likely be Russian, English, or Eskimo. Possibly it might be Spanish, French, Aleut, or of some Indian language. The trouble was that it did not seem to be any of these. Davidson doubtless discovered that the word in English could mean a district in ancient Egypt, but such a derivation was altogether unlikely.

A thorough man, he decided that the British, having first

recorded the name, might know something about it. He wrote to the Admiralty. The chance that, half a century later, anything could be discovered was a small one, but the brilliant success of this letter should be a demonstration to scholars that no lead should be considered too faint to follow. Along with Davidson, however, we must give equal honor to the Admiralty for its preservation of records, and for its intelligent and conscientious answering of miscellaneous correspondence. A clearly written letter settled the whole question:

> When the MS chart of this region was being constructed on board H.M.S. *Herald,* attention was drawn to the fact that this point had no name, and a mark ? name was placed against it.
>
> In the hurry of dispatching this chart from the ship the ? appears to have been inked in by a rough draftsman and appeared as Cape Name, but the stroke of the "a" being very indistinct, it was interpreted by our draftsman here as C. Nome, and has appeared with this name ever since. The information is from an officer who was on board the *Herald* when the chart was being constructed.

In summary, then, the name resulted from an error. It may thus pass as the classic example of a mistake-name, since it so obviously is such, and since the historical evidence, emanating from so reliable and responsible an agency as the Admiralty, is above suspicion.

A name that is much more widely known than Nome seems similarly to have originated from a mistake, though the question has occasioned controversy. In the spelling Ouragon it appears as early as 1765, and its modern spelling as Oregon was first recorded in 1778. Nothing, however, was available as to the origin of the name, and speculation flourished. Derivations were suggested from French, Spanish, and at least four different Indian languages.

In 1943, I was looking at names on a reproduced copy of a map in the Baron Lahontan's *Nouveaux voyages,* a work published in various differing editions in the early eighteenth century. Suddenly the name Ouaricon struck my eye, and its similarity to Oregon seemed suddenly to move the search back half a century. Immediate closer inspection of the map showed that it was R. (that is, "River") de Ouarican, as was only to be expected, since earlier references placed the name regularly on a river. Still closer inspection showed that, on the carelessly prepared map, the letters *sint* occurred under Ouaricon, so that the actual name would have been Ouariconsint, with the last syllable probably being an attempt to render the Algonquian locative ending.

The fact remained, however, that if I could take the name to be Ouaricon, so might another man, and a mistake-name could thus originate. From that beginning, a reasonable sequence of forms can be presented, viz.,

Ouaricon—1703, 1709
Ouragon—1765
Ourigan— 1766, 1772
Oregon—1778

On the Lahontan map R. de Ouariconsint is placed upon a stream which seems to be the present Wisconsin River, and the phonetic resemblance is fairly close. The element *-consin* appears in both names.

Actually, however, the identification of the map-maker's intention is not of immediate importance in connection with the name Oregon. If it originated from a particular spelling, it must be classed as a mistake-name and it thus loses semantic contact, so to speak, with the word or name from which it has diverged by the common process of human error.

Certainly the individuals of all colors, creeds, and languages, throughout all eras, have been subject to making mistakes. As Nome indicates, even the officers of the British Navy are not exempt. We may therefore believe that mistake-names have arisen everywhere and at all periods. The overwhelming difficulty is that the historical record is rarely preserved, and that a scholar, however much he may suspect an error, cannot justify himself in a cutting of the Gordian knot by merely postulating one for his own convenience.

Though an individual mistake is likely to be all too readily recognizable, the general idea of a mistake is somewhat difficult of definition and delimitation. For instance, are not folk-etymologies to be classified as mistakes? Folk-etymologies occurring by unconscious folk-process may certainly be so designated, but many of them arise by wholly conscious process. On the whole, therefore, at least as a matter of convenience, folk-etymology in place-naming is usefully kept as a separate classification.

As thus indicated, mistake-names must always arise from unconscious process and by inadvertence. To proceed toward a formal definition, a double-pronged possibility of origin must be postulated.

A mistake-name is one arising from an unintended failure 1. to conform to an established norm, or 2. to grasp or transmit meaning.

1. When and where no recognized standard of pronunciation or spelling exists, the whole conception of error has no strength. In the medieval period, for instance, there were no firmly established standards for linguistic usage. With spelling the situation is easily shown, because of the numerous variations preserved in the records. In England such a simple name as Bristol (to use its modern form) turns up in such different spellings as Brycgstow, Bristou, Bricstou and Bristoll, some of which are based upon differences of pronunciation. No one, however, can declare that any of these spellings is a mistake. No clear standard being in effect, all of the spellings can be held to fall within the allowed range, and therefore they are commonly classified as variants. Ordinary words showed the same tendency to vary in spelling.

Even as late as the time of the colonization of America, spelling was not fixed. Thus today a county in Virginia is Surry and one in New York is Dutchess, but we must accept these as variants of Surrey and Duchess, not as mistakes of the namers.

The same situation displays itself strikingly in the transfer of names between languages, as between the various Indian languages and English. These names and words generally came first to the attention of frontiersmen, who were either illiterate or nearly so. If illiterate, they passed the names on to someone who wrote them down as best he could. Unable themselves to write the names, these frontiersmen did what they could, each man for himself. Thus, among common nouns, we have *tipi, tepee* and *teepee,* which lexicographers still labeled as variants, all appearing in names.

In many place-names the result was a staggering multiplicity. Dozens of different forms stand in the record for many individual names—Winnepesaukee, with 132, possibly holding the record. Such a simple name as Kansas shows more than fifty different spellings. But, occurring before the establishment of a norm, they must be called variants rather than mistakes.

Eventually, linguistic standards of "correctness" developed, especially in spelling. Today, if we find a Cansas or Kanzas, we are justified in assuming an error, though a conscious rebellion by some devoted individualist is not an impossibility.

Official bodies, such as boards on geographical names and the Post Office Department, have done much to set standards. At the same time, in the United States, the establishment of post offices has done something to entrench mistakes.

In practice, especially in the nineteenth century, the local people applied for the establishment of a post office, and sent to Washington a name or list of possible names. Being written by unskillful hands, these names were frequently undecipherable or nearly so—indeed, they may, to begin with, have included mistakes of spelling. Thus a clerk in Washington might study a certain application, decide that the name was Plaska, and thus officially establish a post office of that name in Texas. Actually the applicant had desired to found another Pulaski, for the Polish hero of the Revolution. The basic desire of the local people, however, was to have a post office, and they probably did not particularly care under what name. With Plaska, as in many such cases, the form as it returned officially from Washington was accepted. The upshot was the establishment by mistake of a new name, a combination of six consonants and vowels in an order which probably existed nowhere else in the world, and probably still remains unique. In this respect, at least, it may even be considered a "better" name than Pulaski would have been.

Other forms produced in the United States by similar confusions of transmission are Tolo for Yolo, Bogata for Bogotá, Divot for Pivot, Hillister for Hollister, Darrington for Barrington. Most of these shifts of spelling are accompanied by marked shifts of pronunciation.

The Spanish word *carrizo*, "reed-grass," has produced Caresso Creek and Carisa Canyon, both in New Mexico. In these instances the shifts apparently occurred from the failure of speakers of English to recognize a Spanish word or to know how to spell it. The process is not that of folk-etymology, because the new forms do not make better sense and are not more familiar in spelling or in pronunciation.

2. As already noted, mistake-names may arise from an unintended failure to grasp or to transmit meaning. Usually a contact of two languages exists.

Approaches of English-speaking settlers to Australian aborigines have yielded some examples. When asked about the name of a certain island, the natives, not understanding, replied with a word meaning "What?" or "Don't understand." Either taking this to be the name or thinking that it would at least serve for a name, the whites called the place Gabo Island. Similarly, the Yarra River took its name from the reply of a native who apparently thought that he was being asked whether the stream ever went dry, and replied "Ever flowing." The explorer, taking this to be in answer to his question about the name, applied it to the river.

The tip of South America was originally named, in Dutch, Kaap Hoorn, commemorating the city of Hoorn in the Netherlands. The English, probably by mere error, made this into Cape Horn, and the Spanish, by another error, render it as Cabo Hornos, that is, Cape Ovens, a highly un-descriptive term.

Mexico yields a famous case. According to the Spanish chroniclers, the Córdoba expedition of 1517 landed at a point where they found the Indians very friendly, and constantly saying a word which the Spaniards took to be Catoche. They assumed this to be the name of the place, and so recorded it. But, as the account continues, it was really a sentence, "Come into my house!" The name survives as Cabo Catoche, one of the chief capes of the Mexican coastline.

Mistranslation may also be considered a kind of error. A famous American case exists with the so-called Staked Plain in Texas, which has been "explained" by several fanciful tales. It is, however, a translation of the Spanish name Llano Estacado, which can actually be so translated in some contexts. Here, however, the correct translation should apparently be "pali-saded," the reference being to a cliff extending along much of the southern edge of the plain. Its rampart-like front apparently suggested to the Spanish explorers the kind of fortification known to them as an *estacada*—in English, a palisade. Curiously, in the United States this term came to be a generic actually meaning a cliff, as with the Palisades of the Hudson.

Two other recognized practices may be classified as, broadly speaking, processes involving mistakes.

Back-formation (a common conception, especially among English scholars) finds its typical instance in the River Cam of Cambridgeshire. It is first recorded about 745 as the Gronte, apparently derived from a British word for bog. Eventually the form Granta established itself, and it still, indeed, survives as an alternate name for the river and in the name of the present village of Grantchester. Actually, the important town on the stream was first recorded, about 730, as Grantacaester, that is, "Roman fort on the Granta." Soon, however, the building of a bridge led to a name-shift to Grantebricc. The name remained in approximately that form until after the Conquest. The Normans, then, occupying the important town, decade after decade, had difficulty with pronouncing it after the Anglo-Saxon fashion, and shifted it to Cantebruge and eventually to Cambridge. The conquerors, however, were little concerned, it would seem, about the small and unprofitable river, and it remained the Granta.

A patent anomaly thus arose. The much-used name Cambridge obviously declared itself to be the place of a bridge over the Cam. But the stream was the Granta. As in war the victory goes to the stronger battalions, so in names the victory goes to the more dominant tongues. Eventually, by about 1600, people in Cambridge were speaking and writing of the River Cam, and Ekwall's *Dictionary of English Place-names* can dispose of the Cam of Cambridgeshire in a few words: "A back-formation from Cambridge."

Another transformation which is connected with the idea of mistake arises from the common human desire for brevity and economy in speech, chiefly in connection with double specifics. We thus have a place which is more exactly named than is common, such as Red Cedar Creek, so called because of red cedars there. By American standards, at least, this is too long a name. If it is shortened to Cedar Creek, no great alteration of meaning has resulted. But some influence (perhaps the existence already of a near-by Cedar Creek) may lead to the shortening Red Creek. Presuming that the creek is not descriptively thus designated, we find here a name which has suffered complete semantic change, for no purposeful reason, but merely by a blind procedure, which may properly be classed as a mistake.

Along the border of the United States and Mexico, a colorful specific occurs with Dagger Mountain in Texas and Dagger Spring in Arizona. It raises romantic suggestions of Mexican banditti. In reality, it is from the presence of the giant yucca, commonly known as Spanish dagger, or dagger cactus, and the present form has resulted from clipping—Spanish Dagger Mountain, for instance, being a longer name than an American frontiersman would tolerate.

The frequent production of place-names by mere human mistake is not surprising. If we can make any sound generalization at all about individual men and women, it is that each of them is subject, on occasion, to error.

10
Shift-names

The term *transfer-name* can be applied broadly to names which have been picked up at one point on the earth's surface, and transplanted to another. All commemorative names from places and many commendatory names are to be thus included. Certain transfers, however, are involved only with the specific, and demand a class of their own. These may be known as shift-names.

They are formed, in the same vicinity, by the shift of a particular specific from one generic to another. Thus the Algonquian term *siskowit* in Michigan refers to some kind of fish. Just how and with what application it first became a place-name is now uncertain. It may first have been applied to the Siskiwit River. Now, however, there exist, in the same vicinity, Little Siskiwit River, Siskiwit Lake, Siskiwit Bay, Siskiwit Falls, the Siskiwit Islands, Siskiwit Outlet, and Siskiwit Mine. There may even be others, since no comprehensive gazetteer is available for the area.

Such a proliferation of shift-names is conveniently known as a name-cluster.

Shift-names are uncharacteristic of older cultures, but even so, in the aggregate, thousands exist across the face of Europe. The case of Cambridge and the River Cam (see Book II, Chapter 9) is evidence of the human mind to conceive in terms of a shift-name. At the time of the Revolution, the French formed most of their new *départements* by means of shift-names which applied to the new entity an already established name of a natural feature, most commonly a river.

At an earlier period but in identical manner the Anglo-Saxons, as they re-conquered the Danelaw, named most of their new shires by the simple process of using the name of a town with the added *-shire,* as with Derby-Derbyshire and York-Yorkshire.

The Russians, seeking a name to replace Stalingrad, shifted the name of the great river, and produced Volgograd. In such cases as this last the possibility may be argued that the naming was conscious, and in a sense commemorative, or anti-commemorative. Certainly, the typical shift-name springs up without conscious process on the part of the namer, or at least out of mere ease and convenience.

Few people, indeed, recognize what might be called the collective chore of naming a new country. An area as large as that of the United States requires, for mere practicality, some millions of names. These names do not create themselves. Excessive repetition is disadvantageous. But explorers, surveyors, mapmakers, and even early settlers are faced with the necessity of supplying many names. Shift-naming is the easiest process, since the selection of one name may provide two or three or half-a-dozen more. Moreover, there is no real problem of repetition, since the generics provide distinction.

In another way, also, shift-names are practical, in that they provide, ready-made, a kind of map or set of directions. They can even be called landmark names. In the United States, more particularly in the West, a man hears the name of a river and then can expect that the valley bears the same name, and so also probably with the lake in the valley and the peak looming up over it.

There are exceptions. Lake Tahoe drains not into the Tahoe River, but into the Truckee River, which empties, not into Truckee Lake, but into Pyramid Lake. In this instance the historical incidents determining the unusual name-pattern are well documented.

Shift-naming meets a certain resistance with descriptives. Because of reddish rocks Red Mountain may be an apt name, but not at all suitable for the stream and lake on the mountain's slope. Nonetheless they may become Red Creek and Red Lake. Highly inappropriate namings may be suspected of having thus arisen—later perhaps to be left as unexplained "orphans" by some change of name of the original feature.

As with Siskiwit, however, shift-naming flourishes best with names of unknown meaning, or, at least, with non-descriptives.

Since feature-names are likely to be established before habitation-names, the general tendency of shifting is from feature to habitation. Innumerable towns and villages in the United States show the result by being called simply Elk River or Grand Lake—or, perhaps, Elkton or Grandville. Shifts in the other direction, however, are also common. Small streams, especially, are likely to remain unnamed in the early stages of settlement, and later to take the name of a village.

In its total effect upon the name-pattern there is much to be said against shift-naming. It fails to create new names, and also produces a general effect of monotony, whether with English counties, French *départements,* or the more elaborated American name-clusters. On the other hand, as long as most human beings are unimaginative and easygoing (even lazy), the economy of effect, as offered by shift-naming, makes the process inevitable. It also contributes, as already pointed out, a certain efficiency by providing name-clusters which remove the necessity of anyone's having to learn and apply a burdensome number of names. In "the old days" people stayed close to home, and knew the names of only a single not-very-large area. With the greater mobility of modern life, efficiency in naming has become more important.

An anecdote of the not-too-ancient past may serve to show the folk-mind at work on shift-naming. Mr. N——, riding in a Pullman car, heard another traveler ask the porter the name of the river which the train was passing, not too far from a town named Jackson.

"That, sir," said the porter agreeably and authoritatively, "That, the Jackson River."

Later Mr. N—— took the porter to task: "Why did you tell

that man it was the Jackson River? It's the Kalamazoo River."

"Oh, sir," was the reply, "I can't keep all these rivers straight on this run. I just use the names of the stations. If they ask me near Jackson, I say 'Jackson River.' If they ask me near Kalamazoo, I say, 'Kalamazoo River.' "

Conclusion

Although the classification here presented is useful and valuable in providing some rough-and-ready compartments for the practical necessity of grouping the many millions of place-names, it is not to be considered scientifically precise. It represents not names as dead things, but the approaches of the namer to his problem, whether or not he is conscious of what he is doing.

Such mental processes are protean, unconfined, and uncompartmentalized. By association the mind shifts quickly from one idea to another. At one moment a person may consider a name merely as commemorative; in the next instant he realizes its commendatory possibilities. When he christens Rock River he is not concerned whether his name is a true descriptive or whether it is better termed associative.

The present classification, then, is to be considered primarily a practical expedient. Most place-names fall clearly into one or another of its compartments. We need not, however, feel any embarrassment at an example which lies upon a borderline. Certain borderlines, in fact, call for special notice.

1. *Descriptive-commendatory.* A name such as Wheatland may be honestly descriptive, indicative of good wheat-growing country, but it may also be merely a land-promoter's device to encourage settlers to purchase acres which are not particularly suitable for producing wheat. But, then, the promoter himself may be honest, although deceived. Ordinarily, we can decide only upon detailed knowledge or by investigation of general probability.

2. *Commemorative-commendatory.* In many instances the two mingle. A town's founder may be genuinely devoted to Washington. Yet, at the same time, he can realize that it is a

"good" name for Americans—familiar, comfortable, confidence- inspiring.

3. *Descriptive-associative.* The connection between these two approaches is close, and the distinction is likely to be blurred. Island Lake can originate in a descriptive effort, but might also arise from mere association; so also with Rocky River, Mud Pond, and Pine Mountain.

4. *Descriptive-incident.* Recurring incidents suggest description. Roaring Run may always, or commonly, be noisy, or it may have received its name because, on one occasion, it was noisy as the result of flooding. Or it may roar briefly after every heavy rain. The naming may thus be either descriptive or from incident, or may fall in between, because of a repeated phenomenon.

5. *Associative-incident.* Rattlesnake Canyon commonly arises from the circumstance that the namer encountered a rattlesnake there. Certain places, however, are notoriously "snaky." The two poles are therefore incident and association.

6. *Incident-possessive.* If a member of an exploring expedition is drowned in crossing a stream and his comrades thereupon name it for him, we have an obvious incident. But how long does a man have to live upon the stream to make the naming possessive—a month, or a year?

Examples of still other borderline cases could be supplied, but such mere proliferation is not necessary, especially since the idea of dual or multiple origin of place-names has been already recognized (see Book I, Chapter 10). Moreover, the necessary acceptance of examples which are not clearly classifiable is not to be taken as a weakness of the whole system. Rather, it should be considered a strength, since it is a recognition of the extreme complication of place-naming, and the accompanying fluidity of human thought.

Finally, we must again emphasize that the system of classification is not of names as such, but of the processes of naming. In a vast number of instances, indeed, the name and the process coincide, so that from the name we are justified, statistically, in deducing the process.

In English, for instance, *red* is to be considered descriptive in a high proportion of its occurrences. Yet Red Creek, as already pointed out, may have arisen from a shortening of Red Cedar Creek. Or it may be a shift-name from Red Mountain. It may have originated, by error, from Reed Creek. Again, it may have once been on the property of a red-haired man, known as Red.

To continue with English as the example, we must recognize that a word may have more than one meaning, both or all of them suitable for use in naming places. The situation is especially complicated by the great number of common nouns and adjectives which also exist as proper nouns and adjectives. To use another word for color, *green* is much more of an uncertain quality than is *red*, because Green is a common family name. No conclusion about this word as a place-name is justified unless we can cite human testimony, written or verbal, or some aptness of color-description.

Another color-word, less common in place-names, but actually more complex in usage in the United States than *red* or *green*, is *orange*. The comparatively few names provided by it illustrate no fewer than five origins.

With Orange Buttes in Arizona it is a descriptive from the color of the rocks. In regions of citriculture, such as California and Florida, the name is a commendatory, suggesting profitable orange-growing. Orangeville in Utah is of possessive origin, from Orange Seeley, an early settler. Orange County in New York is a commemorative of the title Prince of Orange, which King William III brought into the English royal family. Finally, the towns in New Jersey arose by folk-etymology from Auronge, an Indian tribe, recorded as early as 1645.

Without a historical check, the student of names is sometimes, inevitably, left in an either-or predicament. In fact, encountering the situation of Orange, he would face a fivefold uncertainty. Languages, even those of simple people, present ambiguities and multiple meanings. The surprising actuality is that so much (rather than so little) has been done for the elucidation of names. Still more can be accomplished by some historical application of our knowledge of the ways of the namer. This topic provides the subject-matter of Book III.

III
Namers at Work

Introduction

To quote an authority is in a cherished tradition of scholarship. To present oneself as that authority is also not unknown, though not so solidly accepted. Yet, having once composed a passage that seems adequate and suitable, a writer may be pardoned for repeating it.

I offer, then, as a beginning for Book III, the opening of my *Names on the Land:*

> Once, from eastern ocean to western ocean, the land stretched away without names. Nameless headlands split the surf; nameless lakes reflected nameless mountains; and nameless rivers flowed through nameless valleys into nameless bays.

So it was, not only in the Mesoceania which is the United States of America, but, if we pass back far enough into time, so also it was with all lands that lie between all waters, and upon the surface of the waters themselves.

What men gave the first place-names, we can never know. Not when, nor where, nor of what kind. Did the first namers identify the place descriptively, or did something that happened there, some incident, impress itself upon their budding minds?

When records first appeared—on Egyptian stones or Meso-
potamian bricks or Pylos tablets—already the writings
burgeoned with the names of places, whether of streams and
mountains or of towns and cities and kingdoms.

Or again, even further back, into the millennia before writing, scholars may trace sounds and compare generics. By such
methods it becomes possible, or even probable, to believe that
the tradition of place-names goes back to Aurignacian man or
even to the Neanderthalers. Again to quote:

> And since names—corrupted, transferred, re-made—outlive
> men and nations and languages, it may even be that we still
> speak daily some name which first meant "Saber-tooth Cave"
> or "Where-we-killed-the-ground-sloth."

By established methods we can probe back into the past for at
least a number of centuries before the advent of writing in any
region.

The actual records of the past, ancient and recent, preserve
millions of place-names—in treaties and charters, on funeral
steles, in business records, in formal histories and geographies,
in lists of tributary cities and taxable estates, in songs and poetry and folk-tales.

In Book III I will attempt to bring some historical order into
the mass of detail, and to establish some patterns and generalizations. The approach is necessarily two-pronged.

First, in establishing a pattern, is the nature of the land itself.
In a dry country the naming of springs and wells and wa-
terholes takes high priority. In the far North, where the
spruces stretch off for mile after mile, not many names can
arise from trees. But in the tropics, where species are many,
one place may be easily distinguished from the next by its special kind of tree.

Second, as an influence upon the patterns, is the nature of
the people inhabiting the land, and thus giving or maintaining
or shifting the names. Among a people with a culture dominated by religion, as with India, the place-names will be largely
religious. Among peoples with a strong sense of personal prop-

erty, like the Angles and the Saxons, many names will be those of landowners. A people with a strong sense of the past and of what once happened here or there, like the Maoris, give names based on incident. A nomadic tribe spreads its names thinly upon landmark streams and peaks over vast distances, but peasant-farmers plant their names thickly within a half-day's walking distance.

In the account here presented, however, I shall not draw my examples chiefly from among the millions of little-remembered and less-regarded names, but shall focus, instead, upon the great names, those known over the world, those spoken daily and often with awe, those enshrined in the poetry of the nations—the names of lands and of great seas (Egypt, Atlantic), of battles (Thermopylae), of teeming cities (Babylon, London, Shanghai), of famous towns (Bethlehem)—and of many others that have come to be the themes of man's poetry and the symbols of his achievements and of his hopes, and, sometimes, of his disasters.

I

In the Lands of the Rivers

The oldest place-names must occur in some area which has been inhabited for a very long period—perhaps, indeed, since man first developed language. This region must lie in the great land-mass that comprises Europe, Asia, and Africa, and beyond the range of the glaciers of the Ice Age. Any answer as to just where it may have been is, at present, impossible, and is likely to remain so. Comparative linguistics, applied to place-names, can thrust back the limits of knowledge by some thousands of years before history and writing. But far short of this particular goal, it fails. To work with any degree of surety (and even so, not with much certainty), the scholar of names must begin, like the historian, with the records, and therefore with Egypt and Mesopotamia, the lands of the rivers.

The roll of ancient Egyptian names chiefly comprises habitation-names, and the Egyptians themselves seem to have offered no comments upon naming. Still, a few generalizations are possible.

As must always be true, the nature of the environment influenced the name-patterns. The land, watered only by its great river, lacked springs and small streams, and so had no such names. Doubtless the people had names for landmark mountains and curiously shaped peaks that stood up against the sky-line in the dry ranges bordering the valley. That boatmen on the river could specify reaches and bends and eddies we can know, for instance, from a settlement called Khenit, "rowing place," because of a swift current there.

In such a setting, in a thickly peopled agricultural land, the habitation-names necessarily became doubly important to de-note both the city or town or village itself and also the region round about. We know the names, therefore, chiefly of cities and towns, since villages often fail to get into the record. Regu-larly the names are religious, another evidence of the religious domination in the culture. They express the dedication of a place to a cult which centered around some rock, mountain, tree, or animal. Thus we have Atef, "sycamore-town," but cele-brating a cult of that tree, not its mere occurrence.

The suggestion of a once-simpler nomenclature lies behind some of these names. The city of the cat-goddess was Bubastis, meaning "she of the town of Bast." Apparently the local spirits were originally nameless, and were designated by the places of their cult. The town must therefore have been merely Bast before its goddess took over.

During much of the period when civilization was developing around the eastern Mediterranean, Egypt was a closed king-dom, maintaining minimal contacts with other peoples. As a result, the great names (as we now know them) are chiefly "out-side" names, that is, those given by foreigners. Of Memphis, Thebes, Egypt, the Nile, only the first seems to be clearly and wholly Egyptian.

Memphis owes its name to Pepy I of the Sixth Dynasty, who fixed his residence at an old fortress known as The Wall or The White Wall. To his new foundation and his near-by pyramid he gave the religious name Men-nefer-Meryre, "the beauty of Meryre endures." The long name shortened a little into Men-nefer, "the beauty endures," and became the designation of the great capital city. The outside peoples shifted the name to their own uses, the Assyrians recording it as Mempi, the Greeks as Memphis.

In contrast to the comparatively simple development of

Memphis, the other great Egyptian capital has a naming-history which is obscure and must be largely foreign. What we have come to know as Thebes, the Egyptians called Waset, "town of the Scepter district." From its preeminence it came to be known merely as "the city," and the Hebrews referred to it as No for this reason. These names have not the slightest resemblance to Thebai, the form of the Greek city, and much scholarly energy has been expended in trying to discover some possible form which might have led the Greeks to call it that. These attempts have been strikingly unsuccessful. Another hypothesis is that the Greeks (an imaginative people) merely identified the great Egyptian city with their own Thebes, possibly for some mythological reason. In such uncertainty the matter rests, and the name is possibly to be considered as Greek rather than Egyptian.

The derivation of Egypt itself is also obscure. The Egyptians themselves called their land Kemet, "black," apparently a descriptive, from the rich soil of the Nile Valley. The modern name, however, is from the Greek, Aigyptos. One attempt at solution (phonetically possible, but semantically tenuous) has derived this name from an alternate designation of Memphis, which may be rendered in English as Hikuptah. But the great days of Memphis had passed by the time of the Greeks' making contact with Egypt, and the identification of a large country with a second-string appellation for a second-string capital should not be readily assumed.

In Greek the name appears in those earliest documents, the Homeric poems—once in the *Iliad;* more than a dozen times in the *Odyssey*. Moreover, it is also used for the people—and, once, as the name of a man, a Greek, who had no apparent connection with the country of Egypt. But of especial interest, sometimes the name means the country, but sometimes it means the river—as when Menelaus tells:

> We moored the curved ships in the river Egyptos.

Since in Greek the rivers are normally masculine and the lands feminine, there is a strong likelihood that the name, having the masculine form, was first applied to the river and was then shifted to the country. We are therefore justified in searching for a meaning that would be suitable for a river, and here we find the Greek element *aig.* Though in its everyday usage it is connected with *goat,* it also occurs in the archaic *aiges,* "waves," in *aigialos,* "beach," and in place-names having to do with water or the sea, such as Aigaios, the Aegean Sea, and Aigina, an island. It occurs also in personal names, not only in Aigyptos, but in such a one as Aigisthos, with the suggestion that it may also have once been the name of a sea-god. Obviously, *aig-* must in earlier centuries have been in common usage; it may be taken as cognate with the Latin *aqua,* "water," and with the Germanic *aha,* "river."

The possibility then is that Aigyptos arose as a name for the Nile in Mycenean times. It certainly seems to have been well established by the Homeric period.

To continue with a Greek hypothesis, the latter part of the stem is *-ypt,* and the possibility here is to connect it with the adjective *hyptios,* which in a general sense means "laid flat," and is actually applied by Herodotus to Egypt in the sense of "sloping evenly." Used with a river, it could mean "without current," or "having low banks," thus being the equivalent of the common American usage of Flat Creek and, in the French form, of the Platte River.

To the Mycenean Greeks, or even to the Minoans of Crete, who were used to tumbling mountain-torrents, the great river must have been impressive for its apparent lack of current and its general level with the surrounding land, especially in the delta.

To avoid ambiguity—or, as the sceptical Herodotus might have put it "for some other reason"—the Greeks soon limited Aigyptos to mean the country, though maintaining the telltale masculine ending. To specify the river, they used Neilos.

This term first appears in Hesiod's *Theogony,* a work not much later than the *Odyssey.* About this time, which would be approximately 750 B.C., the ancient kingdom of Egypt was opening up to foreign traders, and the Greeks were never slow to seize such an opportunity. Already in the trade, however, were the Phoenicians.

Little is known at first hand of the Phoenician language, but there is enough to assure us that it was much like Hebrew. Classical Hebrew has several words for "stream," and one of these may be transliterated as *nachal*. Apparently the Phoenician traders used this word for the great river, and the Greeks adopted it. Their language, however, had no sound corresponding to the Semitic *heth*, which was probably something like a Spanish *j*. When it stood between two vowels, the natural procedure would be simply to drop it, as the Americans have dropped the *j* in such a name as Vallejo (see also Book IV, Chapter 2). The Greeks would then be left with an *n* and an *l*, and a diphthong between them, to which they could add their own ending—masculine, for a river. This is about as good a description as one could ask for the actual Neilos.

The Romans shifted it to Nilus; the English, still further. But it has remained recognizable through the centuries. It thus provides an example, among hundreds of others, of a river-name which turns out to mean merely "river."

The other ancient river-land is commonly known by the Greek term Mesopotamia, literally, "middle-river-land," but, more intelligibly, "between-rivers-land"—that is, the region between the Euphrates and the Tigris. The name is an approximate translation of the older local Semitic usage, Naharina, surviving in the King James Bible as Aram-Naharim, "Syria of the Rivers." Strabo concluded succinctly and pertinently: "Mesopotamia has its name from what is actually the case."

There has been little study of naming in this area. From what is available the suggestion is that the general practice was religiously based, as in Egypt. Thus Babylon is "gate of the god(s)," though the reference of gate is left uncertain. Also religious is Assyria, from Assur, the city, which itself is the name of a god. Nineveh, the other great capital, remains uncertain, but it may be one of the many habitation-names springing from a local term, in this instance, Semitic, which merely means "habitation." The Greeks, coming after the city was in ruins, invented their usual eponymous hero in the person of King Ninus, and supplied him with an even more famous wife, Semiramis.

The two great rivers themselves have borne different

names—naturally, since they flowed through areas where different languages were spoken. Pliny knew the Euphrates as the Pyxurates near its source and as the Omma where it broke through the Taurus Mountains. The Persians knew it as the "very broad," and their name may be the translation of an earlier one. The Syrians, however, made it into a form that can be rendered "sweet-water," a common name for a flowing stream in desert country.

In the comparatively late time of the Persian Empire that people associated the name Tigris with their own word for arrow, because the river was swift-flowing. The name, however, is traceable clear back to a Sumerian *I-digna,* and is more likely to mean a stream with high banks. If so, the twin rivers may be conceived, reasonably enough, as having counterpart names— the broad-spreading Euphrates as against the closely confined Tigris.

Consideration of these early names may well end with one that looks toward both the lands of the rivers. In most peoples' minds the Red Sea is considered Egyptian; actually, its origins may be with the Persian Gulf.

In fact, only by physical propinquity can the name Red Sea be held to have connection with the ancient Egyptians. They regularly referred to that body of water as the Great Green!

Part of the fixation upon Egypt undoubtedly springs from later translations of the book of Exodus, where everyone reads that the Egyptians were engulfed in the Red Sea. The Hebrew term, however, is Yam Suf, "Sea of Reeds," presumably based upon a growth around the edges of the lagoons at the northern margin.

Nonetheless, through the millennia, scholars and pseudo-scholars have proceeded on two assumptions—that the name is to be associated with the body of water so known at present, and that it is descriptive. Like a pack on a false trail, they have displayed some fine examples of virtuosity, without getting anywhere.

The elder Pliny, who was interested in names, has given a summing-up of the theories current in his own time, the first century A.D.:

The Greeks call it Erythrum, from King Erythras, or according to others, in the belief that the water is given a redness by the reflection of the sun; others say that the name is from the sand and the soil, and others that it is from the actual water being naturally such.

As late as 1954 the descriptive idea was still current. In that year the *London Illustrated News* published an article on the so-called "red tides" in which the author concluded "The Red Sea derives its name from the occurrence."

Another theory—not mentioned by Pliny, although apparently older than his time—is that the name came from pink or red coral. Aeschylus, as quoted by Strabo, was apparently so thinking when he referred to "the Erythrean Sea's sacred stream, crimson of floor."

A name which appears to describe, and yet apparently does the opposite, is to be viewed with suspicion—that is, the explanation of it as descriptive must. We know that the waters of that sea are not naturally red. Men are not given to naming whole seas for such commonplace and evanescent phenomena as a red sunset—or sunrise, as it would have been for the Egyptians. King Erythras is only another of those thousands of so-called eponymous heroes spawned by the personalizing imagination of the Greeks. The red tides might supply an incident-name, but it would be a million-to-one chance. Of all Pliny's theories, only that of the sand and the soils seems to offer a possibility, since shift-names are sometimes counter-descriptive.

The idea, in fact, may be pursued with much hope, until it finally ends in a bottomless pit. The Egyptians, we know, called their own land "the black," and by counterpart, aided by the color of much of the desert rock, the arid regions on both sides of the Nile Valley they called the "red land." Therefore, what could be more likely that they should know that body of water as the Sea of the Red Land? Then, just as Red Cedar Creek may become Red Creek, the name could have shortened to the Red Sea.

Moreover, the theory fits with another fact. To the east of the sea the lands were chiefly held by Semitic-speaking tribes, and one of the regions close to the sea, or even bordering on it, was

Edom. That name—in Hebrew, and probably in other Semitic dialects of the region—can be translated as "red." Therefore, instead of vaguely Sea of the Red Land, it might be Sea of Edom.

The theory is perfect—until you try to find someone on whom to pin it. Not the Egyptians, apparently. Not the Hebrews.

We remain then with a fine solution but no place to put it. It seems, however, too good to throw away. It had better be put aside carefully, to be used later, if more evidence should become available.

Fortunately, we have another theory at hand. If it seems a little fanciful at first, one should remember that unusual names often call for unusual explanations.

As a solid point of departure, we should recall that the term Red Sea, in ancient times, did not refer only to the water now so known. It included also the Persian Gulf, the Arabian Sea, and all the waters that lay to the south and east of the Mediterranean. There is, moreover, no evidence that the name was applied to the present Red Sea any earlier than it was applied to the Persian Gulf—and, indeed, the Persian Gulf may have been so-called earlier.

We shift now to that much-traveling people, the Phoenicians. They, like their Hebrew neighbors, cherished a tradition that their ancestors came from the East. Herodotus notes at the very opening of his great history: "These people came originally from the coasts of the Red Sea." And he certainly meant the present Persian Gulf.

With that much established, we may make a not too bold assumption that the sea by which the Phoenicians lived was known by their name.

To return then to solid linguistic fact. There are two words meaning "red" in ancient Greek. The common term was *erythros,* but there was also *phoenix,* with stem *phoinic-,* apparently referring to darker shades, as the English *crimson* does. This is the term, interestingly enough, that Aeschylus used, in the passage quoted.

There is no question, therefore, but that the Phoenicians

were to the Greeks, literally, "the crimson men." If, then, there was a Phoenician Sea, it was also necessarily the Crimson Sea. And since crimson (*phoinic-*) was a rare and poetic term (or a technical one associated with the dye-trade), the Greeks could have substituted the common term Red (*eryth-*).

It is a theory which leaps lightly over a good deal of time and space, but it solves certain difficulties, and is a possibility.

2

A Land of Many Tongues

The Hebrew Scriptures declare—in fact, they repeat almost *ad nauseam*—that, at the entry of the Israelites themselves, the Promised Land was inhabited by various peoples. Genesis 15 provides a list of no fewer than ten such—to wit, Kenites, Kenizzites, Kadmonites, Hittites, Perizzites, Rephaims, Amorites, Canaanites, Girgashites, and Jebusites. To these would have to be added the later-arriving Philistines and the Israelites themselves.

As far as language was concerned, most of these tribes were presumably of Semitic background, and spoke some dialect of Canaanitish, not too different from the language of the Israelitic invaders. On the other hand, the invaders themselves differed in dialect, as the Shibboleth-Sibboleth story serves to establish. In addition, the Hittites, certainly, used an Indo-European language, and so may some of the others.

The Israelites thus entered into a land which was already thickly inhabited, and had been so for a long period, by various peoples speaking different languages or dialects. Such a land must have been densely set with names. Moreover, the Israelites were a people of simple culture, penetrating among peoples who dwelt in "fenced cities" and followed a more complex way of life. As the biblical account makes clear, the newcomers did not extirpate the earlier inhabitants, but settled down in a *modus vivendi,* even adopting the religious practices. The situation thus displays many analogies with the Anglo-Saxon or Frankish conquests of former provinces of the Roman Empire, and we should expect the resulting name-pattern to show equal or even greater complexity—displaying, for instance, Hebrew folk-etymologies masking the meaning of place-names in earlier languages.

One such (and of a famous name) can be noted. Bethlehem in Hebrew means simply "House-of-Bread." In place-names, however, *beth* commonly meant the house of some god, that is, a temple. House-of-Bread or Temple-of-Bread fails to make very good sense. It seems actually to be a folk-etymology with the specific derived from an earlier Lahamu, the name of a goddess, known from non-Hebrew sources.

The working of folk-etymology should also be at least suspected in Carmel. Meaning "garden" or "orchard" or "fruitful place," it is applied to a mountain, thus seeming counter-descriptive, since mountains are typically barren. Possibly, it may be argued, the wooded heights seemed luxuriant as compared with the dry lands farther inland. Still, the element *-el* seems suggestive of a religious naming, since it commonly means "god."

In spite of the need, at times, to suspect folk-etymology, many of the biblical names are clearly recognizable as Hebrew, though possibly adapted from some earlier Semitic tongue. The namers, whether Hebrews or of one of the earlier peoples, seem to have reacted in the common ways. Descriptives occur in such names as Lebanon, "white," and Zoar, the equivalent of Littleton in England. Possessive names are common by implication, and I Kings 16 definitely records of the foundation of Samaria by Omri, that he "called the name of the city which he built, after the name of Shemer, owner of the hill." Association-names turn up in namings, such as Gath, "wine-press," and the River Kanah, for its reeds, etymologically connected with the many American examples of Cane Creek. The tribe of Dan, conquering a new territory in the north, commemoratively moved their name along with them, and changed Laish or Le-

shem to Dan, "after the name of Dan their father." Commendatory names appear in many religious namings, as with Abraham's naming Jehovahjireh, "the Lord will provide."

As far as the biblical narrative itself is concerned, the most interesting feature is the tendency of the various writers to comment upon incident-namings or to explain namings as resulting
from incident. Many of these, we can only assume, are folk-
tales which were invented to explain the name—the Brook Eshcol, for example. It means "bunch of grapes," surely not a
name to be expected on a stream, and probably a folk-
etymology. The story, however, was that Moses had sent scouts
"to spy out the land of Canaan." These scouts then came to a
certain stream where they cut a bunch of grapes so large that
they had to carry it suspended from a staff borne between
them. Hence, as the story has it, the Brook Eshcol.

If such a story is not acceptable, others point definitely to incident-namings. Such is Bochim, "weepers," which seems to
recall some lamentable event, if not necessarily the one here
suggested. Another one is Gibeah-haaraloth, "hill of the foreskins." If it is not the place where Joshua circumcised the
Israelites "the second time," it at least suggests some definite occasion. (One thinks of the story that David once brought to Saul
a hundred Philistine foreskins as trophies.)

Even when an origin from description is obvious, the Hebrew
commentators may prefer to attribute the name to an incident.
Marah, "bitter," is common for an undrinkable water-source in
the desert, but in Exodus is derived from a particular incident,
when the migrating Israelites arrived there and could not
drink.

Somewhat similar is the more important name Beersheba.
Beer- means a spring or well. *Sheba* may mean "seven." Considering seven as an often-used common number, (thus even in
this passage of Genesis 21) we might consider this oasis to have
been Seven Wells. (The form is not exact, but is probably close
enough for a place-name.) *Sheba,* however, may also mean
"oath," and with such a possibility the narrator, doubtless basing himself on current stories, could have no hesitation. Not
only once, but twice Beersheba is provided with an incident.

Once Abraham swears an oath at that place; the second time, his son Isaac does. Actually there is no special reason to doubt that the name originated so, for the swearing of an oath was a solemn ceremony, and a place might well be thus known.

As the composer of the narrative looked around the land, he found many still-existing names which thus cried out for an origin from incident. Such a one was a well named Esek, meaning "strife." One may compare the American names such as Battle Creek, in which the word "battle" was used to describe a minor dispute between neighbors. Coupled with Esek in the story is Sitnah, "hatred."

Both tie into the story of the patriarch Isaac. While anyone may doubt the validity of this attribution, the question still has to be considered as to just why the connection was with the rather colorless Isaac, instead of with Abraham or Jacob. Possibly some actual tradition was preserved.

Similarly coupled with Isaac is another naming-story. Here we may take it as reasonable enough that there was a place, probably with an old oak-tree, which was known as Allonbachuth, "oak of weeping." Obviously it would spring from some lamentable incident, perhaps in the far past. At least some kind of tradition allowed the narrator to write without qualification, in Genesis 35:

> But Deborah Rebekah's nurse died, and she was buried beneath Bethel under an oak: and the name of it was called Allonbachuth.

Since Rebekah was Isaac's wife, the connection is again with that patriarch. A curious matter, however, is that this nurse of Rebekah's is nowhere else mentioned. She survives only to name a place. (Her occurrence in this one context is an evidence from place-names that the biblical narrative must fail to record a large part of the original body of folk-tales about the patriarchs.)

This interest in the origin of place-names is a striking feature of the Hexateuch, with the exceptions of the books of Leviticus and Deuteronomy. It extends also in Judges. Equally striking is the constant attribution to incident.

The biblical narrators also display an interest in duality of name or change of name. Thus we have in Genesis 31:

> And Laban called it Jegarsahadutha, but Jacob called it Galeed.

In this instance the duality apparently results from Laban using the Aramaic name; Jacob, the Hebrew name.

Most of the shifts can be explained, and many of them are explained in the text. Thus Luz, the probably non-Hebrew name, became Bethel, "house of El," when someone set up a shrine for the Hebrew deity—the incident, in Genesis, being attributed to Jacob, the patriarch. Possibly, however, Luz lingered in popular speech, for the identity of the two places is stipulated three times in the biblical text.

Much re-naming would naturally have resulted from the ravages of warfare, such as Hormah, "utter destruction." But the conquerors also were builders. Numbers 33, records that the tribe of Reuben founded certain cities:

> And Nebo and Baalmeon (their names being changed,) and Shibmah: and gave other names unto the cities which they builded.

Religious scruples resulted in other changes. Thus Kirjath-baal, "city of Baal," gave prominence to a god whom the Israelites worshipped only in periods of backsliding. The name became the neutral one of Kirjath-jearim, "city of forests."

As a contrary example, Bethshemesh maintained itself both in actuality and in name. Meaning literally "house-of-the-sun," it was, in all probability, a foundation named for the sun-god, Chemosh. In Judges 1, the tribe of Naphtali is reproved for not having driven out the inhabitants of Bethshemesh, although forcing them to pay tribute. The name endured, in spite of its being a standing offense to the more pious Hebrews. Both name and city still existed in the period of the later kingdom. By that time they had doubtless become mere names, with no one paying any attention to the literal meaning, for good or for bad.

Never explicitly stated, but evident from practice, was the

custom of re-naming a captured city after its conqueror. Thus in Numbers 32, we read:

> And Nobah went and took Kenath, and the villages thereof, and called it Nobah, after his own name.

Similarly, in the same passage:

> And Jair the son of Manasseh went and took the small towns thereof, and called them Havoth-jair [Villages of Jair].

An interesting passage in II Samuel 12, shows that this custom was strongly entrenched in the folk-mind. Joab, the loyal Captain of the Host, was besieging Rabbah, and realized that the city was about to fall. He therefore sent a message to King David:

> Now therefore gather the rest of the people together, and encamp against the city: lest I take the city, and it be called after my name.

The king thereupon came, reaped the fruits of Joab's victory, gruesomely slaughtered the captives, and made sure that no too-great honor was paid to his loyal general.

Since David himself (again with Joab's essential aid) captured the Jebusite stronghold of Jerusalem, his name was actually placed upon it, and the narrative sometimes refers to it as the City of David.

Not only is Jerusalem a universally known name, but it is also of great antiquity. In addition to being known as the City of David the site is mentioned as Jebus or Jebusi, with the explanatory note, "which is Jerusalem." Obviously this alternate name is to be associated with the Jebusites, whose city it was until its capture by David. Jerusalem, however, was apparently the older name, being recorded as Urusalim in the Amarna letters, preserved from a period well before the Israelitic entry. The name apparently is Semitic, with ur- being the equivalent of the later Hebrew ir, "city." Salim may also be taken as the Hebrew word for peace, but "city of peace" is not a likely naming. Salim may be the name of a king, comparable to that of King Solomon himself. Rather surprisingly, this ancient name survived the long period of Jebusite and Israelite occupancy, and eventually triumphed, to become known throughout the world.

Of all the natural features mentioned in the biblical narrative the most widely known is the River Jordan. It is also an exceptionally interesting name. Its element *-dan* is close to *danu,* a widespread Indo-European term for river, furnishing names all the way from the Don in Russia to the Don in Scotland. The resemblance of a few sounds might be written off as coincidence. But the Homeric poems mention a stream Iardanos in Crete and another in mainland Greece, and Iardanos is a close Greek equivalent to Jordan, with too many letters in common to be credited to coincidence. There is also a record, though late, of a Iardanos in northwestern Asia Minor. It was apparently an established stream-name.

By form and by association, therefore, we can make a case for the equating of Jordan and Iardanos. Its transmission, which must be explained, would seem to be more likely from the Aegean area to Palestine, rather than *vice versa.* One possibility would lie in its transferral from Crete, since various peoples emigrated from that island after the end of the Minoan period, and one of them, the Philistines, certainly reached Palestine, though probably too late to be the carriers of Iardanos.

In addition, during the second millennium B.C., Indo-European speakers were penetrating deep into Asia. Among them were the Hittites, who are regularly mentioned among the peoples inhabiting Canaan. There is thus the possibility that Jordan is a Hittite naming.

The meaning of the first part of the name as yet remains uncertain. Syllables composed of a few common sounds, such as *iar* or *jor,* so readily supply possible answers that the solutions mutually cancel one another. Since the syllable occurs upon such widely separated streams, we may suppose it to be a common specific for rivers. Indo-European roots (with some humoring both phonetically and semantically) yield such results as "swift-flowing," and "separating."

Or the name might be the result of a doubling of generics, with the first syllable another generic in its own right. A widespread and ancient element in river-names is *ar-,* appearing in

Aar, Arno, and many others, and apparently itself meaning river. The river Arnon is not far from the Jordan.

Curiously, to approach from another direction, the two ancient cities on or near the Jordan are Jericho and Jerusalem, both with an opening syllable much like that of the river.

A more solid hypothesis makes use of the Hittite *uru-*, "big." Jordan thus would join the company of the many streams whose names mean "big river." It would also, in a fascinating way, become allied to the great river Eridanos, which appears in Greek mythology and must originally have been applied to some particular stream.

The identification of *-dan* as "river" seems reasonably based. The connection of *Jor-* with Hittite "big" raises phonetic difficulties, but is semantically reasonable. The whole resemblance of Jordan with Iardanos is too close to be mere coincidence.

As for Palestine, it is merely the land of the Philistines. It survived the disappearance of that people, and by various political twistings and turnings has sometimes been applied to the whole region which once was Canaan.

3
The Troublesome Phoenicians

In the history of place-naming, the Phoenicians (along with their colonists, the Carthaginians) may be termed troublesome. They left no voluminous literature, as did the Greeks, and not even one great compilation, as did their neighboring kinfolk, the Israelites. Their history and customs are imperfectly known, and they have provided few harvests for the archeologists. Their language, though closely allied to the contemporary Hebrew, is not well known. Their attitudes toward naming—what might be called their philosophy—we can only deduce from their practice. Under such conditions every attribution of a name is likely to call forth a counter-attribution, every statement a counter-statement.

Unfortunately, the result is that scholars have a tendency to play safe, and to attribute to the Phoenicians only commonplace names. There can be no counterparts of the Hebrew incident-names Well of the Oath and Hill of the Foreskins.

Nonetheless, in their flourishing, the Phoenicians and Carthaginians explored and placed names upon much of the Mediterranean coast, and even beyond it. A good proportion of those names endure and are known over the world.

The famous cities of the Phoenician homeland show simple names, even emotionally moving in their starkness, evidence that these cities were not formally established but merely grew from insignificant clumps of huts.

The modern Beirut still retains, very closely, its original pronunciation, showing its derivation, "wells," from the pural of the same word that appears in Beersheba. The spot provided, on an arid coast, some welcome springs or wells as a source of water.

Tyre, which had its site on the level top of a huge off-shore rock, grew to be one of the ancient world's chief cities of commerce, maintaining its name as merely "rock."

Syria, inland from Tyre, is probably another adaptation of that name by the Greeks, and thus means "country of Tyre," the word for rock being "tsur," its initial sound passing into Greek as either a *t* or an *s*.

Sidon offers some difficulties. The Hebrews supplied it with an eponymous founder—Sidon, firstborn of Canaan and therefore great-grandson of Noah. But he obviously is merely of mythical value. Also dubious is a god named Sid. In ancient times, however, Sidon was traditionally known for the abundance of its fish, and it probably took its name from a word which in Hebrew meant "to hunt," but also in a general sense "to take prey," and so was adapted by a fishing-folk as "to fish." Sidon is therefore "fishing-place."

In general, the Phoenicians turned their eyes to the sea. Malta is one of their names, meaning "refuge," that is, a place where a hard-pressed ship could take shelter. (The Greeks, by folk-etymology, explained the name as being from their own word *mel,* "honey.")

Another Malta, in the Ionian Sea, is much smaller and without a harbor. Still it must have offered, to the small vessels of those times, some welcome shelter under its lee.

Also bearing a Semitic name is the island of Ibiza, close to the Spanish coast, called after its conspicuous pine-trees.

Of the whole Balearic chain, Strabo and Polybius state that it bore a Semitic name, "Slingers' Islands," because the sling was the universal weapon of those people. Now, if the Phoenicians reached Ibiza, they undoubtedly saw and had names for the larger islands of the archipelago. The biblical word for sling, however, is *qela,* while the Greek word for "throw" is from the root *bal.* Possibly we have, as with Malta, a Greek tendency to replace a name by folk-etymology, since an apt meaning could thus be maintained.

The Phoenicians were not assiduous colonizers, and their system, as Thucydides describes it, was to establish trading-posts at strategic locations close to the sea. Their one great adventure at planting colonies was on the African coast, where they began by founding Utica. The name (in concert with the simple ones of the homeland) merely means "settlement." By another theory it is "oldtown," an appellation which seems plausible for what was the original foundation in the area. But it would not have been old at the beginning, and such a name could only occur as a secondary and later naming.

Hippo, used for two settlements, meant "fortified place." The two towns were far enough apart not to be confused in local usage, and bore secondary terms when they needed to be distinguished. Both names still exist, though in highly altered form. One of them, picking up an *n* from its declension by the Romans, survived as Bone under the French rule of North Africa but has now become Anneba. The other city, in ancient times, was differentiated, by means of a Greek form, as Hippo Diarrhytos, probably because a channel divided it into two. Under the Arabs this became Zarytos, and Hippo Zarytos became Bizerte, with the initial two letters as the only remnant of the Phoenician naming—and even those shifted from *po* to *bi.* Near-by Cape Bon is probably of the same origin, but also a good commendatory name for French seamen.

Of ancient foundation but important only in modern times is Tunis. An early form of the name is Tuneta, suggesting strongly a religious origin from the moon-goddess Tanit, one of the patron deities of Carthage.

The outstanding Phoenician settlement was Carthage. As often happened, its founders chose an easily defensible hill for the original settlement, and called it by a name meaning "fortified place"—the mere application of a generic rather than a true naming. As Bozrah, that name occurs on two Biblical cities, and as Byrsa it survived among the Romans as a poetical equivalent for Carthage. The Greeks equated the term with their similar-sounding word meaning "hide, skin," and applied or coined the folk-tale of the founders being granted by the natives as much land as they could enclose with an ox-hide, and then encircling the hill by cutting the hide into a narrow strip.

With prosperity and growth the original site became overcrowded, and an additional circuit of wall was built around the base of the hill, so that a city developed there. This expansion was known as Magalia, "circuit," from surrounding the first town. But in local speech it was simply "new town," and this name came to denote the whole city, appearing in Greek as Karchedon, in Latin as Cartago. It persists in various forms in modern speech.

After the rise of Carthage the situation in the western Mediterranean became more complicated, so that names might be either Phoenician (strictly speaking) or Carthaginian. Linguistically, however, there was no important difference. The Iberian peninsula became the focus of settlements. Its lure was metals, especially gold and copper.

Well beyond the straits and facing the full ocean, the city of Cadiz preserves its Semitic name. The traders, establishing a depot at a strategic spot, threw up some sort of fortification, and referred to it as Gadir, a common designation of a walled place, occurring as the name of several biblical cities.

Though far to the west, Gadir was an early post. We should expect the traders to have pushed farther, both north and south along the oceanic coast.

One likely name is that of a site which offered, attractively for a trading-post, a fine expanse of quiet water and an easy entrance at the mouth of a large estuary. Its Roman name, we know, was Olisippo, so that we may take it for another Hippo, combined with a local specific of unknown meaning. Declining it with an *n,* the Romans made it into a form which, in English, has become Lisbon.

Beyond Olisippo the seafarers may have worked northward toward the prize of Cornish tin. But no more of their names have persisted to mark their stages.

Southward, along the Moorish coast, Agadir may be another

gadir, with the initial letter being what is left of the Phoenician definite article.

Again the sea-trail ends, as far as place-names are concerned, though the Carthaginians certainly sailed farther, as the story of Hanno records. They discovered the Canary Islands, and passed that knowledge on to the Romans, who knew them as the Fortunate Islands, possibly a translation of some Semitic term. The Romans also used the term Canaria, ascribing it to the huge native dogs (from Latin, *canis*). This name also may have been originally Semitic, shifted either by translation or by folk-etymology.

On the Mediterranean Spanish coast at least two important names are Semitic. Malaga probably refers to the original industry of the settlement, the drying of fish. Cartagena was a colony of Carthage, meaning actually (in the unimaginative Carthaginian manner) nothing more than New Carthage, that is, New Newton.

Barcelona (first recorded as Barcino) is less certain, though few investigators can resist the temptation to associate it with the famous Barca family of Carthage, especially with the great Hannibal's father, the almost equally great Hamilcar Barca. He could have planted it as an outpost against the Romans, but record is lacking.

Probably the Phoenicians failed to penetrate deeply into the great peninsula, and the Carthaginian conquests were not thorough or long-lasting. An ardent Semitist can claim Sevilla and Córdoba. But the case is weak, and the native Iberians were capable of naming their own towns.

In Sicily a single important name may be Semitic, though it is usually explained otherwise. The city which is now Palermo appears as Panormos ("all-harbor") in Greek sources, and was thus passed on to the Romans. That name occurred repeatedly through the ancient Greek world, applied to fine harbors. The broad-reaching bay near the western end of Sicily would deserve such an appellation. But the city was thoroughly Carthaginian, and its inhabitants did not speak Greek. Besides, a shift from *n* to *l* seems unlikely.

The answer may be that Palermo represents the original Semitic form, preserved in local speech and eventually ousting the foreign and literary usage. The name suggests a Semitic origin. Its opening *pal-* is close to *bal*, the divine name, borne by Hannibal himself. The whole may even be rendered as a commendatory, "Bal-consecrates." The name would then have been close enough to Panormos to allow the latter to arise by folk-etymology.

Most important of all the possibly Phoenician namings is Spain itself. It occurs in record first as Spania, in Greek. The Romans rendered it as Hispania, with the opening letters suggesting the Semitic definite article.

The name, however, with its three consonants, s-p-n, resembles a Hebrew-Phoenician three-letter root, and one such comes readily to hand is the word for rabbit or cony. Some early scholars eagerly concluded that the early traders had been impressed by the number of rabbits, and thus named the whole country. While not impossible, this derivation is highly unlikely, and these scholars could not even demonstrate that the Iberian peninsula, about 1000 B.C., was notable for rabbits.

When we explore the other applications of the root, however, we find the basic idea to be "conceal, cover," so that the animal may have been itself named for being a burrower. Moreover, in biblical usage the meaning is extended to "something hidden," and even specifically to "hidden treasure."

At this point we should recall that the Phoenicians went to Spain primarily for metals, which were dug from the earth. The country might then be called "the mine." We can recall that a large part of California was long known as The Diggings.

The case seems to be a good one, but there is—surprisingly, for so early a date—an additional confirmation. The whole case for Phoenician names in the Aegean area is a controversial one, and is to be presented later (Book IV, Chapter 2). A few instances, however, seem strongly based. In the southwestern corner of that sea, three islands are Kythera, Seriphos, and Siphnos—all of them displaying three-letter roots. Kythera can be rendered as "Smoke Island"; Seriphos, as "Fire Island." As for Siphnos, it displays *s-p-n*, just as Spain does. Moreover, Siphnos was notable for its gold mines! To establish the meaning of such an ancient name, a better bit of converging evidence is not to be expected. We may, with some confidence, consider Spain to mean "The Mine"—or even, in the California sense, The Diggings.

Nonetheless, the Phoenicians warrant the "troublesome" of this chapter's title. As with Palermo, many of their namings were overlaid by Greek and Latin, and rendered obscure.

4
The Greeks Came Late

A passage in Plato's *Laws* aptly illustrates the classical Greek attitude toward place-names. One of the characters remarks that the colony to be founded will offer no problem of naming, but that the name will be "determined by accident of locality. . . . A river or spring, or some local deity, may give the sanction of a name to the new city." In short, the Greeks' assumption was that every place already had a name, and that their own function was to find out what it might be and to apply it.

The *Odyssey* demonstrates the same attitude. The wanderer arrives at strange places, and may not know where he is, but he never supposes any of the places to be without a name and that he should name it. A detail of the poem reinforces this idea. In Book VI we read that Nausithous made a foundation: "He laid out the walls of the new city, built houses, erected temples, and allotted the land." These activities were apparently considered to be the essentials. He did not give a name. Instead, he used the one that was there already—Scheria.

Clear at the other end of the classical period we come to the voyage of Nearchus. That admiral, under the orders of Alexander, sailed from India to the head of the Persian Gulf, thus performing successfully what we may call the first official voyage of exploration of which there is good record. Nearchus named

Alexander's Harbor commemoratively, but otherwise he merely adopted the local names, putting them into Greek through his interpreters.

This attitude springs from two causes. First, though Greek tribes are supposed to have entered the peninsula about 1900 B.C., the land was already occupied, and had been inhabited for many centuries. Already the name-pattern was old and dense. Though we may suppose the Greeks to have been in some sense conquerors, they must have mingled with the earlier peoples, who were of higher culture. The Greeks thus adopted the names, not needing to create or to apply them.

A second facet of Greek thought reinforced this tendency to adopt rather than to give names. The speaker in the passage that is quoted from the *Laws,* we should notice, mentions "some local deity." Here is an idea that greatly impressed the Greeks, and affected their attitude toward naming. A stream, a spring, a mountain—in fact, any place possessing a sufficient entity to be named—was the seat of one of these local deities, possibly to be called a god, but perhaps to be distinguished by some such word as *daimon.* His power would not stretch far. Still, when you are wading across that particular brook or drinking from that particular spring, you would do well to pay him proper respect, lest you slip and wet your clothing or get the gripes after your drinking. Moreover, the name of the place and the name of the spirit will be the same. So, if you replace a name by giving a new one, you may offend the deity.

Thus, if you are founding a new city on a stream that you need for water-supply, you will do better not to indulge in any fancy work about naming, for fear that the offended local *daimon* dry up his stream in late summer or wash you out with a winter flood.

This practice of the Greeks raises difficulties for modern readers in, for example, Book XXI of the *Iliad,* when Achilles fights against the River Xanthos. But is the opponent the god, or the flooding stream? The modern reader does not quite know what to make of it. But to a Greek that passage must have raised little difficulty, because Xanthos was the name of both the stream and the god.

Literally *xanthos* can be translated as "yellow," and can be considered a descriptive name for a river. To the Greek, it could just as well suggest that the river-god, like Menelaus, had blond hair.

A similar mingling of the ideas of river and river-god shows in Book XXIV of the *Iliad:* "they had come to the ford of the fair-flowing river, eddying Xanthus, that immortal Zeus begot."

Very striking are some situations in the *Hymn to Pythian Apollo.* Granted that we are here dealing with a formalized kind of poetry, still the poet must have been fairly close to the people in his manner of thought. In describing the progress of Apollo, the poet writes (translated as literally as possible):

> So [you] came to the wood-clad abode of Thebe; for as yet no mortal lived in holy Thebe, nor were there any trails or roads on Thebe's wheat-bearing plain.

Thebe seems to shift back and forth between being a place and being a *daimon.*

A few lines further on, the poet again addresses Apollo:

> Then you went toward Telphusa. . . . You came near and addressed her, "Telphusa, here I should like to build a glorious temple."

Again the conception shifts from a place ("toward Telphusa") to a deity, to whom Apollo can speak directly, and who then replies to him.

With such a historical background and with such a manner of thought, the classical Greeks were living in a land of unknown names—just, indeed, as are most of the present-day peoples of Europe.

We can observe the situation by considering the names of streams, about seventy of which are preserved in ancient sources.

How many of these would the ordinary Greek have recognized as meaningful? Not more than half a dozen! And even some of these may have resulted from folk-etymology working upon some earlier, non-Greek name.

Among these meaningful specifics are Campylos, "crooked,"

Cyparissios, "cedar," Glaucos, "shining," and Selinos, "wild parsley."

By a little ingenuity this ordinary, ancient Greek might decide that Krathis could mean a stream formed by the mingling of two tributaries, that Olmeos might be connected with "pebble," and that Sperchios (a repeated name) would probably be "rapid."

Beyond this point the Greek would have encountered no intelligibility, and no method except guesswork. Modern scholars have approached the problem by means of comparative linguistics.

At the first level below the obvious we come to names which suggest archaic or dialectal Greek. The element *ach-* is a characteristic one, its center lying in northwestern Greece, where, as stream-names, we find Acheloos several times repeated, along with Acheron, Arachthos, and Inachos. Obviously *ach-* is an element associated with streams, probably meaning water or river, and representing the same Indo-European root which has yielded *aqua* in Latin. Except for this syllable, however, nothing certain can be made of the names, except that Acheron may be connected with the word for lake which survives in Russian as *ozero.* The Greeks themselves associated this stream with the underworld, and explained it as coming from another root *ach,* to mean "mourning" or "grieving."

Alpheios is another river that may be of older Greek origin. Phonetically it can be equated with the Elbe in Germany and many other stream-names scattered across Europe. A common explanation is to connect it in meaning with the Latin *albus,* "white, shining," but it seems to have come to mean merely "river."

The stratum of stream-names beneath the Greek one is that of the Pelasgians, who apparently occupied the land, or most of it, at the time of the coming of the Greeks. A few remnants of them still lived in some bits and corners of the backwoods as late as the time of Herodotus. He gives the welcome information that they spoke a non-Greek language. Therefore the Pelasgians cannot be considered merely as some early arriving Greeks. Unfortunately, Herodotus did not record any of their

words. Even half a dozen of them, written down in Greek letters, would have removed many doubts. Modern scholars have
generally concluded that the Pelasgians spoke an Indo-
European language.

Undoubtedly many of the river-names are Pelasgian, but only
a few can be identified—and, even those, not with entire certainty. Some of these show elements which are not likely to be
Greek but are common in Indo-European river-names. One
such is the syllable *ap,* occurring in a number of languages as
meaning "water," and in the Greek river-names appearing in
Apidanos and Inapos. As *op* it shows in the repeated Asopos.
The *-dan-* in Apidanos may be another appearance of the widespread Indo-European term for stream.

But even with a few names credited to early Greek and to
Pelasgian, the majority of the stream-names remain unintelligible, and unclassifiable as to language. Almost certainly
they represent a language that may be called pre-Pelasgian,
with many of the names made over and spelled so as to appear
superficially Greek, though not meaningful.

Another group of names of special interest is that of the
islands of the Aegean Sea. Since the Greeks, when they entered
the land, were probably not seafaring, these islands would have
remained in pre-Greek hands for some time, and the newcomers would have had ample opportunity to learn their
names. From the very form of the names, in fact, something
seems to be "wrong" from the point of view of Greek. The
names of islands in that language are feminine, but the most of
the Aegean islands show the typically masculine ending *-os*—
just, indeed, as does the generic for island, *nesos.* A Greek
would have been unlikely to give such an anomalous name,
though he might have no objection to taking it over, already
named.

As might be expected, then, the names of islands ending in *a,*
the common feminine form, suggest either classical Greek or
archaic Greek in their form. Other island-names both end in a
vowel and include the element *aig*—Aigina, Aigaea, Aigilia.
(See Book III, Chapter 1.)

Another interesting element is *par-*, occurring, among islands, as Paros and Peparethos. Even more strikingly it appears on mountains—Parnassos, Parnon, Parnes, Parthenios. By the general principle of repeated generics we can conclude that *par* is especially descriptive of mountains, and most likely means "mountain" or "peak." Possibly also Parthenon falls into this group, having been applied to the hill before becoming the name of the temple. Even the common noun *parthenon,* "virgin," may have been derived from some mountain-dwelling goddess. Since no convincing Indo-European original exists for *par-*, it may well go back to a pre-Pelasgian source.

Examples, however, need not be multiplied. Whether with rivers or with islands, or with any other category of names, the pattern of ancient Greece, even by the time of Pericles, was highly complicated, and at least three strata are discernible. Moreover, the names were, in general, unintelligible to the Greeks themselves, as they still, indeed, remain to us. The great names of that remarkable people survive as historical examples and as poetic symbols. There is, even yet, little but guesswork as to their origin and history.

Athens, we may conclude, stands in some relationship with the city's patron, the goddess Athena. Presumably the city was named, at some point, in dedication to the goddess. Yet there is no certainty. Possibly she bears the name of the city. Like Athena herself, sprung in full panoply from the brain of Zeus, so Athens as the name of the city appears without beginnings.

Sparta is essentially the same as the Greek word for rope, and Aristophanes, shifting it slightly, used it for punning. But a city is not likely to be named for a rope, and Sparta probably goes back to an earlier stratum, and must be considered, historically, as unknown as Athens, and equally as qualified as a symbol.

Thebes has been derived from a very ancient "Mediterranean" stratum, from a word associated with hills and presumably meaning "hill." Thebes stands upon a well-marked hill arising from a broad plain, and so this origin is plausible.

Argos, a repeated name, may well be Pelasgian, that is, pre-Greek but Indo-European. The name is commonly associated with fortified places on sharp hills, and may have connections with the Latin *arx* (*arcis*), "citadel."

Corinth (Korinthos) shows the ending *-inthos*, which has long been recognized as pre-Greek. Probably the name first denoted the high summit known now as Akrocorinthos, and the *cor-* has been taken to be from a word meaning merely "summit," or "rock." (See Book III, Chapter 9). But, again, there is no certainty.

Delphi, for the poet of the *Hymn to Pythian Apollo,* was associated with the word for dolphin, and in that hymn the god declares "[because] I sprang upon the swift ship in dolphin's form . . . the altar itself shall be called Delphinios." But this mythological origin is obviously fanciful. Another possibility exists. Delphi was famous as the navel of the world, that is, its center. But *womb* and *navel* are much the same in their symbolic quality, and the word for *womb* is *delphys* (a borrowed, not a Greek, term). The correspondences of sound and of idea are close. Again, however, as with Athens, we cannot be sure of which came first, and the whole, indeed, may well be pre-Greek.

The terms for the ancient regions, when anything can be determined at all, seem to be tribal names, merely transferred to the area which the tribe claimed to hold. Thus Boeotians probably gave their name to Boeotia. Some, such as Attica, are apparently pre-Greek, and any reference to a tribe can rest only upon analogy. The most discussed of these names is Arcadia, which has often been rendered as "bear-land" from its resemblance to the Greek *arctos.* One may admit that those beasts lingered in that area of rugged mountains after they had vanished from the rest of Greece. Much more likely, however, if a Greek connection exists, we should think of a tribe named for the animal. The tribal name Arcades continued in use. The naming of a country from an animal is extremely rare, but the progression animal-tribe-country is normal. Greece may show other examples. The Boeotians could be the cow-people, and the Phocians the seal-people.

In the end, only a few of the great names of ancient Greece

are clearly Greek, and translatable. The fountain Hippocrene, sacred to the muses, is merely "horse spring." The story that it sprang from the footprint of the winged Pegasus was doubtless suggested by the name rather than giving rise to it. Thermopylae is literally "hot gates," but *therm-* is to be taken in the sense of "hot spring," and *pylai* as the common term for a narrow passageway, here for the place where the road was pinched between the cliff and the beach. Marathon is "fennel," like other demes, the small administrative districts of Attica, bearing a simple name from plant growth. The name, indeed, may have been applied first to the plain, but its intelligibility suggests that it may have come into use in the Greek period, and may have been used, along with other similar names, when the demes were first organized.

Since the Greeks thus, in general, adopted their names rather than creating them, we can approach the study of the Greeks as namers only through special categories.

Hippocrene, Thermopylae, and Marathon, we may note, share a common quality in all being, in themselves, very unimportant and acquiring fame only adventitiously. Such a situation is to be expected. When invaders enter a country, they learn the names of the important natural features and the towns. But they feel no pressure to learn the names of minor features, so that these often lapse, and eventually have to be named again. Anyone looking at an ordinary sized map of the United States would conclude that nearly all the streams have Indian names, but this conclusion would spring merely from the scale of the map. The explorers and settlers learned of the chief rivers from the Indians, but themselves named most of the smaller streams.

So, to return to the islands, we find Greek names especially upon the smallest ones, those lying just off-shore. They bear simple descriptives, such as might be suggested to the mind of a man standing on the shore and looking across a narrow channel. Such islands, particularly in troubled times of piracy, would not be inhabited, though a few herdsmen or fishermen might build shelters there. There would thus have been no one who was really interested in transmitting the Pelasgian name. As a result we find Long Island, Pine Island, Flat Island, Cliff Island—just, indeed, as we find the same names upon similar islands all over the world. But the larger islands bear non-Greek names.

A chain of small islands—once badly exposed to attacks and slave-raids from Carthaginians, Etruscans, and Greeks—lies to the north of Sicily. In the eighth century B.C., when the Greeks began to plant colonies in that region, the islands were probably uninhabited, and no one was there to pass the names on. Thus, more or less of necessity, the Greeks gave them names (and obvious enough ones) such as Strongyle, "round," which survives as Stromboli. They named others Left, Reddish, Twin, and Heather. Another, apparently because of volcanic manifestations, they called Sacred to Haephaistos, the god of Fire. The largest island, now giving its name to the whole group, they called Lipara, which is literally "oily," but was used in the sense of rich soil. An island lying well to the west they named Osteodes, deriving it from their word for bone. The explanation which was later offered was that some Carthaginian soldiers had once been marooned there, died, and were left unburied. Although there is no way by which such a story can be checked, it seems a likely enough incident for those rough times. The name survives as Ustica.

The naming of new colonies generally followed the principle, as laid down by Plato, of taking a local name. In the case of Gela in Sicily the Delphic oracle approving the establishment has been preserved, and it includes the instruction that the name shall be the same as that of the local river. The importance of streams in the planting of colonies comes out clearly in the number of foundations thus named—for example, Siris, Metaura, Akragas, Sybaris, Selinus, Taras. Thurii, however, was named for a spring; Syracusai, for a swamp.

In thus invoking the local divine protection, these namings may be called commendatory. Other methods, however, existed toward the same end. In a few instances the name of the colonizing city was bodily transferred, as at Kyme (Cumae) on the Italian mainland, and at Megara in Sicily. When the tribesmen known as the Locri established their own colony in Italy, they merely used the tribal name. For distinction, the new city was known as Locri Epizephyrii, "The Locrians toward the west." As with the many such transfers of familiar names in the modern colonizing period, Kyme and the others emphasized the maintenance of a tradition, and so were commendatory.

Dedication to a particular god could serve similarly. Thus we find Heraclea and Apollonia. The general idea of what might be called good luck shows in the use of Olbia, from an adjective meaning vaguely "happy" or "blessed," or possibly even "wealthy." A far-flung Greek naming in the south of France survives as Agde, but sprang from Agathe Tyche, literally, "good luck."

Descriptive names are rare, and seem usually to have originated secondarily, after the founding of the official colony. Such a situation shows in the name Neapolis, "new town," which eventually surpassed its mother-city, and, keeping its relative-descriptive name, became Napoli and Naples. One of the farthest off of all the colonies was on the Spanish coast near the foot of the Pyrenees. Its name suggests that it may not have been a proper foundation with the blessing of the oracle, but merely a traders' settlement, though it developed into a prosperous city. Its name, however, remained simply Emporia, the plural of the common word used for a trading-post. It is now Ampurias.

Another important Spanish city owes its name to the Greeks, though it originally was a feature-name—Leuke Akte, "white cape." The Romans sometimes half-translated it as Castrum Album, but more commonly took it over, roughly, by sound, thus making it into Lucentum. After more centuries the Arabs transformed it into Alicante. Thus we have the rare example of a Greek descriptive-naming of a feature which passed on to become the name of a city.

Such a name as Alicante may serve as evidence of what we might otherwise expect, that is, that Greek seamen in far-western waters sometimes had to name their own landfalls before they could make contact with the local tribesmen and learn the native name. Another example is Hemeroscopeion, named for a towering rock on that same Spanish coast. It is roughly equivalent to the American "lookout," but is literally "day-watch-place."

Considering the well-known Greek interest in such portents as the flights of birds, we should expect that some settlements would have been named from incidents occurring at the time of the foundation. One obscure place, indeed, was Soonautes, which can be roughly taken as "saved-seamen." It arose, according to Apollonius Rhodius, because some ships, caught in a tempest, were driven into a safe river-mouth here.

In southern France the name Marseilles originated as Massalia in the usual way, from some local name, probably Ligurian. The near-by Nike, however, probably arose from some unrecorded "victory" against some long-forgotten enemy, even though the immediate source of the name may be from a temple erected to the goddess Victory. In either case, the modern Nice preserves the name. Over against it, Antibes still declares in its Greek name that it is Antipolis, the city on the opposite side of the bay.

When place-names have become unintelligible, explanatory stories begin to circulate. Occasionally the stories may represent a real tradition. More commonly they are fanciful. Though useless for actual elucidation of names, these tales illustrate a people's way of thinking. The ancient Israelites emphasized the action, not the person, so that we have the Oak-of-Weeping. The Greeks, on the other hand, focused upon the person, inventing one if needed.

Helle, they told, was escaping through the air with her brother Phryxius, riding on the back of a ram with a golden fleece. At a certain point, however, she fell off, into an arm of the sea, which thus took its name as Helle's Sea, the Hellespont. The Israelites, we can suppose, would have emphasized the falling, not the personal name.

A whole collection of such stories appears in a work of about A.D. 100, formerly ascribed to Plutarch, and now credited (if such a word can be used about a worthless document) to a so-called pseudo-Plutarch. But, without value for derivation of

names, the work illustrates popular Greek thought about naming, though at a rather late date. The examples are chiefly
river-names, and the treatment follows a formula.

First, a river was formerly called such-and-such. There is no
example of a river having been nameless.

Second, an incident occurs involving a named person. This
incident is violent, and ends with the person drowning in the
river.

Third, the river is then called by the person's name, which
remains as the existing place-name.

The incident often involves incest, an aberration with which
the pseudo-Plutarch seems to have been somewhat obsessed.

Incest aside, the formula seems to be typical of the Greeks.
We may present as an example the account of the River Scamander:

> Scamander . . . was formerly called Xanthos, but changed
> its name upon this occasion. Scamander, the son of Corybas
> and Demodice, having beheld the ceremonies while the mys-
> teries of Rhea were being solemnized, immediately ran mad,
> and being hurried away by his own fury to the River
> Xanthos, flung himself into the stream, which from thence
> was called Scamander.

As already pointed out, the idea that no place was ever nameless is especially characteristic of the Greeks.

We might, in fact, consider that naming for the Greeks was
really conceived as re-naming. The idea certainly sprang from
the fact that the land had already been named before the entry
of the Greeks, but other factors also were probably at work.
The area of the Aegean, indeed, is notable for the preservation
of multiple names for the same place, particularly upon islands.
Thus Strabo records that a certain island was "in earlier times"
(he does not write "originally") called Parthenia, next Anthe-
mus, then Melamphyllus, and then Samos.

These multiple namings must have resulted from a highly
complex linguistic situation. But such procedure is unusual,

and is impossible to explain satisfactorily without historical records. We should, however, remember the practice, evidenced in the biblical record, of a conqueror putting his own name upon a captured city. In a period of warfare and instability, conqueror might well have succeeded conqueror, and the changes of name could have lingered in folk-memory. One may note that each of the islands, even in classical times, was considered a political entity—actually, a city-state—and so might take its conqueror's name. The names by which these islands were known in the historical period could merely be those that were current at the time when the political situation stabilized somewhat, and the custom of name-changing came to an end.

The idea that a place took the name of its king is strong in Greek tradition. Thus Pliny writes of a district in Greece, listing six names for it, and adding: "always taking its name from its kings."

A poetic explanation of dual naming occurs twice in the *Iliad*. In Book XX is mention of the river "that gods call Xanthos, and men Scamander." In Book II there is a mound outside of Troy—"men call it Batieia, but the gods call it the barrow of Myrine."

Just what the poet meant to imply is uncertain, but obviously two names were known. Probably the name in common use was that which was attributed to men. The gods might be conceived as using an older name, vaguely remembered from the past. (But, curiously, Xanthos, "yellow," is a common Greek word, more fitted for common speech than Scamander would be.)

The egomania of Alexander the Great was doubtless the cause of his spreading the name Alexandria. Still, one must grant that he had ample precedent in folk-tale and myth. His successors maintained the tradition, so that they sprinkled the map with Antiochia, Seleukia, Antigonea, Laodicea, and others. One such name has passed on to greatness in modern times. This is Philadelphia, "brother-loving," a name used both by the Ptolemies and by King Attalus of Pergamum. From the latter was named the city that became the seat of one of "the seven churches which are in Asia," and, translated in the abstract as "brotherly love," came to stand on one of the great cities of the modern world.

Nevertheless, though the ancient Greeks were not inspired namers, the modern treasury of place-names owes much to them as transmitters and shapers of names. Egypt, Persia, India, and many others passed through Greek adaptation.

Clear at the opposite end of the Greek world, a native town bore the name Pyrene, doubtless Iberian, but of unknown meaning. The Greeks associated the town with the lofty mountains near it, and the Pyrenees still stand by that name, as transmitted and shaped by the Greeks.

One of the most famous of Greek stories about names sprang from the coincidence that *pyr* in their speech meant "fire." Their storytellers told of a great wildfire, set by some careless shepherds, which burned those mountains over, and thus gave them their name.

Also, the Greeks developed their culture as the centuries passed, and were able to distinguish entities that earlier and simpler people had missed. The names of the individual Aegean islands are typically pre-Greek, but the realization that certain groups of islands could be conceived as nameable entities must have come later, and these groups bear Greek names—Cyclades (for the islands "encircling" Delos), and Sporades (for the "scattered" islands to the south).

Another later Greek coinage is Anatolia, "rising-sun-land," a usefully conceived entity, from the point of view of Greece, to cover Asia Minor as a geographical, not a political, region.

Of much greater significance was the Greek establishment of the entity of three continents.

5
Three Continents

The recognition of the entity of each of the great land-masses could occur only with people who had attained a sufficient knowledge of geography. As a following step, those people could apply names. As far as historical record goes, the first evidences of the process begin to appear among the Greeks of the sixth century B.C., probably among the Ionian Greeks, whose cities fringed the eastern edge of the Aegean Sea.

Two conditions must be kept in mind. First, there is the general custom of the Greeks to adopt names, not to create them. Second, there is the geographical situation of the Ionians. Living on the shore of a particular sea, they saw its island-studded sweep and its microscopic straits as major dividing agents. Though small by global standards, the Aegean and the straits between it and the Black Sea still divide two continents—because things started so.

Assuva, or Assuwa, from which the name Asia seems to originate, made its recorded appearance at what is, for the Aegean area, a very early date. About 1235 B.C., Tudhaliyas IV, king of the Hittites, reported a victory over the "land of Assuva." His enemies were apparently a league or alliance, and the report specifies twenty-two countries or tribes as composing it. The geography is not clear, but a number of arguments seem to make certain that Assuva comprised much of northwestern Asia Minor, bordering the Aegean.

The meaning, as might be expected, is uncertain. The term *assu* meant "good" in Hittite, and Assuva may actually have suggested something like "good land" to a Hittite ear. But there is no reason to suppose that the name was Hittite at all. The Assuvans (if we may use some such term) were enemies of the Hittites, and presumably spoke some other language. Not knowing even what language it may have been, we can do nothing with translation, and can only work a little by analogy.

The very high likelihood, then, must be that the term is not primarily geographical, but tribal. On the basis of its twenty-two component peoples, one must even consider the possibility that the term means something like "allies" or "friends."

In any case, by the year 1000 B.C. both Hittites and Myceneans had suffered catastrophe, and no more documents survive. Presumably the next record of Asia is that which appears as an adjectival form in the *Iliad* (II, 461), where the poet mentions, in a simile, the many geese, cranes, and swans that haunt "the Asian meadow, by the river Cayster."

A single mention in an epic poem cannot be rigorously interpreted in a geographical sense. There is the uncomfortable possibility that "Asian" is a later substitution, or an adjective derived from *asis,* meaning "silt" or "mud," being a natural idea to associate with the habitat of waterfowl.

As it happens, however, two Trojan warriors are called Asius, and in addition some fragments of early Greek poetry contain the name, reinforcing the usage in the *Iliad.* Moreover, Asia was well enough established to have a conventional poetic epithet, that is, "sheep-feeding." In all these instances, also, it is associated with the eastern coast of the Aegean.

Searching for an entity, we may ask, "What was Asia?" There is no suggestion, at this time, that it was a kingdom or a city. Although a tribe of Lydians was known as Asian, that name is very likely secondary, and the usage of the Greek poets does not seem primarily to indicate a tribal name. Instead, we have the suggestions of a vague area, extensive enough to be known for its sheep-pastures, with a sentimental connotation that appealed to poets. We may possibly compare Albion as standing for England, or the common and continuing usage in France of such a politically obsolete term as Normandy; or in Germany, of Swabia.

A vague term has its advantages. Possessing no fixed boundaries, it is subject to expansion.

So it must have been with Asia, when the Ionian philosophers of the sixth century began to sense a new geographical entity. Immediately around them, politically, they knew a score or more of Greek city-states and various non-Hellenic kingdoms and tribes. But, considering the question geographically, the whole westward-facing coast was one—an entity. Moreover, it could usefully have a name. Available was the old term Asia.

The question of its extension is of interest. Traditionally, the name seems to cling to the northern and the central region, where the River Cayster flowed out past the city of Ephesus. The first step might have been to stretch the name to the southern coast as well.

At this point we find a common situation arising, almost to be called a toponymic "law." A nonpolitical name tends to expand if it is planted at the edge of a large territory which lacks a general name. One may cite Canada and Siberia. Juan Ponce used Florida in 1513, probably supposing that he had sighted an island. It was, however, part of a continent, and within a century the name had spread a thousand miles inland. In this instance it drew back under political pressures. But such pressures can work either for or against a name.

Of one part of our ancient situation we can be comfortably sure—that is, that Asia was a term limited to the eastern side of the Aegean.

At the same time, having no set inland limits, it could expand in that direction, under the influence of the vigorous seafaring of the Ionians, interpreted by the philosophers. Gradually a vast land-mass began to take shape—northward, bounded by the Euxine; southward, by the sea to the east of Rhodes. Eastward still the land stretched on, to Syria and Assyria, to Babylonia and Media. Then, from somewhere far to the east, erupted the conquering Persians. Anyone studying geography—or even living actively—needed some organizing principle more than a hodgepodge of kingdoms, city-states, and tribal territories. The name Asia could help supply this need.

Since the essence of a place-name's function is to distinguish one place from another, a single continent cannot, so to speak, stand alone. Otherwise, the old distinctions of *land* and *sea* and of *mainland* and *islands* would be sufficient. Asia demanded a counterpart.

Europe is not of such ancient record as Asia, first appearing in the *Hymn to Pythian Apollo,* which is perhaps as late as 600 B.C. That poem may, however, be older, and obviously the name itself may be. But it does not occur in the Homeric poems, where one would expect it if it had been in common use.

Two lines, once repeated in the *Hymn,* constitute the passage:

> Both those who live in the rich Peloponnesus
> And all those of Europe and of the wave-washed islands.

Logically we should take Europe, as here used, to mean the mainland of Greece to the north of the Isthmus of Corinth, but we cannot hold a poet to accuracy of statement. He may even have used the term in the continental sense. About all of which we can be moderately sure is that Europe, to the poet, was a vague term for a large area in which lived people who could be expected to bring offerings to Pythian Apollo, that is, people who in general were Greeks. In its nonpolitical nature and in its vagueness, Europe of the *Hymn* is, indeed, much like Asia of the same period. Where did the name originate, and from what did it take shape?

In dealing with Europe we have one great advantage over the situation in dealing with Asia—the form is longer. In connection with such an insignificant bit as *As-* almost anything can be written off as coincidence. But the base of Europe (Europa in Latin) has two consonants, a vowel, and a diphthong, fixed in a

prescribed order, so that a good correspondence of sound cannot be lightly dismissed. So when we discover in Greek mythological stories a character named exactly Europe, we have good
cause to investigate. (The Latin form is used below to distinguish
the person from the place.)

Europa was the Phoenician princess whom Zeus, taking the
form of a bull, carried off. She later became queen of Crete.

In the fifth century the Greeks were already telling that the
continent was actually named after the princess. Herodotus
knew the story and scorned it as a folk-tale, and we may agree
with him. But to say that the continent was thus named is not
the same as suggesting that there may be a connection between
the two names. Both name of princess and name of continent
could go back to the same origin.

Considering further the myth of Europa, we find that she
had a famous brother whose name was Cadmus. After her abduction he came seeking her.

Since both brother and sister are specified as Phoenicians, we
might see if their names mean anything in that language—and
we find an interesting result. The tri-literal root q-d-m (what we
have in Cadmus) means "east." There is, listed in Genesis, a
tribe, the Kadmonites, "easterners."

Turning now to the sister, we find that scholars have long
pointed out the possibility of her name being connected with
the Hebrew root *ereb,* originally with a meaning "grow dark,"
and thus "evening," and "west." Phonetically, since *b* readily
passes into *p,* the connection of *ereb* and Europa is excellent.

At the cost of introducing a complication, we must here consider, momentarily, the Greek term Erebus, one of the mythological areas of the underworld, and regularly emphasized for
its darkness. It thus may well be Semitic, maintaining the basic
meaning and displaying a phonetic development different from
Europa. On the other hand, an Indo-European root has been
claimed for its original. Europa, therefore, will here be considered independently of Erebus.

To return, then, to the Phoenician princess, we may consider
the mythological or symbolic connections to be apt. The sister

Europa (darkness, evening, west) precedes into the west the brother Cadmus (east).

Finally, topographically, the association of the continent with the west is exactly right.

If, then, Europa as a personal name could develop from *ereb*, it might also do so as a place-name.

The chief objection that some may raise is that a Phoenician name is not to be expected in such thoroughly Greek territory. Actually, the opposite can be argued. (See also Book IV, Chapter 2.) The Greeks certainly had many names for cities and for topographical features. But a people often has difficulty in conceiving and naming an entity which covers its whole area. Outsiders—viewing, so to speak, from a distance—see the entity more clearly, and Herodotus accepts the idea that Phoenician traders once operated in the Aegean. The Greek mainland could thus have been known to them as "the West," and the Greeks themselves would have found the term useful. Once adopted by the Greeks, the name could spread indefinitely, like Asia, into the hinterland.

That the Greek mainland would have been "the West" to the Phoenician traders comes out more clearly if we consider their probable sailing-route. Not liking open-sea runs, westward-faring shipmasters would have kept along the coast until they arrived at Rhodes. Then they could have gone island-hopping across the southern Aegean, until they came up against the solidity of a large land which was not an island. Since they would have reached it by sailing west, it could naturally, in their minds, be "the West."

The long Persian wars sharpened the sense of distinction between the two continents, by a political application. Plain in Herodotus' great history is the idea: "Asia to the Persians; Europe to the Greeks." Aeschylus also expressed some of this conception in *The Persians,* when he wrote, "Shall the whole barbarian army not leave Europe by the Hellespont?" He wrote "Europe," not "Hellas." By such thinking the line between the two mighty continents was firmly and permanently fixed at the water of an insignificant strait.

The original twofold division into Europe and Asia was sufficient and reasonable enough as a beginning. Only when word had begun to come in of the Red Sea and its divisive break could philosophers think in terms of a third land-mass. Originally the Greeks put the break at the Nile, and Herodotus knew this point of demarcation, although it puzzled him. But, at the beginning, the Nile could be taken as the most outstanding natural feature along that coast.

As for the name of the third continent, its first one probably dates from the time of Hecataeus, about 525 B.C., since he may have been the first geographer to make the three-fold division. Egypt could not aptly be used, for it was a well-established kingdom with fairly definite boundaries. Instead, the name emerging was Libya, whose people, the Libyans, had been fighting with the Egyptians over the course of many centuries. To become the name of a continent it had the advantages of being large and indefinite, stretching into the desert sands. Since the name is that of a people rather than of an area, its possible meaning is not a toponymastic problem. In any case, in spite of its being revived for a modern nation, it was not to continue as the name of a continent, though it remained in such use for some centuries.

The Romans, however, made their entry into the southern continent far to the west of what was more specifically the country of the Libyans. The conquerors of Carthage picked up the name Africa in the course of the wars, either from the Carthaginians or from the native Berbers. It had been applied especially to the district around the city of Carthage, and the Romans used it in that area for their first province south of the Mediterranean. The name escaped this administrative limit. Probably, in the beginning, the province merely extended as far as Roman arms were powerful, and so was indefinite and unrestricted and able to extend.

In language, Africa is probably from the Berber, but may be Carthaginian, that is, Semitic. The usual wild guesses have attempted to derive it from Greek or Latin. With the very language unknown, no satisfactory explanation is possible.

Like its two sister continents, and like so many other of the world's great names, it is a good example of expansion. Planted first on a small area against a vast and unknown background, it had no rivals to oppose it.

Though achieved in a somewhat blundering fashion, the establishment of Asia and Europe as counterpart entities, and their naming, is probably to be considered one of the first triumphs of scientific geography. The establishment of Libya is equally striking, though blurred a little by the later substitution of Africa.

The various shiftings of application of the names are a part of political history rather than of nomenclature.

6

The Ancient Seas

At some far-in-the-future date, studying the map of the ancient Mediterranean area, an investigator should be able to determine, from the names of the seas alone, that the region was then inhabited by a land-animal, not by a creature of the waters. With some exceptions, in short, the names are associative. They express a relationship of that body of salt water to the land that borders it along some part of its shore.

This situation is a common one, world-wide. One sea, looking (and sounding and tasting) much like another sea, offers little possibility for distinction by description. Only in parts of Polynesia, such as the Hawaiian Islands, do the names seem to indicate a race of men to whom the sea was as native as the land. Thus Alenuihaha and Pailolo are passages between islands, but reflect the name of neither island. Instead, they specify the nature of the passage itself—"big waves pursuing," and "rolling waves."

By Hawaiian standards, however, the men of the ancient world, even the Phoenicians and Greeks, were arrant landlubbers, steering from headland to headland. Since the lands already had names, the seas naturally took the same names. Also, since there as yet existed no principle of freedom of the sea, the question of domination asserted itself. Ordinarily, Corinth was an outstanding sea-power, and you sailed the so-called Gulf of Corinth either by permission of that city or at your own risk. In earlier times, however, the name was the Gulf of Crisa, since that was then the dominating city.

Destruction of cities and even of peoples, along with persistence of names, has obscured the basically simple system. The Tyrrhenians have vanished, but the Tyrrhenian Sea still preserves the name of the people now more commonly called Etruscans. On the other side of Italy, the Adriatic is the memorial of the once-powerful Etruscan city of Adria, which apparently dominated those waters so powerfully as to keep Greek colonists away. Similarly the Saronic Gulf preserves the name of a place of which only a temple was left in classical times.

The Myrtoum Sea (to give it the common Latin form) comprised most of the southwestern Aegean, but the only source for the name seems to be a small island, Myrto, at the very northern end of the sea. This islet, just off the southern tip of the large island of Euboia, may have been a landmark and have provided sailing-directions. It could thus have given its name to the sea.

Since the connection between land and people is generally close, many seas merely bore tribal names. Thus Apollonius Rhodius mentions "the gulf named after the Ambracians," and Pliny the Elder declares that the Persian Gulf took its name because the Persians had always lived there. So also Strabo mentions that the Caspian Sea was so called from the Caspii. They were, it may be noted, a tribe living at the southwestern corner of the sea, in a location where they would be the first tribe of that area to come into contact with the Greeks and Romans. Strabo adds, "But the tribe has now disappeared." In this instance, as is common, the name survived the vanishing of the tribe, but apparently the decision was close. The name Hyrcanian Sea, for another tribe, was also in use for a while.

The highly land-based psychology shows in Pliny's passage, "the Romans call [a certain sea] by two names—the Macedonian Sea where it touches Macedonia or Thrace and the Greek Sea where it washes the coast of Greece." To conceive of the sea itself as the entity was difficult.

Certain bodies of water that offer anomalies or unusual histories are of special interest—the Ionian Sea, the Aegean, the Mediterranean, the Black, and the Atlantic Ocean itself.

The Ionian Sea stands out in nomenclature because it is a long way from Ionia. One suggestion is that the name is an ancient one, having arisen before the great Ionian migration, about 1000 B.C., when those people lived on the Greek mainland, and possibly along the eastern shore of that sea. This idea is a useful one to any historian trying to demonstrate that the Ionians once inhabited that area. Actually, even if their ancestors did so, there is no evidence that they then called themselves Ionians, a term which may mean "migrants."

A better possibility is that Ionian Sea means, essentially, Greek Sea and that it is a counterpart to the Tyrrhenian Sea. In the eighth century B.C. the Greek colonies planted at the Straits of Messina were Ionian, and these cities held the gate against the Tyrrhenians. The sea could not well have been known by the name of any one of these cities, but it might have been known by the name of their common tribe. To have called it the Hellenic Sea would scarcely have been possible, since the Greeks had little feeling of unity at this period.

The Aegean Sea probably goes back to the pre-Greek *aig-*, "water," or, by extension, "sea." (See Book III, Chapters 1 and 3.) It would then be another example of a generic in one language becoming a specific in a succeeding language. This procedure would be especially likely in the case of a body of water which for a great number of Greeks in the early period was preeminently "the sea."

The great complex of gulfs and seas now known as the Mediterranean raised difficulties of entity for the ancient peoples who lived on its shore. It was simply, above all others, "the sea." So it remained until expanding trade had advanced into the waters far beyond it.

The Israelites called it merely the Great Sea, thus distinguishing it from the Sea of Galilee and the Red Sea.

The early Greeks either did not grasp its entity or failed to think a name useful, and it remained simply "the sea." Even Herodotus seems to have lacked a specific name, and identified it once as "the sea which the Greeks sail." As often happens with large features, such as mountain ranges, the individual parts could be named before the whole. Once the Greeks had come to know the Atlantic, they sometimes termed the Mediterranean as the Inner Sea. The Romans, having encompassed its shores with their dominion, boldly called it Our Sea. In the time of the empire the term Mediterranean came into use—somewhat ambiguous, but apt, if taken in the sense of "sea in the middle of the land," in counterpart to the Atlantic and the other waters which had no known farther shores.

Of all the bodies of water, the one now known as the Black Sea raised the most nomenclatural complications. It suffered both change of name and duality of name.

It was commonly known simply as Pontus, one of several Greek words meaning "sea." Except as applied to this particular sea, however, the word was rare, occurring chiefly in poetry. Moreover, it appears to be of Indo-European derivation (cognate with English *path*), referring especially to the sea conceived as a means of communication. Yet this sea was always on the edge of the Greek world, and one cannot find a time in history when it could reasonably have been "the path." A borrowing from some local language, possibly Thracian, seems to be demanded.

The two secondary names, Hellespont and Propontis, also suggest local borrowing. Propontis is an interesting one for its point of view. Meaning "in front of the Pontus," it provides evidence that the Greeks approached from the Aegean. If Pontus had been an old name which was brought by the Greeks from some ancient northern homeland, we should have possibly had such a name as Epipontis, "beyond the Pontus."

As for Hellespont, it ought to mean something like "the narrow Pontus," or "entrance to Pontus." But even the language is uncertain, and the Greeks merely told a mythological story about it.

When the Greeks first began to navigate Pontus, its shores were largely inhabited by Iranian-speaking peoples. They sensed the difference in appearance between the water of inland streams and that of the open sea, calling the latter "dark," in their language, *axsaena*. The Greeks adopted this as Axeinos, "inhospitable," and to avoid the suggestion of evil, altered it to Euxine, "hospitable." (See Book II, Chapter 6.) This ancient Iranian name still preserves itself, translated into many far-flung languages, usually altered to mean not so much "dark" as "black."

About the name Atlantic Ocean, one firm statement (and perhaps only one) can be made, that is, that it is *not* derived from Plato's story of the lost island. On the contrary, it was in use at least a generation before Plato told the tale, the name being in the text of Herodotus.

Of course, there is the will to believe, and the followers of Plato (along with proponents of Bacon) seem to have a remarkable share of such will. Such believers can accept literally that the story is an ancient one of Egypt, from which Herodotus and others could have borrowed. Even if we accept Plato, however, we still have the problem of the elucidation of the name.

Atlas (stem: *Atlant-*) enjoyed a secure place as a figure in traditional Greek mythology. Son of Iapetos (the Biblical Japhet), Atlas was one of the elder gods. Close to its opening the *Odyssey* offers the description: "Atlas, of baleful mind, who knows the depths of every sea, and holds the tall pillars that keep earth and heaven apart." In Hesiod's *Theogony* a passage runs: "Atlas through strong necessity supports the wide heaven with unwearying head and arms, standing at the end of the earth, before the clear-voiced Hesperides."

As to the literal meaning, the Greeks themselves derived it from a word "bear, support," thus doubtless giving rise to the story that Atlas, by judgment of Zeus, was condemned perpetually to support the heavens. Actually, the name is probably from a non-Greek source. Since Atlas was the son of Japhet, we may even suspect that name also to be derived from a Semitic source, presumably Phoenician, though nothing definite can be cited.

At this point, however, enough evidence is available from the poems to make at least a plausible case for the naming of the Atlantic Ocean. Atlas was associated with the depths of the sea, and therefore he must have been generally known to seamen. His station was at the end of the earth, near to the Hesperides, who were the Daughters of Evening, conceived in the *Theogony* as living far in the west, even beyond the stream of Ocean. Greek sailors passing through the Straits and into the open water would have every reason to think that they were in the Sea of Atlas, which would yield, in an adjectival form, Atlantic.

The association with the mountains would follow naturally, and they still bear the name.

We lack, however, some links of evidence. Moreover, the case breaks the general rule that the seas are named from the land. As the Black Sea indicates, however, the rule is sometimes broken.

Careful study of the text of Herodotus, moreover, seems to indicate that even in his time the Greeks were not altogether comfortable with the name. He does not refer to it straightforwardly as the Atlantic Ocean, but calls it a "sea" (*thalassa*), apparently still reserving the term Ocean for the mythological river which encircled the earth. Moreover, he does not name it directly as the Atlantic Sea, but uses, uneasily, the circumlocution that for the Greeks sometimes indicates a certain doubt about a name, that is: "The sea which is called (*kaloumene*) Atlantic."

Like so many of the early names that were destined to greatness, both Atlas and Atlantic draw us on by poetic suggestion, but at the end, like the maiden on the Grecian urn, remain ungrasped.

7
The Roman Way

Rome, the name, like all those that are short and simple, lures the linguists onward to plausible guesses, one of which (though not more than one) could be correct. The known vocabulary of Indo-European is voluminous. Any seeker might find some Indo-European root which satisfies the easy phonetic demands of *r-o-m*, and the chances are also good that one or more of these solutions will prove to be semantically acceptable.

There is, for instance, *(e)rem* *, meaning "to rest, to settle oneself," and thus easily extended into "settlement, town." There is also the analogy of the River Rhone, which can be traced back to a root meaning "stream," and would thus be likely enough for a city so intimately connected with the Tiber. These are possibilities for anyone who wishes to accept them, but they offer no compelling evidence. And in the background always rests the good possibility that the name is Etruscan, and thus not Indo-European at all.

One well-founded statement, though a negative one, can be presented. Unlike many early towns, Rome does not seem to spring from a tribal name—simply because Romanus is clearly formed from Roma, not the reverse.

In the context of place-names, one must keep clear the distinction between Latin, for the linguistic tradition, and Roman, for the political and cultural tradition. In their beginnings the Romans were merely one among many Latin tribes, speaking a common language and recognizing some kinship—but often at war.

The few names which survive from this time are thus Latin rather than Roman. Latium itself, for the general area, apparently arises from *latus,* "broad," and means "plain," in reference to the wide-spreading level area south of Rome. If this commonly accepted derivation is correct, the Latins took their name from the country which they inhabited—not the reverse, as occurs regularly. Campania, the district lying farther to the south, offers much the same meaning.

Often mentioned in early Roman contexts is the ancient city Alba Longa. In Latin this means "white-long," and it has often been explained as being the name for a long, white city. The *alba,* however, more likely goes back to a widespread term "height, mountain," which may even be pre-Indo-European.

As the Romans, over some centuries, extended their domination throughout the peninsula and clear to the Alps, they were pushing into territory which had long been settled. The cities that were later to loom so large in history suffered no basic change of name by Roman conquest—whether they were Etruscan (Arezzo, Pisa, Perugia), or Gallic (Milan), or even Ligurian (Turin).

An exception occurred at a site on the River Arno, where the old Etruscan town had been set on a hill for security. The Romans, however, founded a colony on the riverbank, and named it Florentia, which is literally "flowering place." As the repeated Spanish use of Florida indicates, such a naming is not incredible, but it seems unlikely for the practical Romans, especially when naming a colony. Was a man named Florinus or Florentius somewhere in the background?

Pavia shows another Roman naming, being a colony which reflects the presence there of citizens from the Roman tribe Papia.

As their dominion spread beyond the peninsula, the Romans faced differing situations, east and west.

To the east the lands had been anciently and thickly settled. The conquerors needed to establish few names, and most of these were replacements to the already established name.

One of the occasions was under the Emperor Hadrian. At that time Roman patience was sorely tried by the rebellious religious fanatics of Judea, whose center was Jerusalem. In an attempt to settle matters Hadrian established a colony there, even changing the name to Aelia Capitolina, Aelia being from one of his own names, and Capitolina apparently to suggest Capitoline Jove, thus replacing the Jewish deity. Like most such political namings, it survived as long as the political crisis remained, and then the city returned to being what it had been.

By and large, Roman naming throughout the eastern provinces was monotonously commendatory, a city being called after the reigning emperor or by one of the titles, Caesar or Augustus. Readers of the New Testament will remember the city of Tiberias, named for the emperor, and two cities called Caesarea. Since the emperor was officially deified, such names were basically religious dedications.

Like Jerusalem, many of these cities reverted to their previous names. One may mention, however, Edirne and Kayseri, both in modern Turkey, whose names were probably preserved because they were within the nucleus of the long-enduring Byzantine empire. Edirne descends from Adrianopolis, founded and named by the same emperor who attempted to displace Jerusalem. Kayseri is obviously another Caesarea, in this case named by and for Tiberius.

Only in A.D. 330, with the solemn dedication and naming of a new capital city, did the Romans plant a major name in the East. Called Constantinopolis, it used the Greek term for city. The emperor's name, however, was thoroughly Roman. Though the Roman name still survives, it never managed wholly to supplant the earlier name, Byzantium, which the Greek colonists of 658 B.C. had taken over from the local tribesmen, probably Thracian, but which is of unrecorded meaning.

Officially now, under the Turks, Constantinopolis has become Istanbul, a name which a linguist can obviously recognize as a worn-down form of the original Constantinopolis. Insistent popular belief, however, especially among the Greeks, derives it from the petrified Greek phrase *eis ten polin,* meaning "to the city."

Throughout the western provinces population was less dense, and the possibility was greater for the planting of Roman names, though many of these names also failed to survive. The chief trouble was that the Romans commonly established their long and formal commendatories, unsuitable for common use, many of them coupling a Latin and a local element. Along the German border, however, a number of cities preserved at least some trace of their original Latinity. Thus Augusta Vindelicorum, for a local tribe, combined a Latin element with a later-introduced German ending to become Augsburg. Similarly, Augusta Rauracorum has become Augst. Konstanz can still be recognized as named for the Emperor Constantius Chlorus in A.D. 378. Coblenz is from the military post at the Confluentes, that is, the "flowing-together" of the Moselle and the Rhine. Finally—as the most important of these cities, and also the name showing greatest shortening—we have the Roman foundation known officially as Colonia Claudia Agrippinensis. It came to be known merely as the Colony, and now maintains itself as Köln—or Cologne, as the French and English call it.

Elsewhere in the western empire, a number of Spanish cities still go by their transformed Roman names. The oldest of these is Valencia, which in 138 B.C. was founded, in combination with an Iberian tribal name, as Valentia Edetanorum. The name is generally taken as meaning something like "strong city of the Edentani." Possibly, however, some Roman named Valens or Valentius was involved.

Badajoz is from Pax Augusti, "peace of Augustus," the name of a Roman colony. Both parts of the all-Roman name survived, though much altered, having been passed through an Arabic stage as Bax Augos. Similarly, Saragossa preserves remnants of both parts of its Roman christening as Caesarea Augusta. León commemorates the simple fact that the site was the headquarters of the Seventh Legion for many years. One, apparently, began to talk merely of going to the legion. Similarly, Mérida completely lost its imperial name, having been originally a planting of retired veterans (emereti) under a dedication to Augustus. But Augusta Emerita came out as Mérida. Pamplona also preserves some vestiges of having been named, in 68 B.C., for the Roman general who is known as Pompey the Great.

The very center of the western empire was Gaul, its boundaries fairly close to those of modern France. Here we should expect the strongest Roman influence on names, and we actually find it, though in an unusual manner.

The great names of France are rarely Roman. Of the traditional provinces we find only two such.

Provence specifies derivation from "the province," that is, the southeastern part of Gaul which was organized as a province and Romanized a considerable time before Caesar's conquest of the wild Gauls of the north and west. Champagne is from the Latin *campania*, "plain." The exact sense in which the name is to be taken cannot be easily decided, since the province is not notably more level than most of those around it. As often happens, a name applied to a comparatively small feature may have spread to a whole region. The later meaning of "country" as opposed to "town" seems no better suited, since no large city dominates the region.

As with the French provinces, so with the larger cities. Only a few are clearly Roman. Grenoble still shows, if somewhat vestigially, its origin from Gratianopolis, dating from the fourth century, when the Emperor Gratian established a bishopric in the city. By that time the Greek *polis* had been sufficiently used as scarcely to seem Greek any longer. Orleans was formerly assigned as a commendatory naming for the great emperor Aurelian, but modern scholars ascribe it to a certain Aurelius, who is otherwise unknown, but at least had a Roman name. The earliest record, about A.D. 400, gives a name that may be translated as "city of Aurelius's people," suggesting that the city's founder, or re-founder, may have been a kind of feudal lord, such as might arise in the troubled times of the dying empire. In simi-

lar manner, Dijon derives from an unknown Divius, who had a
Roman name, though he may have lived at too late a period to
be considered really Roman.

Among smaller French cities, Autun derives from Augusto-
dunum, in which Augustus was coupled with the Gaulish
dunum, "fortress." Coutances preserves the name of Constantius
Chlorus, who fortified the city about the year 400.

The real thrust of Roman influence on names came at the
village level, and provides in itself one of the chief testimonies
for the history of the period. Under the empire, Gaul became a
region of opportunity, much as did the American West in the
nineteenth century. Worthy Romans—or, at least, men with
worthy Roman names—got land, and set up for themselves,
whether to be country gentlemen or merely farmers. In any
case, each nucleus of such a holding commonly developed into
a village and took its name from its owner, usually with the addition of a suffix. Such names run into the thousands, and
occur in all regions of the country.

The most common suffix was *-acum,* in origin Gallic, but soon
assimilated to Roman usage. In the course of time and under
the influence of local dialects, this ending shifted variously.
Thus Cognac, Cognat, and Cogny all represent an original
owner (whose name is supposed to have been Cunius) coupled
with *-acum.* So also, from Aurelius, we have (besides Orleans)
Orly, Orleat, Orliac, and Orelle. The commoner names led to
much repetition. Julius is the source of twenty or more village-
names, turning up in such forms as Juillac, Juilly, Jullie, Juil-
laguet, and Jullianges. In some instances, the name of the
owner merely stands without suffix—thus, Valence from Val-
lentius.

Though these possessives were the chief Roman contribution
in Gaul, many miscellaneous names are preserved. Aix is from
the Latin *aquae,* for the local springs, and thus a descriptive. Associatives from Roman religious foundations show in such an
obvious instance as Templemars, or less obviously in Fanjeaux,
which is for Fanum Jovis, "temple of Jove." The ending *-etum*
indicated the growth of certain trees or plants. Thus *castanetum,*
"chestnut-grove" yielded Castanet and many others. Neuillac,

Neuilly, Nivillac, and their companions show -*acum,* coupled sometimes with an owner's name (Nobilis or Novellius), but usually with the descriptive *novellus,* to arrive at the English equivalent of Newton.

The Roman period in the West may be said to have ended about A.D. 500, but so to conclude is to consider the matter politically, not linguistically. The people continued to speak a late form of Latin, in spite of barbarian invasions, and names were still given. Even in districts like Alsace, Latin terms worked into the Germanic speech, and hybrid names resulted. Such, for instance, is Strasbourg, "road-fort," so called because of its site on one of the Roman roads. The word, however, had been transferred into German, and the name of the city is therefore Germanic.

In this light the situation in Britain becomes intelligible. From superficial study one would conclude that the Roman influence in their island province was more important than in Gaul. Actually, that influence is so slight that the historians of English place-names come close to ignoring it altogether.

In the province the Romans presumably gave names to estates and farms and budding villages, but these names (and sometimes the villages too) failed to survive the Saxon and Anglian conquest. As a rare exception Lindum Colonia, "lake-colony," preserves, recognizably, its Celtic-Roman name by still standing as Lincoln.

Superficially, indeed, the Roman influence on Britain seems strong, with its often-repeated Chester and Caster echoing the Latin *castra,* "camp." But a curious fallacy exists. Many places now thus named were actually not so called by the Romans. Chester itself was Deva, and Manchester was Mamucion. From the conquered Romano-Britons the early English picked up the word *castra* as a common noun, and applied it, as *ceaster,* to any place where ruins of a fortification were visible. Most of these fortifications were doubtless of Roman origin, but others must have gone back to pre-Roman peoples. Thus originating, these descriptives eventually stiffened into place-names, and gave the map a kind of pseudo-Latinity. The name-element appears as a long roll of what would be considered typical English town-names—Rochester, Doncaster, Chesterfield, Chesterton, Lancaster, Colchester, Casterton.

With the dissolution of the empire the direct influence of Rome came to an end, but the linguistic influence of Latin continued in some degree—as illustrated by Strasbourg and by the many English names. The study of place-names in the territory of the former Roman realm must therefore proceed chiefly against the background of the various Romance languages. Nevertheless, something of what we may call the Roman ideal—its tradition of dignity and unity and power—still remained, and in the course of centuries exerted a world-wide influence, a long-cast shadow of the remembered empire. This influence, we may think, rested upon more than the continued cultivation of Latin as an international language. Latin represented, also, the glory of the empire itself.

Nowhere was this influence more noticeable than among the speakers of English. In the seventeenth century, to illustrate, a new power came to be recognized in Europe. To the Germans this was only one of their own, and they continued to call it Oesterreich, "eastern realm." The French halfway Gallicized it into Autriche. But the English simply Latinized it as Austria.

The English, in fact, became especially devoted to the Latin ending -ia to designate a nation or a district—Russia, Prussia, Silesia, Transylvania, and their own East Anglia. In some instances this Latin form almost constitutes a different name. Thus many people scarcely rcognize the identity of Bavaria and of Bayern, as it stands in German.

Some -ia names may be considered literary revivals of classical forms, as with India and Syria. With such names English preserved and passed on to the modern world the exact Roman form, whereas the other modern languages generally adapted the forms to their own current speech. English, for this reason, sometimes preserves the Latin exactly, where the Romance languages do not—as with Sardinia, which is Sardaigne in French, Cerdeña in Spanish, and Sardegna in Italian.

Because of British exploration and colonization the -*ia* ending became broadcast over the globe.

In the United States the roll of these Latinized coinages includes Pennsylvania, Virginia, Georgia, and Columbia. (California, however, represents a Spanish tradition.)

Nova Scotia, "new Scotland," furnishes another example of a successful naming of this kind, one so well naturalized that its inhabitants find nothing strange in being Nova Scotians.

In Spanish and Italian, however, the -*ia* ending is native, so that names so derived may take the same form as those coined by the English, as with California and Bolivia.

Not all of the Roman tradition displays itself in this particular ending. When the old Spanish Netherlands were organized as a new country in the fourth decade of the nineteenth century, the name was taken from the ancient Gallic group of tribes known as the Belgae. A country thus derived would commonly, in English, have been rendered as Belgia. It became, however, Belgium, using the less common Latin ending seen in Latium. The English preservation of the form is again notable, as against Belgique, Belgien, and other forms.

A common Latin ending is merely -*a*, originally to be conceived as the feminine ending of an adjective, with some such word as *terra* "land," or *provincia*, being understood, or even written. Thus Carolina was originally, in 1629, named for King Charles I with what seems to be a Latin adjective coined from his name, Carolana. In 1663 this was re-spelled as Carolina.

In establishing the American states the ending -*a* became highly popular. In some instances, such as Florida, Louisiana, and Nevada, Spanish influence was predominant. Only in Indiana and Montana can a primarily Latin origin be postulated. Most of the names are from Indian languages, made to seem partly Latin, as with Minnesota, Iowa, Nebraska, Dakota, and Oklahoma. From these beginnings the idea of the ending -*a* as suitable for a place became embedded in the American folk-mind, to produce hundreds of names in which -*a* was joined to almost anything, to produce such results as Daytona and Capitola.

In old and in new Africa, also, the Roman forms loom large.

The ancient kingdom of Ethiopia preserves a name that may be traced from the *Iliad*. Mauretania was the name of a Roman province. The English speech preserves its favorite ending in such names as Algeria, Tunisia, Nigeria, Liberia, Gambia, Tanzania, Zambia, Somalia, and Rhodesia.

8
The Celts of the Continent

On the mainland of Europe the once far-ruling and proud Celts have lost their identity as a people. Their place-names are orphans. Yet these names are numerous, and some of them are of world-wide fame. Moreover, by various scholarly approaches, the language has become well enough known to make possible some explanation of most of the names.

Not too much, however, must be deduced from the insular Celtic, which still maintains itself in Ireland, the Scottish Highlands, Wales, and Brittany. The ancient continental Celtic is not closely related to any modern dialect, so that analogies, though helpful, call for caution. Thus Avon, though the common Celtic word for river in Britain, does not occur in a list of ordinary Celtic name-elements on the Continent.

Scholarship in the middle twentieth century, moreover, has created additional difficulties and complications, with its argument that other speakers of Indo-European preceded the Celts in this area, and left their influence on many names which the Celts later adopted. (See Book III, Chapter 9.) Whether directly or indirectly, however, the Celts left a strong imprint upon names throughout the heartland of Europe.

An ancient home of the Celts centered in what we may roughly term southern Germany. Moreover, they apparently lived there for many centuries. A proof of it is that in that region the names of the larger features are Celtic, or have at least passed through a Celtic form. Especially notable are the names of two great rivers.

The stream which the English know as the Danube was Ister to the Greeks, Danuvius to the Romans. Its having two names is not remarkable. In fact, if we possessed the full record, we should undoubtedly find that it had several others as well. Like most large rivers, it flowed through the territory of speakers of different languages, and would have had various names, just as a dozen may be cited for the Mississippi. In fact, Strabo notes a third name, Matoas.

The Greeks would have learned a name of the river from some tribe living on its lower course—probably, even, at its mouth on the Black Sea. The language, then, would most likely have been Thracian, a little-known Indo-European speech. In fact, the sequence *s-t-r* presents an analogy with the root seen also in the English *stream,* and in Strymon, the ancient Greek name for the modern Vardar of Macedonia. On the other hand, there is a root occurring as *is-* in the names of a number of European streams, such as the Iser and the Isere, with the idea "rapid, turbulent." So, for a prudent man, the Ister must be left as uncertain.

The Romans, on the other hand, must have learned the name Danuvius from some tribe living on the upper waters of the great river—most likely, indeed, from the Celts. The striking feature of this name is the Indo-European element *danu-,* which shows probably in Iardanus and Jordan, and certainly in the whole sequence of Russian rivers including the Don, the Dnieper, and the Dniester. It is also common in Scotland, and occurs elsewhere as well. From being originally a generic for river, *danu* became a specific, as commonly happens, when it was passed on to the speakers of the succeeding language—like Avon and many others. The name as a whole has not been explained, and the *vi-* may represent the remnant of some original specific. Its connection with the Celts is questionable, but it probably, at least, passed through the Celts, thus being transmitted to the Romans.

The other great river of the Celtic homeland flowed out of that region toward the north. As with the Danube, the Celts presumably were familiar with it chiefly on its upper course, where they knew it by a name which they may have picked up from an earlier Indo-European speech. In any case, it is of clear enough meaning, connected with a root "stream," or "swift stream," from which, indeed, after a long passage through Latin the modern English *river* is eventually descended. Thus we have the great international stream known as Rhein, Rhin, or Rhine.

A point is to be noted. The name seems especially to refer to the current of the stream, and so to be given to a swift-running one. Thus it would not have been bestowed upon the Rhine by people seeing it anywhere along its placid lower course. On the other hand, in the region of its swift upper course all the streams are likely to be torrential. Ideally, as the place of naming, one would search for an area where the Rhine was swift but other streams comparatively slow, so that the term would be distinctive. Such finesse, however, would probably be unwarranted, though it might well be more to the point than much of the phonetic juggling to which European river-names are commonly subjected.

The Rhine of history and song does not stand alone as a name. Both in Germany and in France a number of small streams, with different spellings, share the honor. Of purely local significance, they are records of the common process by which a generic shifts to be a specific, usually at some change of language—here, from Celtic to German or from Celtic to Latin.

Important names of Celtic origin follow the courses of the upper Rhine and Danube. Worms stands in Latin sources as Borbetomagos or Bormetomagos, in which -*magos* represents one of the commonest Celtic generics, literally meaning "field, open space," but often "market," because a market would develop where open space was available. Then, around the market, a town would grow. The whole name means "market on the Borbeto (Bormeto)." The meaning of this stream-name is uncertain, though *borm* strongly suggests the common Indo-

European term "warm." An anomaly here is that it is probably the stream now known as Eisbach, "ice-brook."

In the course of time Worms lost its original generic, but Remagen still shows it. Its Latin is Rigomagus, "royal field," or "king's market," presumably because in pre-Roman times it was once a king's residence, or under some king's especial patronage and protection.

Mainz, also on the Rhine, has a Latin form Moguntiacum in which a common Latin ending -iacum has been coupled with the name of a Celtic divinity Mogons or Mogontia. As with Worms, the generic disappeared.

The present Regensburg is German, taking its name from the stream that there enters the Danube. Its background, however, is complex. The official Roman name was Regina Castra, "royal camp." In common speech, however, a Celtic name survived, appearing as Ratisbona in the Middle Ages, and apparently consisting of bona, "house, settlement," with a specific of unknown meaning. The French, and to some extent the English, have preserved this as Ratisbon.

An even more famous city shows the same generic in its earliest form, Vindobona, "white town." Eventually it shortened to Vienna—and, in German, even more, to Wien. If the original naming was because a white house actually stood there, the literal meaning has an interesting analogy with the modern Casablanca.

The Celts finally left their ancient homeland—whether lured away by hope of better country or pushed out by tribes advancing from the east and north. There is no historical record, but place-names yield one bit of evidence, that the immediate successors in certain areas were not Germans, as one might expect, but were speakers of some Slavic language.

The evidence arises from the stream-names along the upper Danube. The chief affluents, those flowing directly into the main river, generally have names of Celtic origin. Secondary tributaries, those flowing into these Celtic-named streams, are likely to have Slavic names. But the small brooks have names of German origin. The situation thus points to an intermediate

Slavic occupation, with the newcomers taking over the already established names of the chief streams, and giving names of their own to others, which they, in turn, passed on to the Germans. Very small streams, however, often are not named at all, or, having names, lose these easily with a shift of peoples. Only with a long and intensive German occupation would such streams finally have their present names.

The Celts, once on the move, swept across the region which was to be known as Gaul—and, later, as France. Restless energy carried them on into the British Isles; in other directions, into Italy and clear to Portugal. One of their far-wandering tribes, then known as Gauls, reached the interior of Asia Minor, where the Roman province of Galatia took their name.

In all these lands the Celts seem to have followed what we may call the usual practice of invaders, that is, they took over many of the already established place-names, especially those of the important rivers. On the other hand, for their own settlements and for many of the smaller features they gave their own names, or evolved them.

Gaul, which became the typical Celtic land, displays their practices, and furnishes most of the great names.

In general, this naming was practical and ordinary. The River Charente, for instance, is merely "sandy." Beavers were still common, and produced many names of small streams, such as Beuvron, Brevon, Beauronne, and Brevenne. Names from property-owners were so common that the Gallic suffix -acum passed on to the Romans. Probably there were many incident-names, and a striking one remains in the city of Caen, which is simply from *catu-magos*, "battlefield." So also to be explained are the village-names Cahan, Caden, and Cahon. In an age and among a people given to war, outstanding encounters must, we should think, have occurred at these places, whether of Gauls against the earlier inhabitants or among Gauls themselves.

Certain of the Gallic names reflect religious beliefs or practices. The Marne is almost the only large stream to show a Gallic name, one which is apparently from Matrona, a dedication to a mother-goddess. The city of Lyon arises from the recorded Lugdunum, "Lug's fort," a dedication to one of the chief Gallic gods. So also came Laon, and other names of towns.

The most striking feature of Gallic toponymy is the influence of the tribal names. Unusual, also, is the fact that many of these tribal names themselves are intelligible, the suggestion thus being that they were not very ancient. Possibly when the people from beyond the Rhine overran their rich conquest, more room was available, so that tribes split into small units and took new and commendatory names. Thus the Lemovices were "elm-warriors," from a tree held sacred, and the Caturiges were the "battle-kings."

Many names of the ancient provinces of France originated from these tribal ones. From the Lemovices came Limousin; from the Arverni, Auvergne; from the Cennomanni, Maine; from the Andecavi, Anjou; from the Turones, Touraine; from the Pictones, Poitou. Since these were not official Roman designations, the conclusion must be that the ordinary people of the region transmitted the name in speech, so that it became attached to the region and persisted long after the original tribe itself had vanished, even from memory. Only after centuries of such transmission did the names become official with the rise of the feudal system.

Even more widespread is the influence of these tribal names on urban centers. Again the procedure is not Roman, and may almost be termed counter-Roman. Under the imperial rule there was a flourishing of cities in Gaul, and some of these took official names, usually with a Roman personal name or title and a Gallic generic—Juliomagus, Caesaromagus, Augustabona. Apparently, however, at the same time the ordinary people referred to these places by some form derived from the old tribal names—Andecavi, Bellavaci, Suessiones. These names seemed suitable, since these places had been the tribal capitals before the Roman conquest.

In the first three centuries of Roman rule the situation was comparable to that which often occurred in the Spanish settlement of Latin America, when governmental or ecclesiastical names competed with popular names, the latter often prevailing. Thus we have San Fernando de Taos and San José de Tucsón, which are now simply and firmly Taos and Tucson.

So in Gaul, after many years of Roman rule and after the Celtic speech was almost extinct, these old names again prevailed. The former tribal capital of the Andecavi became Angers, with Juliomagos lapsing as completely as the saints' names with Taos and Tucson. So also Caesaromagus of the Bellovaci became Beauvais, and Augusta of the Suessiones became Soissons.

This process was essentially the same as that which occurred with the provinces, but much commoner. In some instances, indeed, both province and city used the tribal name, as with Anjou-Angers, and Poitou-Poitiers. In the far south of France the examples become rare, and they vanish in Provence and southern Languedoc, where Gallic influence, apparently, never prevailed. (See Book III, Chapter 9.) In the north, however, the modern political boundaries make no difference. Tongeren in Belgium and Trier in Germany preserve the memory of the Tungri and the Treveri.

Over most of modern France itself a kind of network of more than thirty of the older and more historic towns preserves the tribal names. Included among these are not only such important places as Nantes, Reims, and Bourges, but also the greatest of all French cities.

In the Roman period the town that developed on the little island in the Seine was not a very important place. The Romans wrote its name as Lutetia, the element *lut-* being Celtic "marsh," an obvious descriptive from the low-lying and sometimes flooded island. It was, however, the chief town of a small tribe known as the Parisii, and once stands in a Latin record as *Lutetia apud Parisios,* roughly, "Marshton-at-the-Parisii." It could also be more simply, Lutetia Parisiorum, "of the Parisii." Popular speech reduced the name to an ablative plural as Parisiis, and so to Paris. Eventually the French dropped even the final *s* in speech, though retaining it in the spelling.

The Celts swept on to the south, into the wide-spreading Iberian peninsula. In this region, however, they never became wholly dominant, and they mingled with the tribes already living there, to produce a mixed people, known to the Greeks as Celtiberi. Naturally, under such circumstances, their influence on names was less than in Gaul. A few important places, how-ever, commemorate them.

Segovia, for instance, is from Segobriga, a coupling of the common *briga*, "fort," with a term which has been variously translated as "victory" and "strong." It seems, at least, to have been commendatory. Other towns also show *briga*. One of these gives evidence that the Celts advanced clear across the penin-sula into modern Portugal. There the modern Coimbra is from Conimbriga, joining the Celtic word with the name of a local pre-Celtic tribe.

The whole region still known as Galicia is apparently from one of the Celtic tribes known as Callaici or Gallaeci, a variant of Gaul.

Most interesting of the Celtic names of Spain—at least, as a possibility—is Madrid itself. Scholars somewhat uncertainly ascribe it to *mago* or *mageto*, "big," and the common Celtic *rito* or *ritu*, originally "ford" but later used for other kinds of stream-crossings, such as "bridge." As applied to the small local river, a ford is not notable or likely to produce a name, and "big" is not usually coupled with "ford" unless it can be taken in the sense of "broad." Madrid, however, has not been better explained, and the chances, at least, are that it is Celtic. Even more strik-ingly than Paris, Madrid remained small and unimportant for many centuries, and its name should be one suitable to a small village rather than to a great capital.

In Italy the chief Celtic naming of interest is Milan—its Latin form, Mediolanum. It was an important town of the region which was known to the Romans as Cisalpine Gaul. Literally, it is readily translatable as "middle-plain," an appellation which seems suitable for the great city standing in the Lombard plain. But are we justified in thus assuming "middle-plain," to be also "middle-of-the-plain," and is there not a considerable dif-ference? The difficulty becomes more striking when we dis-cover a dozen places in France that also arise from *medio-lanum*—for instance, Malain, Meolans, Moislains, Molliens. Why this popularity?

The answer probably rests in a greater linguistic accuracy.

The translation "plain," may have to be taken in the sense of "meadow," or "glade," an open space in the forest where religious rites could conveniently be celebrated. Eventually, then, the term could mean "consecrated place," and some scholars so take it. The second term, literally "middle," may then be taken in the sense of "central," or even "principal." Under this heading both the great Italian city and the numerous French towns can easily be included, and we have the image of a level meadow or glade devoted to worship, and so recognized up and down the countryside—the seat, we might suppose, of a kind of Druidic bishopric.

Though a Celtic origin satisfactorily explains many place-names, anyone must end such a chapter as this with a feeling of something beyond. What, for instance, of the chief rivers of France? If they are not Celtic (much less Latin), then what are they? In an attempt to answer such questions, scholars of the twentieth century have turned to the study of what has come to be known as the sub-stratum.

9

The Continental Sub-stratum

As applied to European place-names, the term sub-stratum clearly represents an oversimplification. We would do better to pluralize it, and to consider not only a sub-stratum, but a sub-sub-stratum and even a sub-sub-sub-stratum.

From our mere macroscopic observation of stone monuments and cave-paintings, and, much more, from the multifold testimony of scientific archeology, we know that men have been inhabiting Europe and the Mediterranean basin for thousands of years. From the surviving evidence we can only conclude that they were of a high enough culture to have placed many thousands of names. From our knowledge of the transmission of place-names we must assume that the next-following occupiers of the land took some of these names over, and that the next-comers then repeated the process, until we arrive finally at the present. In their now existing form some of these names fail to harmonize wholly with the modern name-pattern, and thus may be suspected of being ancient. Others, by such processes as folk-etymology, we must suppose, have so completely taken the form of later languages that their earlier origin is not even to be suspected.

Thus far there is general agreement. All of us can accept the beautiful theory. But in any attempt to go further we arrive at controversy and chaos. What particular names are of the sub-stratum? Which ones may be grouped together into a single language? What language, then, and what people? What geographical limits? What groups of languages? What meanings?

Throughout most of a century the controversy has continued hotly, and not without personal acrimony. This scholar, accused of sub-stratophobia, has in turn taunted his assailant with sub-stratomania.

Other sources of evidence besides place-names have been brought forward hopefully—archeological correlations, words preserved in local dialects, the scant remarks of classical authors.

As the controversy has developed, the participants have begun to consider issues greater than the elucidation of some place-names. They have become involved with an important chapter in the development of the human race—that is, the pre-history of man in Europe, and in an area extending to the Caucasus and India. Erudition, especially in linguistics, has developed, and publication has mounted, until—as so often in the modern world—a man must stand appalled before his sources and spend most of a precious lifetime reviewing what has been already put forward.

Fortunately, however, the toponymist need not become so deeply involved. He may rest content and happy with the theory of the sub-stratum in that it seems to supply explanations, or partial explanations, of a considerable number of names, some of which are of much interest and of historical importance.

At its beginnings, during the later nineteenth century, the burgeoning theory drew strength from the two peoples who were known in antiquity as Ligurians and Iberians. In Roman times the Ligurians inhabited the coast in the region of Genoa, which is still known as Liguria. Their territory extended inland through the mountainous region on the borders of Italy and Gaul. Their language, however, was unknown, except for a few words preserved in classical writings. By the early hypothesis their language was something other than Indo-European, and extended over vast areas, thus being the key to the meaning of many thousands of otherwise unexplained place-names. Modern scholarship has resulted in great changes of attitude. The language is now generally considered to be Indo-European, and the people are thought to have been restricted in their territory, more or less to their limits as known to the Romans. Moreover, since little progress has been made with the language, not much can be done with interpretation.

In the case of Po, for the chief river of northern Italy, no less an authority than the geographer Ptolemy wrote that "In the language of the Ligurians the river is called Bodincus." He also declared that its current name, Padus, as spelled by the Romans, was derived from the Gallic word for fir-tree, since many such trees grew near the source of the stream. But, in the same passage, Bodincus is given as meaning "bottomless." Probably the latter explanation is preferable, and the fir-tree idea can be taken as arising from resemblance of words, that is, of *pad-* to *bod-*. The modern name can thus be, with some confidence, credited to the Ligurians, and it may well be from their word for river. The term "bottomless" may also be accepted, even though it is not common. In general, however, to a primitive people anything is bottomless which exceeds in depth the crude methods of sounding available—perhaps anything that is over a man's head or deeper than diving range.

From its phonetic resemblance to Padus the city of Padua is usually connected with the Roman name for the river. Turin shows the name of a Ligurian tribe, having once been Augusta Taurinorum.

As with the Ligurians, the early scholars expected much profit from the Iberians. Their chief habitat was the great peninsula, but they had certainly entered Gaul and were perhaps to be found in North Africa and even Britain. Moreover, their language (the theory held) was allied to Basque and was therefore eventually decipherable. But again came the restrictions. The relationship to Basque proved to be only a superficial matter of borrowed words, and the idea of a vast Iberian occupation faded away.

From one Iberian tribe, the Aquitani, the region known as

Aquitania took its name—the medieval Aquitaine and the modern Guienne. This ending *-tani*, probably "tribe, people," was characteristic of the Iberians, as also in Mauretani and Lusitani. One of these, revived, appears for a new African nation, and the other serves as a poetic name for Portugal. Far to the north, moreover, the Britanni seem possibly to show the Iberian ending. Even so, the evidence would not necessarily indicate an Iberian occupation, but only that this was a name by which that people knew the islanders and their island.

In Spain and Portugal most of the undeciphered names are doubtless Iberian. An interesting one is that of the Ebro, a river known to the Romans as Iberus. Originally, a smaller river in the south of the peninsula bore the name. The natural assumption is that both streams took the name, after the common custom, from the people living there, who were known to the Romans as Iberi. Then from the people the name Iberia (the common Greek usage) originated.

Unless ancient Iberian becomes known, we have little chance of working out the meaning of most of the still unexplained names of Spain and Portugal.

The collapse, as we may call it, of the Ligurian and Iberian hypotheses did not lead to any diminution of research and speculation. Far from it! A group of Italian scholars became the sponsors of a Mediterranean theory—that is, that a single linguistic stock once, in prehistoric times, occupied the basin of the inland sea. On the other hand, northern scholars built up the importance of the Illyrians as spreading a stratum of early Indo-European names over much of central Europe.

In what would seem to many people an unlikely spot—to wit, in Sardinia—J. Hubschmit declared for no fewer than six ancient strata, for which he used the names Eurafrican, Iberian, Hispano-Caucasian, Etruscan, Libyan, and another unnamed one. Yet, as a later scholar has ventured to note, skepticism has not decreased.

Thus, as already pointed out, the idea of the sub-stratum began with the attempt to elucidate place-names, and its chief contribution has been the accumulation of what may be called a vocabulary of prehistoric generics. These have been established, more or less authoritatively, by the traditional process of studying similarities of sound in various names, and discovering the ones which associate themselves with a certain kind of place, usually a natural feature. The assumption then follows that those combinations of sounds, in whatever language they may have existed, actually "meant" that generic with which they are still used.

As checked in many cases of known languages, the assumption is generally to be held valid. Anyone should keep in memory, however, that the most which has been proved is that the element is associated with a particular kind of place, not that it actually has that meaning. (See Book I, Chapter 10.)

Some of the proponents of the sub-stratum have pressed this evidence to the point of becoming fanciful, and have thus created a curious reversal of a traditional situation. In the nineteenth century and even later, the linguists acted as sober and critical judges, by whose conservative scrutiny all fanciful imaginings were to be checked. But in some instances in connection with the sub-stratum the linguists have employed their erudition to create an almost infinite variety, with an approach to fantasy.

As an example we may take one of the most firmly established of the deduced generics, that one which in its most basic form is rendered as *car* or *kar,* with the meaning "rock." It is thus useful and reasonable, for instance, for the explanation of the first part of Carcassonne, a fortress set upon a great rock. It has also helped in the elucidation of many lesser names.

Unfortunately, from the very beginning alternate forms began to spring up. In some names the form could be taken as *kal.* Moreover *k* passes easily into *g,* and so we might have *gar.* Obviously, then, would come *gal.* But the initial consonant not infrequently disappears completely, and so *ar* and *al* become possible. Still not arriving at the end, the ingenious linguists postulated contracted forms—*kl-, gl-, kr-, gr-.* Since vowels are notoriously more subject to shiftings than are consonants, a whole series of forms with different vowels (or even diphthongs) became allowable.

As a final result, all the permutations and combinations produced such a great number of possibilities that many thousands of names could be accommodated.

Semantically, the situation was similarly extended. Since rocks are associated with streams, the element could denote a river, and since people live in rock-shelters and build houses of stones, the element could also be a habitation-name.

All of this may actually be true. At some point, however, one's ability to believe begins to slip, and we sympathize with the scholar who charges that some of his colleagues are merely playing games with the alphabet.

Moreover, since many of the elements are very short, the possibility of coincidence arises. Not often do we meet with such a case as Cereste and Ceyreste in southern France, both of which go back to Citharista of the fourth century and thus echo, at some length, the name of Mount Citheron in ancient Greece. (The problem here, however, is that the name may have been an actual transfer from Greece, since this area was strongly under Greek influence.)

Commonly, however, the elements are very short—as, for instance, *ar*. Its connection with rivers is close and wide-spread. Reduplicated, it forms Arar, the ancient name of the Saone. It apparently occurs in the Aar of Switzerland, in the Ara, the Arga, and the Aragon (all of Spain), the Arno in Italy, the Ayr of Scotland, the Ore of England, and in dozens of other stream-names. But do we here have something real, linguistically and historically, or does the situation partly arise from the fact that *a* and *r* are common sounds in most languages? Their combination can be found in many names not of rivers and far removed from western Europe—even reduplicated, as in Mount Ararat. And what should we think of Arkansas and Arizona?

In all likelihood, however, more than one source is involved. The British examples, for instance, might spring from an Indo-European root which means "flow." Such origin, however, would be much less likely for the Spanish streams. But, as pointed out already, some scholars accept the possibility of *ar* being from *car*.

Still, too great scepticism may be as great an error as too great credulity. Probably we should accept in this simple combination of sounds a term meaning river, perhaps in more than one language.

Even so, the information thus provided is slight. Moreover, it is provided only when the generic happens to be preserved in the recorded name. In France, for instance, three of the chief rivers—the Seine, the Loire, and the Allier—are wholly enigmatic. They happen to preserve no generic, and they can be referred to no known language. They may merely represent specifics.

Another sub-stratum element which is strongly associated with large rivers is the *d-r* combination, as in the Duero of Spain and Portugal, the Dordogne of France, and the Thur of Switzerland.

In addition to rivers, the sub-stratum elements most commonly associate themselves with mountains. The situation is reasonable, since primitive people often find refuge (and, therefore, leave names) in mountainous areas—as in Wales. Usually there can be little certainty as to the exact meaning—elevated country, hill, peak, summit. An element *cuc* appears in such names as Cocumont in France, in which it is tautologically coupled with the modern term for mountain. Widespread, the term appears also in such names as Cumond, Cumont, Montcuq, in combinations that can only be translated as mountain-mountain. Still farther afield, Caucasus may contain the same element. Vesuvius, in its first syllable, shows another such sub-stratum term for mountain or peak.

The study of the sub-stratum has resulted in much satisfactory information about certain place-names. The results, however, are necessarily somewhat limited, when only generics are known—and even those, not with complete accuracy and certainty. We can only receive the impression that the namers of the pre-historic period were singularly limited and conventional, and wholly lacking in color and imagination, when the reverse may actually have been true. The cave-painters and the builders of Stonehenge may well have indulged in many flights of naming-fancy, whereas they have in fact left us as possibly recognizable only a handful of much repeated commonplaces.

The examination, across the board, of the sub-stratum names of a particular area actually suggests much variety. We may thus examine the roster of the historic cities of southern France, for names that are at least pre-Celtic, and may have very deep origins.

In contrast to the plain of northern France, the Midi is hilly and even mountainous. The invading Gauls, we can easily admit, could have defeated the natives in a few pitched battles and then spread quickly across the level country. But the subjection of the south would have been more difficult. Apparently the Gauls never completed that conquest, and the names certainly indicate such a possibility. Through the north and covering about three-quarters of France, the names of nearly all of the cities are demonstrably Celtic. By contrast, those of most of the older towns of the south are prevailingly neither Celtic nor Roman—Bordeaux, Toulouse, Narbonne, Carcassonne, Beziers, Arles, Avignon, Orange, Marseilles, Toulon. We have, for each of these names, the Latin form—Burdigala, Tolosa, Narbo, Carcassonna, Baeterrae, Arelate, Avennio, Arausio, Massilia, Telo.

The Romans, doubtless, took these names directly from the Iberians and the Ligurians, but those peoples, in turn, may have taken the names from still earlier inhabitants.

One interesting point, however, is that the commonest sub-stratum generics appear rarely in this list of cities. Though we cannot fully explain the meaning of any of the names, we recognize in the work of the namers a considerable variety. In all probability, most of the elements represent specifics. The likelihood is that some of the names are from tribes, since the names of primitive towns are commonly so formed. The endings are Latin, and Baeterrae even seems to represent a Latin folk-etymology by taking the form of the plural of *terra,* "land."

In any case, the sub-stratum names of the Midi hold an almost solid front against the names of the Gallic tribes which have attached themselves to the northern cities, and they display also a significant variety. From this list, as from much other evidence, we must conclude that primitive people do not limit themselves to commonplaces in their place-naming.

Among names originating from the sub-stratum, Rhone is of special interest—partly in its demonstration of the way in which facile conclusions may be wrong.

Anyone's natural first assumption would be to take Rhone as being closely related to Rhine. The phonetic similarity is striking. Each is a large river in the same general area, and their headwaters are contiguous.

But an earlier form, as preserved in Latin, is Rhodanus, and this considerably reduces the likelihood of a common origin.

The next conclusion would be that Rhodanus contains the same Indo-European word for river that is found as *don* or *dan* so commonly. Still further study, however, indicates that the significant part of the term is Rhod-, and that the analogy is with a number of smaller French streams, such as the Roudel and the Rodinel, which seem to be based upon a sub-stratum generic associated with rivers and normally taken to mean "river." The Rhone and the Rhine thus turn out to have identical meanings, but different origins. Their near-identity of modern form is thus a striking example of coincidence.

A large and puzzling group of French place-names may possibly find explanation by being taken as having arisen by folk-etymology from a sub-stratum generic. To support such a hypothesis one must reiterate the general principle that an unusual name commonly demands an unusual explanation.

Cantal, the name of a district and *département* of central France, does not stand alone, but as *cant-* has been recognized in other names frequently enough to be designated as a sub-stratum generic, "rock, mountain." One of these names is a diminutive, Cantalou, "hill, hillock."

In some French dialects, however, Cantalou can be taken as from the words *sing* and *wolf,* and it is usually explained as "Sing, wolf!" or "Where the wolf sings." These explanations however, go against all probability. *Sing* is not a word or an idea to be coupled with wolf—the less so indeed, when French has *hurler* for "howl." Moreover, this coupling of a verb of action with the name of an animal to form a place-name seems to be highly limited geographically.

In modern France (and to some extent in neighboring countries, such as Italy) these names are fairly common, as constructions from the verb meaning to sing. Creatures other than the wolf may be substituted, some of them true singers (as with the lark, in Chantealouette), and some of them scarcely singers at all (as with the raven, in Chantecorps).

The most likely onomastic explanation seems to be that the word for "hill" survived on certain places from the sub-stratum term, with the literal meaning wholly forgotten, as would be expected. The name was then taken, by folk-etymology, to be the combination of *sing* and *wolf*. By analogy it then was placed upon other spots—usually, we may suppose, for some association with that common and much dreaded animal. Still later, other animals and birds could take the wolf's place, and we could even have the frog, as in Cantarane.

Just why the name should have become popular must remain uncertain. Perhaps the generic *cant-* itself was common, so that the names involving other creatures might have developed directly. More likely, a certain picturesque, or even humorous, quality in this name-formation appealed to the peasants, by whom these names would normally be given.

Long the topic of controversy, but probably in some way to be connected with the sub-stratum, is that great complex of mountains known as the Alps.

Since a high pasture in certain parts of Switzerland and France is known as an *alp,* some scholars have so derived the larger name. In such a conclusion there is nothing impossible, for in many instances the smaller becomes the larger. One would think, however, that the word for pasture might as well be derived from the general name as *vice-versa.* Moreover, the competition is strong, with two contenders.

Frequently proposed as a source is a sub-stratum **alb-* or **alp-*, meaning "height, high place," and to be seen in a number of French names for towns set on hills, such as Albi, as well as in Alba Longa (Book III, Chapter 7).

One would have to assume that the name, in whatever language it first existed, was a common noun, simply meaning "mountain." Passed on to a following language it would have become unintelligible and merely a specific, though its application must have been vague, the Alps as a whole being not conceivable as an entity to a single primitive man.

Once the speakers of some Indo-European language appeared in the vicinity, a new possibility arose, since they had a term meaning "white," as represented by the Latin *albus*. "White" is a common term for mountains, especially in situations, as in northern Italy, where high mountains rise abruptly from a plain. During much of the year, in temperate climates, men cannot but be conscious of the contrast between the whiteness of the higher peaks and ranges and the darker hues of the foothills. Since some of the Italic dialects said *alpus* instead of *albus*, we find the Roman lexicographer Festus noting: "It is possible to believe that the Alps took their name from the whiteness of their snows." The possibility, indeed, is so good that we may even think of the name as having thus originated in some places without knowledge of the previous sub-stratum term.

A similar confusion is possible with Albion, the early name for Britain. The island could readily have been named from its appearance at the point of closest approach to the Continent. It could even have received a name from people who merely saw it from the vicinity of Calais without having voyaged to it. When they did so voyage, they probably made the shortest possible passage and so approached the cliffs of Dover. These, in some degree like the Alps, are both high and white. We can thus suppose for Albion either an Indo-European background or an origin from the sub-stratum.

The present chapter, however, cannot be rated as more than a sketchy survey of a vast and abstruse subject. In a general work a more detailed treatment is impracticable. The subject, moreover, is one within which scholars still wander in the fog of controversy.

10

The Sub-stratum of Britain

The possibility of a sub-stratal origin for Albion raises the question of other such possibilities in England itself. Until recently, scholars of English toponymy have set their faces hard against the admission of a sub-stratum. They have been ready to propose some far-fetched Celtic etymology rather than to admit the simple likelihood that the name in question was one which the Celts took over from earlier inhabitants. Three ancient names can serve for illustration—Kent, London, Thames. All of these are recorded in Roman writings, commonly as Cantium, Londinium, and Tamesis.

There is widespread agreement that Cantium derives from a Celtic *kant-*, but the meanings ascribed are so various as to take away the sense of anyone's having reached a solution. Ekwall gives *rim, border, border land, coast district.* Reaney, while including the first two of these, adds *white* as a possibility. Cameron derives it from a tribe, the Cantii, of uncertain meaning, but, possibly, *Hosts.* (He does not specify whether this is to be taken in the sense of large bodies of warriors or of a hospitable people.) Still other scholars connect the name with *canton,* in the sense of district, and with the meaning "corner." The result is mere confusion.

Moreover, many of these suppositions tend to become un-tenable if tested against actual naming practices of primitive peoples. We may doubt, for instance, whether any tribesman (lacking a map and transported only by his own feet) would have thought of Kent as being a corner. Moreover, it is not out-standingly the coast district—any more than are the adjacent regions. One has equal difficulty in grasping why it is distinc-tively a border land. A border of what?

The curious fact here is that these scholars have not pro-posed an origin from *cant-,* the sub-stratum generic which French scholars accept in such names as Cantal. Its meaning, *rock* or *mountain,* is not impossible, since the cliffs of Dover are the chief Kentish landmark.

As for London, for many years theories about it scarcely achieved more than did the myth of King Lud. Finally the scholars discovered an Old Irish adjective, *lond,* "wild," but also to be extended to mean "bold." Ekwall declares there to be "no doubt" that London is thus derived—thus using a phrase which, curiously, is never used except when doubt exists.

Since "wild, bold" do not constitute good meanings for a city, the scholars suppose an individual Londinos whose name (or a tribal name) was passed on, in some unspecified way, to the set-tlement.

Such procedure is actually to pile supposition upon supposi-tion. Is Londinos any less mythical than Lud? Even if we should discover an individual so named, what right would we have to assume that he (or some other of the ilk) founded the town or in some other way gave it his name?

As with Kent, we can much more easily accept London as an inheritance from some earlier stratum.

Thames, like London, long defied speculation. (Scholars knew, of course, that the *h* was a mere modern insertion.) Fi-nally someone discovered a river named Tamasa. This stream was a considerable distance off, being a tributary of the Ganges! Still, the situation was not impossible. Linguists recognized that Sanskrit was Indo-European, and so was Celtic. In Sanskrit the term means "dark."

As if thus deriving light from darkness, many scholars accepted this derivation, Ekwall stating categorically, "The name means 'dark river.' " But, given a little more time for thought, scholars hedged, resorting to phrases like "is considered to be," and "is uncertain but may be."

As far as is known, no linguist has consulted with a geologist or a geographer to determine whether the Thames, in its pristine state, was likelier to have been enough darker than near-by streams to have deserved such a distinction.

In actuality, *dark* or *black* is a common enough name for streams, as the often-repeated Douglas still shows throughout Great Britain. A difficulty, however, is that Thames does not stand alone. From what seems the same root come other English rivers—Tame, Team, Teme, Thame, Tamar. By a somewhat liberal interpretation the list may be run up to more than twenty.

One can maintain that all these streams were named from their darkness. A more normal explanation, however, would be to see here another example of the no-longer-understood generic becoming a specific.

Wilhelm Nicolaisen defends this assumption, deriving all the names from an Indo-European root meaning "flow," and therefore the equivalent of "stream." He would then attribute the naming, along with that of many other streams, to a stratum of so-called Old European, speakers of which spread over Great Britain about 1500 B.C., before the arrival of the Celts. (Unfortunately, and curiously, English scholars have ignored Nicolaisen's work, not even listing it in their bibliographies.)

The situation with Thames is thus similar to those of Kent and London. English scholars, traditionally, allow pre-Celtic derivation only as a kind of last resort, the admission being considered the symbol of a humiliating defeat.

The linguistic approach having thus ended in confusion, we may turn to archeology (see also Book IV, Chapter 2). Ordinarily, indeed, scholars of place-names shun that discipline—for the sound reason that names exist in language, an area in which archeology (for a pre-literate people) supplies no information. Here, however, we are investigating the probability of transmission from one language to another, and do not need even to know what the languages actually were. Moreover, we are concerned with successions of languages, and not with absolute dates.

To begin, then—and to omit many details—the first known inhabitants of what was later to be Britain were Paleolithic. A Mesolithic period followed, and two definite peoples, of differing cultures, emerged as Neolithic—the so-called Windmill Hill People (generally, western) and the Peterborough People (generally, eastern). In the Bronze Age two invaders made their appearance. The Beaker Folk overwhelmed the Windmill Hill People, and the Battle-ax People spread widely over the island, mingling both with the Beaker Folk and with the Peterborough People. Next in order, and only then, came the Celts.

By analogy with what is known historically in many parts of the world, we may assume that all of these peoples (no matter what their languages) used place-names. We may also assume a strong probability that each of these peoples passed some place-names along to its successors. We know that the Celts thus transmitted names to the Angles and Saxons, and that the same process has occurred in comparable situations all over the world and down through history—for instance, the European settlers in the New World, whatever language they spoke, readily adopted place-names from various Indian tribes.

Necessarily, then, our assumption must be that the Celts received place-names from their predecessors. Once these names entered the language they would become subject to the development of Celtic, and by analogy would tend to lose the characteristics of the earlier language—again to cite an American case, just as Orange in New Jersey is the adaptation of an Algonquian term.

Thus we are justified in making the conclusion (and would be unjustified in not making it) that the Celts took place-names from the Battle-ax People, and probably from the Beaker Folk also. Similarly it follows that these two peoples had previously taken names from the Wildmill Hill People and the Peterborough People. And there is even the ultimate possibility these Neolithic tribes had in their turn adopted Mesolithic and Paleolithic terms.

In the present state of research, no one has any knowledge of the languages of these Neolithic peoples—and, indeed, it is very likely that we shall never know anything. With the Beaker Folk there is at least the possibility of an Iberian connection. As for the Battle-ax People, there is much evidence that they spoke Old European, a non-Celtic but Indo-European language. Studied chiefly in its Continental manifestations, this language constitutes the upper layer of the sub-stratum over the Rhineland and part of central Europe.

A case that may be strongly argued is that of the many river-names based upon *ar-* (see Book III, Chapter 9). This element, on this hypothesis, is to be taken as from an Indo-European root meaning "to flow" and thus to be used as a generic for a stream. In Great Britain we find Ayr, Oare, Ore, and others.

Frustrating to Celticists have been the names, presumably from a single origin, to be seen in Wye and Wey, repeated in various parts of England. The Old European interpretation derives them from an Indo-European word for water, not existing in Celtic.

Most striking is the case of the various streams called Don, along with Doon, which plainly derive from the same term as the Danube and the Russian rivers, but a term that is lacking in Celtic.

At this point the argument may be brought to an end, since it seems only to be an elaborate exemplification of a thesis that can be accepted *a priori*.

If the case may be considered as established for the transfer of Old European names to Celtic, can the argument be carried further, to include, let us say, a transfer of Peterborough names to Old European? Such a word as "demonstrated" can scarcely be used in this connection, but one can at least suggest a "likelihood." Thus, even when the Anglo-Saxons arrived, the name-pattern of Britain was already complicated. The old conception was that pre–Anglo-Saxon names were Celtic, except for a few Latinisms. Certainly, however, a more accurate term would be "Celticized." Many of the names were probably derived from earlier and non-Celtic languages, but after some centuries of Celtic occupation these names had been fitted into Celtic speech and no longer seemed alien to its peakers. The process was the easier in that no writing existed to freeze the forms at an early stage of development.

Here, indeed, the American analogy breaks down. Indian names in the United States tend to persist in a kind of semiforeign state. Mississippi and Connecticut, though used daily by millions of speakers of English, still remain not quite English. If they had never been written down, they would almost certainly have been shortened to conform to English usage and they might well have been changed in other respects also.

The invading Angles and Saxons, however, were not etymologists. They took the names as they found them. What they heard, though we may propose "Celticized," was all Celtic to the Saxon who came ashore from the Thames estuary and to the Angle who steered up the Humber. And neither of them, we may be sure, was concerned that the names of both the rivers might go far back to vanished peoples.

I I

From Britain to England

The effects of conquest and occupation upon place-names are not to be easily epitomized, since they depend upon conditions, most of all upon whether the language shifted. The British in their two-century venture into India affected place-names scarcely at all. The Franks, overrunning Gaul, somewhat altered the pattern, but basically it remained the same. Spanish and English penetrations of the Americas gave rise to widely differing results. So also, the seizing of the former Roman province of Britain by the Angles and Saxons provides an individual story.

Aside from furnishing a good example of naming, that story is of some special interest, in that many of the names have attained world-wide fame because English explorers and colonists have disseminated them, either as commemoratives or as personal names and titles which were originally derived from place-names. Thus Boston, Salisbury, and many others are of global significance, though not large cities in the home-country.

In addition, the diligence of English scholars has provided excellent material for the uncovering of the story, even though actual records are scarce.

The first invaders landed about A.D. 450, and their descendants at the ninth or tenth generation completed the conquest about three centuries later—certainly not a *blitzkrieg* by modern standards. Somewhat more remarkable—and in the present context more interesting—is that the place-name pattern was, we may say, established by this time. The land was named. In spite of Danish and Norman invasions, and of some inevitable modernization, the hills, streams, and habitations still preserve, broadly speaking, the names which they already bore in 750—or, at least, by 1000.

Such an observation is not, indeed, wholly demonstrable by statistics, because of scanty documentation. One may point, however, to the hundreds of names in Domesday Book, compiled shortly after the Norman Conquest. Moreover, certain linguistic evidence exists.

For example, though *big* is one of the commonest of descriptive terms in the United States, it scarcely occurs among English place-names. The explanation is that *big* (probably a borrowing from the Scandinavian) came into the English language only in the Middle English period, after active place-naming had ceased.

The usage of *great* is similarly indicative. In the first centuries of the invasion period the term maintained its earlier meaning, "thick, coarse," and was not of much value as a topographical term. Gratton, "big hill," and Garston, "big rock," are not cited before 900. Such names as Greatford and Greatham arise from the related word *greot,* "gravel." On the other hand, the term is common in secondary usage, which is necessarily later, as with Great Grimsby.

The common adjective for size was *micel,* which is preserved in names such as Micklefield, Mickleton, and Michelmersh. Though maintained in specialized usage as *much,* this adjective lost its earlier meaning with the shifting of *great,* the introduction of *big,* and the still later introduction of *large.*

Linguistic evidence thus points to early namings which left little to succeeding centuries.

English scholars, minimally concerned with motivation, have failed to give much consideration as to whether the Anglo-Saxon namings sprang up by evolutionary process or were sometimes bestowed by conscious act. The latter possibility should not be neglected. Especially in times of rapid advance and of settlements in new country, the need for names would be immediate, so that a leader could resort to some such formula as, "I name this place!" Standing at the water's edge and seeing the great ash-tree near by, he could thus create the Ford of the Ash-tree—which, after a few repetitions, would be Ashford.

As of primary interest we must consider the Celtic background, that is, what the Angles and Saxons had for a beginning. We need not specify the Roman background, since it must have been already fused with the Celtic.

The careful work of Professor Kenneth Jackson has clearly demonstrated that the degree of Celtic influence varied with the stage of the conquest—Celtic names of rivers becoming thicker from east to west, and to some extent from south to north. Celtic names are thus lacking—or almost so—in the areas most exposed to attack from the eastern and southeastern seaboard. They are at a minimum in Sussex, Norfolk, Suffolk, and Lincolnshire. Geographically and from what little historical evidence is available, we may assume that these were the first areas to be conquered. We may also assume that the overrunning of this sizable area was fairly rapid. Otherwise a Celtic counterattack could have driven the invaders out of their beachhead, back to their ships. But why did the result mean fewer Celtic names?

Explanations are easy to supply, but without historical documentation they carry little authority. The American analogy is not close, but it does provide a generalization: place-names are chiefly adopted in regions where the speakers of the two languages mingle over a period of time in a somewhat friendly relationship. From the name-pattern we may, then, assume that the attack upon eastern Britain was violent, quickly consummated, and even bloodthirsty. The Romanized Britons, having recently lost the protection of the legions, were ill prepared. Besides, they had plenty of land into which to retreat, and it was a hillier and more defensible region.

The entry for 491 in the Anglo-Saxon Chronicle has its implication for names:

> This year Aella and Cissa besieged Andredscester, and slew
> all that lived within, so that not a single Briton was left there.

Under such conditions we can expect a minimum of transfer of place-names, and cannot be surprised that the name disappeared completely as that of a town, though preserved in Andred Forest, on the borders of Sussex and Kent.

After a generation or two, however, the Britons would have learned to fight better, and this stern deed of the South Saxons was not easily repeatable. With an alternation of victory and defeat there would have been enough intermingling, for one purpose or another, to break down the language barrier to some degree. Celtic-named streams are numerous or even predominating in the later-conquered regions, such as Devon, the Severn valley, and the far northwest.

Among the invaders these names must have been just names, without meaning, all to be considered simply British, though some of them might contain Roman elements and others might even be pre-Celtic. As happens universally in such situations, generics in the earlier language passed over into the later language as specifics, so that Avon, "river," exists on at least five individual streams. From a Celtic root meaning "water" sprang a family of rivers—Exe, Axe, Esk. Other names passed over as serviceable specifics—Thames, Trent, Severn—with no one caring to what language these should eventually be credited or what meaning they bore.

The invaders also picked up names for other natural features, such as landmark hills. One of these is the Wrekin, dominating the upper Severn valley, a name known in Latin form as Viroconium but deriving from Celtic (and possibly from an earlier language) and of unknown meaning. Other Celtic-derived names are Barr, "summit," Bray, "hill," and Creech, "hill, mound." When later coupled with an Anglo-Saxon generic they became tautological, as with Penhill. In Pendleton and Pendle Hill, the Penhill first wore down to Pendle, so that the final form is literally "hill-hill-hill."

Highly interesting is the preservation of town-names. Little is known of what actually happened. In some instances the invaders may have occupied the town and lived there. Often, we should think—especially in the first hurlyburly of the conquest—they sacked and burned. Even so, the pattern of streets and the piles of stone and brick would have continued to mark the site and to make a name applicable. To such ruins the invaders applied the term *ceaster,* thus taking over the Latin *castra,* "camp," though many of these sites were towns, not camps, and were not so named by either Romans or Britons. (See Book III, Chapter 7.)

In addition, the invaders adopted some names for towns without resorting to *ceaster,* as with London and York.

As a result, a considerable number of the older and more historic English cities go back to a Celtic form, and so do most of the names for the larger rivers and a scattering of others—especially in the western counties.

We can only assume that many of these borrowed Celtic names have vanished wholly because of absorption into Anglo-Saxon forms. The Celtic *mawr,* "big," would commonly become *mor* and be indistinguishable from the word for *moor.* Thus the repeated Morden can naturally be derived from Anglo-Saxon "moor-hill," but its first syllable could actually be Celtic. An even better case can be made for Monmore, which is derived from the Anglo-Saxon *mere,* "lake," only on the basis of a thirteenth-century spelling.

From early documents (Domesday Book, especially) and from the still-preserved names themselves, some generalizations are possible as to the actual naming by Angles and Saxons.

Like all peoples, they frequently used simple descriptives—long, little, broad, high, low, loud, salty, sandy, rocky. Fulford and many other names use the adjective that in modern times has become *foul,* but then usually meant "muddy." The common color-descriptives were *black, white,* and *red.* Though the landscape in general could be characterized as green, a few features apparently stood out for that special quality—as with Greenoak, Greenford, and Greenwich. Blue and yellow are rare, but *fealu* (still preserved for fallow deer) served to denote a kind of reddish yellow. Thus we have Fallowdon in Northumberland, but lack certainty as to whether the name of the hill refers to flowers, to dead grass, or to some moorland growth.

Relative descriptives are common, and this commonness (leading to great repetition) is significant as probably indicating rapid expansion and a pressure for naming. Under such conditions the namers make use of the already existing name as a point of reference, even if they do not repeat it. Common among such names is *new*. Newton is probably the commonest English habitation-name. In other combinations the term exists in many modern towns, some of them to be dated later than the Anglo-Saxon period—Newbury, Newmarket, Newcastle, Newark, the last being "new work," probably in the sense of "fort."

Anglo-Saxon namers pressed into heavy service the points of direction, chiefly as the often-repeated Norton, Easton, Sutton, and Weston. All of these were doubtless plain enough to the namers, but with changed modern conditions one is sometimes forced to wonder, "North (or east, or south, or west) of *what?*"

Also frequent as relative descriptives are Upper (Upton), Lower (Netherhampton), and the very common Middle (Middlesex, Middleton—the last often becoming Milton and thus difficult to distinguish from the also common Mill).

Numeral and alphabetical arrangements are not to be expected among a largely illiterate people, unschooled in arithmetic. The few numerals are likely to occur in connection with the measurement of land, as with Fifehead, "five hides," a hide being considered a minimal holding for a free family.

The Anglo-Saxon descriptives are commonly simple—sensory or relative. A few subjective names show, however, a people not wholly lacking in esthetic sense. Commonest is *faeger,* "beautiful," which has become Fair in modern English—sometimes, unfortunately, confused with words for pig and fern. (See Book I, Chapter 7.)

Yet another esthetic element is *scir,* which ordinarily means "shire" or "district," but also "clear" or "bright"—appearing as the repeated Sherburn, "clear brook."

Thus, like other peoples, the Anglo-Saxons chiefly employed

a small number of commonplace descriptives, but an occasional one is unusual enough to offer difficulties, as with the name of Liverpool. The generic *pool* is natural for a settlement on a tidal stream. Long considered uncertain, the specific has latterly been referred to an Anglo-Saxon term meaning "coagulated, clotted," and sometimes applied to bodies of water. Unfortunately, the scholars seem to have rested content with a phonetic solution, not attempting to explain just what a clotted pool might be. A muddy one? Or one that is choked with slimy algae?

Many names sprang up, also, over the course of the centuries, by association. One of the interesting ones is *mill*, though allowance must be made for some confusion with *middle*. The water-mill for grinding grain, a basic labor-saving device, was developed toward the end of the Roman Empire. The invaders probably found some mills in operation, and they took the idea over. Five thousand of them are listed in Domesday Book. Naturally, the existence of a mill—especially in times before they had become common—served to identify a place. So the term exists with many different generics—Milburn, Milford, Millbrook, Milstead, Milton.

Associations with trees and other manifestations of the vegetable kingdom produced an enormous number of names, with great repetition. The common Bentley derives from the type of grass. A growth of ferns often served for identification, the term appearing variously as Fernhurst, Farnham, Fairbourne, Farley.

On actual trees, Kipling is apparently right in labeling oak, ash, and thorn as typically English. But other trees also served for names. The elm gave Elmley, Elmham, Olmstead. Though the spruce was not a common tree, we have Sapley. The yew yielded the obvious Yewdale. The beech lies behind Beechburn, Beckwith, and the ambiguous Bitchfield. In the absence of historical record much doubt may arise, as in confusion between the words for alder and elder, and even elm. The linden tree gave its name to many settlements known as Linton and Linford, but also to be considered in such names is the possibility of derivation from *hlyn*, "maple." On the other hand, *maple* itself appears in numerous names, such as Maplestead and Maperton.

The use of *tree* itself as a specific is rare—obviously because most of England was forested, so that the existence of trees was not a distinguishing quality of any particular place. Treeton in Yorkshire must have been in moorland, where trees were distinctive.

Not infrequently, however, a term meaning "tree" occurs in combination, as with Appledore or Mapledurham. Presumably such places were named for a single tree which was notable for its size or for some other quality.

Like relative descriptives, association-names tend to be a labor-saving device. If a tree gives its name to a stream, the ford and the settlement easily take the same specific, so that one name soon does the work of three. Such situations were common in early England.

Of all the methods of creating names, the Anglo-Saxons are most notable for the predominance of the possessive. One feels a desire to equate this situation with the sense of stability and of permanent property which we like to consider typical of England throughout the ages. Possibly, however, it arose from the long-drawn conditions of the conquest, when a man held his homestead essentially by the strength of his arm and the question as to who owned what (or claimed it) was paramount.

The coinage of names from ownership begins at the level of what may be termed nations or kingdoms. At least three counties—Kent, Essex, and Sussex—take their names from the holdings of the kingdoms of the so-called Heptarchy. East Anglia, preserved as a district-name, was another such kingdom.

Below the status of the kingdoms were the tribal units. The Hastings held lands in Sussex and Kent which were almost the equivalent of a kingdom, and might well have so developed. Their chief town still bears their name. The names of several counties are from tribal units. Norfolk and Suffolk arose from the northern and southern people, the two divisions of the East Anglians. Somerset and Dorset are from Sumortunsaete and Dornsaete, that is, the people who were "seated" around the towns, respectively, of Somerton and Dorchester. Devon and Cornwall bear names of British tribes whom the Saxons overran late in the conquest. Westmorland is for the Westmoringas, "western moor people."

Other tribes, important in their day, faded out and left little record. Such a one was that of the Hwicce, which at one time held much territory in the lower Severn valley. Some unregarded names commemorate their possession—Whichford, Wychwood, and a handful of others.

Just as the kingdom fades into the tribe, so the tribe fades, indistinguishably, into a unit which we might call a sub-tribe, or a war-band, or perhaps an extended family. Typically, these units bore not a geographical designation, but a personal one.

Thus we have the large city of Birmingham, though its name is not actually recorded until it appears in Domesday Book. Linguistic analysis, however, shows a very common Anglo-Saxon development. Its first part is from a personal name, which would probably have been spelled Beorma, if anyone had had occasion to write it down. Next comes -ing-, indicating the people associated with Beorma. Finally -ham, a term related to *home* and *hamlet,* means a dwelling-place.

Unfortunately, in most instances, we can go no further. The scanty records preserve nothing about a chieftain called Beorma, or about most of the hundreds of others who have thus left their names. The -ing- may indicate a good-sized tribe, as with the Hastings. Or it may go back to some petty warlord who beached his ship on the sand of the Channel or the North Sea, routed the local Britons, seized a little land, and left his name on Sheringham or Gillingham. By American analogy, we should suspect that the term sometimes was little more than a family name, with Birmingham, for instance, having first meant the place where Beorma maintained his family, perhaps "extended" by a younger brother, two half-grown sons, and a British thrall, along with a quota of women, children, and old men.

Inevitably, therefore, the study of these early English possessives—and even of Anglo-Saxon place-names altogether—degenerates into a study of generics. Thus we may discuss whether-*ingham* is characteristic of the early stages of the Conquest, in what instances -*ham* is really from *hamm,* "river-meadow," and what degree of fortification (if any) is implied in *tun* or *ton* and in *burg* or *bury.* Or what is the significance of "clipped" names like Hastings and Reading?

In a few instances the actual eponym is known from the record. Thus Cissa, who took Andredscester, is mentioned in the Anglo-Saxon Chronicle as a son of the king of the South Saxons. One can reasonably assume, therefore, that his name would be associated with a place on the Sussex coast, and such a name appears in 895 as Cisseceastre, now Chichester. Still, we have no clear idea of why he was connected with this particular site. Did he defeat the Britons there? Did he live there? Was he killed there? Was it a kind of feudal holding? Did he, in some sense, refound it?

Bamborough, on the northern coast, is of special interest. The original castle is recorded as having been built by King Ida in 547. But in the next generation it took its name from Queen Bebbe. Again we do not know why. Most likely it was a special holding granted to the queen, and she probably lived there, at least for a part of the year. Its special interest lies in the fact that it supplies further evidence of the good status of women among the Anglo-Saxons. Many other names can be recognized as those of women, even though the individuals are not known.

These numerous possessives are thus more useful for the study of the personal names than for the study of place-names. Nevertheless, the position that they hold in the English name-pattern may almost be called overwhelming. Though not of such importance in the great names, they predominate among names for villages and small towns, and for the thousands of natural features, either so labeled directly, or secondarily from habitation-names.

By the occasional luck of history, some of these possessives are written large on modern maps—ironically, to commemorate some otherwise unknown person. Thus Nottingham (city and shire) is from Snot, from whose name the Normans happily dropped the *s.* Similarly, among shires, we have Buckingham (Bucca), and Rutland (Rota).

In their way, as names more insubstantial than ghosts, they

still exist—the ones who took the land, narrow or wide, and held it, and assured that their names at least would stand. We salute you, though we do not know you—Beorma, Snot, Rota, Cuca, Bucca, Gylla, and those others.

Since the giving of names from incidents seems to be a universal human habit, we must assume that the Anglo-Saxons thus recorded unusual happenings. The difficulty is that the dearth of detailed documents makes impossible their sure identification. Moreover, English scholars have hardly recognized the category, and even go to extreme trouble to offer other explanations. In addition, shifts of the language over the centuries tend to obscure unusual names, such as those based upon incident usually are. Nonetheless, with all such allowances, the evidence of incident-names remains scanty, and we should perhaps conclude that the Anglo-Saxons were not actually much given to such naming.

American analogy, however, would suggest that many of the personal names did not spring from ownership or residence, but arose from an incident in which a person figured—most commonly, his death. If, for instance, a man imprudently tried a ford during high water and was swept away, his loss might be remembered and his name be fixed to the spot.

One clear case of the sort occurs with the Hampshire village of Charford. It happens to be recorded in the Anglo-Saxon Chronicle as of the year 508 in the form Cerdicesford, and the text states that the name arose from that of Cerdic, king of the West Saxons, who won a battle here. We should find names by the hundred to place with Charford, if diaries and reminiscences were available for early England on the scale that they are for many parts of the United States.

Names taken from those of wild animals very commonly arise from notable encounters, and are therefore to be classed as incident-names. Netherfield, on its face, suggests merely "lower field," but the early forms speak for a derivation from naeddre, "adder," the only poisonous snake of Britain. Ekwall merely notes that the place was "infested by adders." Much more likely the name marks a place where some unfortunate person had an encounter with an adder, was bitten, and remembered the spot accordingly. Or, if he died, his family and friends would remember it.

Names from the wolf, such as Woolley and Woolmer, may have arisen in the same fashion. Names from the otter, which are common, probably sprang up in the same way. Ottershaw, "otter-wood," is an interesting one. Since otters are not normally found in woods, the appearance of one there might have induced the name.

Any unusual event, whether natural or man-made, is likely to produce a name. We may again evoke American analogy. In 1906, we have record, a certain R. S. Shelley was caught in a violent thunderstorm and so gave the name Thunder Rock in Oregon. In England *thunder* is regularly set down as a pagan vestige, a naming for the god Thor. Obviously, it might also be where some Angle or Saxon was caught, like Mr. Shelley, in a bad storm.

Having attained a linguistic solution, English place-name scholars often merely drop the subject. The modern Maidenhead may be cited. It goes back to Maydenhythe, "maidens' landing-place"—"maiden" being a term that had nothing poetic about it for an Anglo-Saxon, but meant merely "girl, young woman." But why, then, should they have a special landing-place? The suggestion is that some particular and striking event (perhaps a drowning) resulted in the name. Maidwell and Maidford could have arisen similarly.

Comparable are names from *child,* such as Childwall, "children's stream," for which Ekwall can only suggest that the reason is obscure, and Cameron supposes that children might have played there. But one may cite the analogy of Boy Lake in Minnesota, a translation of the Ojibway name, given because three boys were killed there by a Sioux war-party about 1765. The Anglo-Saxons might thus have remembered a loss of children or some other incident involving them. (The derivation may also be, in some instances, from a word meaning "prince, young nobleman.")

Though we know little in detail, the Anglo-Saxons for the most part lived in agricultural villages. Except along frontiers, they doubtless lived peaceably. Crime, therefore, would have been notable, and the spot where a striking robbery or murder took place would be remembered. Morpeth, thus, is "murder-path." Many other names begin with *mor-*. These are most commonly given the meaning "moor," but might have arisen from murders—Morestead, "murder-place," being a distinct possibility.

Dethick, according to Ekwall's somewhat tentative rendering, is "death-oak," explainable as a tree from which criminals were hanged. Again we note the tradition of explaining all such names as repetitive descriptives. Actually, a single hanging at that place could have produced the name.

Like murder, robbery is impressive, and several names, such as Satterleigh, seem to present the word *saetere,* "robber."

Unfortunately, in the history of most tribes, battles are common. The Anglo-Saxon Chronicle indicates that the invaders of Britain spent much energy in fighting, both with the Britons and among themselves. We should therefore expect *beadu* to occur in place-names, just as *battle* is common in the United States. Actually, many names begin with *bed-*, but scholars have referred these to the list of possessives, as deriving from the man's name, Beda or Beada. With such a name as Beddington we can accept that derivation because of the presence of *-ing-*, which is regularly coupled with personal names. But we also have names Bedburn, and Bedwell, as equivalents of the repeated American name Battle Creek. The list of names thus beginning is so long that either we must refer some of them to *beadu* or accept Beda as an uncommonly popular name.

One important name, that of the city and shire of Bedford, is here involved. Its earliest form is Bedanford, and has aroused controversy. The historians and archeologists refer it to Bedcanforda, mentioned in the Chronicle as the site of a great victory of the West Saxons over the Britons in 571. The linguists raise objections on phonetic grounds, and call for a personal name, though admitting that such a one on an important ford is unusual. But battles for strategic fords were doubtless fought in many years besides 571. May not Bedford be another naming for a battle?

By and large, however, naming from incidents does not seem
to have been common Anglo-Saxon custom.

Equally striking is the failure to give names that are primarily
commemorative or commendatory. The many possessive names
are apparently those of minor chieftains or landholders, given
merely because he held that land. Namings after kings do not
seem to figure greatly. Even more surprising is the paucity of
religious namings.

Presumably many namings after Wotan, Thor, and the other
ancient gods were suppressed after the conversion to Christianity. If so, however, they were not replaced by saints' names.

The situation, in fact, is remarkable. On the west, the Celts
regularly used saints' names. Across the Channel in France,
such names are thick upon the land. But the English, although
in those times as good Catholics as the others, did not commonly use Saint.

Most such names are a mere transfer to the village of the
name of the saint to whom the local church was dedicated. But
a church is not usually established until people are already
there and the place is already named. In France we can only
imagine that hundreds or thousands of early names must at
some point have lapsed to accommodate another St. Martin or
St. Denis. In England it simply did not happen. Something in
the English social situation prevented it, and perhaps we cannot
do better than to put it down to some traditional English conservatism and solidity. The village just went on being Ashford
or Addingham, though the church might be dedicated to St.
Anselm or St. Dunstan.

The exceptions are explicable as special cases. St. Albans, for
instance, grew up under the shadow of a great abbey which
marked the site of the death of the British hero Alban, who, by
tradition, suffered martyrdom in 209. Most of the English
names of this kind are actually in one county, Cornwall, which
long remained Celtic in language and culture. Similarly, Oswes-
try, "Oswald's cross," is on the Welsh border and may be the
result of Celtic influence. It commemorates, by old tradition,

King Oswald of Northumbria, a Christian, who met his death in the year 641 in battle with the pagan King Penda of Mercia.

The far-spread name of Boston offers a curious case. Again by strong tradition, the name is from a certain Botulf, who gained sainthood. The latter part of the name is the Anglo-Saxon *stan*, "stone," indicating a place at which Botulf preached, or at which he lived, or some other association. In France, we can be certain, such a name would have become St. Botulf. But in England the man was remembered, but not his sainthood.

Incidentally, this procedure resulted in modern greatness. The Massachusetts General Court, bestowing names in 1630, would not have propagated a saint's name, and, apparently in ignorance of its origin, chose Boston.

A question (interesting, but not as yet answerable) arises from the possibility that the invaders used actual place-names for commemorative ends. Such practice may be seen with primitive tribes, such as the Polynesians and some of the American Indians. The name of a continental village may thus have been carried across in the memories of the invaders, and replanted in the new island home. So also, a name existing on the eastern coast may re-occur farther west. Since this practice was so extremely common with the settlers of the English colonies in America, we cannot rule out the possibility that their ancestors behaved similarly.

The whole complexity of the workings of folk-etymology must have affected the situation, not only in the adaptation of Celtic names, but also in the transformation, by the later English, of the names given by their ancestors a few generations back. Unfortunately, the record is often doubtful as to whether the shift occurred in the Anglo-Saxon period or later. Thus Arrow seems a lovely name for a stream, and it occurs twice in England. In each case, however, it goes back to a Celtic original, transformed by folk-etymology.

Closely associated with folk-etymology is the process of so-called back-formation, which seems to have been especially propagated by English scholars. Thus Romford, probably "broad ford," was taken to mean a ford across a certain stream, and that stream came to be called the Rom. In the same way Thetford, probably "chief ford," created the river Thet.

During the later centuries of the Anglo-Saxon domination the population increased, more land was cleared, and some additions must have been made to the name-pattern. Probably to this period may be ascribed the numerous relative descriptives, such as Newton and Easton.

Even an Anglophobe, however, should be willing to admit that the invaders did a thorough piece of work in a comparatively short period. They borrowed moderately from the Celto-Roman past, but, on the whole, they placed their own names, and thus created a name-pattern which has endured.

12
The Arabs

Partly in a great expansion by conquest, partly through the development of trade-routes during many centuries, the Arabs left names upon a large part of Africa and upon some not inconsiderable areas of Asia and Europe. Their language being Semitic, their names are in some cases difficult to distinguish from those of the earlier Phoenicians and Carthaginians.

Arabia itself (Semitic, with a Latin ending) is from a word which is translated in the King James Bible as "wilderness." This archaic term is to be taken in the sense of "uninhabited region," and the equivalent of the word *desert* in the old sense of being deserted. To the ancient Israelites, Arabia was the vast region lying to their east and south, a dry and empty land of wandering tribes who took their own name from that of the place, and came to be known as Arabs.

Mecca, the center of the Arab world, is of uncertain origin, though attempts have been made to connect it with a Semitic term for "ruin." Semantically, such an origin would yield a likely enough supposition, that the city had once been destroyed and had lain in ruins for a while before being resettled.

By contrast, the second holy site has an utterly commonplace name, Medina being nothing other than "city."

Spreading their speech along with conquest and trade, the

Arabs planted many great names. Cairo is proudly "victorious," so called particularly with astrological reference to the victorious planet Mars. Farther up the Nile, the Sudan is literally "the blacks," a shortening of an earlier "land of the blacks." Its capital, Khartoum, is "the snout," with reference to the narrow spit of land on which the city is built, between the two branches of the Nile.

One of the most extensive of place-names, Sahara, is also a simple descriptive, like Arabia itself translatable as "wilderness" or "wasteland."

Advancing across the Sahara and beyond it into central Africa, the Arabs placed some much-repeated generics to mark their progress—Bahr, "water in all its applications," Jebel, "mountain," Dar, "land, region, house," Wadi, "watercourse, river," Ras, "point, cape," Aïn, "spring, well." Occurring often enough to rate as a quasi-generic, Seid or Sidi marks a site where a descendant of the Prophet was the chief of some settlement; it is a title of respect, to be translated as Sir, or Lord.

Taking to the sea like their Semitic kinsmen the Phoenicians, the Arabic traders left names along the eastern coast of Africa, almost to the Cape. Dar-es-Salaam is "house of peace." Zanzibar, like Sudan, means merely "blacks," again, a shortening of "land of the blacks." Sofalá is "lowland."

Since these early voyagers generally hugged the coast, they depended upon prominent headlands as landmarks. So we still find the often-repeated Ras not only on the African shoreline, but far to the east, upon the coast extending to India.

As would be expected, Arabic names are common in the homeland peninsula. Yemen is an interesting point-of-view name, being derived from the word for right-hand, its location with reference to Mecca, for a man looking to the east. Bahrein is "two seas," probably arising from the fact that the island stands in the middle of a gulf with, so to speak, a sea on either side of it.

Not on the peninsula, but still within the Arabic world, the nation of Iraq takes its name from its lowlying alluvial plain, offering a fair equivalent of the Netherlands.

The miraculous Arabic expansion also pushed to the west. At a point on the African coast four small islands lay just off the shore, and the site took the simple name "the islands." Eventually, in English, this yielded Algiers. When it became a city and a capital it extended its name to all Algeria—following the often-repeated process by which political chance shifts small names into large ones.

In Spain and Portugal the Arabs exercised sovereignty, over much of the area, for a period of seven centuries. They conquered a land which was already complexly named—by Visigoths and Romans, by Phoenicians, Carthaginians, and Greeks, by Celts, Iberians—perhaps by even more ancient peoples. Nonetheless, the Arabs left their still-continuing marks, in such a way as to indicate the solidity of their occupation.

A test of thoroughness is the name-pattern of the larger rivers, which in most regions maintain their more ancient names. In the peninsula, however, the element *guad-*, occurring upon more than a score of streams, is the rendering of the Arabic word for river, and thus originally a generic. The Arabs used it commonly with the article *al* followed by a simple descriptive specific, so that we have Guadalquiver, "big," Guadalajara, "stony," Guadalcanal, "of the canal," Guadarrama, "sandy." Guadalupe—like Guadalajara, to become more famous in Mexico—is commonly translated as "wolf river" and is thus a hybrid. To avoid the anomaly, a derivation from an Arabic "gravel" has been suggested. In such situations, however, hybrids are not uncommon. An undoubted case is Guadiana. In *-ana* it preserves an ancient term of unknown meaning, attested from Greek sources.

As is only to be expected, the Arabic influence worked both (as we may put it) at the linguistic and at the onomastic level. Certain words, by pure linguistic process, passed into Spanish and Portuguese as common nouns—for instance, *aldea, aldeia,* "village." It may, therefore, represent a naming by Arabs or a naming by people who were not speaking Arabic at all. Northern Portugal is spotted with Aldeia, but the name probably dates from after the reconquest.

Commonest of all the Arabic name-elements is *al*, the definite article, as we have it in the repeated Alcázar, "the palace"— another hybrid, since the latter part is from Latin *castra*, "camp." It appears in Alhama, "the hot-bath," Alhambra, "the red," Almadén, "the cities," Almería, "the watch-tower," Algarve, "the West," Alburquerque, "the cork-oak," Algeciras, "the island, peninsula." Alicante, however, represents only a false analogy on the part of the Arabs, folk-etymology working upon the Latin name Lucentum. (See Book III, Chapter 4.)

Like the Normans in England, the Arabs raised many castles to protect their conquests, and their word survives as *cala*. The repeated Alcalá is thus merely "the castle." Not infrequently the name was formed from that of the chieftain who was the builder and possessor, as with Calatayud, "castle of Ayyub," and Calatrava, "castle of Rabah." Calahorra, however, is a plain case of coincidence, being from Basque, "house-red."

Portugal itself may contain this Arabic term. Its first element is obviously from the Latin, *portus*, with reference to the harbor at the mouth of the Duero. The whole could therefore be "port-castle," one of the hybrid constructions. At least, Portus Cale could easily evolve into Portugal.

The common term for mountain exists rarely, but appears in Gibraltar, (Geb-al-Tarik), for the leader of the Moslem invaders who entered Spain at this point, either in commemoration of his feat or because he later built a castle here.

Another famous coastal feature is Trafalgar, "cape-white" (or "shining"). As a commemorative of the battle, the name has become world-wide—three examples existing in Australia alone.

In general, the Arabic names are thus descriptives or possessives. To the list may be added Valladolid, "city of Walid," the repeated Medina, merely "city," La Mancha, "the high plain." Out of the ordinary run is Murcia, which is apparently to be rendered as "the firmly founded," and thus a commendatory.

Any full study of naming by the Arabs would have to exceed the range of this presentation. Far to the east, in present Pakistan, the familiar Kalat indicates the presence of another castle. On even more distant horizons we can recognize, in addition to Trafalgar, the household word Gibraltar and the literary echo La Mancha.

13
Ab Tabula Rasa

In the history of place-naming the ordinary situation is that the existing name-pattern is linguistically stratified. Only for a few areas of the world do we have record of a people entering and occupying (and therefore naming) a whole land which was uninhabited (and therefore nameless) at the time of the entrance of the colonizers.

As might be supposed, these areas are usually islands, and two notable and interesting examples may be put forward—Iceland, and New Zealand before the British occupation.

Actually, the two have much in common. Iceland is about the same size as the North Island of New Zealand, where the Maoris made their first and chief settlements. Iceland was settled (by traditional date) in 874, and the Maoris arrived in New Zealand about the same time. Immigration from the respective homelands continued for some centuries. Both peoples were warlike and, lacking "native" opponents, fought among themselves. Both peoples were religious, and—partly by myth, partly by oral narrative—both displayed literary ability.

Most important, both peoples tenaciously preserved their traditions. We therefore can know something of the ways in which they named the nameless land. These records are preserved. For Iceland, there is that remarkable early compilation called the *Landnámabók*. For New Zealand, British observers set down many details not too long after the occupation.

The objection may be raised that these orally transmitted stories are folk-tales, not authentic records. All we can retort is that many of the tales (especially the Icelandic) have the ring of veracity. Moreover, the truth or untruth about a particular name is no more important than the general attitude of a people toward names, since the individual names, *en masse*, will be determined by the attitude.

When the Scandinavians began to make voyages to a large western island, its only inhabitants were a few Irish hermits, and they quickly abandoned the land to the newcomers, leaving behind, apparently, not a trace in the place-names. The situation approaches a kind of scientific purity, by the elimination of one factor of uncertainty. The name-pattern is the result of a natural environment subjected to naming by a people of a single culture and language who were influenced by some historical events.

A comparison with England is interesting. The cultures of the Anglo-Saxons and the westward voyaging Scandinavians—including their naming-traditions—were similar. The Scandinavians in Iceland, however, encountered nothing that corresponded to the Romano-Celtic background, nor did they have to deal with the accompanying military resistance. Moreover, the environment was startlingly different.

The British danger kept the Anglo-Saxons concentrated behind some kind of frontier line, while the Scandinavians could settle anywhere. They took over a land that was rich in birds, but almost devoid of trees and mammals.

The Anglo-Saxons, by being concentrated, could learn to distinguish small differences, and they gave many descriptive and associative names. The Scandinavians, moving freely and widely, would have found the numerous streams and hills much alike. Such words as *clear* and *swift, bare* and *high* could not serve for many distinctions. The absence of trees removed one of the readiest means of naming.

Nonetheless, descriptive and associative names are so basic

that they always occur. We find such common terms as *dark,*
white, red. Lacking terms for trees, the settlers placed the name
Dandelion Fields. Knarrdale makes use of a general term for
brush, not of a specific plant, either because the growth was
mixed or because the settlers had not learned specific names
for bushes which were of little use or interest. Hecla, the greatest mountain, was so called from the "hood" that usually covered its summit, whether of cloud or smoke.

The settlers would have noted particularly the details in
which the environment seemed strange—especially volcanic
and geothermal activity. The capital itself eventually bore the
name Reykjavik, "smoky bay," probably because of volcanic activity, though smoke and mist are sometimes confused. In Iceland, more commonly than in England, "warm" supplies a
name to a stream, and "hot" and "cold" appear as counterparts.

With the suggestion of an esthetic appreciation of the natural
scene, some subjective namings appear, chiefly presenting the
generalized descriptive, "fair, beautiful."

Even names that may at first be classed as descriptives can
turn out to be questionable. Salmon River, for instance, seems
to indicate a stream that teemed with salmon. But those fish
frequented nearly all of the streams, and the question thus
arises, why did this particular one take the name? Most likely
the namers came to it at a moment during the height of the
run, when the fish were leaping everywhere, conspicuous and
easily caught. If the encounter had occurred at some other
season, the name would not have been apt. Or it may commemorate the taking of some notable fish there. From the name itself, there is no reason to suppose this stream more salmon-
populated than the ones near it.

The name of the whole island arose by pseudo-description,
as the actual tradition makes manifest. The men of the third
voyage, under Flocki, climbed a high mountain, and from it
saw a part of the open sea covered with flowing ice. They had
never seen such a sight before. They thus gave the name Iceland—a distinctive name, not descriptive of other regions which
the Scandinavians then frequented. Moreover, the very inhospitality of the name may be called anti-commendatory.

Those who took and named the island preferred, possibly, to have plenty of land for themselves, not to encourage immigration by a pleasant name, such as a salesman might coin. On account of the Gulf Stream, ice is not a notable feature of the island or its adjacent waters, but the name stuck tightly, being catchy if not actually descriptive.

The Icelandic unit of settlement, and therefore of habitation-naming, was a family, under a single male leader. Since there were no hostile natives, the settlers had no pressing need to organize by larger family groups or by tribes. Therefore, the chief entity for naming—as it was already in the Scandinavian homeland—was what is usually called a farm. (An American might find the term "ranch" more fitting, since the holdings were isolated and large, and the people's livelihood was based upon sheep and cattle, pastured on a "range.")

The name of the owner thus soon fixed itself upon the place—as naturally as it did with the settlements of early England and with the post offices across the United States. The commonest suffix was -*sted,* "place." Lacking family names, the Icelanders had to allow for name-changes as the ownership shifted from father to son. The name of the first settler did not in all cases become the fixed one. Nevertheless, possessive naming was the rule.

To illustrate, we read of Hrani who lived at Hranisted, and of Stafn Grimm at Stafngrimsted. But, of the latter, the note follows in the *Landnámabók* that it is now called Sigmundsted. The family relationship may be clearly stated, as when we learn of Raud who lived at Raudsgill and his sons—Ulf at Ulfsted and Aud at Audsted.

Incident-names are common all over the island. When we read that certain men met in Fightdale and fought there, we need not look further for the origin of the name, even though we may grant the fact that the name was presumably applied after the fight and not before it. Or, again, there is Battledale, where Onund and three of his men were killed, and one of Gunnar's men. (We here merely give the translations.)

Other names arose from peaceable incidents, though they

might be fatal, even so. Einer, being drowned along the shore, left his name on Einer's Skerry. His wooden shield and his cloak floated in, and places were called Shield Island and Cloak Island.

Also drifting ashore, on one occasion, was a gigantic spruce-tree which must have floated with the Gulf Stream from some American forest. Afterwards the islanders knew the place as Spruce Cape, though no such trees had ever grown there. (The implication is that these people recognized a spruce-tree from knowledge that they had before arriving in Iceland.)

The Icelandic animal-names (both for the rare wild animals and for the numerous domestic ones) arose largely from incident. Flymoor is for Fly, a notable fast horse, who was caught in a bog there and died. A certain Ingimund lost ten swine, but found them after several months; he knew the spot where he retrieved them as Swinedale. Where a boar named Beigad died, the place became Beigarsknwoll.

This Ingimund came upon a white bear, such as drifted in occasionally on the ice. She had two cubs with her, and so the place became Bear-cub Water.

When some men lost an ax at a certain stream, it was known as Ax River—a kind of naming which may be paralleled across America.

Illustrative examples could be multiplied. Gösta Franzen, in his study of Laxdaela names, comments upon the "strikingly large number of names" that have arisen from the misfortune of people or animals. In that lonely and rugged country they smothered in bogs or drowned at river crossings or froze in the winter storms.

Some incidents yielded names without being specific. A small stream with a name that may be translated as "mischief" suggests a definite happening, and may be compared to the repeated Troublesome Creek in the United States. Charming in its implications is Delightdale, but there is no means of telling whether it springs from a particular incident or is a generalized subjective-descriptive.

Developed wholly within one language, the name-pattern of Iceland is a simple one. Even within that language, the motivations of the namers were few. Thus, no commendatory names seem to have been brought from the homeland, and only a few may be called religious dedications. About equally, the names seem to have sprung from description, from possession, and from incident.

The Maoris—like the Icelanders, being offered the blank sheet of an unnamed land—solved their problem somewhat differently. Their name-pattern arose by description, incident, and commemoration.

Negatively speaking, the most striking feature of the Maori pattern is the absence of possessives. It is thus in sharp contrast with the Icelandic, and, indeed, with the systems of many cultures. As with most situations in name-study, reasons are easy enough to suggest, but difficult to demonstrate or to prove.

We cannot defend the proposition that the Maoris, as with many primitive societies, had failed to conceive of the human ownership of land. On the contrary, that conception was basic to their thought, and was reinforced by religious sanctions. Ownership, indeed, was based not upon the individual, but upon the tribe and the chief. In that case, however, we should expect names from the tribes or the chiefs, like the Anglo-Saxon names ending in *-ing*. One of these, actually, can be held to persist in Taranaki, which may be "mountain-people." In general, however, tribal boundaries shifted constantly, because of wars. The names thus would have applied to the tribes rather than to the fixed area, a common situation.

As for the villages, these seem merely to have assumed the appellations of the natural features at which they were built. To the Maoris, apparently, the stream or hill was the real "place," and the village was merely something that men happened to construct there. Accordingly, the word *pa*, "village, fortification," seldom appears as a generic, and is even then generally used under British influence.

This conception is the opposite of the one which has been traditionally current in European place-name study—that is, that the habitation is really the "place." Of the two conceptions, that of the Maoris seems the more primitive, and also the more logical.

In any case, the absence of possessives is striking. A few may

be so classed, such as Waerenga-a-Hika, "clearing of Hika."
Even this one, however, may be an incident-name, indicating
not his ownership, but something that happened to Hika at that
place—or it may be a name of the British regime.

Descriptive names are extremely common—much more so,
indeed, than in Iceland. Also, they offer much greater variety.

Two causes were certainly at work. First, the Icelanders lived
on their sheep and cattle, and were thus in some degree removed from nature. The Maoris, though they practiced some
agriculture, were largely hunters and gatherers, and so necessarily were minute observers of nature. Thus they had words by
which to call different varieties of eels, and the place-names
made these distinctions.

Second, a general principle of biology is that the number of
species is highest in the equatorial regions and decreases toward the poles (see Book III, Chapter 15). Certainly the contrasts of Iceland and New Zealand are striking. The one was almost treeless; the other had numerous varieties. Iceland
supported a few mammals, whereas New Zealand had only
seals and whales. But it had 120 species of birds, which gave
rise to hundreds of recorded place-names. As we might put it,
the gap resulting from the lack of possessives was easily filled by
the descriptives.

As regards incident-names, Maori and Icelander show much
in common, and one would hesitate to suggest in which island
such names were more frequent. H. W. Williams, in his *Plea for
the Scientific Study of Maori Names* (1912), comments that "in the
vast majority of cases" mere translation of the names is possible,
but that the name would still "remain inexplicable" unless the
circumstances were known. He goes on, "the incidents commemorated will in many cases appear to us trivial or irrele-
vant," thus making it clear that his reference is to names arising
from incidents.

The importance of incident-names is to be inferred, also,
from the numerous folk-tales which regularly ascribe names to
incidents. Many of these etymologies are fanciful, but they

firmly establish the naming from incident as basic to Maori thought.

Many names, as is to be expected, indicate their origin in their actual meaning or by a reasonable story. The word *toto,* "bleed, blood," occurs in Waitoto, "stream-blood," and in Maniatot, "plain-blood," in both instances presumably the site of a battle or at least of some bloodshed. Iwikatea, "bone-bleached," indicates another battlefield; Kokowhakarere, "body-cast-away," preserves the record of a fight where the bodies were left lying on the ground. The twice-used Ahimanawa, "fire-heart," goes back to circumstantial stories of the cooking and eating of an enemy's heart in ritualistic cannibalism.

Not all the incidents were warlike. Aromoho preserves *ara,* "path," and a word meaning to force one's way through brush, the whole recalling a certain man's being lost in a dense thicket and dying there.

As elsewhere, names have arisen from minor happenings, as with Manurewa, "kite-floating," given because an escaped kite floated a long distance.

In their third type of naming, the commemoratives, the Maoris show not only a great difference from the Icelanders, but also are in some ways unique. Namings from places "in the old country" are common enough in many parts of the world, but are usually associated with habitation-names. But the Maoris gave to the hills and streams many names that they had brought from other islands.

The situation is not simple, and in a particular case the name may be doubtful. Evidence, however, can develop from three different sources. First, the name may actually occur in some other island or islands of Oceania. Second, Maori legend may state that the name is commemorative. Third, the unintelligibility of the name, or its failure to be accurately descriptive, may suggest its commemorative origin.

Illustrative examples come readily to hand. Williams notes that Waimea and Maungaroa are to be connected with names found in Hawaii, and that Matawai is of Tahiti.

Even though some of the seeming imports may actually be

descriptives, the use of commemoratives must remain as one of the distinctive features of Maori naming. It leads us on, moreover, to an even more unusual relation of this people to their names, that is, the involvement with mythology and folk-tale.

Most people—the ancient Israelites and Greeks, for instance—tell stories about name-origins, but probably no other people has equaled the Maoris in this field. These stories, as may be expected with folk-tales, are generally fanciful and not to be trusted for literal truth. On the other hand, they are of great importance as showing attitudes toward naming, and we have, in most instances, no reason to doubt that they spring from a modicum of reality.

A striking example of such a story (existing in two versions) is that of the voyage of a vessel called Arai-te-uru. Caught in a vicious storm off the east coast of North Island, the shipmaster ran southward to avoid being cast on the rocks. At some point a crewman named Moko-tere-a-tarehu was swept overboard. His body was found later at the mouth of a river, and a rock there received his name. The storm, continuing, blew the vessel along the coast of South Island, where the voyagers suffered shipwreck on a reef. A man named Pohu died in the wreck, and his name was placed there. The rest of the people, men, women, and children, got ashore, wandered about, and were able to support themselves from the country. Thus wandering (as the tale takes pains to record), they gave numerous names—chiefly, if the story is to be trusted, from incidents and from the names of people who suffered some incident at that place.

Although some details of this story are not clearly explicable, on the whole it seems circumstantial—what might well have happened to some early immigrants. The emphasis upon the giving of names supplies the typical Maori touch.

The other version of the story is far removed from credibility, but even more striking in its emphasis upon naming. During the run before the storm a whole series of people "went overboard." Most of them are conceived as having swum ashore. Some of them were then changed into mountains bearing their names. Others merely had some natural feature named for them. The listing includes 140 entries dealing with place-names!

A historian or a folklorist may make his own interpretation of such a story. To the onomatologist, however, the emphasis upon the naming is of significance because it shows a people extraordinarily concerned with both the giving of names and their later explication. In the simple version the explanations may well rest upon genuine tradition. In the elaborated and formalized version the explanations must generally be conceived as being fanciful reconstructions. But the Maoris' interest in naming is inherent in both versions.

Many other tales make even more certain this emphasis upon naming. The chief Ihenga, as one story tells, went on a journey along the shore of a lake and gave names to various places. Again, Ihenga traveled by way of Waiomio, giving names to places as he went—either descriptives or from incident.

As already noted, the incident might be minor in itself. A river is still known as Waingongora, "stream-snoring," and a folk-tale explains it as the place where a certain chief once slept and snored.

Maori folk-tales also consider the imported names. Thus at a certain point along the coast the early voyager Paikea found himself reminded—apparently by the shapes and positions of the mountains—of similar features in his homeland, which is supposed to have been Raiatea (Society Islands). He therefore named the places accordingly, saying, "The names I have given . . . are the names of places at my old home, and these places are like them." Again, there is good reason to suppose a genuine tradition.

In this last example, as with Maori naming in general, the fact that the land was wholly unnamed is of importance. Without a network of names, people have difficulty in keeping orientation. At the very least, a lack of names is a great nuisance. Naming is thus a kind of taking possession, a way of producing a sense of being at home. The use of commemoratives from the homeland increases this sense of familiarity.

Also to be noted is the fact that immigrants to an uninhabited country are in need of a large number of names very quickly, and are thus likely to establish, consciously or unconsciously, some system—as Spanish voyagers reproduced the calendar of saints. One can point to two possible Maori systems, as they display themselves in the folk-tales. First, their explorers transferred names commemoratively; second, they placed personal names, not with a sense of ownership, but because something happened to the person at that spot—often, indeed, his death.

The inference which can be drawn from the far-from-perfect study of Iceland and New Zealand would indicate that the absence of an already existing stratum of names is not in itself a highly determining factor in the establishment of a new name-pattern. In short, the Icelanders and the Maoris, though each starting with an unnamed land, arrived at very different results.

Of much greater weight, apparently, are the environment offered by the new land and the traditional culture of the new people. We may notice that the Icelanders' name-pattern resembles that of the Anglo-Saxons, to whom they were closely related in language and culture.

On the whole, the absence of pre-existing names seems to have had little effect upon Icelandic naming, while it had much upon Maori naming, in ways which have been noted.

14
Of Farther Asia

Across the vast arid reaches of Asia and across its broad river-valleys, thick with people, place-names stand by the million. Little is available, however, in place-name study. Only from general dictionaries may something be learned of the origin of the Asian names that are famous over the world, together with a little of the naming-habits of the various peoples.

In actuality, we need not entertain any exaggerated idea of differences between European and Asian name-patterns. An illuminating work is *Geographical Nomenclature in Siam,* by Helen L. Smith. This essay shows the names, with allowance for language and environment, to be just about what are to be expected from our knowledge of other parts of the world. Many descriptives occur, among them many relative descriptives, such as *north, south,* and *upper.* Associatives spring from the native flora, and along with them, either as associatives or as names from incident, stand names drawn from the fauna, such as *crocodile* and *elephant.* Such an imposing name as Ban Chorakhe Sam Phan, "three-thousand-crocodiles-village," is doubtless not to be taken as arithmetically exact, but at least suggests an incident involving an extraordinary concentration of crocodiles. The author notes that many of the larger towns have names that "indicate a hopeful and idealistic attitude on the part of the

founders," just as American towns such as Concord and Rich-
land.

East and west alike, names may be involved in accident, as the
capital city Bangkok serves for illustration. It is literally "village-
olive," the name of a humble Chinese trading-post. The new
foundation on the site was officially Krung Thep, "capital of
the angels," but the older and simpler name survived in foreign
usage.

Siam itself goes back apparently to a Chinese source, but with
lost meaning. With patriotic motives, in 1939, the people of the
country adopted for it their tribal name, Thai, "free." In thus
seeking to "improve the image" they were acting in a manner
that may be paralleled elsewhere.

Thus, in Thailand, when good translations are available, the
names appear to be comparatively simple, and no more unusual in manner of origin than are names elsewhere.

As for India, any concise treatment of its place-names must
consider it in the areal sense, as the subcontinent, not as being
composed of the different independent nations now dividing
the region.

India is a name of ancient record, and of unusually clear origin and history. It begins with a Sanscrit word, *sindhuh,* meaning, "river," which was originally applied to the great stream on
the western edge of the peninsula. Doubtless the people of the
land themselves used the term as a generic, and had also a specific. Invaders, however, are notoriously inclined to accept the
commonly used generic as the actual specific, and the invaders
were the Persians, who, under their great King Darius,
marched in shortly before 500 B.C. The name thus passed on,
and eventually it reached the Greeks, many of whom were
under Persian rule at the time. In Greek the river came to be
Indos and the country near it India.

The name, in fact, is one of those displaying an extraordinarily successful career. Moving to the east, it passed beyond
the Indus valley to include the whole subcontinent. Then it
moved to the great islands known as the East Indies or Indonesia, and even established a kind of half-interest in Indo-

China. To the west the name spread over the West Indies (often known simply as The Indies), and came to include other entities, such as the state of Indiana.

Moreover, through later Persian influence, the name developed into Hindu, for people and language, and by linking to itself a Persian suffix for a place, it became Hindustan. Closer to its point of origin and remaining much what it had first been, it was preserved as Sind for the district near the mouth of the river. Far to the north, it also kept the memory alive by the Hindu Kush, "Indian mountains."

Finally, to include the Indian Ocean, we have this name of a river (not so large or famous as a number of others) thus spreading over most of the globe—partly by historical accident, but partly, also, because of the glamour of the name and of the country for which it stood.

By still another anomaly, as the result of a quirk of political development, most of the course of the Indus River is not now through India, but through Pakistan.

In the subcontinent, languages are numerous, topography varied, settlement ancient, people numerous. Such a multifarious situation as this not only ensures a thick implantation of names, but also provides a complicated stratification, together with a complex linguistic pattern. Obviously, a single worker could easily expend all his years upon some small facet of the region.

As an example of a complexity—one not yet surely solved—we may take the name of the great mountain-system, the Himalaya. Traditionally, it has been explicable as from Sanskrit, placed by the Indo-European invaders as they saw the massive and towering peaks to the north, snow-covered—*hima*, "snow," and *álaya*, "dwelling-place, home," or merely "place." Why would anyone need to doubt this, or desire to do better?

By an almost perverse semantic trick, however, in Dravidian (a language already existing in the region at the time of the Aryan invasion) the word meaning "mountain" occurs in the form *malai*. We face then, as an undeniable possibility, the constantly recurring situation of invaders taking an established generic and applying it as a specific. Although the Dravidian theory fails to explain the syllable *hi-,* the correspondence of the two names seems difficult to write off as mere coincidence.

To turn to some of the better-known names, one finds those of natural features to be, in most instances, comparatively commonplace. The stream known as Mahanadi is simply another "big river," such as is to be found over all the earth. Ganges is a Sanskrit word for "stream," which has been specialized to identify the chief river of the region. Its large tributary, the Jumna, is probably "twin"—a fitting name, since the Jumna parallels the main stream for many miles.

Regional names are similarly direct. The Deccan is merely "the south." The Punjab is "five rivers." Bengal is from Banálaya, the land of a tribe known as Bang.

On the other hand, the names of important cities are generally commendatory in a religious sense. Very rare is an exception such as Pondicherry, which is merely "new town." Regular is the inclusion of the name of some god. (See Book II, Chapter 6.)

Not only are the Indian gods numerous in themselves, but also each of them may have various epithets, or bynames, which are also usable. Thus the land is thickly set with these names as specifics, usually coupled with a generic—as with Rampur, the holy name joined with the common *-pur,* "city," a cognate of the Greek *polis.* Thus also we have numerous names with Vishnu, Hari, Brahma, Kali, Sri, Krishna, and Shiva.

Though religious names are more characteristic of habitation-names, we also come upon them for natural features, as with Brahmaputra, "Brahma's son," for the third of the great rivers. So too it goes with Ramganga, "Ram's river," and Srikanta, "Sri's mountain," Kalinádi, "Kali's river," and many others.

The religious fixation in India, however, is by no means unique. In many countries of medieval Europe the namings for saints are comparable. Even more closely similar is the situation in the many parts of the Americas which were colonized under Catholic influence. The name-pattern of much of California, for instance, is religious—with the cities and larger towns generally beginning with San or Santa, except when some other religious conception has taken over, as with Los Angeles, Sacramento, and Carmel. Even natural features are largely thus named—Santa Lucia Mountains, San Joaquin River, Point Reyes. Both in India and elsewhere the chief motivation for the religious namings is the same, that is, the desire for a commendatory name.

Given China's more than three and a half million square miles, given its wars and its invaders, given its ancient and continuing culture, and given (most of all) its dense population of peasants—under such conditions the total number of its place-names may well pass a hundred million.

Insofar as the backgrounds of Chinese place-names have been presented, they show a preponderance of the generic-specific structure with the specific preceding, and are simple and clearly meaningful descriptives.

We can almost reduce the giving of Chinese place-names to a kind of game. Take, first, a few good generics, such as *king,* "royal residence, capital," *hai,* "sea," *shan,* "mountain," and *ho* and *kiang,* "river." Then take some simple specifics, such as *pe, nan, tung,* and *si,* "north, south, east, west," *tsing,* "blue," and *hoang,* "yellow," and *ta* "big." By means of the two lists any intelligent person can form some good Chinese names, or (on the other hand) analyze numerous names already in existence— Peking, Nanking, Shantung, Takiang, Hoangho, Hoanghai, Nanhai, Taho, Tsinghai, Tunghai. The order of the elements may be altered to give a different meaning, the generic, by a process of association, becoming a specific. Thus Sikiang is "west-river," but Kiangsi identifies a place as being west of the river.

Undoubtedly such a presentation indicates an oversimplification which would vanish if we carried the work into some detail. Nonetheless, the simplicity and logicality of these major components of the name-pattern are remarkable.

Even among the better-known places, a few call for special comment. Shanghai contains the common *hai,* and the whole is to be taken as denoting a place near the sea. Hong Kong may be taken colorlessly, as "pleasant port," but an older idea, "fragrant port," is not impossible, since references to the good smell of land were common among early seamen.

The Yangtze, greatest of Chinese streams, has been the subject of much contradictory interpretation. Some have taken it to bear the name of a former province, Jang. Others, lured by semantic appropriateness, have translated it as "big," or "long." A more romantic approach has rendered it as "son of the ocean." Most probably, it can be taken as "twin," because of its two branches.

Canton is a result of a shifting, under foreign influence, of the province-name Kuangtuang. The process is apparently the familiar one of folk-etymology, since *canton* is a common word in several of the European languages.

Like Canton, the great name China itself is the result of foreign shaping. In the earlier centuries of Chinese history the land lacked natural boundaries and stable political unity. There was therefore no obvious entity to be named. Under such conditions the outsiders are more likely than are the natives to see the need for distinguishing a whole. The Chinese themselves were likely to use the name of the reigning dynasty for whatever fraction of the area was under that particular rule. Finally, however, the Chin dynasty, shortly before 200 B.C., established a rule over the whole country.

This "empire" then could be known by the dynastic name. Like other dynasties, the Chin passed away, but the conception of an entity remained—at least among the outsiders, who would, most likely, have been Malay traders trafficking in and out of the mainland ports. At the other end of their run, then, these traders told their counterparts in India about the great land of Chin, and the term became established. Since Indian traders maintained relations with the Roman Empire, the name passed on into Greek and Latin, with its initial consonant shifted to *S*. As a result, though the geographical reference has been lost, we still refer to a *sinologist,* and use such a phrase as *Sino-British relations.*

The original form, however, maintained itself in India, and

still remained to greet the Portuguese voyagers who rounded Africa. Apparently feeling more at home with a place-name ending in a vowel, the Portuguese added one, and the result was China.

Nevertheless, unlike India (though the two names seem in many respects to be counterparts), China has remained a foreign name. Its own people seem actually to have struggled unsuccessfully to fit a name to their country, having worked through such uncertain descriptives as Middle Kingdom and Flowery Kingdom. From an early period, moreover, political name-changing has been a practice. The city. known now as Peking has formerly been Ki, Yuchau, Chungtu, and Yenking.

The Japanese, crowded upon their intricately embayed islands, have developed a naming-style much like that of the Chinese and somewhat influenced by the language and usages of China.

Japan itself—also in the alternate form Nippon—may be originally from the Japanese "fire-land," but is generally taken as the Chinese adaptation, "rising-sun-land." One can note that the actual inhabitants of the islands would hardly have given the latter name, since they would have had no more reason to associate themselves with the east or the rising sun than would any other people. On the other hand, the Chinese necessarily thought of the islands as lying to the east, and would easily give such a name.

The typical Japanese place-name represents the naming-process already noted for Chinese place-names, that is, it is a simple descriptive with a generic and specific.

Thus we have Tokyo, with *to*, "east," and *kyo*, "capital," named in counterpart to the earlier Kyoto, which seems merely to have been "capital." Nagasaki is *naga*, "long," and *saki*, "cape." Fujiyama shows *yama*, "mountain"; *fuji* should probably be taken merely to mean "big." The four main islands show equal simplicity. Hokkaido, farthest to the north, is "north-land." Honshu, the main island, has a name indicating as much. Shikoku is so called from its being composed of four provinces, and the somewhat larger Kyushu from having nine provinces. Such unpoetic number-terms suggest naming by a central authority.

An Ainu stratum exists, especially in Hokkaido. Thus Sapporo, the largest city of the north, is from an Ainu river-name, a descriptive meaning "big-in-drought," apparently indicating a stream which maintained its flow even in dry weather.

By and large, the names of the Orient fall easily within the scheme of classification here presented in Book II.

15
A Little of Africa

Shedding light upon what is still, onomastically speaking, a dark continent, one unusual and excellent treatise is available—the study of Spanish Continental Guinea (*Toponímia de la Guinea Continental Española*, 1947) by Dr. Luis Báguena Corella.

The area, now a part of Equatorial Guinea, is about 110 miles in length from east to west and 80 miles in breadth. It lies a few miles north of the equator, fronting on the Atlantic. The land, even where it rises into low mountains, is covered with dense, tropical rain-forest. It supports only scattered villages, inhabited by tribesmen speaking the Pamue language. They practice subsistence agriculture, but depend largely upon hunting and fishing. The population is sparse, about twenty to the square mile.

A study of the naming of this area is of importance, as it gives an insight into what a primitive African tribe accomplishes against the background of an equatorial environment.

Dr. Báguena lists and expounds 3477 names—1169 of villages, 2021 of streams, 287 of mountains and hills. He makes no claim to being complete in his listings, but he certainly provides an adequate sampling of the more important names. His own classifications, moreover, make clear what is named—that is, just about what is named anywhere.

Faint traces of a pre-Pamue stratum exist, as with a stream-name, Esantua, derived from a tribe which formerly dominated the area. At the other end of the time-scale, a few European names exist. This influence, however, is superficial and negligible, being limited to transplanted and altered names, such as Baselona (Barcelona) and Kadis (Cadiz) and to some introduced words, such as Ekabala (for Spanish *caballo*, "horse"). The great body of the nomenclature, however, is solidly Pamue. It is, moreover, intelligible in a literal sense—probably an evidence that it is of comparatively recent origin. But in attempting to discover the reasons for some naming, Dr. Báguena frequently had the answer, "just a name!" and the excuse that his informant had the name from his grandfathers or ancestors—the word used in the text being *abuelos*, which is, unfortunately, ambiguous in Spanish usage.

In a manner that might surprise many people, the naming-practices of this primitive tribe are, in themselves, far from primitive. Both in practical distinctions and in vivid and even poetic qualities, they might well be judged to surpass those of most of the civilized nations.

The generic-specific usage is not only in effect, but also is carried to a high degree of efficiency. Two terms are available to distinguish between large and small streams (as with *river* and *creek* in most of the United States). But generics are also available to indicate the source of the stream, its headwaters, and its main course. Thus the speakers can readily achieve accuracy, when it is desired, although they also retain the ability to refer to the whole stream by a single term. Shift-names are much in use, adding to the efficiency, though tending toward monotony because of repetition. Thus, almost regularly, a stream bears the name of the mountain from which it flows.

As in all parts of the world, descriptives are common. Muni, from which the term Río Muni is sometimes applied to the whole area, is simply "big." Other descriptives are those indicating a stream with rapids, one which goes dry in the rainless season, or one displaying certain rocks or other minerals.

In spite of such overlapping, anyone who considers European or American usage to be normal will find the Pamue descriptives differing greatly. Certain qualities of places apparently make little impression. For instance, color-words are almost lacking. Relative description is rare—partly, it would seem, because the country is so heavily forested that the position of one feature with respect to another is difficult to observe. Thus the compass points are not readily discernible and apparently do not occur in place-names.

On the other hand, certain types of descriptives are highly developed, especially subjectives, that is, those that describe by indicating the effect upon the namer. The possibility of such naming is further enhanced by the nature of the language, which permits verbal expressions as name-specifics. It may also spring from a more emotional nature of the people, or at least a lack of cultural tradition of objection to the expression of emotion. Thus one village-name may be rendered as Sadness. Another is I-Weep, which should be distinguished from He-Weeps, the latter being applied to a stream whose scarcity of fish is discouraging to the fisherman. Another is He-Who-Cries, which refers to the number of babies there. Still another may be translated as Has-Everything, for a place which is (according, perhaps, to covetous outsiders) "rich in goods, money, and women."

Associative names are common. Though bridges are rare, the people cross many streams or gullies by means of the trunks of fallen trees (known in some parts of the United States as footlogs). Many small streams are thus named with the quasi-generic Nche, coupled with some further descriptive. One stream has an unsavory name—from the location on it of the village latrine. What is apparently a trysting-place (compare the American use of Lovers' Lane) bears the uncompromising African term which may, with some civilized reticence, be rendered as Fornicate. Dr. Báguena expounds: "Where the young people go bathing, and, now and then, secret encounters occur among lovers."

As for Enana, also from the presence of a latrine, the careful doctor renders it as "action of defecating," and adds that it is an onomatopoetic term, suggestive of groaning or grunting.

By far the most numerous of associatives are those drawn from trees and other natural growth, but their discussion is a topic to be reserved for fuller treatment later.

Numerous incident-names occur, many of them difficult to distinguish from associatives or descriptives, especially subjective-descriptives. Thus Hold-Me-Fast and Hold-Me, both applied to streams with fords, may indicate the usual dangerous nature of the stream or may spring from a particular incident. On the other hand, I-Lost-My-Way and Young-Man-Drowned seem clearly to be from incidents. Many informants, indeed, told Dr. Báguena the stories of what had happened at various places. The clarity of many of the stories suggests a fairly recent origin, and in such cases there is the likelihood that the current name has replaced an older one.

As always, the incident-names are colorful. They record where a leopard was captured; where the body of a leopard (killed by wild pigs) was found; where a woman, out fishing, was abducted by some wandering strangers; where pestilence decimated a village. One stream may be rendered Marry-by-Rape, having been the scene of an abduction which was later regularized by means of the customary payment.

Among animals the elephant, naturally enough, has been most productive of place-names. Here the body was cut up and distributed to people of different villages. Here a large specimen was captured. Here the immense, rotting carcass polluted the forest air.

Destruction of property and crops being taken for granted, peaceful encounters with elephants produced stories to be remembered. Some fishermen, having placed their traps, were appalled to see some elephants crossing the stream, but the monsters passed without causing damage. A village is Pass-Quietly-Elephant, because a band once wandered along the edge of the village without harming houses or crops.

Like namings from trees, the namings from animals are interesting enough to call for special treatment later.

The lack of possessive names is striking. It cannot altogether be attributed to absence of a sense of ownership. On the contrary, some names refer to boundaries of areas over which individuals or groups exercise prerogatives. The actual identification of land and individuals, however, seems unrecognized. Only in a very few instances is a tribal ownership more or less suggested.

Commemorative names, though a few occur, are of little importance. Most of them are names which may have been introduced by Europeans, though changed to a Pamue pronunciation. Nanepo, for instance, represents a considerable alteration of Fernando Po, a name which was first brought to the mainland by a village-founder who had worked on that island. The village known as Oyem bears a name which was brought from Gabon by African immigrants.

Commendatories are of some importance, although these are not of religious suggestion, the Pamue not having a useful catalogue of gods or saints to serve their purposes. Their closest approach is such a name as Nseelang, from the mythological story of a leopard-demon. The Spanish stratum provides a few names such as San Benito.

More characteristic of the Pamue are commendatories, such as may be rendered Good-Village—or, with negative application, Bad-Luck. More elaborate is I-Shall-Conquer-in-the-Strife, which serves as a good omen for hunting.

The name-pattern of any area results from a complicated interreaction of culture (considered also in its historical aspects) and of environment. The Pamue names serve as an excellent demonstration, especially upon the environmental side.

The dense tropical rain-forest has various effects, one of them curious. As Dr. Báguena has noted, anyone walking under the canopy of foliage, even if following a trail, can scarcely see the sky, and is quite unable to discern the general contours of the country and even the existence of particular hills. Unseen, a hill cannot be recognized as an entity, and remains nameless.

Much more striking as an environmental influence is that of the native flora, especially of the trees. As noted in the comparison of the Icelanders and the Maoris, variety of species is greatest near the equator, and in the Pamue country the number of species must approach its maximum.

There is no need to be theoretical. In his summation Dr. Báguena lists 178 species of identified plants which appear in the place-names, and in addition he lists 76 names which he believes to be those of plants, though he has not identified them botanically. The total is thus 254!

This figure, one should note, is for names, not for named places. Although good compilations of other countries are not available for comparison, the figure seems extraordinarily high, especially when compared with our general idea of the situation in the temperate and arctic zones. One would think that not more than a score or two native plants occur in English place-names. As a result, we have excessive repetition, specifics such as *oak* and *ash* appearing scores or hundreds of times.

A similar situation, though somewhat less extreme, occurs with the fauna. Serving as specifics are nine terms which designate varieties of ape or monkey, besides an additional one meaning monkey in general. Altogether, forty specified mammals figure in the name-pattern, and there are seven others not clearly identified.

Though birds and reptiles fail to provide a comparable number of species, toads and frogs appear with a total of five. The fish present fifty-seven species.

Actually, in establishing this name-pattern, we find that the factor of culture interacts with that of environment, and a brief comparison with England is again fruitful. The Angles and Saxons, at the period of the invasion and conquest, had long since come to a stage of depending upon the cultivation of cereals and the exploitation of livestock. Hunting was little more than a sport, and gathering did not go much beyond picking some blackberries and collecting hazel-nuts. The people had therefore, to some extent, lost touch with their environment. The Pamue, to the contrary, still base their lives largely upon hunting and fishing. Therefore, not only the number of species, but also the people's dependence upon them, determine the result.

In the end the basic principle of entity and use is crucial. To illustrate, the species of insects near the equator are very numerous, but only nineteen of them appear in the list. Moreover, five of these refer to bees or ants, species important enough in themselves to be likely to serve to identify places. Even more strikingly, only one species of the great spider-family produces a place-name, and that is the tick! Obviously the Pamue had no reason to be interested in arachnids, but they had had the unpleasantness of ticks impressed upon them, and could thus identify a place.

Similarly—crocodiles being creatures not easily ignored—the Pamue had words to distinguish two varieties, and therefore the places where they lived, or places where one of them had once been memorably encountered.

As so often in the study of the culture of a "primitive" people, the result indicates a high degree of complexity, efficiency, and even sophistication. The name-pattern of the Pamue is well adapted to the people's needs, and displays great variety, along with some touches of poetry.

16

The Transition

Even before Columbus set sail, as a kind of prelude, had come the thrust of the Norsemen to the west, and the probing of the Portuguese to the Atlantic islands and along the African coast.

Eric the Red, about the year 1000, sailed west from Iceland until a mass of land—whether island or continent he had no means of knowing—blocked the way ahead. He at once faced the questions which would engage so many explorers in the centuries to come—that is, not only what was this land, and what were its relations with other lands, but also what was its name, or was it nameless? Eric, on his own responsibility, gave it a name, and a most interesting one, which stands in English as Greenland.

It was doubtless good enough as a descriptive, since the southern end of that great island was richly grass-grown during the cycle of warm weather which the world was then enjoying. But the saga which supplies the record states plainly that he so named it "because men would the more readily go there if the country had a good name." Thus the idea of commendation made its appearance, at the very opening of the Age of Exploration.

On the other hand, Eric's son, Leif the Lucky, who continued the exploration along the American coast, was a straightforward namer by description. He was responsible (in translation) for Slateland, because it had slate-like slabs of rock; Woodland, because of the forests; Vineland, because of wild grapes there.

These names all designate large areas, and so are somewhat unusual, since sea-voyagers are likely to name small features which can be readily seen and thus grasped as entities, such as coves for safe anchorage, and offshore rocks which can serve for landmarks. We can only surmise that Leif gave such names also, but that the saga-composer failed (as would be likely) to include the full list—or that the names had been lost from the tradition before the composition of the saga.

Also lacking is any name derived from Eskimos or Indians, since neither voyager had peaceful contacts with the native peoples, or possessed any knowledge of their languages.

The Portuguese sea-voyagers of the fifteenth century faced situations comparable to those of Eric and Leif. They were discovering unnamed islands and coasting along strange shores. The islands were uninhabited, and the shores were sparsely peopled by generally hostile tribesmen speaking unknown languages. The Portuguese, like the Norsemen, had no established tradition of naming, and found themselves suddenly under the necessity of supplying names for practical purposes. As dependable methods they turned to description, association, and incident.

Madeira is merely "wood," or "timber," since the discoverers, their own land nearly denuded of trees, found the island's forests a bonanza.

Azores is, in the plural, for the sea-hawks which were very plentiful around the islands. Since the Portuguese, like other early voyagers, would have been careful observers of bird-flight, the reality is, doubtless, that the seamen noted the direction in which the birds flew at twilight, and thus had an indication of where the not-yet-sighted land was to be found. The association of the first-discovered island with the hawks would therefore be very close, and would tend to have the concreteness of an incident.

Along the Atlantic coast of Africa the Portuguese started with some knowledge of names gained from the Moors, who in turn preserved a few names which were originally Semitic, that is, Carthaginian or Arabic.

Such a possibility exists with Cape Non, also appearing as No, Num, and Não, but taken by both Portuguese and Spaniards as merely representing the negative. Las Casas, recording the tradition a century later, states that they called it "the cape of No, as if saying that, from there on, there was no more land, or that it was not possible to pass beyond." The Portuguese seamen—superstitious, as seamen always have been—took the name as a plain warning that voyaging farther to the south would be unlucky. This belief may actually have blocked exploration for a short time, until some shipmaster, bolder than his fellows, violated the taboo. In reality, the name is more likely to be derived from the Semitic word for "fish," and may merely record a fishing-ground or a good catch near this point of land—a likely place, indeed, for fishing, because of shoals extending out from the cape.

In their voyages along the coast the Portuguese focused their attention largely upon capes that marked turns in the general trend of the land and served for landmarks. To these they were fond of giving color-names, such as Cape Verde, "green," for its abundant vegetation. The shade of rock yielded Cape Branco, "white," Cape Roxo, "red," and Cape Negro, "black."

As they became more familiar with the land by means of trade, the Portuguese established some other world-famous names. Guinea, taken from one of the local kingdoms, spread over the large, though ill-defined, area. Senegal, applied to both river and region, sprang from a tribal name. The Portuguese, however, adopted Gambia from a local dialect, but in doing so, as has frequently happened, they merely took a term meaning "river."

The Portuguese also adopted both Zaire and Kongo, applying Zaire to the great river and Kongo to the region. They thus followed native usage, both the names being of local origin, and of uncertain meaning.

The other great stream of that coast, the Niger, had been

vaguely known under that or a similar name since classical times, and there has been an unescapable tendency to derive it from the Latin "black." More likely, however, it is a Berber word, and (again) should be taken as meaning "river."

By and large, however, the Portuguese had no interest in penetrating inland, and a curious name-pattern thus arose, each section being named for the product which was considered most typical of it, with Coast as the generic. So on the modern map we have Grain Coast, Gold Coast, Slave Coast, and (probably a later addition) Diamond Coast. There is also Ivory Coast, a name borne by one of the new nations. The modern map also shows the sinister-sounding Skeleton Coast, which cannot have arisen from any article of trade, and is probably (like other names of the sort) from the finding of a skeleton.

On the whole, the Portuguese of the fifteenth century displayed what might be called a reticence and timidity in naming. They were Europeans, just emerging from the Middle Ages, working upon the usual assumption—as ancient as the early Greeks—that places were already named. But if you sighted an outstanding cape from your ship and lacked contact with local people, you might be forced to name it. If so, you did something easy and practical, as by recording its color.

The third major group of islands to be discovered by the Portuguese suggests that timidity. Though the archipelago lies isolated, its most easterly peaks rising from the Atlantic some hundred of miles from "the green cape," the discoverers failed to give it a name of its own. As a far-flung example of association-naming, this of the Cape Verde Islands may set a record.

In ordinary speech the specific probably shortened to Verde, and we may thus explain the note made by Columbus when he touched at the islands on his third voyage—"a false name, since they are so barren that I saw nothing green there." (But the situation serves merely as another example of the manner in which associative names may be deceptive.)

In the naming of their settlements in the various islands, the Portuguese showed themselves to be quite unskilled. The local names run largely to some of the principal saints—Mary, Anthony, George, James, Lucy, Nicholas—in most instances probably echoing the dedication of the local church.

Terceira got its name in straightforward fashion, as being the "third" of the Azores to be discovered, an early example of naming by number.

What is absent from a name-pattern may be as illuminating as what is present. The Portuguese seem to have lacked the idea of commemoration, except as applied to the dedication of churches. Names fail to echo those of the homeland, or to honor the king. Most remarkable of all, there is no island or archipelago bearing the great name of Prince Henry, though most of the voyages were made under his patronage.

Norsemen and Portuguese alike, in these early years of discovery, seem to be at a loss as to how to go about naming the new territories that they had the good fortune to find.

One Portuguese naming, however, deserves commemoration, especially since it survives upon a modern nation. Apparently lying close to a mountainous coast, the seamen felt the effects of a tropical storm raging ashore. The thunder beat upon them, reverberating among the peaks and ridges, and dying out in long grumbles. Someone observed that it was like the roaring of lions, and they gave the name Serra Lioa, "lion-mountain." Partially shifted to a Spanish form, it remains as Sierra Leone.

I 7
Columbus and Revolution

On October 12, 1492, that eccentric near-genius Christopher Columbus had himself rowed ashore to a small island which had previously been unknown to Europeans. He then and there took possession on behalf of "his sovereigns and masters the King and Queen." He also gave a name—or we might better put it—a new name, calling the island San Salvador, "Holy Savior."

Columbus, almost a religious fanatic, thus naturally expressed his gratitude at having been granted the attainment of the objective of a boldly conceived and perilous project. But why did he name the island? And upon whose authority?

Primarily, we should think, he named it as a practical matter. Islands have names, and so should this one. A name is handy to have standing in any act of taking possession. It is useful for sailing directions. Columbus's instructions did not, indeed, specify the right or duty of giving names—perhaps on the principle that you had better catch your rabbit before worrying about how to cook it.

Nonetheless, we may think it of some interest and even of some historical importance that Columbus so acted. The practice of naming places had been moribund in Europe for centuries. Hills and streams, islands and lakes—insofar as they

were important enough to bother with—had long possessed established names. Columbus must indeed have known something of the Portuguese practice. Or he could merely have assumed that the right of naming goes along with
possession—and on that latter point Columbus had royal instructions.

Doubtless, the Admiral would have been glad to learn the already existing name for the island, and might even have been
glad to employ it, since the use of a long-established name
would give some advantage, legal and otherwise. But, even
though the handsome brown-skinned natives came around
curiously, no Spaniard could speak a word of their language—
not even that Spaniard who could talk Hebrew and Chaldee,
and thus, hopefully, establish communications with the Ten
Lost Tribes.

Later, after having established some linguistic contact, Columbus learned that the natives called the island Guanahani.
He considered this name as of enough interest and importance
to be recorded. Eventually, however, both Guanahani and San
Salvador disappeared, and the world had only the colorless
Watling Island, named for some now-long-forgotten Englishman.

By and large, this first incident of New World naming shows
many details which would be repeated later—the giving of a
commemorative name, the interest in (and frustration about)
the native name, the heavy rate of casualties which resulted in
the loss of both names.

A passage in one of Columbus's letters shows that he was
both conscious of naming and interested in it:

> I named the first-discovered island San Salvador, in honor
> of our Lord and Savior who granted me this miracle; the In-
> dians call it Guanahani. The second island I named Santa
> Maria de Conception; the third, Fernandina; the fourth, Isa-
> bela; and the fifth, Juana. Thus I renamed them all.

In this first run of names the working of the namer's mind
shows well enough. After paying his religious respects to the

Son and the Mother, he shifted to his patrons of the royal house—king, queen, and prince-apparent, to the last of whom he seems to have had some special attachment, since another place became Puerto del Principe.

Like explorers in general, Columbus in his later namings (to include here all his four voyages) proceeded with what we may call a straightforward and straightline practice of naming, by which he set a precedent for those who followed him. About a hundred of his namings have been preserved in the somewhat defective records. Probably many more were originally entered in his now-lost logbooks. The reason for the naming usually must be inferred from the name itself and the circumstances, but in a few instances, fortunately, the reason is given in the source, and such comments are numerous enough to serve as a general check upon mere speculation.

When a natural feature stood out clearly, Columbus was likely to use a descriptive, as with Puerto Grande, Cabo Verde, Islas de Arena, and Río de las Cañas, which in English must be rendered as Big Harbor, Green Cape, Sand Islands, and Cane River. Subjectively descriptive was Cabo Hermoso ("it is indeed beautiful"). Cabo de Palmas suggests that a headland over-grown with palms was unusual enough to serve for identification.

A channel called Vacas "cows" might have been from an encounter with sea cows, but the text indicates that the name sprang from seven islets which apparently suggested a herd of cattle.

Namings from incidents are also common, especially when we include calendar-namings, which occurred when a name was needed on some particular day. Thus arose St. Nicholas, St. Thomas, and St. Catherine, as well as Concepción, which was named for the popular feast of the Virgin Mary, celebrated throughout Europe on December 8. So also, the first-founded settlement was Navidad (an alternate form of Natividad), for the Christmas season. Dominica, the island, was discovered on a Sunday.

Another naming from incident was Golfo de las Fleches,

"Arrow Gulf," because of an encounter there with hostile Indians. Tortuga, applied to an island, probably indicates by its form the sighting of a single turtle there.

Commemorative namings are the commonest of all, and many of them have commendatory overtones—such as the first namings, for religion and royalty. The names of saints are particularly common, partly because of namings from the calendar. On the other hand, strict naming from the calendar results in the honoring of many minor saints, and those appearing in Columbus's roll are major figures, such as Martin, Martha, Magdalena, Elmo, Juan, Mary. Along with the original San Salvador, we may note Monte Christi, a Spanish-Latin hybrid. Also, in addition to Santa Maria, we have Concepción and the Sea of Nuestra Señora.

There occur also a certain number of vaguely religious names—Cabo Santo, Río de Gracia, and Beata Island.

The important Cabo Gracias a Díos expresses thanks to God at the rounding of a point which enabled the voyagers to shift course and thus to be no longer at the mercy of the headwind which they had battled for days.

Commemorative namings for places in the homeland occur, but rarely. The profile of the island of Montserrat seemed to resemble that of the famous mountain, with its monastery, in the north of Spain. Cartagena, in its physical features, was reminiscent of the Spanish city. One stream became Río Guadalquivir.

The second largest island was at first known by its native name, but it soon became Hispaniola, "Little Spain." The founding here of the first settlement doubtless had something to do with the suggestion, and the appearance of the landscape was noted to be similar to that of Spain, but the particular reason was that some sailors caught various kinds of fish which much resembled those of their home waters.

Although Columbus was a man of unusual or even bizarre mental traits, he permitted himself only a few fanciful namings. The two difficult and dangerous channels of Trinidad he called Boca de la Sierpe and Boca del Drago—"The Serpent's Mouth" and "The Dragon's Mouth."

The disputed naming of Trinidad itself is illustrative of the explorer's mentality. On the third voyage he had apparently made up his mind to name his landfall after the Trinity. His narrative, however, runs that a sailor reported sighting three peaks, a circumstance which Columbus would certainly tend to interpret as divine indication. Some modern observers have reported only two peaks, but we do not know whether Columbus's own superstitious mind shifted to the more suspicious number or whether the sailor saw what he had been instructed to see.

An incident of the second voyage shows how naming could become not only commonplace but also a burdensome task. Off the southern coast of Cuba so many islands appeared that Columbus gave up individual naming and merely lumped them as El Jardín de la Reina, "the Queen's Garden."

Columbus also proceeded upon the common assumption that places in inhabited lands already had names, and that the duty of the explorer was, when possible, to discover and use these existing ones. Columbus took a few Indians on board his ship, and he almost immediately managed to have some communication with them, or to think that he did. Within a week, apparently, he had got the idea that one large island was called Colba, and that another was Bohio. In the latter instance the native word seems to have meant "house," and we can scarcely be surprised, under the circumstances, that a mistake had been made. We have no greater assurance that Colba was really the name of the other island. It also may be merely a mistake, arising from the almost total lack of communication. Nonetheless, in the form Cuba, it has survived.

Havana, Haiti, and Jamaica are Indian terms which Columbus took to be place-names, whether they actually were or not.

In history, what a man did not do can often be as interesting as what he did. Columbus, for instance, seems to have remained insensitive to new fauna and flora which he was encountering. In his list of names there is not one derived from the alligator. In fact, the turtle is almost alone among animals, together with two namings for the snake. Since there are also some references to snakes, we might even assume that Columbus had a certain interest in serpents. Cabo de Palmas seems to represent the only naming from flora.

Possessive names are also lacking, unless a few may lie concealed in some of the untranslated Indian names. Columbus conceived of the local Indian chiefs as "kings," but he did not—as later explorers often did—make use of them for place-names. A halfway move in that direction appears in the one reference to "Guacanagari's harbor."

Perhaps strangest of all, Columbus named nothing for himself or for any of his comrades. Since he appears to have been a man of considerable egotism, this failure is somewhat curious. It may have sprung from a general sense of awe, but it may also have been from fear of infringing upon the royal prerogative, as if you could make a feudal claim by planting your own name.

Thus, with the discovery and naming of San Salvador, we pass a revolutionary moment. From what we may term a decadent period we pass into one which burgeons with creativity. Millions of names would be established in the centuries to follow—whether by the direct process of bestowal or by the usually more difficult procedure of discovering the aboriginal name and transplanting it into European nomenclature.

The thousands of individuals who participated in this wholesale naming were themselves as diverse as the names that they gave, and the situations in which they worked were similarly various.

Many of these names, however, were given by men who were seamen, like Columbus, looking ashore at strange lands and making notes on their charts of newly seen islands, river-mouths, rocks, capes, and landmark-hills. Typically, again like Columbus, these later shipmasters went ashore but did not penetrate far, and they generally failed to look at plants and animals very carefully.

When opportunity afforded, they gave a descriptive or associative name, which had the additional advantage of being a landmark-name to identify the place for a later occasion. Thus Columbus himself had named Cape of the Pond and Cape of the Islets, both being good associatives and serving for identification.

A well-commanded ship supplies few daily incidents of enough importance to be perpetuated as names. Calendar-naming, however, was always common with the Spaniards, particularly if there was a priest aboard. One could always check the calendar of saints against the date in the logbook, and so come up with a name.

Commemorative names also came to flourish. Columbus had confined his to the royal family, but later voyagers paid off debts of gratitude to patrons and political bigwigs, and not infrequently complimented themselves and their comrades.

Finally, again unlike Columbus, the later voyagers were likely to transfer the name of the local chief to his village or even to a natural feature.

The basic question as to authority was never well settled. The Spanish crown, in its commissions, sometimes included instructions about giving and recording names, and thus gave royal sanction. Since the kings held also by papal grant, the names too might be said to be so based. In practice, however, Spanish instructions would be of no importance to Portuguese or French or English sea-captains, and naming from the sea came to be largely a catch-as-catch-can affair. Even a later Spanish voyager was likely to pay a minimal attention to the work of a predecessor. Thus the Cabrillo voyage of 1540–41 along the west coast resulted in careful naming, but Vizcaíno, in 1602–3, replaced those names wholesale.

The process of shifting shows even in Columbus's time. Thus, on his second voyage, he named a cape for St. Michael. But, as the younger Columbus reported later, "because of the ignorance of sailors, this cape is now known as Cabo del Tiburon." Apparently some incident involving a shark had caught the seamen's imagination, and led to the replacement of the commonplace saint's name. Incidentally, both names have now disappeared, though a village in the area is still Tiburon.

18
Half the World

A saying among European toponymists is: "The more important a place, the more difficult the explanation of the name."

Though not to be taken more than half-seriously, the generalization has some validity. We may note that thousands of
names of Italian, Spanish, and English villages are clearly explicable, but that Rome, Madrid, and London remain in controversy or obscurity. The reason undoubtedly is that the more
important places in general preserve older names.

The second largest land-mass of the earth, in one manner, illustrates the principle, and, at the same time, in another way,
may be cited as an exception. In short, the name may be held to
be clearly understood, but it preserves the generalization in that
it displays a fantastic history and would certainly remain un-
solved but for careful and devoted scholarship, and the lucky
preservation of rare records.

The story must start with Columbus and his lost opportunity.
He began with the idea of reaching Asia by sailing westward,
and he obstinately refused to change. Certainly after his second
voyage he should have recognized that he had had the glory of
discovering a continent hitherto unknown to Europeans. He

should have grasped that there was here a new entity. Being an entity, it could bear a name, and being one of enormous size and obviously of enormous importance to the human race, its name would be of tremendous use.

Unwilling to admit the existence of the entity, Columbus could not give it a name. One is led, therefore, to speculate what might "normally" have happened.

One possibility is that some European potentate, regal or papal, would have given a name—consciously and by his own supposedly divine authority. The name would almost certainly have been religious. Columbus called his first island San Salvador, and the whole continent might well have been so called, and be Salvador today. That it would have been a viable name its existence for a present-day republic attests.

A second reasonable and likely possibility would have been that a name which had been established locally, at some point on the seacoast, would have spread inland, and, lacking natural boundaries, would have eventually embraced the continent, or even both continents. Venezuela, Mexico, Canada—all represent names that have moved far beyond their original domains.

Still another possibility existed in the use of the term "New World," most commonly in its Latin form, Novus Mundus. Again, it did not happen. Perhaps the Latin form was phonetically unpleasing. Perhaps the term was too inaccurate, since not a world but two continents were actually involved. "New World" remained as a potent oratorical and poetic term, but not as a name.

Latin, however—serving then as a much-used international language—offered other possibilities, and its feminine form for "New" was less cumbersome than those of the masculine and neuter. Many names so formed appear on early maps, such as Nova Hispania and Nova Francia. No doubt, Nova Asia or Nova Europa might, similarly, have served for the continent.

Granted, we might say, sufficiently bad luck, even Columbus's original idea might have survived, in more than merely the modern West Indies. We might—with infinite ambiguity and inconvenience—have had Nova India.

Appearing in the earliest years of the discovery, Newfoundland might well have gone on to apply to the whole land-mass. But all we can say is that it did not.

With such reasonable possibilities eliminated, anyone would hesitate to advance an altogether fantastic one—that is, that the magnificent and world-famous name America came into exis-tence from the brainstorm of a German pedant who had never crossed the ocean, and probably had never even seen it. Yet the written record is so conclusive that scholars have had no re-course but to reject all the reasonable ideas and to accept the fantastic one.

We know little enough about him. He was, in 1490, a student at the University of Freiburg, and he lived on into the next cen-tury. Obviously he would have studied Latin, and apparently he was an enthusiast for the Greek studies, which were popular at the time. If there is a single fact of which we can be certain, it is that he was one of those individuals under the fascination of names. We can see as much in his manipulation of his own name, which was Martin Waldseemüller, the family-name to be translated as "forest-lake-miller." He set out to put this into Greek, as some scholars did in those times. The result must have been something like the repugnant and impractical *hyl-lakko-mylo-os*. But, for his own ends, he ingeniously manipulated this monstrosity, and, as the custom was, Latinized it. He got then, finally, Hylacomylus. Obviously, such a man is not to be trusted with a name.

At this point we must turn to that other character of this fan-tasy, a Florentine who usually spelled his name Amerigo Ves-pucci—Latinized as Americus (or Albericus) Vesputius. He was what has been called, somewhat enigmatically, a "controversial" figure, which means, in this case, that his stories of voyages across the Atlantic have been assailed as fabrications, especially by the highly respected early Spanish historians Las Casas and Herrera. Later investigators, however, have defended him. On the whole, we can conclude that he had really voyaged to what was the northeastern coast of South America. As a result, he took the position, as more and more people were beginning to do, that Columbus was wrong; that this was not India, but a new continent.

In 1503 or the following year he published, under the name Albericus Vesputius, a Latin pamphlet, its title *Mundus Novus*. In it he stated his belief about those regions—"They may be called a New World, for there was no knowledge of them among our ancestors, and it is a wholly new thing to all who now hear of it." Here was the idea! Here, the declaration of the entity! We need not be concerned with later works, some of them dubious, which are ascribed to him.

Exit, now, Amer(r)igo or Americus or Albericus, and whether or not he was a faker makes not the slightest difference in the outcome.

Back to Hylacomylus. By the year 1507 he had done well for himself, in a provincial way. He was a member of what we might now call a scholarly institute, a "think-tank," in the town of St. Dié in Lorraine, under the patronage of the local duke. The time was the burgeoning Renaissance; Greek studies were in vogue; one of the "fellows" had a printing press; even in far-inland Lorraine there was interest in the amazing discoveries of strange lands.

By this time the star of Columbus had sunk low and grown dim. His idea of the Indies was not convincing. He himself had lost favor at court. Was not Vespucci a better guide?

In any case, the little institute at St. Dié decided to reprint one of the Florentine's pamphlets, with a map, the title to be *Cosmographiae Introductio.* Who should be chosen to write the preface to the volume? No other than one of the members who was beginning to establish himself as a geographer—that is, Waldseemüller/Hylacomylus. Rarely have the need and the man arrived at a more fitting union.

Written in Latin, his pertinent statement may be translated thus:

> Now, indeed, these parts [the three "older" continents] have been broadly explored, and a fourth part has been found by Americus Vesputius, as will be shown later. I do not see why anyone should rightfully object to calling this part for Americus (its discoverer, a man of intelligence) to wit,

Amerige, that is, Land of Americus, or America—since both
Europe and Asia got their names from women.

At this point in history a great name is, we may say, struggling to be born. But just what form will it take? The first
suggestion is for Amerige. In the name-obsessed mind of Hylacomylus this spelling had some justification because of the Italian form Amerigo. More definitely, however, it is to be analyzed as Ameri-ge, with the Greek word for land thus fused
with the Italian personal name. In fact, the actual spelling in
the text is Amerigen, the form of a Greek accusative case.

The other suggestion is America—a name destined for
greatness far beyond any imagining of its creator. Its origin is
simple, since it is merely a Latin feminine form, derived from
the already established Americus. By analogy with the other
continents, as also from the usual Latin practice of having
names of islands and countries in the feminine, that gender was
the natural one. In this original text America takes second place
(or may, indeed, be taken as a mere explanation of Amerige),
but it seems to have been its creator's final choice, or else he
yielded to pressure from others. In any case, on the map which
he published the name stood as America.

The outcome can only be viewed as both amazing and fortunate. In itself the one form may seem as good as the other. But
the -a ending was unambiguous in pronunciation, drawing
strength from thousands of established names. The -e ending
was much less familiar, and would have resulted in countless
difficulties in being passed from one language to another.

But America had still other advantages. To anyone, it actually looked like the name of a continent. Europe, Asia, Africa—
each begins with a vowel and ends with one. If we take the
Latin form, all of them end in a. Africa and America share the
syllables -rica. The new name slid easily into its place.

Moreover, it was an easily slidable unit—euphonic, with its m,
its r, and its plentiful vowels. Either an orator or a poet could
use it readily—as many thousands of both have done. It comprised only common sounds, used in all European languages.

Another advantage (for people of the Renaissance, if not for moderns) existed in the analogy which the original passage notes—that is, that no one can well raise objections, "since both Europe and Asia got their names from women." Here, weighted with the tremendous authority of the ancient Greeks, was the justification for naming a continent after an individual. The author was proposing, apparently, that with two continents named for women, no one can well object to having one named for a man.

Also of importance was that America was, from the beginning, essentially a proper noun, without meaning, since its association with a particular person was easily ignored or forgotten, and did not, in any case, constitute a valid "meaning." There was no call for translation; in fact, translation would have been unwarranted. Here lay the great weakness of such a name as Newfoundland—that it demanded translation, and thus failed to be international. But America, from the beginning, was international.

The greatest point in favor of the new name, however, was merely that it filled a need. The preconceptions of Columbus were going by the board. An entity—and among the greatest of earthly entities—was appearing among men. They must have a name for it. By great good luck a German pedant, living in an out-of-the-way town, produced a name which was at once practical, universal, and beautiful.

The pamphlet had fairly wide circulation—the map, probably, with it. In a few years the name was established. Hylacomylus must have thought that he had loosed a whirlwind.

If any distinction is to be made, we must admit that the name was applied first to the southern continent, and it is thus placed on the map of 1507. Later voyagers and explorers by land outlined a second narrowly connected land-mass. The use, for it, of another name would have been advisable, but this time luck did not serve, and no ingenious namer turned up with an idea. So we have the cumbersome North America and South America.

In one way, however, the northern continent has stolen the

name. With the establishment of the first independent nation of the Americas, its government and people, by common practice rather than by any definite action, began to use United States of America. Some voices were raised that it should really be United States of North America, but that substitute was too long, and was not, in itself, wholly accurate, since the new nation did not include all, or even most, of the northern continent.

A worse situation arose when common usage began to consider that America was sufficient in itself, and that "American" was all that was needed for an adjective or for a citizen of that country. By the time, about half a century later, when other nations arose in the Americas, the situation was so well established that nothing, practically, could be done about it, in spite of some protests, both from inside and from outside.

In naming-history, America thus began with great good fortune, but in the end suffered a certain blunting of that success.

Its fantastic story, however, may serve as another example of the difficulties associated with the elucidation of many of the great names.

19
New Oceans and New Seas

The onward-pressing discoverers revealed not only new lands, but also new seas—some of them enticingly studded with green islands, some of them inhospitably clogged with floating ice. Like the ancient seas, these new ones were to mean much in the history of man, and their names were to be known, world-wide.

As with the new lands the namers did not develop any system or general plan. The question here, one should note, is of the greater seas, and even oceans, not of the myriad little bays and coves and harbors that speckle the coastlines. These, being essentially features of the land, usually bear such names, and are often, indeed, named from the land, so that we have Calfpasture Cove and Mussel Sound. But the oceans and the wider seas—they too needed names, and such names were not always easily established.

As in ancient times, description—that standfast help of the namer—was of little avail. Except for floating ice, one sea, the fact is, is much like another sea, and any shipmaster knows that the qualities of a body of water may change sharply under the influence of weather and season. The situation for the Chinese, apparently, was somewhat different. We still use their term the Yellow Sea for that one so colored by the outflow of the great rivers—though actually the name may be a transfer from Yellow River. The Chinese, also, by relative description, used East Sea and South Sea, so that European voyagers adopted those names, adding further distinction, as in South China Sea.

A common method of naming these large bodies of water was, however, just that which the ancient namers had used— that is, to call them, by association, after some tribe or country which they bordered. As we have the Caspian Sea after the Caspians, so we have the Caribbean after those warlike and much-feared cannibals the Caribs. The Gulf of Mexico echoes Mexico, the chief goal of early voyagers. So also there is nothing that needs to be said further about such examples as the Gulf of Panama and the Bay of Bengal. Even a city—usually the chief port—could yield the name by association, as with the Gulf of Quayaquil and the Sea of Okhotsk.

Almost unique, in that it bears a saint's name, is the Gulf of St. Lawrence, but it also arises from association. On August 7, 1535, the explorer Jacques Cartier, seeking shelter from bad weather, found refuge in a small bay, and thankfully called it after St. Lawrence, whose day it was. Thus planted early, the name spread to the whole gulf, and eventually to the river.

As is to be expected, some anomalies seem to exist. Thus the Gulf of California appears to be far removed from the area most commonly associated with that name. Perhaps for that reason substitute names for it have come into use, such as the Sea of Cortez and Vermilion Sea. Historically, the name first arose by association with the long peninsula that is now known as Baja California.

As if recognizing that a discovery established a kind of possession, or else wishing to pay a tribute, the world, not infrequently, put the discoverer's name upon the body of water. Hudson and Bering were thus permanently inscribed upon the map—partly, perhaps, because they died in the course of the explorations. Other explorers to be honored, either contemporaneously or in retrospect, include Barents, Baffin, Foxe, Weddell, Bellinghausen, and Tasman. Narrow waters connecting oceans and seas were also likely to take the names of the discoverers—Davis Strait, The Strait of Magellan (see below), Drake Passage, Cook Strait.

Rarely—especially as compared with land-features—did sea-voyagers give the names of patrons. The Philippine Sea derives from King Philip II of Spain, but only at second hand, the name having been first bestowed upon the islands. An exception is the Beaufort Sea, to the north of Alaska, which honors Admiral Francis Beaufort of the British Admiralty, a great forwarder of Arctic exploration. Another such was Felix Booth, patron of John Ross's expedition, who subsidized the explorer with funds derived from his prosperous distillery. In Latinized form the Gulf of Boothia commemorates him. One can also note that both Beaufort and Booth, like other patrons, were more commonly honored by the naming of numerous land-features, such as the Beaufort Islands, and Cape Felix.

The explorations also set up what we may consider a new category of names by necessitating a new conception of *ocean*. The mapping of the globe's surface eventually revealed what had been considered as merely "the ocean" was actually divided into at least four parts, each of them of sufficient size to warrant the general name. With the Atlantic, however, no problem arose for a specific, since the ancient term could merely carry on (see Book III, Chapter 6).

As for our Indian Ocean, the ancients had merely thought it to be the Red Sea. With its recognition as an ocean it took its name, after the common custom, from the most important country bordering it (see Book III, Chapter 14).

The Arctic Ocean shows a series of transfers. Arctic, originally from an Indo-European word meaning "harm, injury," was first applied to the bear, possibly as a so-called taboo-name, so that one would not have to risk the monster's displeasure by mentioning his real name. The ancient Greeks then applied it to the constellation which is also known as the Big Dipper, and which holds the northern part of the heavens. Before long (as early, indeed, as the time of Herodotus) the name had attained geographical significance as the region of the earth "under the Bear." The Arctic Ocean, therefore, was merely in a global sense "the North Sea," and thus raised no problem of nomenclature.

Antarctic (whether applied to an ocean or a continent) arose by learned counterpart, "opposite the Arctic."

Of all the oceans, the largest in size is also the most interesting in its name. The Spanish conquistadors, probing upon the coast of what they did not as yet know to be an isthmus connecting two continents, heard from the Indians of a great sea which lay to the south. Soon their leader, Balboa, reached a height of land and saw this water, to which he and other Spaniards gave the name South Sea, a term which was locally applicable and even obvious. The explorations of only a few years, however, were sufficient to show the inadequacy of this name for what had to be recognized as one of the oceans, lying more to the west than to the south. Yet the highly inappropriate name survived with much tenacity. The "South Sea islands" and "the South Sea" itself are still current as generalized and poetic expressions.

One might think that the inexactitude of the name eventually led to its displacement. But, curiously, its replacement was also questionable in application.

This name of the largest ocean was one of several great names to spring from the voyage of Magellan in 1520 and 1521. One of these is that for the dangerous strait which he was the first to navigate. Modestly enough, he himself called it Todos los Santos, as if intimating that the collaborative efforts of all the saints had been necessary for a successful passage. In later years the Dutch de Wert called it Stormy Strait, and the Spanish Sarmiento named it Strait of God's Mother. In the long run, however, these yielded (by a kind of justice not always seen in world opinion), and it became merely the Strait of Magellan.

Passing out of the western end of the strait, Magellan came into a sea of peculiar appearance, so that the voyagers considered that they were not in the open ocean, but in a large gulf. Perhaps there was method in this conclusion, for, being in a separate gulf, they could give a name that would not conflict with South Sea. Quite possibly, they began to refer to it as a calm sea. The mild and favorable weather continued, as if truly all the saints were working together. At what point the new name was formalized we have no direct information. The good weather itself continued through all the passage—three months and twenty days! Navarrete records "they named it Mar Pacifico, because in all the time that they sailed across it, they had no storm."

Actually the adjective, as applied to a sea, is of Latin rather than of Spanish association, and the first form may well have been in Latin, Mare Pacificum.

The largest of earthly features thus bears a name for which we can postulate mixed motives. From Magellan's experience he was giving an honest descriptive name, but as a seasoned navigator he can have had little confidence that a vast expanse of open water could be fairly described as being without storms. In another sense, then, the name is from the incident, that is, that this particular voyager had the good fortune of an easy passage. In the formal Latin naming there may also, in the namer's mind, have been a touch of the commendatory, an encouragement for others to sail that way. Finally, there may well have been a little of sailor's superstition—that, by speaking favorably, a man might encourage good weather to continue.

20
Pattern of Latin America

Viewed historically, the establishment of the millions of names necessary for the Americas looms as a gigantic task. In practice, it was shared among thousands of diverse people, working over centuries.

Historians are likely to emphasize the difference among the varying nationalities of the occupiers (and therefore the namers) of the Americas. True, they spoke different languages, and supported (at least, after the first half-century) different churches. The blue-eyed Englishman or Norman stood in contrast to the dark Castilian or Portuguese. One called his queen Isabella; the other, Elizabeth.

But Isabella and Elizabeth are the same name, developed from the Hebrew, just as Spanish and English are cousin-languages by descent from Indo-European. Most of the common traditions of Christianity remained strong, among both Catholics and Protestants.

All the European newcomers found native peoples in the newly discovered lands, and took names from them. The number and kinds of names thus adopted seems to depend not so much upon the nationality of the Europeans as upon local conditions. The degree to which the Indians were few, low in culture, and hostile, was likely to influence adversely the transmission of names. Change any of these factors, and the Indian name more easily passed the language barrier, no matter what the nationality of the Europeans.

As for names actually bestowed, the namers saw the world in much the same way, whether they said Sugarloaf or Pan de Azúcar. When they killed some dangerous animal—be it a grizzly or a jaguar—the little stream there was likely to take its name from the incident. The French remembered their king in Louisiana, and the Spanish theirs in Ferdinandina, and the English theirs in Carolina—but basically it was all one. In Argentina as in Iowa, where a pioneer made his settlement his name was likely to survive on a village.

Men of all of the nations, moreover, made much use of transfer-names—obviously, in the interests of economy. So name-clusters arose everywhere, with what had been a stream-name coming to stand also on the hill, the village, and even the district.

Naturally, there were differences, and interesting distinctions of detail. The Protestants tended to avoid saints' names, and the Catholics to propagate them, often transfering the dedication of the church to the village. Also, the Catholics used the convenient system of naming a place by looking at the calendar and taking the name of the saint whose day it happened to be. But even this disinction tended to die out. Spanish explorers in the eighteenth century had apparently grown tired of saints. On the other hand, English explorers of the same period, such as Cook and Vancouver, sometimes looked at the English calendar of saints and planted those names.

One may maintain that the English, sentimentally, reproduced more profusely the names of their homeland, as with Boston and New Hampshire and Chester County, but one can also cite the Spaniards' Guadalajara, Córduba, Nuevo León, and many others.

The manufacture of names is something of a speciality of speakers of English. Even so, Mexicali seems to thrive. As another detail of difference, Latin American usage employs long and formal namings, such as the small towns of Argentina, among them Libertador General San Martín and Comandante

Luis Piedrabuena. In ordinary usage such names are shortened, but Anglo-Americans would not allow them even formally.

In the present project, I must desert and ignore that rich
nomenclatural field of the United States of America, on the
ground that I have already treated it in *Names on the Land,* to
which all those curious about the matter are referred and even
recommended. I will here attempt to present, in a single chapter, some flavor of the naming of parts of the Americas from
Spanish and Portuguese traditions. Actually, indeed, the Spanish tradition has exercised a basic influence upon Texas, California, and other states.

Since Latin America presents some millions of names, here I
shall concentrate upon a few world-famous natural features,
and upon the continental nations and their capital cities, for
these names, which are of special interest in themselves, are
also to some degree typical.

The Indian languages of Latin America are many and
various, representing even different linguistic families. Such a
work as this cannot go into detail, and must in general be content with specifying merely "the local Indian language," rather
than pin-pointing Guarani, Kechua, or some other scientifically
established unit.

The usual method of such a presentation as proposed here
is to make the division linguistically, between Indian names and
European names. In some instances, however, the Europeans
used a term of native derivation, but themselves performed the
naming-process—sometimes, apparently, even replacing a previously established native name. As examples, we can cite Nicaragua and Bogotá (see below). As a result, the present presentation will classify the names by their method of origin rather
than upon a linguistic basis.

Unfortunately, but only to be expected, the significance of
many of the native names is uncertain. In some instances, these
may have been so old as to have become unintelligible to the In-

dians who lived in those places at the time of the European arrival. Or, careless transmission may be to blame (see Book I, Chapter 4).

The greatest single land-feature of the continent is the mountain system known as the Andes. The chronicler Garcilaso, himself half-Inca, writing less than a century after the Conquest, should be accepted as a good authority. He stated that the derivation was from a tribal name which he spelled Anti. These people lived to the east of Cusco, and so their name might easily, by association, have come to denote the local mountains. Later proposals have been Copper Mountains (because that metal was there obtained), and East Mountains (as seen from the capital city of Cuzco). Once established locally, any of these names could readily have spread, north and south, along with the course of Spanish communications.

The well-respected general principle that large rivers bear the oldest names scarcely holds good for South America, that land of remarkable streams. To be sure, Orinoco is pre-European, with -co meaning merely "river," orino-, possibly, "clay."

The most common element in river-names is from the widespread Quechua languages, that is, pará, a term which can mean, in different dialects, anything from "rain" to "water," and is often applied to large streams. In simplest form, it stands as the Pará in Brazil, but it also appears with different endings which are probably attached specifics, often so worn down as to preclude elucidation.

Four of the greatest stream-names, however, are of European origin. The Magdalena and the São Francisco are clearly religious, and arouse neither difficulty nor much interest. La Plata (often The Plate, in English) is the Spanish word for "silver," but applied to a stream which is neither silvery in appearance nor productive of precious metal. The present name sprang from the voyage of Sebastian Cabot, who sailed there under the Spanish flag in 1526. He found the local Indians in possession of a certain amount of silver. Actually, they were not exploiting any mines, but had come by their modest wealth by plundering a Portuguese expedition. Cabot, however, assumed that he had made contact with a rich source of silver, and so christened the stream.

The name is thus of complicated origin. It might be said to be from false description or false association. But the discovery of this silver was a kind of incident, and the name a commendatory, certainly the result of wishful thinking and the desire to enhance the importance of the discovery. Perhaps for this reason, or perhaps merely because it was a catchy name for its attractive suggestions, Cabot's christening displaced several earlier Spanish names, and it still maintains its triumphant career.

The story of the greatest river also springs from an incident. In 1541 Francisco de Orellana made an amazing voyage down a great stream, which seemed endless and grew ever larger and larger. The chronicler Garcilaso may be allowed the narrative:

> Francisco de Orellana, in descending the river, had some skirmishes with the Indians inhabiting its banks, who were very fierce. In some parts the women came out to fight along with their husbands. Therefore, and to make his voyage the more wonderful, he stated that it was a land of Amazons, and asked his Majesty for a commission to conquer them.

Herrera, writing some years later, was skeptical, but he permitted the explorers to state their case:

> Father Carbajal affirms that . . . he and the other Spaniards saw ten or twelve Amazons, who were fighting in front of the Indians, as if they commanded them. . . . These women appeared to be very tall, robust, good-looking, with long hair twisted over their heads . . . and bows and arrows in their hands with which they killed seven or eight Spaniards.

The Europeans of this period found the ancient tale of warlike women to be extraordinarily intriguing—partly, doubtless, because it was sexually challenging, and partly because certain stories associated Amazons with precious metals, as in the earliest account of California.

There is, in itself, no reason to doubt that a few energetic and desperate women joined with their men in resisting a Spanish attack on their village. From this the story could have grown, and we note Garcilaso's cynical comment, "to make his voyage the more wonderful."

As with La Plata, therefore, the name of the great Amazon sprang from a minor incident, and one which may, indeed, have been largely fictional. But the Amazons, like silver, made good publicity and supplied an excellent commendatory. In those times everybody knew, or liked to believe, that Amazons used no metal but gold and that gems were "like stones of the field for abundance." So, once Amazon had been placed, it remained.

To turn to the nations and their capital cities, we may list six examples with which the naming-process appears to be wholly indigenous. About one of these, Tegucigalpa, so little is known that it can merely be cited as Indian. Managua has been noted as possibly from a tribe, but remains uncertain. One may point out, however, the apparent Spanish folk-etymology with -agua, "water."

Also indigenous is Mexico. The Spaniards found it a current term for the city and valley with which it has ever since maintained a particular association. During the Spanish regime the great province was officially New Spain, but in the early nineteenth century the emerging nation took the old and commonly used name. As for its derivation, Gutierre Tibón, whose dicta always demand respect, translates it as "moon-navel-place," with *navel* probably in the idea of "center." On the other hand, some connection with the Aztec war-god Mexitli (and other spellings) seems almost unavoidable, the question being, "Which is derived from the other?" It is a situation which is comparable to that between Athens and Athena. As to probability, we can merely comment that hundreds of places are named from gods (especially if we stretch a little to include demigods and saints). On the other hand, anyone sets himself a hard task if he tries to find a god that has appeared as a deification of the name of a city. By mere probability, therefore, Mexico may well mean something like Mexitliland.

Guatemala has the honor of a full linguistic explanation in the work of the early chronicler Lopez de Gómara: "Cuahtemallan, commonly called Guatemala, means 'rotten tree,' for *cuauh* is 'tree,' and *temali* is 'rotten.' " As if not wishing to sponsor this uncomplimentary rendering he added an alternate, that it might mean "place of trees." The second possibility, however, does not fit the etymology as well as the first one does, nor does it give an apt semantic interpretation, since in a generally wooded country "place of trees" is not distinctive. In addition, the somewhat later historian Herrera, who displays much interest in names, presents only the meaning "rotten tree." Some later commentators have rendered this as "woodpile," thus trying to make sense, as if it were a lumbering operation, such as the Spaniards themselves sometimes indicated as Corte Madera. Topologically, however, there is no need for anyone to shy away from "rotten tree," which could identify some place, such as where a trail crossed a stream, and thus become the name of a village, which could become a city.

The name is of interest in its later history. It was first applied to the capital city, founded in 1524, and then to the province. In 1541, however, a cataclysmic flood of water from a near-by volcano almost wholly destroyed the city. The dangerous site was thereupon abandoned and a new capital founded, some twenty miles away. The curious feature is that the name, detached from its true site, was applied to the new foundation, where it still remains. The ruined city, partially rebuilt, came to be known as Old Guatemala, but exists now merely as Antigua.

Quito is from an Indian naming, which was applied to an inhabited site before its taking-over by the Spaniards. It apparently was then in a somewhat ruinous condition, and its older buildings (according to the always-to-be-respected Herrera) were known as *quito*. But other early authorities identify the Quitu as an ancient tribe which had conquered this country some five centuries earlier. The testimonies are not wholly irreconcilable, since the old buildings might have taken the name of their legendary builders.

Panama is a local name for a village which the Spaniards merely took over. Las Casas, who wrote at an early date, gives it as meaning "place where many fish are taken." This reasonable idea for a village on a coastal bay seems to find confirmation in later investigation. The extension, by association, to the isthmus and the region follows common practice.

To proceed to the second group, the more numerous instances in which the Europeans themselves accomplished the essential work, we may begin with two descriptives, both of somewhat unusual nature.

Venezuela furnishes an excellent example of small-to-large. In 1499 Alonso de Hojeda, leading a party of Spaniards, came to an unusual Indian village:

> Its houses are built, ingeniously, in the water, supported on stakes driven into the bottom. Communication from one house to another is by canoe.

The Spaniards, for obvious reasons, called the place Venecia. Later it took the diminutive form, and as Venezuela, "little Venice," spread to include the whole region—and, eventually, the nation.

Ecuador is also to be classed as a descriptive, though of unusual nature (see also Book II, Chapter 1). Meaning simply "equator," the name is apt for a country lying squarely on that line. An imaginary line, however, is not anything that a person can see or otherwise sense, and the name thus falls into the class of intellectual descriptions.

Three of the names may be classed as possessives.

Caracas is a tribal name for some of the Indians holding the region: the s is probably the Spanish sign of the plural.

Herrera, again useful, explains another case:

> Although this whole country is called Nicaragua, that is not its real name. But [it is so called] because Gil González Dávila and Francisco Hernández de Córdova began its conquest in alliance with the chief who was named Nicaragua. . . . So they called all the region so, although it was divided into many districts, each with its own designation.

Such a puppet-king was useful to the conquistadors, since they could enter upon the reduction of the region with the idea (or fiction) that they were supporting the rights of the monarch against his rebellious subjects. At the same time, they found an advantage in extending his theoretical rule as far as possible, and so obliterated the other local names. Since the assumption also was that the king was the owner of the land, the process of naming may be considered possessive.

Closely similar is the case of Bogotá. Gomara mentions "the king Bogotá," and Herrera gives the interesting detail that he was not only lord of the country, but also had four hundred wives. In this instance the Spaniards made use of his name for one of their towns, again using the idea of possession.

Only one of this group of names is to be credited to an incident. On August 15, 1536, which is Assumption Day, Juan de Ayolas captured a certain Indian town. To the foundation which he later made on the site he gave the name Nuestra Señora de la Asunción, because of his victory on that day. It remains, shortened, as Asunción.

Since incident-names and commemoratives have much in common, the seven names of this list to be classed as commemoratives might, in some instances, be considered as arising from incidents—and might the more likely be so classed, if the occasions of their naming were better authenticated. Most of them are of religious significance. The considerable number indicates not only Spanish religiosity of the period, but also the formal nature of their political organization, which dictated that such events as the founding of a new town should proceed with due ceremony. In such a situation, the accompanying incidents or what the place looked like or what the Indians said its name was—all these were secondary as compared with the propriety of the name for a Spanish town which might eventually be the seat of a viceroy or governor and would have to be mentioned in reports to the archbishop and even to the king. (In taking possession of a new territory and establishing upon it the name New Mexico, Juan de Oñate in 1598 expended a full day in ceremonies, religious and lay, including both the preaching of a sermon and the presentation of a comedy.)

An obvious example of a religious name is Santiago, founded far to the south, in 1541. It commemorated not only St. James, the patron of Castile, but also an actual Spanish town, well known as a goal of pilgrimage. San José in Costa Rica honored St. Joseph, also a major saint.

El Salvador shows another occurrence of a name which was, elsewhere, the first to be given in the New World, and was then bestowed by Columbus himself.

Buenos Aires is of special interest in being so deceptive as to confuse even such an acute scholar as J. J. Egli, who merely wrote it off as being named for its "good breezes." Herrera, however, is authority for a religious naming in honor of Nuestra Señora de Buenos Aires—"Our Lady of the Favorable Breezes." As not infrequently happens—Asunción, indeed, offers an example, and so does Los Angeles—the unduly common main part of the name went out of use, or may never have been in ordinary use, and the distinguishing epithet remained for the place-name.

La Paz, the capital of Bolivia, dates its foundation from 1548, when it was first named in a kind of double commemoration. Not only was it for Nuestra Señora de la Paz, "Our Lady of the Peace," but also it celebrated an end of hostilities between two warring factions among the conquistadors themselves.

Commemorative, but wholly unconnected with religion, are Bolivia and Colombia. The former was named, after the success of the struggle for independence, in honor of Simón Bolívar, the hero of that conflict. Colombia, which, after independence, replaced the Spanish name Nueva Granada, fastened upon a name which had already been widely used as a commemorative in the United States—as with the District of Columbia and the Columbia River. Actually there had been a strong movement to adopt that name as the official one, thus replacing the awkward and lengthy United States of America. That movement might eventually have succeeded, except for the adoption of the name by the South American republic.

Only one of these names can be classified as definitely commendatory. The roots of its naming go back to Columbus, on his fourth voyage. Along a certain stretch of coast he obtained some gold from the Indians, and called it Costa del Oro, "Coast of the Gold." Later the name was generalized as Costa Rica, a

term not so much based on description or reality as suggestive
of future possibility for wealth.

No fewer than seven of these names arose by transfer. The
proportion is significant as another indication of what may be
called the general laziness of mankind, that is, the tendency to
avoid giving a new name by spreading an old one around to do
duty on a new generic. We also meet the general principle that
the first names to be established in a country new to the namers
are those of the chief streams. Five names of South American
nations and one of a capital city arose from rivers.

In 1515 the Spaniards penetrated some distance to the south
from Panama, and came (they thought) to the village of a chief
named Biruquete. Actually, that may merely have referred to
the village, and meant something like "granary" in the local
speech. Naturally (confusion in language being normal in such
situations), the Spaniards assumed that Biruquete also served
for the village and for the river there. It shifted on Spanish
tongues to Peruquete, and then was shortened to Peru, and
applied generally to the regions lying to the south. Thus the nation got its name from a small river which does not even lie
within its present boundaries.

Founding a capital city for their new province of Peru, the
Spaniards dedicated it, on January 6, 1535, as Ciudad de los
Reyes, "City of the Kings," thus commemorating the Three
Kings, whose day it was. As sometimes happens, however, this
formal naming failed to succeed, being perhaps difficult on the
tongue. The stream there was known as Rimaco, meaning "one
who speaks," since there had once been on the banks a heathen
temple and oracle. Or, since other Peruvian rivers bear the
same name, it may merely refer to the noisiness of the stream
itself, which can easily be called "talking." Rimac, severely handled in its transition between languages, came out eventually as
Lima, displaced the official name, and established itself as viable and even poetic in Spanish.

Chile has produced much speculation and much playing with
the roots to be collected from various Indian languages, as well

as the usually plausible idea that it is a tribal name. These suppositions ignore Herrera's statement that it is from a river which had been so called since the time of the Incas. As for the etymology of the river-name, that still remains open for a guessing game.

Paraguay and Uruguay suggest a common element in -*guay*, but this identity may be only the result of attraction bringing the names together in the Spanish period.

Though Paraguay seems to contain the frequently appearing Guarani element *pará-*, "water, river," some scholars see -*y* as being the element with that generic meaning, thus also occurring in Uruguay. Possibly, however, -*guay* can represent a worn-down form of *guaso*, "big," so that we have merely another "big river." Also invoked is the local word *paragua*, meaning "crown of feathers," but scarcely fitting for a river. The most satisfactory explanation is probably that of León Cadogan, who takes -*y* as "river" and *paragua*- as the name of a chief who collaborated with the Spaniards in the conquest of some local tribes. In this case, Paraguay follows the course of Nicaragua and Bogotá.

Uruguay is even more uncertain, by mere resemblance of sound being explained as "bird," "snail," or "mollusk." A better possibility seems to be that offered by A. J. Peralta, that is, it is a coupling of -*y*, "river," with *irugua*, "chief channel."

Although also arising by transfer from a river, Argentina is unique among the names of this list in that its history is wholly within the European languages. As already noted, the great stream of that region came to be known as La Plata. With the establishment of the new republic the name was merely shifted to that of a more Latinate form of a Spanish adjective, with the meaning "of silver, silvery." The resulting Argentina, in the feminine, served well for a region, and was at once practical, poetic, and less commonplace than the ordinary word, which continued to designate the river.

The only name of the list to be named by transfer from a feature other than a river is Honduras. As Herrera tells, the first Spanish ships to sail that coast could find no anchorage near a certain cape, even though they were close to shore. They were thus in a dangerous situation. Drifting or sailing along, however, they eventually found shallower water, as opposed to the depths (Spanish, *honduras*). They then remarked "God be praised, that we are come out of those depths." Though no one can guarantee such exact words, the general situation seems acceptable enough. By natural association the near-by cape became Cabo de Honduras, a designation that served at once as a landmark and a warning. Eventually the whole country took its name from the cape, in spite of the inapplicability of the term to dry land.

Two names from the list of nations and capital cities remain for discussion. These two, Montevideo and Brazil, present special points of interest.

Montevideo may be confidently assigned to the list of incident-names. On January 10, 1520, Magellan was on that coast, which is generally flat and lacking in good landmarks. At some point, however, a lookout called down that he saw a hill. If he had been an ordinary Spanish seaman, he would naturally have said, "Veo un monte!" but he might have shouted in excitement "Monte! Veo!" He also added something about the hill being shaped like a hat (sombrero), since the record preserves that detail.

But to derive a place from an exclamation of this kind is very rare, and what happened is even more confused. "We gave it the name Monte Vidi," writes the chronicler Albo. But that would be half Spanish, half Latin, and would mean "I have seen a mountain." Just what was happening here? We may fall back upon the general principle that an unusual name requires an unusual explanation. What the lookout said apparently impressed people enough for them to fix the strange name—doubly strange, in fact, being of a type rarely given and of a mixture of languages which is almost unparalleled. The possibility is that the lookout was some foreigner (Catalan, perhaps, or Italian) who did not speak Castilian fluently, and on occasion mixed up his words and his word-order. What he said may have impressed those on deck as very unusual, perhaps very funny. A break in the ship's monotony! That he should have known some Latin is not incredible in those years of the Renaissance. He may then have called down, "Montem video!" or even the mixture "Monte video!" He could then have added that it looked like a hat, and that too could have come out in laughable form. At least we can be sure that something unusual happened, and the strong suggestion is that a lookout mixed up his languages in some ludicrous fashion. In any case, the city preserves the strange name.

Brazil is one of those names which seems to present a simple case. Anyone, in fact, trying to suggest something else might well be accused of needlessly stirring up the mud in the water. Even such an early historian as Herrera could write: "now called Brasil from that sort of wood brought from there." Still known as brazilwood, that timber remains a valuable article of commerce. It is also true that primitive countries, particularly those with shorelines, may take their names from their chief product—as with the Ivory Coast and the Gold Coast.

Pedro Alvares Cabral, the Portuguese navigator, first saw this land on April 22, 1500, but gave it its name as of May 3, which was the feast of the Finding of the True Cross, so he called it Terra de Vera Cruz. The usual accounts declare that Brazil came later, and they may, indeed, be correct. But other questions arise. Why did the not-very-notable name Brazil replace the earlier name? Can it be that Brazil was, from the very beginning, the name in the common speech of the seamen?

Anyone, indeed, may raise the point that Brazil was an old name, among seamen, many years before Cabral. It was a name applied to one of the legendary islands which were thought to exist in the Atlantic somewhere. Those islands appeared regularly on maps, and Brazil or Brasil was generally located far to the west of Scotland or Ireland. The legend might have arisen, one would think, from a glimpse of fog-obscured St. Kilda, by a hard-pressed shipmaster, blown off course and trying desperately to claw off from the wave-pounded cliffs.

In those years, we must remember, Columbus and others were constantly imagining that they were discovering lands that were already known. Another legendary island was Antillia, and it has actually survived in the islands known in English as the Antilles. So, why not Brazil?

In retrospect, and even when considered by means of a short list, the names of Latin America exhibit much variety. Linguistically, they appear to be more or less equally derived from the various Indian languages and from Spanish, with Portuguese exerting its influence in Brazil, and Latin supplying occasional aid. All the methods of the namers' approaches are exemplified, with the exception of manufacture. Even so, such a name as Bolivia is after some fashion coined, with the aid of a Latin suffix. The pattern of naming must in many ways, be considered comparable to that of Anglo-America.

21

The U.S.A. and the World

Although the history of place-naming in the United States, being the topic of *Names on the Land,* is not integral to the present subject matter, we should at least present some sketch of the position which the names of that country display in comparison with other parts of the world.

As would be expected, the pattern displays what may be called the universals of place-naming (see Books I and II). It exhibits nothing unusual in its use of descriptives and associatives; its nomenclature is rich in folk-etymologies and in names from incident. By its frequent employment of possessives, either from tribes or from individuals, the pattern associates itself with the areas—such as most of Europe—which have developed under the influence of the idea of private ownership of land.

The United States differs from most of the world (at the same time associating itself with certain special areas) by its considerable use of commemoratives, often with an associated commendatory idea. These names include those brought from the "old country," as with Boston, New Orleans, and Harlem. In the western parts, however, such names usually go back to places in the eastern states. Thus, anywhere west of the Appalachians, Lexington can generally be put down as derived from

Massachusetts, and Winchester as being from Virginia. Commemoratives for men, however, usually refer directly to the person.

Also setting the United States off from most of the world is a whole group of names which may vaguely be called "literate," since they spring from the written and printed language rather than from speech. Although many of the frontiersmen were illiterate, especially before the nineteenth century, yet most groups included some literates, and such a process as naming was likely to be the responsibility of the leaders, who were also those most likely to be able to read and write. We meet here a great contrast to most other parts of the world, which were named before the invention of writing or before its introduction into the particular area.

Sometimes the evidence of literacy and its influence is surprising. Thus Daniel Boone during one of his mid-eighteenth-century explorations into the region of Kentucky had with him a copy of *Gulliver's Travels* and from it named a stream Lorbrulgrud, a name which survives as Lulbegrud.

What may be called the exotic commemoratives likewise arose from reading—hence such names as Toledo, Memphis, and Lima.

The highly characteristic manufactured names are also dependent upon literacy. Occasionally, someone may have analyzed the sounds of a word and constructed a new name from them, but the regular process was visual, working from an inspection of the spelling. Only by manipulation of the written or printed letters would anyone have been likely to produce Tesnus from Sunset or to have fused Bickham and Jerome into Birome.

Mistake-names, also, are usually mistakes in spelling rather than in pronunciation, though in turn the spelling may affect the pronunciation. This whole result of the spelling has been, in fact, to create what are, in effect, new names. Thus Berlin (accented on the first syllable) and Athens (with a long vowel) are so transformed that in speech they may be considered as something new.

Though literacy has made possible these unusual names, it

did not actually supply a motive for them. Undoubtedly the most important factors working toward that end were the tremendous rapidity of settlement and the accompanying growth of population, especially throughout the nineteenth century. Necessarily, under the conditions, a great number of names were needed.

Faced thus with the necessity of giving many names, the Americans developed a kind of facility, even an expertise. There was no need to make a great task over giving a name. It might be an occasion for humor—for a pun or a private joke. You might pick a name out of the atlas, the Bible, a Shakespearean play, or the novel that you happened to be reading. Railroad officials named stations by the dozen, sometimes in alphabetical order. Miners contributed the flamboyant titles of their mines—Golconda, Anaconda. Ranchers provided brand names, such as Ucross and Teedee.

The final result has been what is possibly the most variegated name-pattern of the world.

A special interest attaches to the likenesses and differences of the name-pattern of the United States in relation to that of the home-country—here to be considered in a linguistic sense, and therefore chiefly England.

The similarities are striking. We may note, for instance, the great number of possessives—the names of Anglo-Saxon tribal and family leaders being equivalent to those of pioneer landowners, Indian traders, and postmasters.

The actual transfer, commemoratively, of many habitation-names has resulted in a striking resemblance, though at a somewhat superficial level.

Considered, however, with respect to mechanism, the high number of commemoratives and commendatories constitutes a striking difference between the two regions. Moreover, the lack—or apparent lack—of incident-names in England also produces a notable difference. The differences such as those resulting from manufactured names have already been considered.

Linguistically, the greatest difference lies in the general in-

telligibility of American names as contrasted with the obscurity
of British names—at least to the ordinary person. The causes
are obvious. The British names commonly arose in the Anglo-
Saxon or early Middle English periods, but the emergence of
the American pattern lies wholly within the Modern English
period. The process of growing unintelligibility (see Book I,
Chapter 6) has thus had little opportunity to work in the
United States.

The result may be considered, aesthetically, as somewhat
mixed. Names of unknown meaning possess or readily absorb a
poetic value, as with Avon, Arden, or Runnymede. But intelligible place-names may in their very meaning "tell a story," or
raise a suggestion, as with Broken Sword Creek, Golden Gate,
and Providence. The United States, moreover, especially because of its Indian names, is by no means devoid of mystery
and the accompanying romance, as with Chickamauga, Mississippi, Chicago, or Atchafalaya.

A common conclusion—or accusation—of British observers
of the nineteenth century was that the American pattern displayed excessive repetition, and therefore monotony, in comparison with that of England. How this curious idea could ever
have arisen is difficult to see. One factor undoubtedly was that
the observer was comparing the whole United States with England on the principle of one-horse-one-rabbit. Thus, if a name
occurred a dozen times west of the Atlantic and only twice to
the east of it, the conclusion was thus made, with no allowance
for the much greater size of the United States. England, in fact,
is only about as large as the state of New York.

In its variety and multiplicity of place-names, the United
States is actually remarkable—especially as compared with England. Several forces were at work toward this end.

In the first place, the density of place-names in the United
States is low, so that the mere statistical possibility of repetition
is lessened.

Second, the individual American has been footloose and mo-
bile. The Anglo-Saxon peasant, attached to his land with its
village, did not move farther than a few miles, and so did not
know—much less care—that the name of his village was re-

peated ten miles to the south and again twelve miles to the east. Such iteration would have been an intolerable nuisance to the free-roving American.

The situation was even formalized when the Post Office Department, early in the nineteenth century, firmly prohibited repetition within a state. This ruling, indeed, had little influence upon the names of natural features, and the land developed a multiplicity of streams known as Clear Creek, Sand Creek, and Beaver Creek. Minnesota has (or had, about 1900) at least a hundred bodies of water known as Mud Lake. At the same time, we must comment that Minnesota is about twice as large as England and that the state has an estimated ten thousand lakes, so that some repetition was inevitable. Mud Lake in most of its occurrences was small and unimportant, scarcely needing a name at all, rarely mentioned except in its immediate vicinity. Since the census of Mud Lakes was compiled, many of the names have probably been replaced or the lakes themselves have been drained for agriculture.

England has five rivers known as Avon, and many other repeated river-names. Much more striking, even, is the multiplicity of habitation-names, such as Charlton, Stoke, and Ashton. The commonest such name is supposed to be Newton—at least one example occurring in nearly every county. In England (and in most of the European countries) such repetition has led to the device of considering the original name as a quasi-generic, as with Stoke, for instance, it undoubtedly was. Thus considered, the name attracts an additional element to serve as a distinguishing specific. Thus we have, for example—gaining precision at the loss of succinctness—Newton Blossomville, Newton by Daresbury, Maiden Newton, and Newton Regis.

Repetition is also the cause of the length of English addresses, as evidenced on almost any letter. The name of the county regularly occurs, and in many instances some other distinctions.

The comparison of the United States with the newer English-speaking nations—especially with Canada, New Zealand, and Australia—raises interesting details. Such comparison follows, in the next chapter.

22

The Briton Overseas

During the second half of the eighteenth century and the first three-quarters of the nineteenth, the inhabitants of the British Isles accomplished the exploration and settlement of Australia, New Zealand, and English-speaking Canada. In the same thrust they fixed, implanted, or created the place-names.

The geographical diversity of these lands and their separation by wide reaches of ocean might seem to preclude any common quality in their name-patterns. Actually, however, the patterns are highly similar, because they arose from the same motherland.

Most important as an influence was the English speech, which was not much affected by the numerous Scottish and Irish settlers. Moreover, except in French Canada, there was no seriously competing European language. The three name-patterns came to depend upon a substratum of aboriginal speech—Indian and Eskimo, Maori, Australian.

In culture, moreover, the settlers in the different lands all sprang from the British tradition—sometimes, indeed, from the same family. The names themselves (so many of them commemorative) testify to an intense patriotic loyalty to the homeland.

Negatively, as a lack in the British inheritance, the colonists failed to possess any tradition of naming. Whether English, Scottish, Irish, or Welsh, they came from regions where the names had long since been established, and where the bestowing of names was no longer actively practiced. Even the new cities which had sprung up with the Industrial Revolution were merely, like Birmingham and Sheffield, built upon the sites of Anglo-Saxon villages, and preserved those names.

In this respect the situation differed from that of the people of the United States. By the later eighteenth century the Americans had already been naming places over the course of two centuries. (The first English namings, Virginia among them, date from 1584.) The Americans, as the previous chapter has noted, had thus acquired what we may call a proficiency. Such experience was absent among the new immigrants into Canada and the southern lands.

As may happen, such a lack of tradition worked, apparently, in two ways. In one direction it gave a chance for creativity and originality. In another, it led to playing safe, and therefore to dullness, parochialism, and monotony.

Moreover, a few special namers actually possessed a well-developed tradition of naming and its responsibilities. These were the explorers by sea, whose technical ancestry went back to the captains whom Prince Henry had sent out from Portugal. The great English discoverers around the edges of the southern ocean (especially Cook and Flinders), knew from this tradition that repetition of names should be avoided, and that unusual names, therefore, need not be altogether eschewed.

Nonetheless, these captains saw no harm in the repetition of a name if a sufficiently long interval of space intervened, and these repetitions in themselves speak eloquently of the far-ranging English explorations of that time. Thus the names and titles of the British royal family were sown over the face of the earth.

Lesser figures, also, might find themselves thus honored in far places. Such a one was Sir John Barrow, second secretary of the Admiralty for forty years, a promoter of exploration, and a man of warm friendships. Among a whole generation of British voyagers, to name some natural feature for Barrow was almost as much taken for granted as to name one for Queen Victoria. His name now holds the northern point of the American land-mass. His friends also implanted it elsewhere—several times in the Arctic, in the Antarctic, in Australia, in Korea, in South Africa, in Oceania.

The names of the three nations themselves are of interest. About Canada only a little is sure—that is, that its first record-ing is in Cartier's narrative of his 1535 voyage, and that he took the name to refer to a large and indefinite region around the St. Lawrence River. Since communication between explorer and Indians was dubious, we can have little confidence in the accuracy of even this conclusion, and no one is certain of what Indian language gave rise to the term. It is most commonly supposed to be Iroquoian and to be from *kanata,* "village, town," or even "house." But with any of those meanings it is not a suitable term for a whole region. Besides, the Iroquois, as far as records go, lived farther inland than the spot where Cartier heard the name. Altogether, then, Canada must be put down as only another of those early-transferred Indian terms about which we are reduced to mere guesswork.

And of guesswork there has been plenty, including one famous and often-repeated story. The Portuguese explorer Cortereal in 1500 got into this region, but became discouraged at not finding much that was interesting. He or his men then said, "Cá nada!" which means, "Here nothing!" As with so many such stories, the likelihood is that some humorist was the originator, and that only later was the tale taken seriously. Its acceptance demands that the local Indians should have pre-served the Portuguese exclamation, and fed it back to the Frenchmen a whole generation later! Onomastically, the moral to be drawn is that correspondences of sounds and spelling are not always to be trusted (against judgments based on history and common sense) even in names with as many as six letters.

Australia furnishes a good example of an apt descriptive, evolved rather than bestowed, springing from the tradition of Latin as a universal European language. (See Book III, Chapter 7.)

Magellan, in his passage of the straits, had seen many fires burning on the land to the south. These had been lighted by the natives, who were doubtless excited by the sight of the ship. From this incident Magellan gave the name Tierra del Fuego, "land of the fire." His use of "land," rather than "island," indicates his ignorance, since what he saw might be an island, or might, on the contrary, be the last northern extension of some continental mass. The modest name, moreover, may be taken as an indication of the natural modesty of the great captain and of a strong sense of not going beyond the evidence.

Contemporary geographers, however, were not so constrained by fact, and seized upon the possibility of the continent—that idea being in harmony with some of their theoretical conceptions of cosmology. World maps of the sixteenth century began to show this continent, which touched South America except for the narrow line of the strait, came within some hundreds of miles of Africa, and then swept around the southern hemisphere, full circle. The great Ortelius map of 1570 displays this land, with Terra [sic] del Fuego a small part of it, and the whole labeled Terra Australis, "land-southern." A whole line of notable voyagers—from Drake to Cook, and even more modern ones—were to be engaged in cutting this continent down, until eventually a small part of it survived as the presently recognized Antarctica.

Its name, however, clung to a large island, or small continent, which for a time bore the name New Holland, as initiated by Dutch voyagers. About the year 1800, under English auspices, and largely by the usage of that great explorer Matthew Flinders, the name of the now-discredited continent was applied to what might be considered a remnant. It assumed the Latinized form Australia—a name at once descriptive, practical, and poetic.

New Zealand, unlike its neighbor, preserved its Dutch name, which had appeared first in 1665 when geographers were beginning to realize that the area was probably not a mere part of the Terra Australia, but could be considered a nameable entity in itself. Zealand being taken from a province of the Netherlands, the naming (with the distinction New) was a com-

monplace for the period, New Netherland in North America
having been named a few years earlier. The original Dutch
province bore a rare name, and one that is definitely unusual,
since that region had no more an exclusive claim to being "sea-
land" than did other places bordering the sea. Possibly the nature of the region produced a kind of specialized descriptive,
since Zealand is delta country, at the mouths of the Rhine,
where low-lying land and tidal estuaries may have seemed to its
early settlers to give them some particular proprietorship in the
sea.

Though its bestowal upon those far-lying islands may have
been wholly for commemorative reasons, there is also a certain
justification and applicability. No country stands more lonely in
the oceans and has better right to be a land of the sea than does
New Zealand.

Unfortunately, no one thinks of it in its literal sense, and in
earlier times the English settlers considered it a foreign name,
meaningless and inappropriate, fit to be replaced. When the
Irish came upon the scene the two chief islands, for a while,
were New Ulster and New Munster, only to shift, later, into the
utterly commonplace North Island and South Island. In the
end, however, the Dutch name survived in English spelling—a
highly appropriate and even poetic name, if its origin is remembered.

The general place-name pattern of Canada offers an occasional poetic grotesquerie such as Medicine Hat and Moose
Jaw. (Both of these are apparently translations of Indian
names, but the reasons for their application are uncertain.) On
the whole, however, the name-pattern is conservative and even
monotonous as compared with that of the United States.

The great names of Canada are almost exclusively either of
Indian origin or are commemoratives of patriotic suggestion.
Quebec is the "narrows," from its situation on the St. Lawrence
estuary. Ottawa, Erie, and Huron are tribal. Toronto is much
disputed, but seems to contain the Iroquoian word for "log,"
and may be so called from another of those many streams
which were named because of being obstructed by a logjam.

Winnepeg is "water-dirty," but may be mythological rather than descriptive. Manitoba is "water (of) (the) prairie." Saskachewan is "swift-current," a name surviving in English translation on a tributary stream.

The patriotic commemoratives begin in the Maritimes with New Brunswick, Nova Scotia, and Prince Edward Island. They end on the Pacific coast with British Columbia, Victoria, and Vancouver. Far in the frozen north one finds King William Island, Prince of Wales Island, Prince Patrick Island, Victoria Island, and the Queen Elizabeth Islands. In between stand Regina and Alberta. Edmonton echoes, indirectly, the town of that name in England.

In a fit of temper one might well class these names as the brandings of colonialism. Whether lacking heroes or not inclined to honor them, Canada displays few names comparable to Washington, Franklin, Lincoln, and dozens of others which have turned the map of the United States into a demonstration of popular heroes.

Closest to attaining such a rating is Alexander Mackenzie, Scotland-born, but Canadian in his career. As one of the greatest of all overland explorers, his name, fittingly, stands upon the mighty river which he discovered, as well as upon the vast territory through which that river flows.

Second to Mackenzie, but still eminent as a river-voyager, we must rate Simon Fraser, also commemorated by the great stream which he explored.

The place-names of Australia and of New Zealand display enough similarity to be jointly presented, although certain differences are also of significance.

In both of the areas the explorers and settlers adopted many names from the natives. As might be expected—the higher culture of the Maoris being considered—these names are more numerous, or, certainly, more conspicuous, in New Zealand, where streams repeat to the point of monotony the syllable *wai*, "stream, river." On the other hand, river-names in Australia commonly preserve the English name of an early explorer or of some governor who was commemorated. Thus Stuart and Cunningham, having discovered a large stream, named it for Governor Sir Ralph Darling, who had encouraged their undertakings.

Natural features in New Zealand other than streams, as well as habitations, more commonly bear native names than they do in Australia. The chief exception to be noted is that the Australian capital preserves an aboriginal name. The reason in this case is that Canberra, as a city, is a recent foundation, which merely assumed a local name, recorded since 1826. An additional reason may be that the original Nganbirra, "meeting-place," is an apt term for a capital of a democracy.

The Murrumbidgee is the chief Australian native-named river, and it is merely another "big water." Many of these English-named streams, however, preserve native names for various sections—probably an indication that the aborigines, as commonly happens under primitive conditions, lacked a sense of the whole long river as an entity, but had names for its different reaches, pools, and rapids.

The southern lands display, as may be expected everywhere, a scattering of simple descriptives, such as Hummock Island and Round Mountain. More interesting (and one might even say more characteristic) are the descriptives of the more unusual types—intellectual, metaphorical, subjective. Many of these are namings made by the early voyagers, especially Cook and Flinders. These men, having to enter new names on their charts almost daily, developed into professionals, not content to repeat such clichés as Big, Black, and Rocky. So we find Mount Lofty and Streaky Bay—both specifics being definitely unusual.

Botany Bay itself (for a time, almost synonymous with Australia) is an excellent example of an intellectual descriptive, being given by Cook on account of the numerous species of plants found there.

Subjective, describing the namer's feeling rather than a sense-impression, are such names as Mount Hopeless, Anxious Bay, and Doubtful Sound. Mount Aspiring even seems to rest upon a personification of the mountain itself.

Such subjective-descriptives are closely related to names derived from incident, but names to be definitely so classified are also common, as in the United States. Some are obvious, as with Catastrophe, Deadman, Danger, Disaster. Mount Zero was named during bitterly cold weather. Mount May Day was first ascended on May 1, 1827. Because some early explorers camped by a certain stream on Sunday, we have Sunday Creek. Flinders, at Encounter Bay, sighted a French ship. Cayley's Repulse denotes the place where George Cayley, an early botanist, erected a cairn to mark his point of turning back. Farewell Hill similarly serves for another explorer.

Some of the namings from incident become complicated in motivation. Mount Deception had raised hopes of a water supply, but in this the namer "was deceived." The Ophthalmia Range springs from the eye infection which troubled the namer at the time. Pandora's Pass arose when a hard-pressed explorer thought of the Greek story, and trusted that there might still be "a hope at the bottom." Going ahead, his party discovered the pass, and named it.

Many names are clearly incident-derived, but without trustworthy record of the occasion. Thus we may take it for granted that a man named Wilson met with some trouble at Wilson's Downfall, but various stories are told.

Manufactured names are rare. The American custom of border-naming, as with Texarkana, never developed.

J. C. W. Wilmott, a surveyor of Victoria—surveyors are professionally involved with place-names—is responsible for half a dozen such names. At one time there was much local interest in which of two young ladies would capture the heart and hand of a certain bachelor. Someone phrased the question, "Will Laura or will Helen do it?" At this opportunity Mr. Wilmott produced two original and serviceable names—Willaura and Helendoite (see also Book II, Chapter 8).

In New South Wales, on one occasion, the name Billabong (meaning "pool") was deemed too common, and Illabo was coined by cropping at both ends.

The largest area to be known by a manufactured name is that of the Nullarbor Plain, a name which the explorer Alfred Delisser coined in 1866, basing it upon the negative descriptive in Latin—*nullus arbor,* "no tree."

Unfortunately, during its colonial period, a very blight of commemorative naming fell upon the land, so that the pattern became a monotony of dullness because of flattery bestowed on undistinguished governors, minor officials, and their wives. Creativity fell to a low point. Even the rivers took such names, though the Tasmanians chose rather to transfer bodily the names of English and Scottish streams.

The highest mountain partly escaped this blight by being named by a Pole for a national hero and thus becoming Mount Kosciusko.

If we consider the Australian states and their capitals, we can appreciate some of the banality.

One naming for the reigning queen might be justified, but we have not only Victoria but also Queensland.

West Australia and South Australia bear such colorless names as scarcely to be names at all.

Tasmania is better off. It was first known as Van Diemen's Land, after having been thus named by a Dutch explorer for his governor-general. But the name acquired a bad connotation by its association with transported criminals. In addition, *diemen* was too close to *demon*. With the the ending of the period of transportation of criminals in 1853, the island took the name of Abel Tasman, who had actually discovered it and given it its original name. A Latin ending, on the analogy of Australia itself, completed the establishment of a workable, and even apt and poetic, name for a man who well deserved such honor.

In the worst condition of any of the states is New South Wales. Captain James Cook, in many instances a talented namer, had an off day on August 21, 1770, when he took possession for George III of a certain strip of land and named it New South Wales on the ground that the broken skyline reminded him of the coast of southern Wales. Certainly the principality deserved its commemoration among the numerous names which were being fixed throughout those years. But the limitation to only the southern part was a curious and almost unfriendly act, and the doubly qualified name has remained cumbersome.

With a partial exception in the case of Perth, the capitals of the Australian states display a complete monotony of commemorative naming. Most of the names were bestowed out of compliment (or flattery), and preserve the memory of someone who had little or no interest in Australia—much less in the particular place. Thus Adelaide bears the name of the queen of King William IV, being bestowed at his request. Also to be identified are Lord Melbourne, eminent for many years in the British government; Lord Sydney (see Book II, Chapter 5); Lord Hobart, who was Colonial Secretary. Brisbane displays at least a little more genuine reason for its existence, in that General Thomas Brisbane was serving as governor of New South Wales when a northern river was discovered and given his name; by easy transfer the town took the name of the river.

Perth was named in honor of Sir George Murray, Colonial Secretary. His name, however, had already been used elsewhere, on the Murray River. Doubtless for this reason the namers used Perth, from Murray's birthplace in Scotland.

The name-patterns of these three modern nations display much in common, in addition to the basic use of the English language. All three suffer, in comparison with the United States, from a kind of monotony, especially in the use of patriotic commemoratives, all given in a spirit of flattery, and not for connection of the individual with the place being named.

23
The Present Status

Now, in the later twentieth century, one might well believe that the great period of the giving of place-names has come to an end. That conclusion may be justified for such highly developed countries as those of western Europe, but even with them there may be some doubt. Over the whole earth the new names are now, quite possibly, being given at an unsurpassed rate. Map-makers fill in the less-known regions. The work proceeds in Antarctica and on the ocean-bottom. Most of all, by the principle "the more people, the more place-names," the developing areas bestow names for new communities and for the smaller natural features, which in times of less pressure of population went nameless. And naming continues on the moon, and elsewhere in space.

Even such a seemingly well-advanced country as the United States is highly primitive in its name-pattern, and is unlikely to remain at the ridiculously low figure of one name per square mile. There are still, even in the "lower forty-eight," many thousands of the smaller natural features with clear entity, but without names.

Contemporary naming strikingly displays two phases, which are, in some degree, working in opposite directions. On the one hand, we have official or formal naming, and, on the other, popular naming.

Official naming is commonly under the supervision of governmental boards on geographical names, whose work proceeds in a primarily practical manner. Variant spellings are normalized. Repetitions and obscenities are purged.

Such political bodies, national in their point of view, have some tendency to employ steamroller tactics. Thus a French writer on names protests:

> The official surveyors, without asking advice of the local inhabitants, have taken great liberties with the names. Some names have disappeared; others have suffered shifting of place—a sacrifice of our dear old names, which are, a little, the soul of the land.

Sometimes, however, as has happened occasionally in the United States, stubborn local opposition may overthrow the official decision. Thus, on the death of President Kennedy, Congress memorialized him by shifting the name of the Florida cape from Canaveral to Kennedy. But, as the result of prolonged local objection, the sixteenth-century name has now been restored.

In connection with official naming, we may also state that for the first time in the history of the world the emphasis has shifted away from the primitive approaches of description, association, and incident. The official namers seem to think, almost exclusively, in terms of commemoration and commendation. All the newer countries, as already demonstrated for Australia, have shown this tendency.

Antarctica exists as the extreme case. Almost every name showing on the contemporary maps is of this type, placed either for sentimental or, more often, for patriotic or nationalistic reasons. (We hesitate to use such adjectives as adulatory or sycophantic, though the temptation sometimes exists.) One does not begrudge the naming for explorers, who subjected themselves to the hardships of the land, and even lost their lives there. But another occurrence of the name Victoria seems hardly necessary. More interesting is Edward VIII Bay—perhaps the only memorial name for that short-reigning monarch. We even have Executive Committee Range! Under this

new dispensation of officialdom explorers no longer gave
names for what they saw with their own eyes or for what adven-
tures they encountered. Little America offers a touch of ironic
humor, but it too is commemorative.

Such names as those of Antarctica, many of them with strong
political suggestions in their commendatory quality, are close to
propaganda. In general, however, political messages are not
common in nomenclature. Revolutions may unseat one regime
and establish another, a few names may be shifted, but the
millions of names remain unaltered. In fact, the wholesale
change of place-names is too much of a task for even the most
enthusiastic bureaucracy to assume.

The Soviets have made attempts to alter their names in accordance with their post-Tsarist ideology, but their efforts, nu-
merically, are negligible. The Ukrainians, for instance, have felt
some concern at some of their names being Russianized. One
writer, however, points out that some hundreds of Ukrainian
names may have been thus changed, but twenty million remain
the same.

Politically, indeed, most names are neutral. Round Mountain
and Big River are neither imperialistic or communistic. Sentimental attachment to such a symbol as the Volga River easily
carries across a revolution, and is not readily subjected to a political test.

The communistic regime has actually allowed nearly all of
the older names to stand. Among these, as an interesting
group, are the names on the Black Sea which go back clear to
the era of ancient Greek colonization, such as Sebastopol and
Fiodosiya.

A few important names have been shifted. The capital that
was founded by Peter the Great was named for his saint, with
the German *burg* as an ending. In 1914, with a bitter war being
fought against Germany, the name was shortened and Russianized to Petrograd, still preserving the Tsar's name. In 1924,
however, on the death of the greatest hero of the Revolution,
the city became Leningrad.

Places preserving the word *tsar* have been subject to change.

One of these was Tsaritsin, a city on the Volga, which was apparently named from another local river and had nothing to do with the tsar, unless it had been attracted to that form by folk-etymology. In 1918 a revolutionary general named Stalin defended that city against the White army. Conveniently, by one move, to commemorate the defense and to get rid of the imperialistic suggestion, the name Stalingrad was applied. Any name, however, thus used for political reasons, is subject to further change as political conditions shift. During World War II this city became of vast strategic importance, and the German advance upon it resulted in a conflict which must rate as one of the decisive battles of history. Anyone would have thought that Stalingrad would be, forever, a symbol of patriotic devotion. Eventually, however, the name Stalin became anathema to the ruling group in the government, and the name was shifted again, this time becoming neutral by bearing the name of its great river and being Volgograd. Thus, most surprisingly, a name which had become a national or even international symbol yielded before the exigencies of political and personal antipathies, and by transfer took the commonplace name of a stream, which was merely another "big river."

Naming has also continued in the modern world, because of the progressing discovery and recognition of new entities. Homer terms the sea "fruitless," but he could even more aptly have used "nameless." Until the nineteenth century the surface of each of the larger bodies of water remained, in human thought and imagination, merely a broad-stretching plain, requiring names merely as it stood in relation to the neighboring lands. Only within soundings did the sea-bottom offer the reality of known places, where a mariner might conclude, by uncertainly dangling a sounding line, that here lay an underwater reef, and there a deep chasm. Within this narrow limit the fishermen often gave names to submarine landmarks, especially to those near which fish could be taken.

Then, in the nineteenth century, and even more in the twentieth, vigorous exploration of the sea-bottom finally developed. Entities soon became recognizable—basins, seamounts, ridges, trenches. Once thus realized, the entities needed names for the

convenient distinguishing of one from another among those
which represented the same generic. Generally speaking, the
oceanographers who discovered the entities also gave the names,
though that process, apparently, was of little interest to them.
They generally took the easy and safe way of naming by association or transfer. Thus the Philippines Trench merely echoes
the nearest important body of land. The Mid-Atlantic Ridge is
now recognized as one of the earth's major features, but it can
scarcely be said to have a name of its own.

To date, the under-sea features are distinguishable only
when very large, so that the total number of such names is not
appreciable by world standards. Already, however, there are
beginnings of projects for the recovery of metals from the sea-
floor. Once such undertakings are developed, certain areas will
be necessarily more minutely discovered and utilized. The
"miners" then will recognize new entities and give names more
numerously—just as, in Alaska, a discovery of gold would lead
to the naming of all the near-by creeks and gulches, though
outside of the mining area no one named such small features.

Nevertheless, even at the present time, the names of under-
sea features are more numerous than most people would imagine. *Gazetteer No. III* (1969), approved by the U.S. Board on
Geographic Names, lists them to the approximate number of
8500.

But the modern world also recognizes new entities, sometimes by combining smaller units into larger ones. In many respects primitive man was as well qualified in the recognition of
physical features as is modern man. He could note small ones
just as well. Thus, seeing a rock or sand bar entirely sur-
rounded by water, he easily grasped the conception of "island."
But a large island left him somewhat uncertain, since he could
not tell, except after long and tedious walking or paddling,
whether that land was joined to other land at the farther side.
Such a conception as an archipelago was even more difficult.

Therefore we must consider as a modern triumph the recognition of the entities and the practical naming of Indonesia,
Polynesia, Micronesia, and Melanesia—all coined from the

Greek *nesos,* "island," with the modifiers equivalent to "Indian," "many," "small," and "black." Two of the names, indeed, are purely descriptive, and two arise by historical or anthropological association. But perhaps a lack of precise system is to the good. Certainly the names have proved to be highly successful, and they display something of the dignity and beauty which often accompany Greek and Latin formations.

Notable in the history of the post World War II period has been the emergence of new nations. Since each of these has had to furnish itself with a name, the treasury of the world's names has expanded noticeably. These names, on the whole, seem to have been taken with a minimum of consideration, as if in the throes of establishing a new government any name might serve and no time need be wasted over one.

In some instances a name raises ambiguities between geographical and political application, as with India, where the most populous of the nations has preempted the name of the whole subcontinent. Also, anomalously, India uses the old name, though its linguistic origin and its first application were with the Indus valley, and that region is now no longer a part of India.

Thus Pakistan might have some claim to being the true India, but that nation, instead, has taken a name coined from the Persian, containing *stan,* the common term for "land." The rest of the name can be translated as "of the pure," and its application, at its coinage in 1933, was to a theoretically "pure" Moslem state. In the course of time, however, many of the Pakistanis have come to regard the name as coined from the initials of the various regions or peoples composing the nation, that is, Punjab, Afghan, Kasmir, Sind, coupled with *-tan* from Baluchistan.

The recently emergent Bangladesh follows the common tradition by which the name of a people becomes that of the country, being literally "Bengal-nation," and preserving the early tribal name Bang.

Africa, the nursery of new nations, displays several methods of naming. In many instances the old colonial or imperialistic name has been continued—at least in English usage—as in

Algeria and Nigeria. Or the name may arise by transfer from a natural feature, as with Chad from the lake and Zambia from the Zambesi River. Names of tribes have usefully supplied Botswana, Somalia, and others.

Cameroon is one of the more interesting names, literally being from the Portuguese word for shrimp, an early name bestowed upon a river there by Portuguese voyagers. The region, then, by common process, took the name of the principal stream, in this case happening to be a somewhat incongruous one for a nation.

On the emergence of the new nations the great river Congo gave rise to both the Republic of Congo and the Democratic Republic of Congo, creating an unfortunate and almost intolerable opportunity for ambiguity. In a way the conflict was apparent in the first accounts of the area by Diogo Cão, the Portuguese explorer, in 1484. He then reported the kingdom there as Congo and the river as Zaire—both unexplained local names. During a considerable period the stream appeared on maps as the Zaire, but eventually Congo replaced its rival, which really disappeared. Recently, however, the Democratic Republic of Congo, with great increase of specificity and convenience, has changed its name to Zaire.

On the whole, the African republics have shown little interest in their names, and the circumstances of their origin may well be forgotten. Letters of inquiry written (1971) to their embassies in Washington went unanswered in most instances, though a few evoked perfunctory replies, and a few others were carefully answered.

To illustrate popular naming in the modern period we may present two far-removed examples, both of them in the English language.

Mr. Hood Roberts has preserved the situation resulting from American namings on the front of the Second Infantry Division during a static period of the Korean war in 1952–53.

From the point of view of giving names the situation may be considered peculiar. The local names were in the Korean language, of which the Americans were ignorant. Still, an important stream continued to carry its native name, and was known as the Yokkok-Chon River, when it could not merely be The River. Folk-etymology gave rise to Poke-eye Ridge, from a Korean name, Pokkae—the folk-etymology, however, being more striking in the written than in the oral form. So also, Hasakkol became Hadacol, an American trade-name. In addition, the name of a village, No Dong, was preserved—partly, no doubt, because it was a simple one to pronounce, but chiefly, as Mr. Roberts suggests, because of its touch of friendly obscenity, *dong* being one of the soldiers' words for penis.

The situation was also peculiar because of its topographical limitations. As usual in static warfare, the lines faced each other across a vague unoccupied area. With the view thus restricted, the Americans could name only the features that they saw, chiefly those in no-man's-land. Within their own lines there was no need of place-names, since reference was commonly made to the unit holding the ground area, such as "Third Battalion's area." Thus limited, the soldiers gave comparatively few names.

Most of the namings were descriptive. Arrowhead Ridge took its name from shape, though more definitely from the curve of the river around its base. Other names from shape were Hook (for a ridge) and Star Hill. As might be expected, these isolated Americans dug back into folk-practice for familiar names which would be not only descriptive, but also even a little nostalgic. Bunker Hill, for instance, showed bunkers built as fortifications by the enemy, but the name is also rooted deep in the American consciousness. Camel's Back is also conventionally descriptive, demanding no actual camel. Old Baldy, its top having been denuded by artillery fire, is another name occurring at least once in most of the states. The Three Sisters, for a group of similarly shaped hills, would also have been familiar from use in Oregon and elsewhere.

Two unusual names, while genuinely descriptive, were obviously influenced in their selection by the infantryman's fixation on food—Porkchop Hill and T-Bone. Influenced by another fixation is Betty Grable, a series of ridges named for the favorite actress and pinup girl, but also descriptive in that the silhouette suggested a reclining and nude female figure.

Metaphoric description appears in Death Valley, for an area under enemy observation and thus dangerous.

Mr. Roberts has suggested that Little Gibraltar may have been originally named by the British Commonwealth Division, which had formerly held the position. Gibraltar, however, is a much used name in the United States.

Monk's Hood Hill, though listed among the descriptives, may be actually an associative name from the growth there of the plant so known.

Since the naming occurred from fixed positions and was applied to more-or-less distant features, there was little chance for incident-naming. Apparently the only one is Silver Star Hill, which was explained to the investigator in what seems reasonable fashion—"where Lt. Henry got his Silver Star."

Mingled with these grass-roots names were some which had been adopted by the front-line men but had originated by headquarter's usage. Alligator Jaws was thus named because of the pattern of contour lines on a map. Ten Sixty-two (usually written 1062) was probably from altitude. Other names were originally code designations, such as Uncle and Check-point Easy.

Technicalities and complications aside, the situation indicates what may be called a universal human trait. As nature abhors a vacuum, so do human beings; if faced by a region which is nameless to them, they will fill it with names of their own.

In the preceding chapter the conclusion was promulgated that the English had lost their tradition and that their naming had become quiescent, or even decadent, merely because there had been little need for that activity over the course of two or three centuries. In one respect, however, an exception must be made—for house-naming in the twentieth century.

The tradition is clear and cogent. In the feudal period the estates bore names which might or might not be those of villages or natural features. As the squire and the country gentleman succeeded the baron, they also, naturally, named their seats of residence. As a next step, one which was only to be expected, the retired professional man or the prospering greengrocer, having bought a lot with a five-room house on it, gave it a name, even though it already had the identification of a street number. In some degree the motivation may be called snobbish. More generally, however, it shows pride in ownership and the desire to attain some warmth of designation—which a name provides better than a number.

The tradition in the United States, we may note with interest, has worked in just the opposite direction. In the English and general European tradition, the large landowners—as in the Hudson valley and throughout the South—regularly named their estates, but ordinary one-family farms bore only the owner's name and shifted as the ownership might change. Large holdings in the West, such as the Spanish grants in California, also bore names, and the tradition carried on to some American ranches. In the nineteenth century, however, the current set in the other direction, apparently because the naming of private holdings seemed ostentatious and snobbishly Anglophile. The climax perhaps was reached when the White House itself became officially 1600 Pennsylvania Avenue.

In England, although a certain anti-snobbery is a restraining factor, the naming of even very modest holdings is a common custom. Though they may be classified as minor, they have all the necessary qualities of place-names, that is, they identify a certain geographical entity. Many of them, indeed, by their very nature show their reference to be to the site as well as to the house—Homeland, Sunacres, Oak Dell.

No estimate is available as to the number of these names, but Leslie Dunkling has catalogued about 2500 actual names, and makes no suggestion of completeness. Their dates have not been studied, but they generally are of the twentieth century. Most of them represent the work of what may be considered the lower middle class, and most of the houses are modest.

As with all habitation-names, those of the English houses spring basically from commendatory reasons. Any owner, and especially when there is a family, wants a name of pleasant suggestion, and we have thus the repeated use of the ideas of view, height, contentment, brook, garden, and trees. A few bold house-owners go by opposites, and we have examples of the indomitable Englishman facing a rough life—Frosty Hall, Hurricane House. Others take refuge in humor, as with Creepy, which is in the town of Crawley.

Many commendatory ideas also relate to description—Twin Chimneys, High Corner, Edgewater, Rose Cottage, Cherry Trees.

A certain number suggest naming from incidents—Moon Rise, Hawks Stoop, Squirrels Leap.

Commemorative names show chiefly in the transfer of already established names to the new setting. Since Lamorna is a resort for homeymooners, the name appears frequently on houses. Similarly Aarhus, the name of a Danish town, is a house-name in Derbyshire, because the couple had honeymooned in Denmark, but also because it seemed to stand for Our House.

This last suggestion leads on to the most remarkable feature of this whole development, the fixation upon manufactured names. Such names really do not exist in the traditional English nomenclature, and by what means this type of naming became popular for houses is as yet unexplained.

Blend names of two elements are common. These are usually indicative of the couple inhabiting the house—Alaneileen, Alfbar, Donann. Belscotia is for a Belgian wife and a Scottish husband.

Almost every possibility of manufacture is present. Cufesi is the home of a student of chemistry who wrote a thesis involving copper, iron, and silicon. Olcote, which might pass for an Anglo-Saxon name, is from the initials of Our Little Corner Of The Earth. Odtaa conceals One Damned Thing After Another. Dun is a frequent Scottish prefix for "hill, fortress," but functions for "done" in Dunroamin and Dunrovin, homes of retirees.

Mere shifts of spelling are frequently sufficient. Certainly no great skill in cryptology is necessary to decode Omagain, Koz E Kot, Allourown, Itzours, R-Ome. Dryrotia suggests, probably with wry humor, that the house is suffering from dry rot.

Probably in more instances than can be actually known some kind of incident at the time of moving into the house has been taken as an omen. Thus Jin-Y-Wood was derived from the remark "Jinny [recently dead] would have loved this place."

To end a sober historical investigation on such names as It-zours and Jin-Y-Wood may seem almost sacrilegious. But the message is clear. The giving of names is a basic human trait. With need and opportunity the names will come—whether by a dedication to a sun-god or by a commemoration of a honey-moon.

IV

Place-names as Sources
of Knowledge

Introduction

Place-naming, itself rooted firmly in language, ramifies into many branches, thus entwining with other human activities. It is a bequest from early periods of man's development. It is never likely to cease entirely, even though the process may be reduced to naming strong points along a battlefront, or honeymoon cottages. Particularly involved are explorers (whether by land or by sea), settlers in new lands, and patriotic memorialists.

Once the naming-process has been active, the names themselves remain as a heritage for future generations, preserving the record of what may be called, in its broadest sense, human history—preserving that record, too, through illiterate centuries. Geographers and historians find clues in place-names. Researchers into the cultural record may discover, for instance, what domestic animals a people once possessed and what crops they cultivated. Folklorists collect, without end, stories "explaining" place-names. Archeologists and students of language, from different points of view, subject the names to study. Poets, from the earliest times, have endeavored, in ringing lines, to evoke from the use of names something of their phonetic beauty, their historic associations, and their mystery.

The outstanding quality of place-names which enables them to preserve the record is their long endurance, to the point of

what may be called permanence. They are passed from generation to generation, even without the aid of writing. Thus—at
least in theory—they offer keys to pre-history and to nooks and
crannies which have been left dark in periods of scant records.

But he who follows this path treads upon slippery ground.
By and large, the justification of the study of place-names lies in
itself—that is, in the satisfaction of our own curiosity about the
names and the processes of naming. The argument that we
thereby open up new approaches to other fields has not been
wholly convincing.

Certain such attempts seem to go to great lengths to demonstrate or prove what can be more easily established by other
methods. In some instances, too much confidence has been en-
trusted to a single name or to a small group of them. In such
situations the possibility of mere coincidence renders the argument uncertain. As in all fields, moreover, place-names are
picked up to support some already promulgated theory,
though the meaning of the names themselves has not been independently confirmed. Too many scholars have felt themselves competent to argue from intriguing place-name evidence, though they have never studied the actual manner in
which names are given.

Yet, properly used, place-names can serve, legitimately and
significantly, to extend knowledge. Toponymy must be allowed
to exist as a discipline in itself, but it can also at times serve as a
useful auxiliary to historians, geographers, linguists, archeologists, folklorists—and, I can even maintain, to poets.

The concluding chapters of this volume will present some examples.

I

Names and History— the Anglo-Saxons

The evidence of place-names has proved highly effective in the reconstruction of the history of the Anglo-Saxons. Such auxiliary help is of especial value since actual historical records are meager throughout those tumultuous and largely illiterate centuries.

One possible example, in connection with Celtic river-names, has already been presented in Chapter 11 of Book III. Two others may serve here.

As one illustration we may choose Augusta Longnon's demonstration of the Anglo-Saxon names in France—a discovery which is characterized by Albert Dauzat, another great French scholar, as "one of the most striking in toponymy." These names, clearly recognizable in linguistic form, are scattered here and there along the Channel coast of France. Their chief concentration is in the region lying inland from Calais and Boulogne, and for present purposes we may thus confine the discussion.

Chiefly of interest—as indisputable proof—are the names ending in *-thun*, the French equivalent of the common English *-ton*. Thus we have Alenthun, Audincthun, Bainethun, Darlincthun. Not only is *-ton* clearly in evidence, but also *-en* and *-inc* represent the common Anglo-Saxon *-ing*. Then, by what seems more than usual scholarly luck, the whole names as they stand in France have their equivalents in England. Thus the four names listed above are, in modern English form, Allington, Oddington, Bainton, and Darlington. There is therefore no possibility of error, the number of names being sufficient to preclude coincidence.

Longnon's discovery is the more remarkable and the more illuminating in that history, except for one passing reference, makes no mention of a settlement of Anglo-Saxons here. The exception is that Gregory of Tours notes Saxons in this area in the sixth century, a statement which in itself would be too vague to be of much value.

As a demonstration, we may here list the justifiable conclusions to be drawn from this group of names, and then add a few notes upon what conclusions cannot properly be drawn— that is, upon the limitations of the toponymic approach to history.

1. The discovery proves the actual occupation by people of Anglo-Saxon speech.

2. The area of occupation is at least roughly defined. This definition of place is, in fact, one of the most reliable features of place-name evidence.

3. Some possible light may be thrown upon the date at which the names were placed, since both -*ing* and -*ton* appear in very early names. They also, however, appear in later names, so that no sure conclusion can be drawn.

4. We may make some reasonable inferences about the nature of the settlement. A mere raid or even a succession of raids will not result in the establishment of habitation-names. We must assume that the speakers of Anglo-Saxon actually held these places over a period long enough to allow the fixing of the names so firmly that, even when the French language was reasserted, these Anglo-Saxon names did not revert to the still older forms of the Roman period, but were preserved and reshaped. The situation seems to demand the general use of the Anglo-Saxon language (at least in these particular villages), and therefore

the presence of women and families, since, over the course of a few generations, women control language.

But what cannot be deduced from the names is equally striking. Their evidence, for instance, is not even sufficient to make certain that these settlers were Saxons and not Angles, though the French scholars mention them as Saxons. They may even have been Jutes, since that tribe held the part of England just across the Channel.

Moreover, the names tell nothing as to whence these settlers came, whether direct from the continental homeland or as a reflux from Britain. They tell us nothing about the motivation of the settlement. In modern terms it looks like an attempt at sea-power to be obtained by holding both sides of the Straits of Dover, but we can hardly assume such wide-sweeping strategy in the fifth century. The names thus yield certain information, but cannot be pressed very hard.

Further information may be extrapolated from the scant evidence of the history of the Franks. That powerful people swept across present-day Belgium and northern France in the later fifth century. One of their chief seats was at Tournai, only some seventy miles from Calais. In all probability, therefore, the "Saxons" must have made their incursion before the coming of the Franks. In the following years, also, the Frankish kingdom was strong and aggressive, and undoubtedly imposed its rule on the small Calais-Boulogne region. The takeover, indeed, may have been peaceful. The "Saxons" were not strong enough to fight, and they were, also, Germanic and closely related to the Franks, both in culture and in language. In any case, the fates of the two invading peoples were similar, both of them adopting the language of the country and amalgamating with its people.

Only the single reference in Gregory remains as an uncertain historical record. The scattered place-names supply the convincing evidence.

We draw the second illustration from the insular Anglo-Saxons, around the year 900. At that time the Danes had overrun and were holding most of northern and eastern England, and the Saxon kings of Wessex were strenuously attempting to regain their hegemony by winning back the lost territory. The men of Wessex, thus involved, had little interest in what was happening in a large and isolated northwestern section of the island—in modern terms, the coastal land extending northward from Chester to the Scottish border. This region had been conquered rather recently from the Britons, was still somewhat British, and had been a part of the Anglian kingdom of Northumbria, which the Danes had shattered. Mountains almost cut the region off from the rest of England, and many of its traditional ties were with the Scottish Lowlands. During these years that remarkable work, the so-called Anglo-Saxon Chronicle, kept the record of what was happening between Wessex and the Danes, but the chroniclers apparently considered the northwest as out of their sphere of responsibility, and make no mention of it.

At this juncture (by what may be considered another bit of scholarly luck) the evidence of the place-names becomes clear and important.

Basically the name-pattern of the northwest is much like that of the rest of the country, that is, English names overlie a Celtic stratum. There are also a good number of Scandinavian names, which one would attribute, at first thought, to infiltration from the Danish settlements to the east of the mountains. Closer examination, however, determines that many of these names are not Danish, but Norwegian. Moreover, mingled with them are some of Irish origin. Thus, to a remarkable degree, the place-names enable us to reconstruct history, without what are usually called historical sources.

After the Danish destruction of the Northumbrian kingdom, the isolated Angles of the northwest probably escaped Danish occupation because the Danes had no especial need or desire to live in that not too hospitable region. They doubtless raided it occasionally for cattle. The local Angles, lacking a king, probably organized themselves under petty chieftains, and of necessity became tough fighters.

During these same years the vikings from Norway (leaving

England chiefly to the Danes) had been sweeping around Britain, and raiding Ireland. Eventually they occupied much of that island, and established kingdoms—at the same time, as usually happens, mingling with the native inhabitants. When they set out to make settlements in Britain, along with them went their Irish allies (and their half-Irish illegitimate sons.)

Undoubtedly the situation over a period of years grew complicated, and place-names yield few details. Probably some of the Hiberno-Norwegians came as invaders with conquest in mind. But they themselves were not overwhelmingly strong, and apparently they were not successful in conquest. On this point the names—in a most curious and helpful manner—supply evidence.

The Norwegian and Irish names are mostly upon villages, as would be expected, since most of the natural features would already have received names. These names cluster upon unattractive sites, such as what must have been marshlands at the time. This is not the pattern of conquerors!

There would seem to be two possibilities. By one, we can conceive that an invading army was crushed, and its remnants were then permitted to settle in those odd nooks and corners which were unoccupied. Or else the settlers from Ireland might have been essentially refugees, driven out by some local convulsion—either a counterattack by the Irish, or a factional dispute among the Norwegians. On the whole, the slight evidence of the names would point to a kind of peaceful infiltration. Thinly settled lands, such as the United States during much of its history, encourage immigration as a source of strength.

Without too much fancy, we may envisage a ship from Ireland putting in, here or there, along the coast. Its captain bargains with the local chief for land and a chance to settle, promising staunch allegiance and some good axmen for the local wars. Perhaps there is a suggestion of threat—that what is not given freely may be taken. But names themselves do not provide such vivid details—except for occasional incident-names, and these are lacking in this present connection.

By another lucky fall of the dice of scholarship, this name-pattern of the northwest not only affirms some history, it also seems to confirm the historicity of a document which had been considered, before the study of the names, to be merely a fictional tale. This is the story of Ingimund.

He came, as the tale goes, from Ireland. He commanded a ship with a crew of Norwegians—along with them, some Danes and Irishmen. They were refugees from some disturbance, and some other ships were either with this one or closely cooperating.

Ingimund made petition to Aethelflaed, the so-called Lady of the Mercians, that remarkable woman whose power was scarcely beneath the king's. She granted him permission to take lands in the Wirral, that is, the part of Cheshire which is a peninsula between the Mersey and Dee rivers. It was apparently land which was unoccupied, and for that reason we may consider it to have been second-rate land. After a few years, however, the settlers from Ireland played false, and attacked the near-by city of Chester.

Though the story is told with some fanciful embellishments, in its main events it rings true to what we have already had reason to believe from the evidence of the names.

On the whole, then, the place-names of any people—as here, with the Anglo-Saxons—are potential witnesses for history. Their testimony should not be pushed too hard, but it may aid in reinterpretation of actual written sources.

2

Names and Archeology—
Phoenicians and Greeks

A much-disputed question is that of the nature and extent of Phoenician influence upon the Greeks during the two centuries following the year 1000 B.C. No historical records of the period exist, and it was presumably illiterate. Tradition, however, spoke strongly for the Phoenicians, even attributing to them the foundation of such a leading city as Thebes. The Homeric poets (especially in the *Odyssey*) accepted this general idea, making mention of Phoenicians and their articles of trade. So did Herodotus and Thucydides—the former, for instance, stating that the Aegean island of Thera was in the hands of Phoenicians for eight generations. The earlier modern historians followed naturally in the path of their classical predecessors.

But, with widespread archeological research, doubts arose. The most meticulous excavation failed to reveal anything of importance. The archeologists, therefore, found themselves unable to accept the idea of any notable thrust of Phoenicians into the Greek area. They decided that the tradition must be untrustworthy—at the least, highly exaggerated. They converted many historians. The weakness of the archeologists' position, however, was that it rested upon wholly negative evidence.

A kind of impasse thus exists between the positive though scanty testimony of the tradition and the negative testimony of

377

the spade. In such a situation, with more evidence badly needed, a study of place-names may be of aid.

Unfortunately, the problem is of the utmost complexity and difficulty. The classicists have not studied the names exhaustively, so that there can be no good references, as there are with the Anglo-Saxons, to research already completed. (The bulk of what is here to be presented has been assembled for this particular project.)

In addition, the place-name pattern of ancient Greece, though many names are recorded, is of complicated linguistic background, a large proportion of the names being non-Greek and presumably pre-Greek, derived from languages for which no reliable vocabularies exist. (See Book III, Chapters 4, 5, 6, and 9.)

Any attempt to isolate Phoenician names from this mass is extremely difficult, especially since that language itself is not exhaustively known. In addition, no particular phonetic combinations serving to identify the names have so far been tabulated. As a result, the possibility of coincidental identity is always present. The mere resemblance of a single name to a Phoenician word or root cannot, by itself, be taken very seriously. The name must stand in association with others, must represent a translation, must display a singularly apt meaning, or in some other way qualify. In particular, we must be able to demonstrate some means by which Phoenicians and Greeks established contact in such an intimate way as to permit the transfer of names.

The last requirement can be considered in the light of what is generally known about the Phoenicians. They were skilled navigators. They were traders rather than conquerors or colonizers. They operated by setting up trading-posts at points strategic for such trade. (The analogy with the European "factories" of the sixteenth and seventeenth centuries is close.) As the meanings of Cádiz and Hippo indicate, these posts were fortified. They were held semipermanently, and might eventually become towns (see Book III, Chapter 3).

Under such conditions, fairly close contacts would exist between the two peoples, and words and names would pass from the one language to the other. Thus *chrysos,* the Greek word for gold, is Semitic and probably Phoenician. Commonly, the new-comers would adopt the already established place-names, but they might also give new names, which would be in their own language, just as European traders, for their own convenience, often gave their own names to places in America or Africa. Such names, once established, have a chance of being adopted by the natives.

Developing this hypothesis further, we can make another assumption—that is, if the Phoenicians had the skill to sail the long distance from Phoenicia to any part of the Aegean, they were able to traverse the much shorter distances into all parts of that sea, and to reach even beyond it into the passages to the Black Sea. Once we realize that the ships had sailed to Greek waters, in short, we can no longer consider distance as a limiting factor, and we must take a place-name of the northern Aegean equally as cogent as one of the southern Aegean. On the other hand, since the Phoenicians typically kept to the sea, place-names of such an interior region as Arcadia are inapplicable.

Our procedure will now be to test this hypothesis by means of place-names—perhaps also, we might say, to test the validity of the toponymic approach in such a situation.

We may begin with an example which can indicate what *not* to do with place-name evidence. The high promontory forming the southeastern prong of Greece was known as Maleia. It is mentioned several times in the *Odyssey*. In trying to round it, Odysseus met the violent head-wind that drove him back and sent him upon his wanderings. Since the Phoenicians were essentially sea-farers, they must have had a name for this notable landmark. With interest, then, we discover that a common Biblical word for *hill* is *maalah,* and any eager tracer of name-trails would suspect that we have a Phoenician name, or the remnant of one. Immediately, however, caution would warn anyone that the element *mal-,* short and composed of very common sounds, is simply not sufficient in itself to support any conclusions. Moreover, *mal-* is to be found in areas of inland Greece, where Phoenicians presumably did not penetrate. All this counter-argument, indeed, does not remove the possibility of our original suggestion. It does, however, reduce the strength of the argument, approximately, to nothing. The attempt to maintain such a case can only lead to the arousal of mistrust in place-name arguments generally.

Yet the possibility of mere coincidence fades rapidly with longer names. Thus, for this reason chiefly, a much stronger case can be presented for the city of Lampsacos. Testing a Phoenician origin, we can analyze the name as from the root *p-s-ch,* "crossing, ford," to which has been prefixed the preposition-article *la,* "to the," the *m* being a phonetic insertion and the *-os* a Greek ending. There is also the analogy of the well-known ancient Syrian city Thapsacos, with a different prefix.

The situation would be of little interest, however, except for the remarkable semantic relevance. Thapsacos stood at the point where travelers commonly crossed the upper Euphrates. To return to Lampsacos, we find it a town on the Dardanelles, where it also would have been a point for crossing that narrow arm of water. The name, then, is translatable as "to the crossing," showing the not uncommon absorption of a preposition occurring along with the name's becoming unintelligible.

There would seem to be some probability that the Phoenicians would have founded one of their trading-posts at this point where they had the double advantage of water-transport and of land-trails which would have converged from both the European and the Asian sides.

To a four-point consonantal agreement we thus add practical reasons for a Phoenician settlement at this point. The case may not be considered to be settled beyond controversy, but at least it cannot be lightly dismissed.

The name Samos occurs not only on an important island, but also as Samothrace on another island, and as Same, a recorded older name for Cephellenia. Strabo, curiously, gives two different explanations for the name, mutually contradictory. One of these has been already cited (Book III, Chapter 4). The other is merely that "high places are called *samoi.*"

The repeated use of the name suggests that it was, at some period, a generic. Strabo, however, fails to suggest what language it may have been, though he may imply that the word was once so used in Greek. Actually a Phoenician origin is clearly possible, since the biblical *samah* has the basic meaning "to be high."

As already pointed out in connection with Maleia, little confidence can be placed in a very short linguistic element. In this particular instance, however, the occurrence of the element in several names suggests a generic, and the specification of its meaning by Strabo greatly strengthens the evidence.

The widespread and common name Minoa shows one example in Sicily, another in Palestine, and no fewer than seven in the Aegean area. The Greeks themselves connected Minoa with Minos, the famous king of Crete, though Minos himself has never been clearly proved historical, and has, on the contrary, important mythological connections. Diodorus, writing about 50 B.C., accepted the idea of a colonization of the Aegean islands by Cretans during the reign of Minos:

> And this circumstance explains why harbors on the islands as well as on the coast of Asia have the same designation as those of Crete, being called "Minoan."

Diodorus, however, lived almost a millennium after the time of which he was writing, and his conclusion may be merely his own guess. Such late testimony is not to be highly regarded.

Even so, the ideas of Diodorus have proved very useful to modern historians. They have looked upon the name as providing evidence for the historicity of Minos. Like Diodorus, they have seen evidence of a Minoan empire. They have cited the analogy of modern times, when British explorers spread far and wide such names as Victoria, to honor their own monarch.

Strictly considered as a naming-problem, however, the lovely structure collapses. First, we must remember that Minos himself has not been proved historical, so that the whole basis of the argument remains in doubt. Second, the proponents of the idea seem to argue in a circle by assuming that the existence of the names strengthens the case for the existence of a King Minos, at the same time deriving the names from him. Third, the proponents neglect to consider the nature of the

places named. British colonizers bestowed Victoria upon dig-
nified and important natural features or upon settlements
which were designed for greatness. But the places named
Minoa are obscure, and always were so. Even Heraclea Minoa
in Sicily was hardly better than a third-class town.

From the onomastic point of view the methodology to be
applied to a repeated name is well established. The whole series
of sites should be examined on the hypothesis that the common
qualities will reveal something that would allow the name to be
accepted as a descriptive or as a generic.

With Minoa, the results are nothing short of startling. First,
all the sites are on the seacoast. Second, most of them are habitation-names, but of villages, not cities. Third, there is a strong
association with harbors. Many of them are described in Pauly-
Wissowa's *Realencyclopädie* as harbors. So also, indeed, Diodorus
designated them. In a minor way, moreover, the existence of
two of the sites on Crete itself is an argument against the origin
from Minos. In empire-building, the names of monarchs are
not typically bestowed in the homeland.

Inevitably, because of the repeated "harbor," the idea arises
that we have here another of those common cases of a repeated
generic which has been passed on to a succeeding age as a specific of unknown meaning. At the same time, any onomastist
would begin strongly to suspect that the generic once meant
"harbor."

By what seems almost more than to expect from fortune,
such a term occurs in two biblical words (*manoha, manuha*) both
connected with the idea of "rest, repose." Since these are fairly
common words in Hebrew, their existence in Phoenician is
likely. Phonetically, for adaptation in Greek, the terms offer
only superficial difficulty, as to what would happen to the consonantal sound represented by the Semitic *heth*. This sound was
unfamiliar to the Greeks, as is evidenced by their failure to use
it for a consonant in their standard alphabet. Instead, they
employed that place in the alphabet for a vowel, and thus created *eta*. We have here a common situation. When an unknown
sound occurs, especially between vowels, it may merely be
omitted altogether, as already suggested in connection with the

derivation of Nile (see Book III, Chapter 1), and with the modern Spanish *j* sound in such a name as Vallejo. If we allow such a common process, the Semitic words could stand in Greek in a form which would appear in English as Minoa.

On this basis we may conclude that Minoa was derived from a Phoenician term, and that it means "rest, resting-place," that is, from the maritime point of view, "harbor." Moreover, this meaning is exactly the one that it should have—on the basis of geography and also, even, upon the testimony of Diodorus.

The situation thus seems obvious enough—that Minoa was a name meaning harbor and propagated by the Phoenicians during a period of infiltration and possibly of some dominance in the Aegean area. Without resorting to mere speculation, one may even go a little further. In this early period, if the Homeric poems may be taken as a guide, the Greeks normally would have had little interest in harbors, because they pulled their vessels ashore, stern-to, upon any beach—a practical enough procedure with small ships and a tideless sea. The Phoenicians had a longer voyage to make from their home-ports, and they needed space for cargo, being traders. Their standard craft may have been the one mentioned in the *Odyssey* (ix, 322f). Such a "broad-beamed merchantman" would have been difficult or impossible to beach, and would have been dependent upon a harbor for landing and for riding out periods of bad weather. The Greeks may thus have come to associate the term with the Phoenicians and to preserve it as a place-name without taking it into the language.

This interpretation is not, incidently, dependent upon the assumption of a Phoenician hegemony or empire, as a modern analogy may demonstrate. The Dutch have never dominated the Shetland Islands, but Dutch fishermen have been accustomed to visit those waters. Two place-names there contain *dokke,* a Dutch word for "harbor."

The case will be stronger if we can discover a cluster of place-names indicating that we might have there a focus of Phoenician influence. One such may exist in the region of Megara.

Megara itself is commonly derived from the Greek *megaron* in the plural, thus to mean "halls, houses." This case rests on phonetic similarity only, and is possible, but far from conclusive. At the same time, we may cite the Hebrew *magur,* "temporary dwelling-place." Such a name would be obviously suitable for a trading-post, a place not designed—at least in the beginning— as a permanent settlement.

One of the places called Minoa is close to Megara. As used in Periclean times, the name was applied to a small island, but the island forms one side of a remarkably sheltered harbor, and a transfer would have been natural.

The island of Salamis lies close to Megara. Its close resemblance to the common Semitic term meaning "peace" has often been noted. That word occurs not infrequently in place-names, under Semitic influence, as in the modern Dar es Salaam, "house of peace" (see Book III, Chapter 12). Such a name is likely to arise from an incident, and such an incident might well have been the establishment of a treaty for peaceful relationships between the sea-borne traders and the local inhabitants. Another ancient Salamis was in Cyprus, an island in which Phoenician influence was strong. Unfortunately, no actual evidence has been preserved as to the cause of either of these namings.

Pausanias, that indefatigable antiquarian, records that Megara was originally called Caria. Although some have taken this name as evidence of a settlement of Carians, it is also a very common Semitic element, occurring in Carthage and Carchemish, and (as *kir-*) in a number of Biblical cities, with the meaning "town, citadel."

The port of Megara in historical times was Nisaia. The later Greeks, with their usual fixation on deriving the names of places from those of people, told the story of a certain Nisos. Not to spin the tale out, he was finally transformed into a hawk or sea-eagle. A curious fact is that the Hebrew word *nes* actually means "hawk." Such a point cannot be pressed hard, but namings from birds of prey are fairly common, and doubtless were much more so when such birds were taken as evidence of divine portents. Possibly, therefore, the Phoenicians knew the place as Hawk Beach, and that the name helped to supply a detail for the later Greek folk-tale.

As an independent argument we must emphasize the striking suitability of this area for Phoenician infiltration. Megara was one of the Greek crossroads. Situated on the Aegean side and at the northern end of the Isthmus of Corinth, a post there could receive land-trade from north and south, and from the eastward-reaching peninsula of Attica. It had a port on the Aegean for sea-borne commerce. Overland communications were also possible with the Gulf of Corinth, and thus with western Greece.

In fact, with the possible exception of the vicinity of Corinth, Megara offered the best site in Greece for a Phoenician post. Their apparent failure to occupy Corinth may be attributed to some political problem—for instance, the existence of a strong city which did not want foreign competition. Moreover, by its possession of an excellent "minoa," Megara was probably superior to the eastern end of the site at Corinth, and such an advantage may have enough to swing the scale. Historical probability thus adds its strength to that of the remarkable number of phonetic similarities.

Names which appear to be Phoenician in form are thus widespread and common in the Aegean area. By their very numbers they reinforce one another. Moreover, the semantic background is, in many cases, striking. Already mentioned, for instance (Book III, Chapter 3), is that likely grouping of the southwestern area—Kythera, Seriphos, and Siphnos—that is, "Smoke Island," "Fire Island," and "Mine Island."

On the whole, therefore, the testimony of place-names in this controversy seems to support the historical tradition, not the archeological evidence.

3
Place-names and Poetry

Place-names serve the poet for their romantic appeal and their evocative quality, and, sometimes, for their inherent meaning.

The romantic appeal springs from sonorous syllables, and from a sense of the strange, bizarre, and wonderful. Thus to be moved, one need not know the origin of the name, nor be concerned with it. In fact, one may be better off so. The classical story is that of the old woman who was moved by the mere repetition of "the blessed name Mesopotamia."

Caroline Norton, the English poet and novelist, read in Longfellow's *Evangeline* the name Atchafalaya, strange of sound and, to her, meaningless—the stream where the lovers failed of their meeting. Apparently taking it as a symbol of fate, she had it cut into a seal. Later she discovered that the king of the Belgians felt the strange power of that same word.

Actually, some kind of appropriateness seems to have guided, unconsciously, both lady and king. The meaning of the Indian name is simply "long river," but that idea furnishes also a good symbol for life, or for fate itself.

Some of the poets themselves seem to have grown almost intoxicated with names, sometimes reducing a poem to a kind of quasi-magical chant. Sydney Dobell's *Ballad of Keith of Ravelston* is one of these, with its repetition of Ravelston. James Clarence Mangan felt an equal fascination with Karaman. Even more extreme is John Todhunter's *Aghadoe*. It may, in fact, set some kind of record—Todhunter used that place-name thirty times in a poem of twenty-eight lines.

More subtle is Walter James Turner, in *Romance*, but he also depends upon this charm of the strange and unknown, in this poem, developing the theme from the three names—Chimborazo, Cotopaxi, and Popocatapetl.

That way, also, lies the power of names conceived as magic.

As commonly happens with any discussion of poetry, classifications become vague. The romantic use of place-names passes over into the evocative. Who can say how much the power of a certain name—Jerusalem, for instance—depends upon the resounding ring of its own syllables, and how much upon the memories associated with the place and therefore with the name?

Of the major English poets, Milton is outstanding for his use of names, usually with a mingling of romantic and evocative feeling. In Book XI of *Paradise Lost* he departs into a rhapsody of strange but also evocative names in a run of twenty lines— Samarchand, Oxus, Chersonese, Ecbatan, Mombaza, Quiloa, Congo, and a dozen others.

In Book III of *Paradise Regained* he again called up many place-names, as in the lines:

> From Arachosia, from Candaor east,
> And Margiana to the Hyrcanian cliffs
> Of Caucasus, and dark Iberian dales;
> From Atropatia and the neighbouring plains
> Of Adiabene, Media, and the south
> Of Susiana to Balsara's hav'n.

In that same Book III he also produced—with personal enjoyment, we may think—a single line which is wholly composed of place-names:

> Artaxata, Teredon, Ctesiphon.

Paradise Lost, Book I, offers the resounding passage:

And all who since, baptiz'd or infidel
Jousted in Aspramont or Montalban,
Damasco, or Morocco, or Trebisond;
Or whom Biserta sent from Afric shore
When Charlemain with all his peerage fell
By Fontarabbia.

With the evocative use of names, as with the romantic, the etymology or literal meaning of the name makes no difference. These names stand, one might say, as shrines on the long pilgrimage of man, symbolically for good or for bad, for heroic deed or for disaster—Rome, Babylon, Athens, Thermopylae, Bethlehem, Runnymede, Sybaris, Sodom, Cape Horn, Gibraltar, America, London.

The evocative use of place-names is no modern invention, nor is it any specialty of English poetry, although in the present context it is most easily illustrated from English poems. One of the most striking examples, however, is from the *Hymn to Delian Apollo,* from the early Greek *Homeric Hymns,* a passage which spins the names of lands and islands into meter, as Leto seeks a birthplace for her son, against the threats of an angered Hera. Though translation, lacking the hexameters, cannot be satisfactory, the passage runs:

Whoever inhabits Crete, and the land of Athens;
The island Aegina; ship-famous Euboea;
Aegae, Eiresiae, sea-girt Peparathos;
And Thracian Athos, and the lofty heights of Pelion;
Samothrace, and the shady summits of Ida;
Scyros and Phocaea and Autocane's lofty hill;
Imbros, the well-built-upon, and inhospitable Lemnos;
Most holy Lesbos, home of Macar, Aeolos's son;
And Chios, most fruitful of all the isles of the sea;
Rugged Mimas, and Corycos of the high headlands;
Gleaming Claros, and the sheer mount of Aesagea,
And well-watered Samos, and the steep heights of Mycale;
Miletos also, and Cos, city of Meropian men;
Steep Cnidos, and windy Carpathos;
Naxos and Paros and rocky Rhenaea.

On the whole, the evocative quality seems to be stronger, for most people, than the romantic, so that it may even make a

name seem beautiful, though such a name might otherwise be
considered cacaphonic. If we take—across the board—any
group of names with strong evocative quality, we find that
nearly all of them are in themselves euphonic, or at least seem
to be. Consider the provinces of old France that seem to sing
themselves eastward from Brittany to Lorraine. Or take the English counties from Northumberland, thunderous at one extreme, to Cornwall, quiet at the other. In the United States
most of the states bear names that seem to have been consciously chosen for oratorical purposes—indeed, the reports of
discussions in Congress prove that certain of them actually
were. But even Massachusetts and Connecticut, by their associations, escape from their phonetic harshness.

The converse can also be true. Names like Golgotha and
Buchenwald give the effect of being ugly in themselves. But it
may be that we merely find ourselves prejudiced by the sense of
evil in the evocative quality.

Finally, place-names touch poetry in their own actual meaning and the associated suggestions. Incident-names, especially,
thus tell the deeds of men. The power of such names, as opposed to the romantic and the evocative aspects, springs thus
from the meaning, and rests upon the availability of proper explanation.

I cannot do better, in this connection, than to quote, once
more, from *Names on the Land:*

> The United States seems particularly rich in such names—
> Sweetwater, Lone Pine, Gunsight Hills. In this lies the charm
> of Cape Fear, Cape Flattery, Cape Disappointment, and
> Cape Foulweather; of Broken Sword, Broken Straw, and
> Broken Bow. These are the names which seem to have
> stories of life and death behind them—Roaring Run, Dead-
> man Creek, Massacre Lake, Rabbit Hole Spring.

Such qualities of names must have led Stephen Vincent
Benét to write his *American Names,* certainly the most widely
known of poems springing from place-names.

The United States, however, has no monopoly on such
names, and a possible advantage only in that a large proportion

of them are intelligible. Especially in the chapter on incident-names, but also scattered elsewhere throughout this work, are numerous examples of such suggestive examples in many languages.

Even in the United States many such names yield their poetic quality only after translation or historical explanation. In the Southwest a ruined pueblo is Callemongue, which becomes, when translated, "where they hurled down stones." It thus becomes effective in itself.

As such a name illustrates, we need not know the details—who hurled down stones at whom. Was it a desperate siege or only a minor happening? We may even entertain the suspicion that the name arose by some mistake, or by folk-etymology. But the effect can remain. In fact, it may remain even if the error is demonstrable.

Such an example is Cape Wrath, at the northwestern point of Scotland, facing the wild seas of the North Atlantic. It seems an inspired naming, taken in its English sense. But it is in a region where namings from that language have scarcely left a trace, as against Gaelic and Norse. More reasonably, Cape Wrath may be taken as a late English folk-etymology from a commonplace Norse term meaning "turning-point." Even so, the translation fails to destroy the splendor of the name, and we can still envision the turmoil of breakers upon a dark headland.

Similarly, if a name implies more than the record allows, that situation need not trouble us. Starvation, in itself, suggests crisis and human extremity. The record in the United States, however, shows that people may merely have been temporarily hungry at a place which by hyperbole they gave the stronger name.

A similar name in England is Hungerford, which Ekwall glosses as "ford where people had to starve." But to have people gather at a ford in time of starvation seems peculiar, and we may equally well think of some early Anglo-Saxons missing a meal and then giving the name. The uncertainty, however, may be taken as enhancing the appeal of the name, not destroying it.

Another suggestive English name is the simple Cowbridge.

To explain it Ekwall merely takes refuge in linguistics, glossing it as "Self-explanatory." But, considered as a question of name-giving, it is *not* self-explanatory, and arouses, in fact, some interesting ideas. Surely some incident involved a cow (or more than one of them) with this bridge. Did a cow fall from it, or balk at crossing it? The name provides no answer, and is surely not "Self-explanatory" except in mere words. Thus, a little more deeply considered, even the simple Cowbridge stirs the imagination.

This book—perhaps imprudently—has taken as its topic the whole human activity of giving names to places, over the globe and through time. Such a study can never be complete, and must merely end. Doubtless as good an ending as any is with the homely image of a cow crossing a bridge—or, perhaps, refusing to cross it.

The End

Author's Note

Now in my eightieth year, having written for about thirty books those eloquent words "The End," I somewhat reluctantly turn my thoughts once more to composing something which is, anomalously, post-terminal. Partly for practicality—but largely also by convention—authors and publishers seem to conceive the proper text of a work of nonfiction as a kind of jewel to be set in the dull metal of a preceding Preface and Acknowledgments and a succeeding Bibliography, Notes and References, and Index.

In my own writings I have generally eschewed most of this so-called scholarly "apparatus," and have contented myself with an Author's Note. I have trusted that my text speak for itself, and have believed that a reader should not be asked, first, to read a dull preface. An Index is generally indispensable.

The *raison d'être* of Bibliography, Notes and References, and so forth is partly to facilitate the work of the next scholar in the field. Even more, however, they represent an attempt, so to speak, to keep the writer honest, and at the same time to provide an opportunity for him to flaunt his erudition, or apparent erudition.

Actually, no device ensures honesty, much less good judgment and imaginative insight. Such qualities derive from the character of the writer.

394 AUTHOR'S NOTE

In my own case, I believe that I may stand upon the record of scholarly works already written. As an additional testimony I present some history of the present book's genesis.

Whether by some innate quality or by some environmental quirk, I felt at an early age the charm of names and their elucidation. In adolescence I read Isaac Taylor's *Words and Places,* and it deeply moved and impressed me. I still find it readable, though it can no longer be accepted as authorive.

In 1940 I started work on the project which appeared five years later as *Names on the Land.* This history of place-naming in the United States was the most difficult task of any that I have ever attempted. As an acute professor once remarked of the book, "Both the analysis and the synthesis had to be done at the same time." Moreover, there existed no model, and I had to create the form into which the elaborate details must be fitted.

In the end, however, I was able to do much of what I had set out to accomplish. Because of difficulty but final success the book has become perhaps my own favorite among my writings.

In later editions I corrected a few minor errors that had chiefly sprung from my acceptance of inexact sources. On the whole, however, the scholarship of the book still stands intact after thirty years.

About 1945 I began to feed a file on place-names all over the world. I read widely in the literature that gave examples of how namers function. Note-taking was difficult, since I could not possibly record everything. Neither had I, at first, shaped a criterion of judgment enabling me to select or to reject. Gradually, however, some conception of the present work began to take shape in my mind. Probably by 1950 I was already using the present title, a counterpart of *Names on the Land.* I was still, however, somewhat baffled as to what *Names on the Globe* would really become. I let the ideas develop slowly.

There was no need to hurry. Throughout the 1950's and into the 1960's the book stood (as I might put it) somewhere in the tail of a lengthy waiting line of projects to be accomplished—or, at least, considered. In this period I wrote some articles on place-names, prepared a new edition of *Names on the Land,* served a year as president of the American Name Society, and continued my reading and my increasingly directed note-taking.

I winnowed the classical writers, such as Herodotus, Pliny, and Strabo. A slight operation immobilized me for most of one summer, and I spent much of the time on Arctic voyagers. Explorers, whether by land or by sea, are zealous givers of names, and they are likely, in addition, to furnish good reading. I picked for my notes anything that seemed pertinent, although I noted much more than I could finally use. From this long-continued reading I was able to quote, when apt, from dozens of authorities who, here or there (sometimes as a *hapax legomenon*), might furnish examples—Livingstone, Arsenjew, Flinders, Pigafetta, M'Clure, Apollonius, and the others.

During the later 1960's I prepared my dictionary, *American Place-names*. That activity gained me much insight into the ways of namers, still further supplied examples for my file, and helped to mature my ideas. With the completion of that book in 1970 I realized that *Names on the Globe* had finally come to stand at the head of the waiting line.

I began systematically to review, insofar as I found possible, the scholarship of name-study. Besides the restriction of my own energy, the mere mass of material made selectivity necessary. In addition, not even the vast resources of the University of California Library were wholly complete.

The language problem also set limits. Though I prefer to read English (both for greater speed and for fuller comprehension) I also reviewed materials widely in French, Spanish, and German, and could employ Latin, and classical Greek and Hebrew. I even, in a minor way, used Italian, Portuguese, and Dutch. Linguistically, my chief regret is my inability to use Russian and Japanese. Fortunately, much information upon names in languages which I could not read was available in languages which I could. Thus, the material upon Maori names exists in English.

As I progressed with my research, my ideas became firmer. I came to realize that my focus must be upon the namer and the naming, not upon the mere listing and elucidation of particular names. Selectivity became the key word. Thus my ideas suffered change as to what was important—that is, what must be included. I found myself able to de-emphasize, for my purposes, the whole voluminous topic of the European substratum. Originally I had envisioned a whole chapter upon the names of France and another upon those of Germany, largely because much material was available upon them. In the end I did not systematically present either of these fields, although much material (especially upon France) is to be found under various headings.

As a primary project I reviewed the chief journals, such as *Revue Internationale d'Onomastique, Zeitschrift für Namenforschung, Beitrage für Namenforschung,* and *Names.* The vast bulk of the material should have been discouraging, but its actual detailed nature allowed me to eliminate most of it.

I then turned to the also voluminous studies of book-length, usually less detailed and more useful to my ends (see below).

As to my precise sources, I may claim Books I and II to be essentially my own, and not to owe much, as to ideas, to any other work. The examples are drawn from my own experience of namings and namers, as derived from the background of research here detailed.

Book I is a kind of philosophy of place-naming—a topic upon which I was thinking as early as 1940, when I published an article, "What Is Named?—Towns, Islands, Mountains, Rivers, Capes," in *Essays and Studies, University of California Publications in English,* vol. 14. Also, for Book I, Chapter 5, I acknowledge a great debt to Professor J. B. McMillan's "Observations on American Place-name Grammar," in *American Speech,* vol. 24. I also make acknowledgment to V. A. Nikonov's "L'Étymologie? Non. L'Étiologie." in *Revue Internationale d'Onomastique,* vol. 12.

Book II is essentially an elaboration of my article "A Classification of Place-names, " in *Names* vol. 2, which also developed, along the way, into "Names (in Linguistics)," in the *Encyclopedia Britannica* (14th ed.), and the "Introduction" to my *American Place-names* (1970).

My use of particular writings is great in Books III and IV.

Many of these indebtednesses are sufficiently identified in the text. I here list others.

As a general work of reference I express my unlimited debt to J. J. Egli's *Nomina Geographica* (German text); I have used the 1973 reprint of the Second Edition of 1893. Although having passed its century mark (originally of 1872), this remarkable work of scholarship is still usable. Its survival I would credit to its linguistic spread and to its verbatim quotations of hundreds of original sources on naming. Naturally, it must be used, as the phrase goes, "with caution." It is obviously of no value for discoveries made since its time—e.g. the sub-stratum.

Another general work is Sturmfels and Bischof, *Unsere Ortsnamen* (3rd ed., 1961). I have not, however, in spite of its comparative modernity, found it to be wholly satisfactory, and I have used it chiefly for clues to be elsewhere confirmed.

Another group of "general" works is composed of those studies, chiefly dictionaries, dealing with a particulàr country. Since *Names on the Globe* required a sweeping approach, not an intensive study of a few names, these works were of the utmost importance, though they themselves vary in quality. For brevity I cite them by author only: Eilert Ekwall (England), P. W. Joyce (Ireland), W. C. Mackenzie (Scotland), Albert Dauzat and Charles Rostaing (France), Auguste Vincent (Belgium), Adolph Bach (Germany), A. E. Martin (Australia), A. W. Reed (New Zealand), G. H. Armstrong (Canada), Charles Pettman (South Africa), and G. R. Stewart (U.S.A.).

I list my chief sources by chapters—without, however, making further acknowledgment of the general sources already noted. Nor do I repeat, when the source is sufficiently identified in the text.

Book II, Chapter 1. H. L. F. Lutz, "Topomastic Patterns of Ancient Egypt," in *Names*, vol. v. Personal communication with Professor Klaus Baer.

Chapter 2. Chiefly based directly upon the biblical narrative.

Chapter 3. Egli is useful. Also of value is Albert Dietrich, *Phönizische Ortsnamen in Spanien* (1936).

Chapters 4, 5, and 6. There is no comprehensive study of ancient Greek place-names. The scattered references in the text are probably clear enough. When the argument touches the sub-stratum, see the listing under Book III, Chapter 9. D. J. Georgacas supplies the exhaustive treatise, "The Name Asia for the Continent," in *Names*, xvii; I differ from him on certain judgments. I mention also my "Europe and Europa," in *Names*, ix.

Chapters 7 and 8. There is no general study of the Romans and Celts as namers, but there is much comment and explanation of these names in the general works on the various European countries. Here may be included the valuable treatise on French river-names by Paul Lebel, *Principes et Methodes d'Hydronymie Francaise* (1956). Excellent, though brief, are Charles Rostaing, *Les Noms de Lieux* (1948), and E. Nègre, *Les Noms de Lieux en France* (1963). Also under the general heading see Dauzat and Rostaing, Bach, and Ekwall.

Chapters 9 and 10. I have not attempted to penetrate deeply into the maze of writings upon the sub-stratum. I am indebted to Professor J. R. Craddock for his *Latin Legacy Versus Substratum Residue* (1969), which supplies an outstandingly clear exposition of the development of the sub-stratum controversy. He is inclined toward a skeptical or "conservative" attitude toward the sub-stratum, and supplies the phrase "skepticism has not decreased." Another conservative is Nègre, who supplies the background for Cantalou. Rostaing presents a much more enthusiastic acceptance of the sub-stratum. I have made guarded use of A. Carnoy, *Dictionnaire Étymologique du Proto-Indo-European* (1955). In Britain my anthropological summary derives largely from Jacquetta and Christopher Hawkes, *Prehistoric Britian* (1953). The chief proponent of a British sub-stratum is W. F. H. Nicolaisen, "Die Alteuropaischen Gewässernamen der Britishen Hauptinsel," in *Beitrage zur Namenforschen*, viii.

Chapter 11. The publications of the English Place-name Society, county by county, over many years, are outstanding. Although I have long been familiar with them, their highly detailed nature made them nonessential for the present work, much as I regard them with a feeling scarcely less than reverence. Several comparatively recent books are excellent: K. Cameron, *English Place-names* (1961); P. H. Reaney, *The Origin of English Place-names* (1960); W. F. H. Nicolaisen, M. Gelling, and M. Richards, *The Names of Towns and Cities in Britian* (1970); and C. M. Mathews, *Place Names of the English-speaking World* (1972). Somewhat more popularly conceived is H. G. Stokes, *English Place-names* (1948). Also useful on Celtic background is K. Jackson, *Language and History in Early Britain* (1953). My indebtedness to Ekwall has already been acknowledged.

Chapter 12. The chief special study is Miguel Asín Palacios, *Contribuciones a la Toponomía Arabe de España* (1944).

Chapter 13. Ellwood's translation of the *Landnámabók* (1898) has served me well, and I have also received essential help from the English summary in Gösta Franzen, *Laxdaellabydens Ortnamn* (1964). On the Maori names, see A. W. Reed, *A Dictionary of Maori Place Names* (1961); J. Andersen, *Maori Place-names* (1942); H. W. Williams, "A Plea for the Scientific Study of Maori Names," in *Transactions and Proceedings of the New Zealand Institute,* vol. 45; and Edward Shortland, *Maori Religion and Mythology* (1882).

Chapter 14. Smith's work (see text) is in *Geographical Review* (1946).

Chapter 15. See text.

Chapter 17. Columbus's own reports and letters provide the essential basis.

Chapter 18. I have relied upon M. S. Beeler, "America—the Story of a Name," in *Names,* vol. 1. Also to be noted is Gutierre Tibón's treatise *América, Setenta Siglos de la Historia de un Nombre* (1945).

Chapter 19. The narratives of the explorers provide the basis.

Chapter 20. The chroniclers (often basing upon the explorers' narratives or log-books) supply most of the material, viz., Herrera (especially interested in names), Gómara, Las Casas, Navarette, Oviedo, Pigafetta. Local scholars have carefully studied Indian names but, unfortunately, have paid little attention to European namings, viz., Tibón (Mexico); Lemos (Ecuador) Rona (Uruguay); Valle (Nicaragua); Durand (Peru, Bolivia); Valenzuela (Chile); Cadogan (Guarani names); Peralta

(Guarani names). Nils Holmer provides a general survey with his "Indian Place-Names in South America and the Antilles," in *Names,* viii and ix.

Chapter 21. Based chiefly upon my own writings.

Chapter 22. For sources, see the general works listed above and the Maori studies as presented under Chapter 13.

Chapter 23. The French protest is from M. Cury and G. Baillet, *Toponymie de la Commune d'Archon.* For Roberts, see "G. I. Place Names in Three Sectors of Korea" in *Names,* vii. See also Leslie Dunkling, *English House Names* (1971).

Book IV, Chapter 1. I have based primarily upon A. Dauzat's *Les Noms de Lieux* (1928), and F. T. Wainwright's "Danes and Norwegians in England," in the publications of the Fourth International Congress of Onomastic Sciences. The sources of the rest of Book IV are sufficiently clear in the text.

I should also mention a number of works which I have studied with admiration, but of which I have been unable to make much use because of lack of space: Fischer, Eichler, Naumann, and Walther, *Namen deutscher Städte* (1963); A. Slawik, *Die Ortsnamen Der Ainu* (1968); M. Olsen, *Farms and Fanes of Ancient Norway* (1928); E. W. Gifford, *Tongan Place Names* (1923); F. Boas, *Geographical Names of the Kwakiutl Indians* (1934); E. R. Seary, *Place Names of the Avalon Peninsula of the Island of Newfoundland* (1971).

My path of scholarship is characteristically a lonely one, but I have had some pleasant meetings, and give my thanks, especially, to Madison Beeler, Kendrick Pritchett, and Charles Jones, for kind words and sage advice (sometimes heeded). So also I thank my editors James Raimes and Caroline Taylor. Finally, I acknowledge still another debt to Theodosia, who might well be given the title Encourager of Books.

G.R.S.

San Francisco
November 1, 1974

Index

To keep this index within practical limits, I have omitted from it the many place-names which are mentioned in the text only as examples and in themselves designate unimportant places. The index does include important and interesting place-names, as well as names of people and books, and of ideas and concepts. If variant spellings exist, the one I have used is generally that of contemporary American English. In transliterating from languages other than English, I have let practicality rather than absolute consistency be my guide.